The 98-99 Housebuilder's Bible

Mark Brinkley

Published Nov 1997

ISBN 0-9524852-2-2

Rodelia Ltd

Post	*POBox 853*
	Weston Colville
	Cambridge CB1 5NZ
Phone	*01223 290230*
Fax	*01223 290985*
E-mail	*housebuildersbible@compuserve.com*

We run a mail order sales service. Phone for details.

Printed by Burlington Press Foxton Cambridge

Contents

Tables

About the Author

The following is adapted from an article by Brian O'Sullivan which appeared in Professional Builder, June 1994.

Some wise sage said that everyone had a book in them, a story to tell. Lucky then for the readers of the Housebuilder's Bible, because Mark Brinkley's volume is not only a good read but also an informative and thoroughly researched source of reference.

As both a professional and a selfbuilder himself, Mark is well qualified to write the book, having fallen into many of house building's pitfalls and paid the price for inexperience.

Having read for a degree in Social and Political Science at Cambridge University in the early 70s, Mark entered the building industry by accident in 1980. A small inheritance enabled him and some friends to renovate the house he was living in and this was a job he really enjoyed. So he decided to make a career of building and went off and did a TOPS course in carpentry and joinery. "It's the best bit of education I've ever had!" he laughs. He then formed a business alliance with friend Robin Gomm who was gaining a reputation for designing high class alterations. The pair subsequently spent the prosperous 80s working on domestic renovations, studios, stable conversions and the like, eventually forming a housebuilding business called Complete Fabrications which has spent the last ten years designing and building one-off houses and small developments for private clients and for developers. Most of Mark's material and much of the price information in the book is drawn from this business which he continues to manage on a part time basis.

With the slowdown in the early 90s Mark decided to use a building plot he owned to erect a house for his growing family — the end product was a brick/block ground floor with a timber frame top hat first floor. "With a 200m² floor area and a build cost of only £80,000 we went for most space for least bucks," Mark remembers. "But it was that process that made me decide to write the book. With my previous building experience you'd think I'd find it a doddle but I didn't, I struggled. All sorts of basic questions that I ought to have known the answers to I found I didn't," he said.

But in order to write a general book on housebuilding Mark didn't regard his house as representative of a standard new house so he asked a local developer if he could use one of his as a source of reference, a benchmark. He then amassed hundreds of quotes on various items to get guide prices and then set about writing down his experiences.

"You don't have to be a brain surgeon to build a new house," continues Mark "but there are an amazing number of component parts — something like 10,000 — and getting them all assembled correctly and in the correct order is enough to tax anyone's managerial skills. Most builders approach it from knowing one trade very well — for example a carpenter knows all about hanging doors and skirtings but knows nothing about heating and plumbing systems — and vice versa for a plumber. There are very few ways of getting that knowledge rather than through hard experience — and that can be expensive!"

To help readers along the way, the book is written in a user friendly non technical manner. "That's because I don't understand the technicalities!" Mark laughs. "I don't really care how a condensing boiler works and I don't know the ins and outs of the wiring regs. My criteria is dead simple: Is it any good and what does it cost? I don't claim to have all the answers either, but when I finished my own house in 1992 I was aware of how much I didn't know and set out to rectify those faults."

Two shots of the house we built. Above: rear view — note ground level is above first floor height. The added costs of a sloping site are detailed in Chapter 6. Below: kitchen, mostly handpainted MDF.

About this Edition

The Housebuilder's Bible is unusual and perhaps unique in that it crosses the divide between price guides and handbooks. Traditionally, building price guides have been great fat tomes which come out annually and cost an arm and a leg: I've never been able to fathom how they work because I haven't trained as a quantity surveyor and I don't understand many of the terms they use. Yet in our building business we regularly bandy about metre rates for this, that and the other and would be at a loss without this information so, whilst writing the first edition, I was aware just how much really useful price information there was floating around which remained largely inaccessible to casual builders. The professional price guides pride themselves on just how big they are and just how many prices they include but by doing so they also make it very hard for the untrained user to ferret out any useful information. Not so the *Housebuilder's Bible*. Most of the cost information is contained in a series of tables and the emphasis is on simplicity so that, though they are undoubtedly much less detailed than the information in the price guides, they are much more accessible to non-technical people who are looking for ballpark comparison costings.

On the other hand, the general building handbooks (and in this category I include the D-I-Y manuals) go to great lengths to avoid any mention of prices because to do so was always said to be publishing death as this would hopelessly date a book within a very short timespan. Yet by avoiding all mention of costs, these books usually leave out what is usually the most important and useful bit of information that people actually want. It's a bit like a mail order catalogue with no prices; interesting but ultimately frustrating. To me, the logical thing was to write a handbook with prices in it and damn the consequences. Publishing suicide it may have been but I have survived to update a third edition.

The background against which the first two editions were written was one of a torpid building trade slowly emerging from a horrible recession. Price rises were a rare event and this made for a relatively easy time of it in putting together price tables. However—as of late 1997—the economic climate is very different and in many areas construction appears to be booming again. Land prices are up markedly in the SouthEast and labour rates are on the increase—indeed there is much talk in the trade press of labour shortages. One of the key benchmark rates in the building trade is the price charged by bricklayers for laying a thousand bricks—it's a sort of thermometer of construction activity. In the 1980s it topped £200/k; it collapsed to around £160/k in 1991 and didn't do much for five years. However this year it started at £180/k, it reached £200/k by June and is headed for £225/k at time of writing. Bricklayers are in demand and they are seemingly few and far between. So for the first time I go to press against a background of price rise—albeit still very gradual when compared to what we have known in the past—and I would urge more caution than before in basing your budgets on my figures. It would appear that the south of the country is possibly now overheating whilst the north and the Celtic fringes are much quieter and so anticipate a bigger than normal (10%) price variation.

Upgrades Abandoned

It is my intention to keep the *Housebuilder's Bible* abreast of the times and to this end new editions shall be appearing every two years. However, unlike some yearbooks, the content will remain largely the same and will only change as I feel it is necessary to either improve the coverage or alter prices, phone numbers or regulations. A number of people asked me whether there could be some sort of upgrade offer available and I actually ran a half price upgrade offer experimentally in the last edition. However fewer than 1 in 12 sales took the trouble to register for the upgrade offer and I now anticipate great difficulties weeding out genuine second-time buyers from people who have just come across an upgrade card. So whilst I will attempt to honour the upgrades from the 96/97 edition to this current one, I will not be continuing it this time around. It's a nice idea— it's just proved to be impractical for something with a relatively low price. The cost of administering such a scheme effectively is out of proportion to any perceived benefits. Instead I will aim to keep the cover price low.

Feedback

Housebuilding is such a large subject that it is impossible for one person to keep abreast of every product, every technique and every regulation and there will inevitably be areas of the book that can be improved upon in subsequent editions. I see myself primarily as a compiler of useful nuggets of information and the more golden nuggets that are unearthed, the more useful the book will become to its readership. I was frankly amazed at the response to the first two editions, especially from professional builders and developers. I had initially thought that they would be distinctly sniffy about something that purported to tell them all about their livelihood but, in the event, many turned out to be extremely appreciative that someone had bothered to write all this stuff down. I have learnt a great deal and have incorporated many of the best suggestions into this current edition. So please keep the feedback coming, especially where you encounter inaccuracies or think I've oversimplified a complex problem.

Mark Brinkley, October 1997

Acknowledgements

Electrics .... Andrew Bailey, Peter Graver

Plumbing and heating .... Norman Cox, Bob Fryer

Roofing .... John Barnes

Design .... Julian Owen

Benchmark House .... Robin Gomm of Complete Fabrications

Editor .... Sean McSweeney

Book design .... Nick Ellis

Front cover illustration .... Jack Brinkley (my son, aged 8)

Gorilla cartoons, back cover faces ...... Andy Davey

Primary Reference Sources .... NHBC, Building Research Establishment, Financial Times, Hutchins' Priced Schedules, Centre for Alternative Technology, Which?, National Home Energy Ratings.

Project management .... Charlotte Brinkley

Impossible without .... Diana Brinkley

General Thankyou .... Numerous tradesmen and businesses which have taken the time and trouble to provide informations and quotations. Good prices and useful information will frequently have resulted in a mention and I hope this somehow repays the trouble you have all taken.

Also to the many people who have mailed, rung, faxed or e-mailed me with new information and corrections on current data

Also worthy of mention is the Individual Homes internet discussion group which has been running since 1997. A valuable resource for me and for the hundreds of selfbuilders and building professionals who frequent it. Open to all with an internet access. URL is http//www.ihomes.co.uk

Dedication .... David Thomas, a fine writer and a close friend since schooldays. His untimely death in a car crash in Kuwait, where he was reporting on the aftermath of the war in 1991, provided me with the inspiration to get cracking on this project.

Chapter 1
Introduction

HOUSE BRICKS

SUPER VANADIUM STEEL REINFORCED SALT-RESISTANT LOW FROST ENGINEERING BRICKS

Builders Dilemma

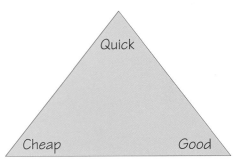

This triangle represents the age-old conundrum for all builders and would-be builders. It is said that you can have any two of these points in a building job but only at the expense of the third. Thus you can have a good, cheap job done but it won't be quick, or a cheap, quick job that won't be any good.

So when you hear claims — as you may — of people having built (or more likely "put up") a house in just eight weeks you can reply, confidently, "Ah, but how much did it cost you?" And, similarly, if you meet someone who claims to have built a house for £17/ft², you can look them in the eye and exclaim "I bet it took you years" — and you'll be right. So before you set out to build a new house, first examine your motives and see where you fit into the triangle.

The Cheap House

The average new house is constructed entirely by builders; it takes about 6-8 months to complete and costs around £40/ft² (that's £430/m²). It is built to standards that meet — and do *not* exceed — the current building regulations.

If you want to maximise the financial return on your new house — in all but the most upmarket areas — it pays to keep it dead simple. Whether you plan to actually be a hands-on builder or not, the following advice should be carried out to the letter.

- Dispense with any notions of individual design. Aim for a four-square box drawn up by a technician or a surveyor or better still from some already existing book of house plans — in fact anyone except an architect.
- Avoid all of the following:
a) Layouts with any more than four external corners
b) Anything round or curved
c) Anything poking out through the roof (dormers, chimneys)
d) Anything other than concrete pan tiles on the roof
e) Anything other than face brickwork on external walls
f) Anything other than straight stairs
g) Complicated sites (unless bought for bargain price)
h) Fancy Continental plumbing systems
i) Timber frame
j) Trying to build a "green" house
k) Underfloor heating
l) Central vacuum cleaning systems
m) Kitchens that don't come from MFI
n) Bathrooms that don't come from Plumb Center
o) Anything but Magnet Standard casement windows
p) *Low E* glazing
q) Handmade anything at all (bricks, tiles, pavings)
r) French doors/patio doors
s) Garages — especially ones with remote-controlled doors
t) Porches and entrance canopies
u) Any roof not shaped like
v) Built-in cupboards
w) Hardwood floors
x) More than six rows of ceramic tiles
y) Any lighting that doesn't hang from a pendant in the middle of each room — especially if it's got the word halogen in it.
z) Almost everything second-hand — it's only been salvaged because it's worth more than the new replacements.

Your sole remaining decision will be whether to paint or stain your woodwork. Received wisdom is divided on this topic; stain is quicker and easier to apply but it's more expensive to buy and the joinery needs more careful preparation.

What you will end up with will have all the charm of a 50s council house. But if space for bucks is your main motive in taking on a construction project, then you'll be very happy. Much of the book that follows is concerned with the options that might turn a cheap house into a good house and therefore much of the book will be of little relevance to you. I have, however, always tried to indicate what the cheapest option is in each element of the house.

The Quick House

The quick house will almost certainly be a kit house which is largely prefabricated in a workshop or factory. It will also, very likely, be a timber framed house. Timber frame kit houses tend to be rather more sophisticated than standard houses both in terms of specification and in the way they are built, but they are not cheap; even the simplest box-type designs are likely to add significantly to construction costs. Also note that while the timber superstructure goes up with alarming speed, what really takes up a builder's time is the finishing tasks and these are pretty much the same whatever your chosen building methods.

The Good House

Most would-be individual housebuilders are not hard up nor in a hurry — at least they're not when they're just planning it all; they might beg to differ when they're halfway through building. They can afford to browse and contemplate and research. They will look at many different options before embarking and will probably be keen that the finished product should somehow be an expression of their personality as well as a way of meeting their individual needs in a way that an off-the-peg house couldn't hope to. Even if you are building for resale rather than personal occupation, you are more than likely to want to build an attractive house that passers-by will come to admire and occupants will love to call home. After all, the house is likely to be standing long after any transient profit is banked and spent, and may well still be there when they are burying your grandchildren. To build well, the client (you?) has to know what's going on and not just rely on experts: the more you are involved in the design, the more you will appreciate the outcome, and the more you are involved in the building, the better that outcome will be.

Is this book for you?

What follows is an easy-to-dip-into trawl through the world of housebuilding. It is *not* a D-I-Y manual (there are enough of those) and it is not a disguised advertisement (I'm not selling anything apart from this book). It *is* a gentle introduction to many of the choices you, as a housebuilder, will be faced with. Although primarily concerned with new housebuilding, there is also much information specifically tailored for people converting or restoring existing properties. Wherever possible I have tried to show comparative costings and I have tried to avoid construction jargon (though I have a fondness for building site slang, which keeps cropping up). Many of the tricks and tips described I have learnt the hard way, starting as a selfbuilder in 1980 and working both speculatively and directly for clients ever since. As the old saw goes, experience is the best education but it is also the most expensive. My hope is that some of my "experience" and research will help you avoid expensive pitfalls, many of which I've had the doubtful pleasure of falling victim to myself. In short, the aim of this book is to enable you to build a good house cheaply and quickly. Now hang on a minute, I thought that wasn't possible.

Housebuilding in the UK

Housebuilding in Britain has always been a boom or bust activity, and this has never been more clearly illustrated than in the last few years. The early 80s saw a huge surge in private housebuilding caused partly by the postwar baby boomers entering the housing market for the first time and partly by people choosing to live in smaller groups — and this increased demand led to a huge increase in house prices. This in turn encouraged more and more people to jump onto the bandwagon of home ownership, and this trend was encouraged by the Thatcher government which made the supposed benefits of property owning a key plank of its programme.

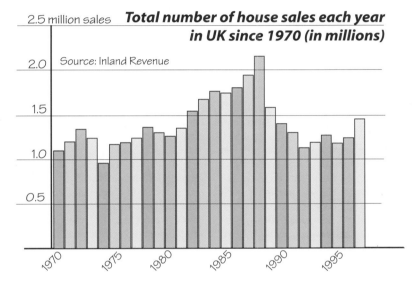

Total number of house sales each year in UK since 1970 (in millions)

Source: Inland Revenue

The Slump

This bandwagon came juddering to halt on August 1st 1988 when Nigel Lawson, the chancellor, stopped offering double mortgage tax relief to unmarried couples. The removal of this tax perk had been flagged in his budget speech in March and the housing market, which was already toppy, went haywire in the rush to complete sales before the August deadline: people who in more normal times would never have considered house purchase together were being bounced into it by a fear that it was now or never for the housing ladder. In SouthEast England, where most of the action was, prices went up 30% in the seven months leading up to August 1988.

When the party stopped, prices began to fall. At first this decline was gradual as sales came to a standstill, all buyers having been sucked (some would say suckered) out of the market. However, during 1989 it became apparent that all the estate agent's talk of the market "just taking a breather" was bull and, as the number of sales continued to decline, the rout set in. From spring 1989 to spring 1990 average prices fell by 20% and even then, with talk now of the market being at "realistic" levels, sales remained sluggish and prices continued to fall, albeit at a more modest rate. It wasn't until 1993 that the market began to recover, by which time house prices had fallen

25% from the peak of the price bubble and, as if that wasn't enough, 1995 was another nasty year for housebuilders with the number of sales going into reverse once more. The bar chart on the previous page is a reasonably good indicator of the heat of the housing market and the indications are that 1997 (as yet uncompleted) is a year of strong recovery after many years down in the dumps. The phrase "negative equity" which has haunted us since 1990 looks like it may soon be history but hopefully the lessons of the past ten years will not be forgotten in a hurry. The property market is capable of springing traps and you would do well to understand the rudiments of how it works.

Mini-markets

The housing market varies enormously across the country. Generally speaking, the further away from London you travelled the less spectacular the bursting bubble was. Price rises had been much more muted in the 80s and sales activity far less frenetic; consequently, the market didn't fall off a cliff in 1989. In Northern England and, in particular, Scotland, prices continued to rise gently for some time.

This is an important point to grasp because there is really no such thing as a national housing market, really only a collection of local markets each succumbing to different expectations and factors. For instance, in SE England everyone blamed the collapsing housing market on the high interest rates which the government imposed — the base rate was 15% from October 1989 to October 1990; however, these same base rates applied in Scotland and there the market remained steady if not buoyant. Statistics published in the media about the housing market are, therefore, usually next to useless because they tend to conceal the different trends going on in the various regional markets. To really get the feel for a market, it must be studied at a local level.

New housebuilding has never accounted for more than a small proportion of all house sales (usually around 10-15%) but its fortunes are still inextricably tied-in with the fortunes of the market as a whole. In good times, professional housebuilders borrow money, buy land (*the landbank*) and then sit back and watch profits grow effortlessly as land prices rise. In bad times — well the bad times are so bad that I think it would be altogether too distressing for me to go into them here. Suffice it to say that banks (that's money banks not landbanks) don't like lending to businesses with few, if any sales, and with existing loans supported by assets which are falling rapidly in price. In the recent slump, not only did prices collapse but the total number of sales fell to a level last seen in the 70s. Whereas the late 80s saw nearly 250,000 houses a year being built, most of them by private developers for resale, the 90s has seen this number falling to below 180,000, and of those 40,000 have been built by housing associations. Selfbuilding or individual building has risen from being a fringe activity to become a substantial part of the market — estimates vary between 15,000 and 25,000 homes per annum. The number of houses built by speculative developers — as op-posed to social housing and selfbuilding — has therefore fallen to nearly half of what it was in the boom years.

Price and Character

The housebuilding market has changed ir-revocably. People are no longer buying houses as an investment; they are buying a place to live. There are two attributes that they are looking for: either 1) it should be cheap or 2) it should somehow be different. People will only tolerate living in a mass-produced char-acterless box if it makes economic sense: it either has to be cheaper than renting or the price has to be going up by at least 10%/an-num. Having been bitten in the 80s down-turn, people are naturally reluctant to buy just for speculation, the former has come to the fore and this has meant that there has been a concentration on building affordable starter homes and flats. Developers working upmar-ket have been caught cold by people's unwill-ingness to pay more for houses which are per-ceived to be dull and unremarkable, whereas estate agents still report a good business in "character" properties, most of which are more than a hundred years old. This desire for character (whatever that means) has been in part responsible for the surge of interest in selfbuilding, where people are saying "To hell with the developer, we'll do it ourselves."

Selfbuild

Selfbuild is a catch-all phrase that encom-passes many different poisons. Time was, about ten or fifteen years ago, that selfbuild was thought of mostly as a bunch of hippies getting together to build their own homes and to live in new age bliss in communities with names like Lightmoor or Zenzele. The em-phasis was always on building cheaply, sim-ply and in an environmentally sound way, which usually meant building the Walter Segal way. Walter Segal was an innovative ar-chitect who designed and promoted a very simple method of building timber frame houses which could be easily mastered by novices. The Segal Trust (0171 831 5696) con-tinues to promote his work and methods. The emphasis is now on what is termed commu-nity selfbuild and if you are financially chal-lenged but still harbour dreams of building your own home, then you would be well ad-vised to contact them or the Community Self Build Agency (0171 415 7092) who keep abreast of up and coming schemes all over the country. Other useful contacts are the As-sociation of Selfbuilders (Angela Youngman 01604 864013), a charity set up to provide support for both individuals and community builds and Constructive Individuals (0171 377 6763) who run hands-on courses for self-builders.

Whilst this specialised niche is alive and thriving, it is now dwarfed by the mainstream selfbuild market which consists of people acting as, what the Americans call, *paper con-tractors*, that is do-it-yourself property devel-opers. This group tend to be fairly well-off and tend to build relatively high spec. houses; some estimates reckon that over a third of all detached housing in the UK is now selfbuilt.

For many of this new breed of selfbuilder there will be little or no physical involvement in the construction of their homes; they are instead providing the nous (and money) to get a plot of land purchased and to build a new home on it. Throughout the postwar years, this group was typically buying and doing up old wrecks of houses, but as the wrecks with the most potential have mostly been snapped up now, their attention has moved on to building from scratch. Now it is recognised that there is such a thing as a *self-build industry* which supports many special-ist businesses, three national magazines — *Build It, Selfbuild* and *Homebuilding & Reno-vating* (formally *Individual Homes*), two an-nual national exhibitions as well as many smaller regional roadshows and the like. Whilst the early 90s have been a grim period for housebuilding as a whole, it's witnessed huge growth in individual selfbuilding with a record number of people taking on the chal-lenge fuelled by an ever-increasing number of press articles explaining the basics of how it's all done.

Much of the sales literature which is used to attract individuals to build their own homes is based on the fact that there is a large, tax-free profit to be had. Whilst the responsible end of the market likes to reign in such claims, you still come across examples of this hype. Typical of these is one that appeared in July 95 in the magazine *Nationwide Proper-ties.*

"Interested in a management activity for your spare time which should gain you more in a year than your regular salary? With the benefits completely tax free? If so, you are looking at selfbuild. It is all based on the fact that the cost of a serviced building plot added to the cost of building a house on it using subcontractors is significantly less than the finished value of the property. Typically the savings will be around 25% and on a £160,000 home this can be £40,000."

Sounds too good to be true? You guessed it. Let me put the other side of the case so that at least you are aware that all that glistens is not gold.

Until 1989, everyone in housebuilding (be they Tarmac, Barratts or Mr. and Mrs. X) was making a very tidy return, thank you. This was almost entirely due to rapidly appreciat-ing land prices and owed very little to busi-ness acumen. Since the collapse of the hous-ing market, very few have made any worth-while money out of housebuilding; indeed, the reckless, the over-borrowed and some-times just the unlucky have been bankrupted. The building trade's response to the slump in demand for their services was to cut prices and slash overheads. In good times, builders hope to make a profit of 20% over and above their costs; in slumps, many builders quote work at cost (or even slightly below) in the knowledge that they may be able to screw down their subcontractors' prices even fur-ther.

Land Costs are the Key

The way in which prices for building plots are set is based on subtracting the building costs from the estimated value of the completed house. For example, if the estate agent or surveyor marketing a plot reckons that a nicely finished house there might fetch £150,000 and that it might cost around £75,000 to build, then he will probably recommend that the plot be sold for around £60,000, maybe more. There is obviously a return here but the problem is that there are many more costs involved than just the plot price and the building costs. If house prices increase by 15% during the time it takes you to build, all appears well and good and you do appear to get a fantastic return on your efforts; but in the early 90s house prices did not increase at all and even as I write (Aug. 97) price rises are still pretty muted and you'll have to throw an almighty number of hours at your building project if you are to keep costs down to a level at which you appear to make a profit of more than a few percent.

The bulk of the profit in a greenfield housing site tends to go to the landowner who succeeded in getting planning permission to turn whatever was there before into building land. In most places in the UK, agricultural land is worth less than £2000/acre; in contrast, in SE England, building land can still fetch £500,000/acre (down from £1million/acre in 1988 — but still an expensive commodity). One effect of this relationship between land costs and finished housing costs is that building plots tend to go up in value faster than house prices when house prices are rising; conversely, plot prices fall further than house prices when house prices slump. However, one of the demonstrable effects of the selfbuild boom is that the prices for single building plots have held up much better than prices for multiple developments: in other words, because of the increasing demand for single plots, they are relatively expensive compared with other building land and of course the effect is to make that easy money just that little bit more difficult to make.

Understanding the Costs

Table 1a compares the development costs for a professional developer and a selfbuilder using a timber frame kit house on an averagely profitable site. The costings reflect something akin to our standard house — see Chapter 2 *The Benchmark*. If you just add plot costs and building costs together you'd see a 20-30% profit (this is the margin that the press get so excited about), but a more thorough analysis reveals that the figure is nowhere near this amount. In particular, the finance costs eat into the gross profit at an alarming rate and the effect of a) interest rates going up and b) failure to obtain a quick sale are disastrous. Anyone who borrows to finance a project as large as a new house is extremely vulnerable to changes in interest

rates — see Table 1b to see just how catastrophic these effects were for developers at the end of the 80s. Table 1b assumes that around £80,000 is borrowed in four stages to finance the building of a house, fairly typical of this kind of development deal. When interest rates start to rise, professional developers tend to get squeezed not just by the extra cost of this finance but also by the fact that the level of sales tends to decline, sometimes accompanied by the dreaded fall in house prices. Housebuilders are very vulnerable in these circumstances and what looks like a healthy profit on a house can evaporate within a matter of weeks. A selfbuilder is in a subtly different situation to a speculative developer and this may mean that they are able to hang on to more of this gross profit margin. The selfbuilder doesn't need to find a buyer and therefore has no selling costs; also the selfbuilder can keep construction costs down by carrying out supervision and some construction work. Against this, however, it is unlikely that they can build as cheaply as a professional developer, whatever construction methods they use.

The DIY Approach

DIYers are, in any event, a race apart from the conventional building client; they are drawn to take on challenges like a moth to a flame and will use any handy facts and figures to back up what is really an emotional decision. The majority of building projects are designed and commissioned along the time-honoured lines of sending out the plans for quotation to a number of builders and then selecting the best option from them. D-I-Y builders are very unlikely to use this macro approach (although they will keenly search for best material and subcontract prices) because they will assume that their endeavours will produce a cheaper and probably a better job. Maybe they will, but how could one ever tell?

Richard and Valerie Dring: one of the 15,000-odd self builders who graduated in 1997. Their project involved lots of hands-on work from both of them and from other family members. What's so special about the Drings? Mrs. Dring just happens to be my bank manager.

Common sense dictates that selfbuilding, whether just project management or carrying out some of the work as well, should achieve some savings on employing a main contractor for the whole job. But if you value your labour at all, you will probably find that you are worth a depressingly small amount per hour worked: I would anticipate around £2-3/hr for a beginner, rising to double or at most treble for an experienced builder/speculator when house prices are stable.

Real Savings

The costs of the average residential building job are made up of around 50% on-site labour and 50% materials. (Obviously this varies from project to project but is almost always within the 60:40 and 40:60 ratios). In theory, you could therefore achieve savings of around 50% on construction costs if you carried out all the labour yourself — but here we have to look at some rather complex actuarial calculations about the value of your time and the cost of borrowed money. Only if you are both rich and unemployed can you afford to ignore these calculations.

1a: Comparison of Costs: Developer v Selfbuilder

	DEVELOPER	SELFBUILDER
Plot	£40,000	£40,000
Stamp Duty	400	0
Legals	400	400
Survey Fees	500	500
Design Work	3000	0
Planning Fee	160	160
Building Control	207	260
Structural Warranties	400	800
Quantity Surveyor	500	0
Infrastructure Charge	430	430
Water Connection	600	600
Electricity Connection	350	350
Build Costs	£60,000	£70,000
Insurance	500	450
Selling Costs	3000	0
Legals/Agents Fees	2000	0
Finance @10% for Plot (18months)	6125	6065
Finance @ 10% for Build Costs	2500	2917
Total Development Costs	£121,072	£122,932
Projected Sale Price	£135,000	£135,000
Net Profit	£13,928	£12,068

No stamp duty on purchases under £60,000

Design fees included in kit house purchase

£70,000 covers a kit house on which everything is paid for. Savings could be enhanced with D-I-Y works.

Most D-I-Y projects are of low value (say, less than £1000) and have little effect on house values. They are carried out because the occupants appreciate their amenity value. However, larger building projects — extensions, conversions, rehabilitations and especially new housebuilding — call for much closer assessment of your labour input. By taking on even part of the work yourself, you are in effect becoming a speculative builder whose work will be rewarded by enjoying an increase in the value of your property. The more work you carry out yourself, the less you pay to others and the greater your eventual profit (in theory). The problem with this sort of work is that your labours are far more likely to be rewarded in line with property price movements rather than with how hard or well you yourself work. In boom times your rate per hour may appear to be enormous (and you'd probably think yourself very clever for embarking on this nice little tax-free earner); however, the slump has put all that into a new perspective, and many D-I-Y builders will

have found that they have actually lost money — and the more masochistic will have converted that into a loss per hour which begins to make slavery look like an attractive alternative.

Most people would not consider carrying out all the work themselves. In fact, the vast majority of people would have no more wish to take on such a task than they would choose to educate their children at home; life simply isn't that long. There are, however, many people who find their work is seasonal, intermittent or out of normal working hours, to whom a high level of involvement in a building project makes good sense. They will tend to be practical and experienced in problem solving and those that are already running their own business will have much of the organisational backup in place already. The extra costs involved will not be enormous and even if their work only nets them £2.50/hr, that's still more than they'd get doing nothing.

However, for many people selfbuilding may just prove to be a lousy option. They will be committing themselves to 2-3000 hours work — often very hard and dirty work — putting up an overpriced structure to a design that isn't very good in the vague hope of making a "dream home" and a "fantastic windfall profit" to boot. Ask yourself two questions:

· If it was that easy to make money, why don't more selfbuilders turn into professional property developers?

· If builders' profits are so exorbitantly high, how come so many of them keep going bust?

I started as a selfbuilder (albeit with a renovation not a new build) and went on to become a "professional" (in that other people paid me for my labours), often working alongside selfbuilders. It'll come as no surprise when I report that the hours are long, the work is backbreaking and the pay is crap. Actually, when I started building in 1980 the pay was quite good: a good builder would earn more than most manual workers and as much as many professionals like teachers and junior doctors. However, pay rates have basically remained unchanged since about 1984 and now builders have fallen way down the list — you now get more working on a Tesco's night shift. There are no huge profits in the building trade — it's a very competitive business, and though thousands of small builders have gone under during the reces-

1b: Effect of Interest Rates

BORROWING RATES	10%	15%	20%
Stage 1: £20k for 8 months	£1,333	£2,000	£2,667
Stage 2: £20k for 6 months	1,000	1,500	2,000
Stage 3: £20k for 4 months	667	1,000	1,333
Stage 4: £20k for 2 months	333	500	667
Total interest after 8 months	£3,333	£5,000	£6,667
Interest for each extra month	£667	£1,000	£1,333

sion, there is a seemingly never ending stream of hopefuls waiting in the wings to fill their shoes. Most building work is done by loosely affiliated gangs of subcontractors (subbies) organised by a gaffer: most subbies reckon they are doing well if they pull in £15,000/annum (though plumbers and electricians have always earned more) and in recent years gaffers have fared little better.

Yet despite both the low wages and near-zero inflation in building materials, building work is still perceived to be expensive. Perhaps this is an accurate perception; after all building is still a very labour intensive operation and labour — even cheap labour — never seems cheap when it's you that's paying for it. The point I'm trying to get around to is that whilst you will naturally be saving yourself the cost of that labour if you carry out the work yourself, you might well be better employed earning a tidy sum elsewhere; after all not many individual builders earn less than the subbies they employ.

Management with a Broom
For every seven or eight hours spent on construction, one hour has to be put into servicing the site. This can involve any and everything from sweeping up and unloading lorries to meeting building inspectors and buying materials. Many selfbuilders take on this "management with a broom" role thinking that they may not be able to plaster a wall or fit a staircase, but they had no trouble organising the school run therefore... Be warned. You'd be right to think that the organisational skills are not in themselves exceptional, but their efficient execution is very dependent on a thorough working knowledge of the building trades and the local building practices and prices. After three or four projects, you'll start to get halfway good; if it's your first time, you'll find it an almighty struggle and you'll be unlikely to do it well. Your subcontractors will very quickly realise they are working for a novice and the less scrupulous ones may be very tempted to take advantage of this and to cut corners or to bodge, particularly if you've negotiated "keen" labour prices. Whilst your building inspector should ensure that the structure is adequate, very little professional checking takes place above foundation level and, in any event, most of the finishing trades are not covered by building regulations.

Furthermore, don't kid yourself that you're doing away with the overheads of employing a main contractor by managing the project yourself. Your phone bill will be up by £100-£200/quarter; your mileage will increase two or three fold, even if you are living on site;

you will need site insurance; you will suffer damage to materials which will have to be replaced at your own expense; you will end up with leftovers that you cannot easily get rid of; and at the end of the job, you'll have to chase yourself to get all those little snags finished. Over half of a main contractor's mark-up goes on paying overheads that would be common to professionals and amateurs alike. And, as the pie chart on this page hopefully makes clear, there is still the tricky little matter of finance to pay. There are many other costs besides plot and building costs, and they are all conspiring to eat away your paper profit.

Still wanna Selfbuild?
I would argue that the rewards of selfbuilding are not chiefly financial. What it really allows people to do is to have the freedom of choice to design and build a new house to their specifications, something that you will not be able to do by any other route. For many people it represents one of the great challenges in life. The more they are involved in the project, the more they get out of it and the whole attraction of selfbuild is the pure adventure of it all. If this is your motivation then more power to your elbow and all that. You'll find that the only disappointment that results is that you'll never quite be satisfied by what you've done and will be haunted by a whole host of "what ifs" and "if onlys." Fear not, this is an experience common to all designers and builders. You'll just have to do it all again.

However, if your motivation is mainly financial then I warn you to look very carefully at the sums involved.

- Yes, you can save money selfbuilding but it may not be as much as you might first expect.

- Don't ignore the well-trodden route of hiring a designer (who in turn manages the job for you) just because you think it is bound to be expensive.

- Never forget that property developing (for that is what you are doing) is a very risky business. Unlike many financial products which are now sold with warnings attached, building plots and the houses that go on them are sold on the understanding that the buyer knows the risks involved. You are assumed to be a sophisticated investor; make sure that you actually are.

American Viewpoint
In the States, the concept of selfbuilding (or *owner build* as they call it) is as old as the hills and is much more widespread than it is in the UK, in some areas accounting for over half the new homes constructed. There are many people who build this way primarily to save money but there the expectations are generally much more realistic. I am indebted to several US builders and owner builders who have e-mailed me about selfbuild in the USA and here are two of the typical responses.

Where the Money Goes

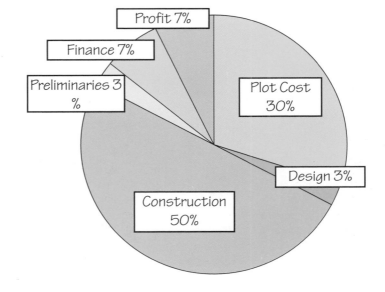

Clay Thompson of Minnesota: "There is a strong contingent of people who Act as their own General contractor here in the States. This practice, to the uninitiated, is a frightening experience at best. The problem for most is that they find there is no way to keep the small details from slipping through the net. They do boast a cost savings of about 10 percent, I think they are lying, though the ones who have some business savvy and the time to work out the details do okay."

Denis Hathaway: "I'm a general contractor in Los Angeles, and I've heard (and seen) various horrors visited upon homeowners who undertook to act as their own contractors. My advice is to forget about it unless you've got a lot of time and energy to put into selecting and supervising subcontractors. You've got to make sure they're properly licensed and insured, you've got to make sure they'll do the work to your satisfaction at a fair price, you've got to know how to schedule them if you don't want the job to take forever. Having been in the building business now for 15 years, I can tell you that proper supervision is the key to the successful completion of any project, and that this supervision requires a significant investment of time and energy."

This last sentence hits the nail on the head. Houses don't build themselves and the subcontractors that build them don't all gell together like a well-oiled machine; they need a huge amount of chivvying, chasing and challenging.

In fairness to the other side of the argument, I should point out that there are American owner-builders who claim to have saved a whole stack of money by organising it themselves. But I suspect that what is really going on here is a variation on the old saying that an optimist sees a glass as being half full whilst a pessimist sees it as being half empty. The selfbuilder has an emotional investment in their project and really wants to believe that all that work actually made sense financially; on the other side, the professional builder has good financial reasons for *not* wanting to exaggerate the profitability of any scheme they undertake — to do so would be to hand money over to the taxman. Thus the professional builder will account for every cost they possibly can whereas the selfbuilder will be inclined to overlook many of the legitimate overheads in order to make the final sum look more pleasing to their eyes.

Nowhere is this discrepancy greater than in the area of finance. To a developer, finance is just another job cost, essentially no different than the cost of the land or the building costs. When the house is sold on, they will total up all the loan interest they have paid and add it in as a legitimate business cost. The selfbuilder is in a rather different position. They may — probably will — already have a mortgage before they even think of taking on a major project like a new house or a major renovation. By transferring this mortgage from an existing house to a building plot they are not necessarily altering their cashflow at all and do not have to add this cost into their calculations. What they are doing is exchanging a year or two's hardship (such as living with the in-laws or in a caravan on site) for the opportunity to live in a bigger or better house than they could otherwise afford. Whilst a cost accountant would probably say

that the selfbuilders are deceiving themselves, it seems to me to be a perfectly legitimate approach to things.

If there is a danger for the selfbuilder in all this, it is that they will tend to get greedy and to overreach themselves. It is notoriously difficult to accurately predict building costs and the world is full of people with a vested interest in making building costs look cheaper than they actually are — and also to inflate the value of the completed houses. Getting prices out of builders and subcontractors is often much easier said than done and the chances are that most selfbuilders will have to commit themselves to a building project before they have a clear idea of the actual costs of the project. Often people realise at a comparatively late stage that they can't afford the scheme they have embarked on and desperately start seeking ways of reducing the costs. Many will complain bitterly just how expensive builders are when the root of the problem is that they always had inflated expectations of what they could achieve with the money at their disposal. Many people are bounced into becoming project managers because they think it is bound to be cheaper to build directly with subcontractors. This is not the way to become a selfbuilder, it's the way to become a headless chicken. Even hardbitten professionals have problems reconciling their dreams with their budgets and it is essentially in response to this problem that I wrote this book — to help put you, the person paying all the bills, back in control of the situation. Read on.

1c: How Big is that House?

	m²	ft²	Range of building costs
One-bedroom flat	40	430	£12,000-£20,000
Terraced two-bedroom house	60	650	£18,000-£30,000
Semi-detached, 3 bedrooms	90	970	£27,000-£50,000
Detached 3/4 bedrooms, integral single garage	130	1,400	£40,000-£70,000
Large detached 4/5 bedrooms, detached double garage	200	2,150	£70,000-£150,000

Beware Building Costs

You may have a very good idea of what you can afford but, unless you are an experienced developer, you are unlikely to have much idea of how much and what sort of house that money will build. Novice builders often make the mistake of clutching at building costs, usually measured in £/ft² (that's pounds per square foot) and assume that they should divide their budget by the going rate (often around £40/ft²) and the answer is the size of house they should build. For instance, if your building budget is £60,000, then — by dividing £60,000 by 40 — you could build a 1500ft² house. You may be very happy with this outcome, but it is also just possible that a 1200ft² house built to a much higher specification would have suited you better. You don't judge cars by their size and you shouldn't judge houses that way either.

Trouble is that all of these figures which are casually bandied about — none more so than this £40/ft² figure — are themselves very casually defined. There is no British Standard number to define what a building cost actually is and there isn't really such a thing as an industry standard either. Neither is there complete agreement on just how floor areas of houses should be measured. Different businesses use different methods and this makes a minefield out of the task of comparing costs and setting budgets.

Measuring Floor Areas

You might at first think that how you go about measuring a floor area is a little bit academic. It is, if you aren't basing your budget and/or designs on some cost/unit area, but the evidence is that a huge number of builders do just that. And for those contemplating buying a timber frame kit, the floor area measurements are habitually used to compare one supplier's product with another, despite the fact that there is every chance you will not be comparing like with like.

The most widely used floor area measurement in Britain is the one which refers to the internal floor area of the house. It expressly excludes the area of the external walls, although (largely for convenience when carrying out the measurements) the area taken up by the internal partition walls is included. This measurement is also known as the net floor area.

Gross v Net

There is another floor area measurement commonly in use, the gross floor area, which includes the area of the external walls. The effect of including the external wall areas in the calculation is to increase the apparent size of the building by up to 15% as external walls are, these days, usually constructed at thicknesses of 240-300mm. On the continent, it's the gross floor area that people usually refer to and many of the kit home suppliers use gross floor areas in their sales literature without being explicit about the fact and there is often no way of telling which area they are talking about other than by measuring it up yourself with a ruler. Using a gross floor area will appear to reduce cost/ft² by 15% — an illusion.

Garages

Garages should not be regarded as living space, even when they are integral to the rest of the house. Again, there is no check other than you and your ruler and you need to be very careful when evaluating sales literature to see that any integral garage is not included in the overall floor area. In contrast, detached garages are unlikely to be included as part of the floor area of a house in such literature, but here the trick is to exclude their building costs from any overall budget calculations. As a garage will typically cost between £5000 and £8000 to build (which may be as much as 20% of the total building cost), either its inclusion in floor areas or its exclusion from building costs will have a dramatic (and wholly misleading) effect on apparent build costs/m².

Net Floor Area v Gross Floor Area

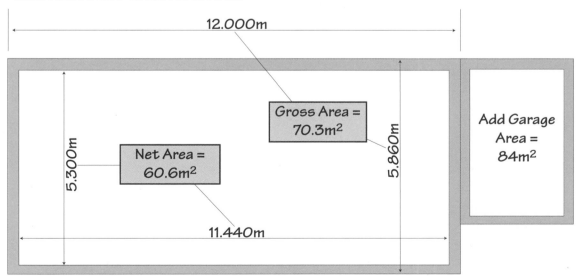

External Walls are 280mm thick, usually 12-15% of the gross floor area

Added to possible confusion over net and gross floor areas, the lack of a consistent benchmark for measuring floor areas of houses means that a four-bedroom house with an integral garage could be said to be 150m² by one method and as much as 200m² by another.

Grey Areas

There are a number of other features worth examining. When you get into the swing of measuring house sizes off plan, you will undoubtedly come across features which are not clear cut. Again there are no hard and fast rules but I would suggest the following assumptions are fair.

Cupboard Space

Storage space such as under-eaves cupboards which are common when your upper storey is built into the roofspace, should be excluded from internal floor area. However, built-in full height wardrobes should be included as normal living space.

Utility Areas

Normally these would be included as part of the living space. Sometimes it is hard to judge where a utility/storage area ends and a garage begins; if you're in this position don't worry too much because at least you understand what the issues are.

Internal Walls

Conventionally, these are measured straight through and they are included as part of the internal area.

Stairwells

Normally measured straight through on both floors and therefore included as internal floor area as if it was regular circulation space. The exception comes when you have a large open plan arrangement, not often seen in new houses but common in barn conversions where large openings have to be preserved. How do you decide when your ordinary stairwell becomes extraordinary? The rule is that if the upper floor opening is restricted to just the functioning stairwell, then measure straight through on both floors: if the open

area extends beyond the immediate staircase, then you must exclude the entire stairwell area from the upper floor area.

Building Costs

So much for defining the internal floor area. The "building costs" are even harder to define. There is no official standard but there is a sort of British way of defining building costs, as detailed in the accompanying Table 1e. Making long lists and producing definitions is all very well, but what I am trying to get at is that building costs are really just a subgroup of development costs and that to concentrate on building costs to the exclusion of other costs is potentially disastrous. Like building costs, development costs can vary enormously and in this respect there is no greater variant than the price paid for your building plot. Some building plots are far more expensive to develop than others; problems can arise with bad ground, slopes, difficult service connections, difficult access, trees, legal covenants, intransigent planners — you name it! Now, the art of property developing is to be able to predict these problems and to negotiate a price on the land which reflects the cost of getting around them: if you stick to the well-worn mantra of "Forty pounds a square foot, forty pounds a square foot" then you stand a real chance of being shafted by a whole range of costs which you may feel are totally out of your control but in reality should have been easily predictable.

All housebuilders must pay close attention to these extra costs. One advantage a selfbuilder has over a professional is that they have more potential to control the project cashflow. For instance, you may not need to build a garage at all which could bring substantial savings. You can defer certain non-essential works such as landscaping for many years if cash is tight. You can substantially reduce your financial commitments by roughing it a little bit whilst the house is being built. And, of course, you can reduce costs by undertaking some of the work yourself. But all of this will pale into insignificance if you fail to budget the project correctly in the first place; to achieve significant savings, you need to buy and develop your plot appropriately, be very organised and be able to stick tightly to a budget.

1d: Building Costs v Development Costs

WHAT'S INCLUDED	WHAT'S EXCLUDED
House Superstructure	Building Plot
Electrics, Plumbing and Heating	Legal Fees
Kitchens and Bathrooms	Finance
Cooker and Hob	Insurance
Services Laid On	Design Fees
Working Drains	Planning Fees
Limited Paving	Building Regulation Fees
Garaging	Infrastructure Charge
Driveway	Service Connection Fees
Turfing	Floor Finishes
	Fitted Cupboards
	Laundry and Dishwasher
	Light Fittings
	Landscaping and Planting
	Curtains and Blinds
	Furnishings

Chapter 2
The Benchmark

The front door of the benchmark house is, confusingly, located at the back of the house overlooking the small estate which was developed on an old farmyard site.

The Housebuilder's Bible bases itself on the idea of a benchmark house around which all the alternative techniques and costs can be examined. For this edition, I have selected a house which I personally had a hand in building, albeit rather an indirect one. This has one big advantage in that I have had full access to the design and construction cost data, but this advantage comes at a cost in that it's not actually typical of what developers are currently building, as the business which I work with is rather specialised. Not that it's so *very* unusual — there are no experimental features, it's not an eco-house, it's neither an ultra modern design nor something that looks like it's 300 years old. It's just that it's not quite the house which a spec developer would have built.

Built in Cambridgeshire in nine months starting in July 96, the house itself is a large three bedroomed-affair — I've given it away already, spec. builders do not build large three bedroom affairs. Why is it a large three bedroom affair? Although it went on the market (in 1997, at just under £150,000), it was not originally envisaged as a speculative development at all but was commissioned by a local farmer as a residence for his farm manager. However, during the course of the build, the farmer found another cottage in need of renovation in the same village and his objectives changed so that our house became a speculative development halfway through the building program. Its origins as an individually designed home mean that in many ways it fails the acid test of the spec. developer or, to put it another way, it is over-specced for the site it occupies and its build cost is well over the 50% of the sale price which is the type of ratio deemed necessary locally to make a living from housebuilding. In particular, it's floor area (166m² or 1786ft²) is almost enough to warrant a five bedroomed house — spec. developers usually switch from three to four bedrooms at about the 100m² mark — yet it boasts just three bedrooms. So what? Aren't there loads of people out there wanting three large bedrooms rather than five small ones? Well, maybe but most housebuilders don't take such risks preferring to stick to tried and tested formula.

In terms of amenity, the house is really very close to conventional standards. It is situated on a tiny plot (nothing unusual there); it has an attached double garage which together with the paved area takes up most of what garden space there is. If the garage had been allowed to open onto the side road, the house could have had a small but private garden space but the planners insisted that there had to be a turning space on the plot and this turning space effectively takes up the garden. There is nothing unusual in this: planners as a rule insist that you can't back out into an adopted road.

Inside the house, downstairs is split by a hall/stairwell. On one side is the living room, on the other side are two doors, one opening into a room described as a dining room (but which will probably get used for other purposes) and the second door leading into a large kitchen which itself unfolds into a "Meals Area", a utility room and finally a door through to the double garage. Upstairs there are two bathrooms besides the three bedrooms. Oil-fired heating is via a boiler in the garage and radiators in all the rooms. The kitchen is a natural wood finished Shaker-style made by Arena, the white goods are by Neff, the internal finishes are lots of magnolia paint; the doorknobs are white porcelain. All nice, but nothing out of the ordinary.

Above: immediate neighbour is a timber clad barn (top photo) and the external house design draws from this (bottom shot after completion). Below: little touches like this access door are typical of Complete Fabrications attention to detail. Bottom: Shaker-style kitchen by Arena.

Externally, it's a little unusual in that the majority of the walling material is timber boarding and the roof is natural slate (at the insistence of the planners).

Why timber boarding? Well the house is one of a number to be developed on an old farmyard site and immediately adjacent is a timber barn conversion, all weatherboarding and dark stained windows. The benchmark house is a visual echo of this barn: in fact, stylistically, it sits halfway between a standard 90s developers house and a standard 90s rural barn conversion. There are certain features like the chimney and the dormer windows which you wouldn't expect on a barn: other features like the extensive timber boarding and the *Narrow Module* windows which you wouldn't expect on a regular house.

The Builders

Complete Fabrications is a design and build business run out of a small office in a street of terraced houses in Cambridge. Its proprietor is Robin Gomm who has been building and converting homes for some twenty years. Robin and I have been business partners in the past and I still take an active role in setting up some of the building work and so I know how the business works. The workforce is usually around about the eight mark and most of them have been with Robin for several years — in many ways it's not that unusual a small building business though the fact that the proprietor is also the scheme designer is still a little uncommon. The workload consists of a mixture of one-off houses (almost always built for individuals rather than done on a speculative basis) and a varied mix of extensions, loft conversions, kitchens and pure planning work.

This particular house was built by a mixture of the regular crew and a number of outside subcontractors almost all of whom have worked on Robin's projects before. The groundworks is now always carried out by the in-house crew following some less than satisfactory experiences in the past where subcontracted groundworks have gone badly wrong. The brick and blockwork is always subcontracted out as are roofing, scaffolding,

plumbing and electrics. The bulk of the in-house work goes into carpentry and finishing.

Building Costs

The following tables summarise the costs of construction of the benchmark, split wherever possible into labour and materials with a section at the end on design and management. It was not a particularly cheap house to build; whilst most sections are very close to industry averages:

- Groundworks is high due to the soil being clay and the trenches having to be excavated to a depth of 1200mm
- First fix carpentry is high due to the complex roof design
- Roofing is very high due to using second hand roofing slates as cover
- Overall labour element is high in some sections due partly to the use of a direct labour crew for some elements of the work. Direct crews are always more expensive but usually result in better standards.

Taking all that into account, it sounds like its going to be completely over the top but it's not. The build cost is £469/m^2, the overall development cost (excluding land) is £536/m^2; the final bill to the client was £587/m^2 including the design work and the fees — what is sometimes called the "full turnkey service." Given that selling prices in the area in 1997 were nudging the £900/m^2 mark, you can see that this would have hardly ranked as a big money spinner for the client. I reckon that had the scheme been designed as a speculative house from the ground up, it could have been built for perhaps 10% less without effecting the sale price. Perhaps more importantly it would have been designed very differently and probably would have been quite a bit smaller than it ended up. No matter…it serves its purpose well enough for a benchmark.

It is also worth pointing out that every house is different and each site presents different problems. Complete Fabrications constructed a 200m^2 timber frame house during this same period, again using their own designs and their own crew to carry out the work. Despite this other house being 20% larger, the design and build cost was not significantly different to this benchmark house — i.e. the unit cost of the works was much less. The important point to grasp here is that it is always very dangerous to generalise and that building costs can vary quite dramatically on apparently similar projects. Please bear these words in mind as you read the rest of the book.

2a: Benchmark House Building Costs: Table 1 (of 3)

Item	Quantity		Rates			Totals			
		Mats	Labour	Plant		Material	Labour	Plant	Costs
Clearing Oversite	62 m³	0.33	7.00	8.90		20	434	552	1,006
Excavating Foundations	65 m³	0.33	7.00	8.90		21	455	579	1,055
Trenchfilled Concrete	50 m³	50.00	14.20			2,500	710	0	3,210
Footings	85 m²	6.50	5.00			553	425	0	978
House Beam & Block Floor	95 m²	12.70	4.20			1,207	399	0	1,606
Garage Beam & Block Floor	30 m²	12.70	4.20			380	130	0	510
Garage Floor Structural Slab	30 m²	9.00	6.00			270	180	0	450
Foul Drains	30 m	18.00	12.00			540	360	0	900
Main Drain Connection						100	200	0	300
Rainwater Drains	48 m	13.00	10.00	2.00		624	480	96	1,200
Service Trenching/Ducting	35 m		9.00	2.00		0	315	70	385
GROUNDWORKS						**6,215**	**4,088**	**1,296**	**£11,600**
Inner Skin Blockwork	158 m²	6.00	6.00			948	948		1,896
Outer Skin Blockwork	158 m²	6.00	6.00			948	948		1,896
Garage Blockwork	51 m²	6.00	6.50			306	332		638
D/S Internal Walls Blockwork	47 m²	6.00	6.00			282	282		564
Chimney Blockwork + Lining	30 m²	16.50	16.50			495	495		990
Chimney Brickwork	12 m²	15.00	20.00			180	240		420
Plinth Brickwork (House)	60 m²	16.00	12.00			960	720		1,680
Plinth Brickwork (Garage)	20 m²	16.00	12.00			320	240		560
Garden Wall (Curved Brickwork)	10 m²	16.00	18.00			160	180		340
Regular Lintels	15 No.					500			500
Steel Beams	3 No.					300	250		550
Cavity Wall Insulation	183 m²	1.80				330			330
MASONRY						**5,729**	**4,635**	**0**	**£10,364**
First Floor Joisting	70 m²	6.70	6.90			470	480		950
First Floor Cover	70 m²	4.90	5.00			340	350		690
Studwork Walls, Bridgings	62 m²	7.60	8.10			470	500		970
Window Cills	14 m	6.40	14.30			90	200		290
House Trussed Roof	132 m²	9.50	9.50			1,250	1,250		2,500
Utility Area Roofing	30 m²	8.30	33.30			250	1,000		1,250
Dormers	2 No.	75.00	150.00			150	300		450
House Fascias/Soffits	42 m	4.80	8.30			200	350		550
House Bargeboards	41 m	2.40	3.70			100	150		250
Porch Roof	4 m²	12.50	37.50			50	150		200
Roof Insulation	93 m²	3.10	4.30			290	400		690
Garage Roof Carpentry	44 m²	6.80	17.00			300	750		1,050
Garage Fascias/Soffits	12 m	2.10	8.30			25	100		125
Garage Barge Boards	16 m	1.60	6.30			25	100		125
Weatherboard Cladding	95 m²	8.90	10.50			850	1,000		1,850
Floor Ducting	25 m	9.50	5.00			50	125		175
FIRST FIX CARP						**4,910**	**7,205**	**0**	**£12,115**

2a: Benchmark House Building Costs: Table 2 (of 3)

Item	Quantity		Rates			Totals			
		Mats	Labour	Plant	Material	Labour	Plant		Costs
House Windows	16 No.				880	100			980
Garage Windows	2 No.				95				95
Velux Rooflights	2 No.				360	100			460
External Door Frames	3 No.				300	50			350
External Doors	3 No.				350				350
Garage Doors	2 No.				470	60			530
House Glazing for Windows	10 m²	24.00	12.00		240	120			360
Toughened Door Glazing	2 m²	35.00	12.00		70	25			95
Garage Glazing	1 m²	14.00	12.00		15	10			25
Staircase	1 No.				475	300			775
Door Linings	10 No.	12.00	15.00		120	150			270
Internal Doors	10 No.	32.00			320				320
Airing Cupboard Doors	1 pr.	45.00			45	40			85
Airing Cupboard	1 No.				20	50			70
Door Hanging (Int & Ext)	15 No.	20.00	25.00		300	375			675
Skirting	185 m	1.80	1.00		340	190			530
Architrave	133 m	1.20	1.00		160	130			290
Pipe Boxing	6 m				25	250			275
Vanity Units	3 No.				50	150			200
Loft Hatch	1 No.				25	50			75
Snagging						300			
JOINERY, GLAZING & SECOND FIX CARPENTRY					**4,660**	**2,450**	**0**		**£7,110**
Roof Tiling (House)	166 m²	24.00	8.50		3,980	1,410			5,390
Roof Tiling (Garage)	44 m²	25.00	8.40		1,100	370			1,470
Rainwater Goods (House)	50 m	3.60	3.00		180	150			330
Rainwater Goods (Garage)	20 m	4.00	3.50		80	70			150
Scaffolding (House)							680		680
Scaffolding (Garage)							170		170
ROOFING & SCAFFOLDING					**5,340**	**2,000**	**850**		**£8,190**
External Render (House)	13 m²	2.70	6.50		35	85			120
External Render (Garage)	33 m²	2.70	6.50		90	215			305
Plasterboard and Skim	287 m²	2.60	4.50		740	1,300			2,040
Internal Render and Skim	230 m²	1.50	3.70		350	850			1,200
Underfloor Insulation (inc prep)	92 m²	2.70	2.20		250	200			450
Screeding	92 m²	3.30	4.30		300	400			700
PLASTERING					**1,765**	**3,050**	**0**		**£4,815**
Power Circuits	24 skts				420	500			920
TV/Telecom Wiring	5 skts				50	100			150
Lighting	21 outs				360	690			1,050
Fans	3 fans				150	180			330
Smoke Detectors	2 No.				60	30			90
Alarm System					150	250			400
ELECTRICS & ALARM					**1,190**	**1,750**	**0**		**£2,940**
Oil Tank					200	180			380
Central Heating & DHW					1,860	1,760			3,620
Bathrooms & WC					1,005	1,132			2,137
PLUMBING & HEATING					**3,065**	**3,072**	**0**		**£6,137**

2a: Benchmark House Building Costs: Table 3 (of 3)

Item	Quantity		Rates			Totals			
			Mats	Labour	Plant	Material	Labour	Plant	Costs
Kitchen Units						2,000	400		2,400
Worktops						360	150		510
Sink/Plumbing						180	200		380
Appliances(inc VAT)						940	150		1,090
KITCHEN						**3,480**	**900**	**0**	**£4,380**
Mastic Frames/Sanitaryware						150	250		400
Fire Surround						180	200		380
Painting Ext Render House	13	m²	1.90	6.90		25	90		115
Painting Ext Render Garage	33	m²	1.80	7.00		60	230	0	290
Staining Joinery House						140	800		940
Staining Cladding	95	m²	3.00	4.00		285	380		665
Staining Joinery Garage						30	120		150
Emulsion Walls/Ceilings	490	m²	0.40	1.20		200	600		800
Internal Glosswork						150	1,200		1,350
Wall Tiling	25	m²	20.80	18.80		520	470	70	1,060
DECORATING & TILING						**1,740**	**4,340**	**70**	**£6,150**
Ground Preparation	200	m²	1.80	3.30		350	650		1,000
Paving	106	m²	6.50	8.50		692	900	20	1,612
Fencing	27	m	18.90	13.00		510	350	30	890
Border Fencing	22	m	5.50	6.80		120	150		270
Turfing	80	m²	1.70	1.90		135	150		285
EXTERNALS						**1,807**	**2,200**	**50**	**£4,057**

	Material	Labour	Plant	Total Costs
ALL BUILDING COSTS	**39,847**	**35,690**	**2,266**	**77,982**

Build Cost/m²	166	m² net floor area	£469
Build Cost/ft²	1,789	ft² net floor area	£44

	Material	Labour	Plant	Costs
Planning Drawings	100	1,650		£1,750
Planning Permission	160			£160
Other Design Work		2,000		£2,000
Building Regs	340			£340
Structural Engineer		300		£300
NHBC Warranty	400			£400
CDM Planning Supervision	225			£225
Water Connection	180			£180
Infrastructure Charges	410			£410
Electricity Connection	350	110		£460
Site Security Fencing			990	£990
Site Management	170	2,920	460	£3,550
Office Management		390		£390
DESIGN and PROJECT MANAGEMENT COSTS	**2,335**	**7,370**	**1,450**	**£11,155**

ALL DEVELOPMENT COSTS			**£89,144**
Development cost/m²	166	m² net floor area	£536
Development cost/ft²	1,789	ft² net floor area	£50

Above and right: road view as building work progresses.

Below left: beam between kitchen and meals area.

Below right: relatively complex roof carpentry results from building with a "room in the roof" design.

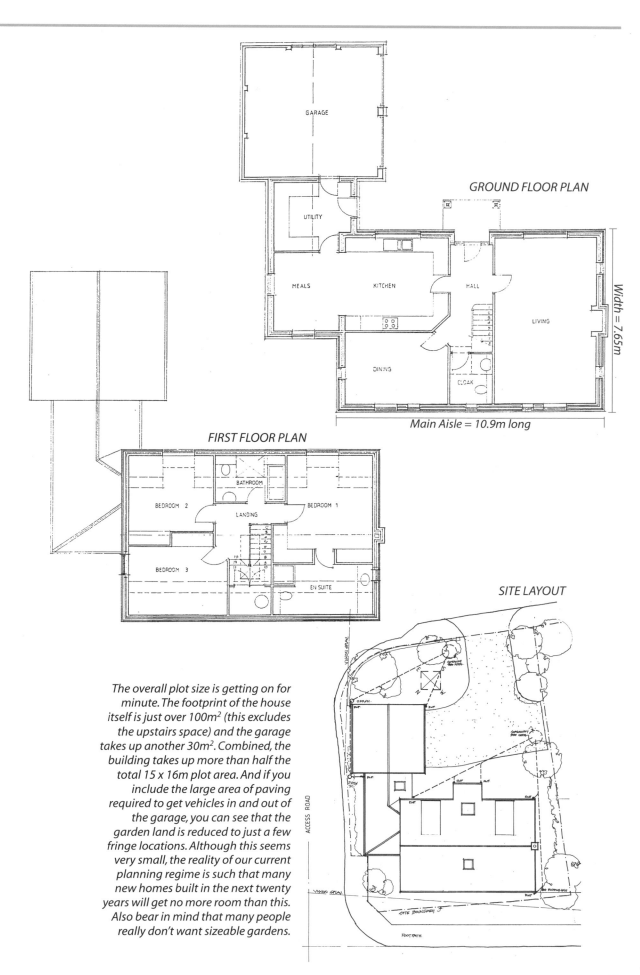

GROUND FLOOR PLAN

GARAGE

UTILITY

MEALS

KITCHEN

HALL

LIVING

DINING

CLOAK

Width = 7.65m

Main Aisle = 10.9m long

FIRST FLOOR PLAN

BATHROOM

BEDROOM 2

LANDING

BEDROOM 1

BEDROOM 3

EN SUITE

SITE LAYOUT

ACCESS ROAD

The overall plot size is getting on for minute. The footprint of the house itself is just over 100m² (this excludes the upstairs space) and the garage takes up another 30m². Combined, the building takes up more than half the total 15 x 16m plot area. And if you include the large area of paving required to get vehicles in and out of the garage, you can see that the garden land is reduced to just a few fringe locations. Although this seems very small, the reality of our current planning regime is such that many new homes built in the next twenty years will get no more room than this. Also bear in mind that many people really don't want sizeable gardens.

Benchmark Blues

The benchmark house chosen for this edition is not totally typical of what you might buy from a plc housebuilder such as Wimpey Homes or Barratt. Though the initial spec. is not greatly different, there were one or two unusual features, already described, which made it rather more expensive to build than the housebuilding industry's standard. What the table on this page does is to compare this industry standard with an immensely expensive version of the same thing. So the first column will appear to be a bit cheaper than our benchmark, the second column will be twice as much.

What manner of things could cause you to spend twice as much money? Some may be beyond your control:

- A sloping site set 50 metres back from the road
- Difficult ground conditions needing special foundations
- No main drains or gas available
- Located in a conservation area requiring natural stone walls and roof coverings.

Add to this recipe some extras that you might select for your project in order to have a very high class home:

- Hardwood joinery throughout
- Expensive kitchen and bathroom fittings
- Inglenook fireplace
- Moulded covings, architraves and skirtings
- Professionally designed lighting system
- Super-efficient insulation levels throughout
- Energy-efficient, safety glazing throughout
- Underfloor heating combined with condensing boiler
- Mains pressure hot water delivery
- Intelligent alarm system.

Outcome

Refer to table below.

Much of the rest of the Housebuilder's Bible is concerned with exploring all these options and problems in much greater detail, frequently referring back to the benchmark house. But before I move on, it is good to take a brief look at just what damage all these accumulated changes could do to an ill-prepared budget.

2b: How To Double Your Building Costs

	Developer's House	Expensive Alternative	Reasons
Clearing Oversite	£600	£4,000	Sloping Site
Foundations	1,770	5,000	Difficult ground
Foul Drains	900	3,000	On site treatment
Service Connections	980	4,000	Site > 50m from services
Driveway Foundations	800	1,600	Site> 50m from road
External Skin	4,500	14,000	Build in natural stone
Cavity Wall Insulation	300	1,100	Use 50mm Styrofoam
Chimney	1,200	3,500	Have two chimneys/fancy brickwork
Timber Windows/Doors	2,000	4,500	High performance hardwood
Glazing	500	1,100	Laminated, Low-E glass
Trussed Rafters	1,000	3,000	Cut roof, ready for attic, plus more complex design
Roof Tiling	2,400	11,000	Handmade tiles or Welsh slate
Rainwater Gear	500	1,200	Cast iron or seamless aluminium
Plasterboard/Dry Lining	2,400	4,400	Use Fermacell board
Coving	390	750	Use moulded coving
Underfloor Insulation	250	500	Use 50mm Styrofoam
Staircase	500	1,200	Made to measure
Skirting/Architrave	750	1,400	Specify hardwood
External/Internal Doors	730	1,800	Hardwood doors
Door Furniture	300	800	Specify higher quality
Lighting	1,050	3,000	Specify low voltage halogen lighting scheme
Ventilation	280	1,500	Whole house ventilation and heat recovery
Heating system	3,050	5,500	Oil-fired condensing boiler/underfloor heating
Fireplace	300	4,000	Specify an Inglenook fireplace
Alarm	650	2,000	Specify a TotalHome switching system
Kitchen	4,100	12,000	Specify Smallbone style kitchen
Sanitaryware	1,050	3,500	Specify Continental bathrooms
Wall/Floor Tiling	700	2,500	Specify handmade tiles
External Paving	1,500	7,500	Site> 50m from road
Fencing	270	1,800	Site> 50m from road
Unchanged Elements	35,000	35,000	
Total Build Cost	£71,000	£146,000	
Cost/m² on 166m² house	£428	£880	

Chapter 3
Pitfalls

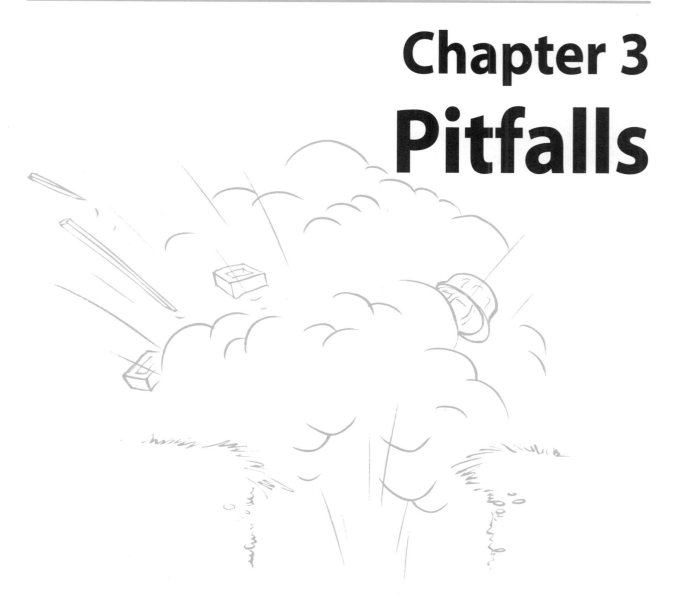

Buying Land

"Where do I find the land?" is the most commonly asked question by wannabe builders. All the many selfbuild exhibitions have stands dedicated to selling building plots and often I am to be found just a few feet away, busy signing and selling this very book. And yet still the most frequent question I am asked "Where do I find a building plot?"

"Have you looked over there?" I reply.
"Oh yes, but they're all expensive."
"Well, land is expensive."

Shoulders shrugged. Conversation ends. Once or twice the conversation doesn't end there but develops along the lines of "How do I get building land for the price of farmland?" I say I wish I knew, if I did I wouldn't be here flogging my book. Then conversation ends with more shrugged shoulders.

People aren't dumb. They realise that the only way to make a killing at this property game is to get hold of the land for nothing or next to nothing. Time was back before they had such strict planning controls (I'm talking 50 years ago) that land changed hands cheaply pretty much regardless of development potential. Houses were built with large gardens because people appreciated large gardens; farmland with road frontage changed hands because people wanted to grow things; barns were barns, not development opportunities. But these days anybody owning such a piece of land or an old outbuilding is well aware that these are considerable financial assets worth far more than their intrinsic value and they don't let them go for peanut prices. The planning policies adopted in England and Wales in 1947 – which have grown ever stricter since – have deliberately restricted

the supply of building land in order to protect the landscape and one of the many side effects of this policy has been to force up the price of building land to exorbitant levels. Every village, every street is subject to a local plan which involves drawing lines on maps around each and every settlement and deciding which infill spaces can be built on and which can't. Visit your district reference library and check out your Structure Plan (usually referred to as the *Local Plan*) and you'll understand how little land there is on which development will be permitted. Then you will understand just why building land is so expensive.

You may find odd advertisements in the press for outfits claiming to be able to locate untitled land, the implication being that you need only register it yourself to be able to lay claim to it. If only it was that easy. There is no un-owned land in this country, certainly none you can build on. Other advertisements claim to be able to help you identify potential building plots; there are undoubtedly plenty of potential building plots about but just because you identify one doesn't mean that the owner will sell it to you for a song. Afterall, if someone offered you £500 for the back-end of your garden, wouldn't you be a bit suspicious. One thing this book is not going to tell you is how to get hold of cheap land this side of the Channel. France…now there's another book altogether.

Mechanics

The actual process of buying land (or derelict buildings) is similar to that involved in buying houses. And indeed the principles are exactly the same, though the detail is very different. You don't buy a house if you think it's too expensive or if you think it's going to fall down; you normally employ solicitors and surveyors to ensure that you are not buying a pig in a poke. Likewise with plots, you want to ensure that you can build what you want on it at a price you can afford. Having said that, the whole process of buying plots (and, especially, *renovation opportunities*) is more complex because there are more things that can go wrong. When buying an existing property at least you know that it is there (even if it might just fall down next week!); with a building plot you are buying nothing more than a field which comes with a promise, a hope for the future. And unlike the conven-tional house market, the chances are that you will have to purchase your chosen plot without knowing exactly what you can build where.

Professional Help

If and when you find a plot or a barn that you would like to purchase, then your first objective is to agree a price with the seller (or *vendor* as they get called in these circles). As with houses, always make any offer you make "Subject to Contract" which means that your offer is not binding until contracts are exchanged. NB The situation in Scotland is rather different; the offer to buy (if accepted) is actually deemed to be a binding contract from which you cannot walk away so you have to undertake all your preliminary investigations before making an offer. This state of affairs also applies in the rest of the UK if you are buying at an auction.

Hire the services of a solicitor (or a licensed conveyancer). A good one, if you can find one. Certainly look for a property specialist who knows which questions to ask and who knows the area well. If you are buying in an area new to you, you'd be well advised to look for a local rather than sticking with someone you've used before who might be 200 miles away from the action. Now is the time you need as much information, official and unofficial, as you can get. A good solicitor will uncover more than just that which is revealed by undertaking searches and checking for legal complications and boundaries. But even the best solicitor is not going to be able to advise you as to whether the plot is an A1 purchase because there are a number of other areas that wouldn't concern even the most scrupulous legal beaver. To get an overview of these concerns, and it's no more than an overview, I have summarised them as human problems and physical problems on the following pages.

In truth, land buying is a very technical and complex subject and there is no one expert you can turn to to get it all worked out. Gen up: you could do worse than read *How to Find and Buy a Building Plot* by Roy Spear & Michael Dade — phone 01273 843737. The biggest problem for many people is that the really nice plots and renovations tend to be sold in a matter of days and that very often you are in a hopeless position unless you have finance available and ready to go before you even hear about an impending sale. As I write, the property market in SE England is buoyant and most of the estate agents in my area had hardly any small development opportunities on their books at all during the year and, when they did, they usually sold them within a couple of weeks at or above the asking price. Narrow market, tough market. Undoubtedly the main reason why selfbuild is not even more popular than it already is. If you are choosy about where you are going to live, then you have to be prepared to a) act fast and b) pay over the odds.

Human Problems

The prospect of buying a duff plot is a nightmare that haunts professional builders as much as amateurs, and the consequences of doing so are likely to be with you for many a year to come. There is no absolute foolproof way of avoiding the lemons but a little bit of diligence (and a good lawyer) employed at the pre-contract stages of negotiations should uncover most of the problems. These problems broadly fall into two camps; the first to do with the technicalities of ownership and planning permission, the second with problems encountered on site.

Legal

Covenants

Building plots are often sold with legal constraints over what may and what may not be done to them. The most common form of constraint is the covenant whereby the vendor (i.e. the person selling the plot) requires that the purchaser should fulfil a number of conditions. Many of these might not cost a penny — i.e. no caravans to be stored in the back garden or no trees to be planted where they might block someone else's view — but others can involve substantial costs. The commonest type of covenant deals with boundary fencing and would read something like this:

The purchaser covenants to erect 6' high fencing to the south and eastern boundaries of the plot before any building work takes place.

Sometimes the covenant will be very much more specific and ask for a brick wall nine inches thick or something like that. A condition such as this is expensive to meet and should really be reflected in a lower plot price.

Rights of Way

There are any number of complications that should, repeat should, be uncovered by your solicitor's search: rights of way crossing the plot, existing wayleaves for services and cables to cross the plot, complex shared ownership of access roads, to name but three. Even if you can live with these arrangements, they may well affect resale values and may well make finance much harder to get and insurance more expensive. Many of these problems can be sorted out by throwing money at them — but the canny buyer should ensure it's the vendor's money not theirs.

Plot Access

Another likely cause of problems occurs when part of the land needed to successfully develop the plot is owned by someone else. Normally this would show up at an early stage of legal enquiry and would be down to the plot vendor to sort out, but one thorny problem that might get overlooked is the local highway authority's requirement for visibility splays at plot entrances. A visibility splay is a wedge of uninterrupted view either side of a driveway entrance which allows vehicles pulling out to see what is coming. Just how large this area needs to be is down to individual authorities and you would be well advised to check this matter personally with them before proceeding with a purchase. A typical snag here would be that planning permission has been granted for a house with access which is legally unbuildable; either you have to purchase a wayleave over a neighbour's land or you must alter planning consent.

The important principle to understand here is that the legal constraints on building a house (or access to that house) will not necessarily be the same as the planning constraints — and vice versa. A solicitor's or conveyancer's brief is to sort out the legal complexities surrounding purchase, not necessarily to advise on planning problems. Never assume that the development will be trouble-free just because it has detailed planning permission.

Options

If it is any consolation, this is an area that causes big headaches to major professional developers as well as virgin housebuilders. If you are in any doubt about these issues, my advice is to use what muscle you have as a plot purchaser and, if possible, take out an option to buy your chosen plot rather than formally exchanging contracts.

What is an option to buy? The bare bones of a contract might look like this: you agree a price on a plot of land (though even this doesn't have to be fixed in stone). This remains in place for say 2-3 years (the length of the option is entirely up to you). During that time the vendor is prohibited from selling to anyone else. Some contracts involve interest payments to the vendor: this acts as a spur to the purchaser to get on with it and protects the vendor from time wasters. The big plus from the purchaser's point of view is that an option protects you from gazumping and other forms of treachery.

How much would you be expected to pay for an option? Well, that depends. If the planning angle is difficult and you are taking on the costs of obtaining planning permission (which could be several thousand), then there may well be no payment made to the vendor at all. They would be very happy for someone else to do all this work for them. However if market conditions are buoyant, then you may have to part with up to 5 per cent of the plot price just to tempt the vendor into an option. Also the buyer may want to make the plot price conditional on what you manage to squeeze out of planning so that the price is £60k if you get one house but £100k if you get permission for two.

If there is a pitfall in all this, it is that you can spend a lot of money and get nowhere. But that's a pitfall that all property developers have to face.

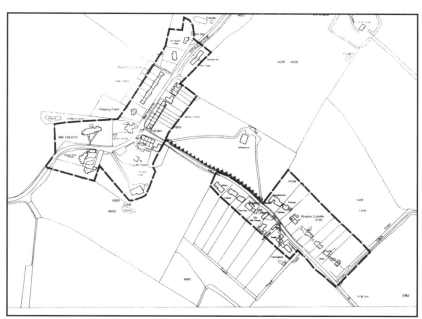

Every village has a framework boundary to restrict new building

Planning

It is paradoxical that 18 years of Conservative government dedicated to "rolling back the frontiers of the state" presided over ever-toughening planning laws. As I write, our new Labour administration is still in its honeymoon phase and it is not clear if any changes are afoot. If they are, it's odds on that the state frontiers will be rolling forward some more. The planners — albeit accountable to elected local councillors — now have considerable and arbitrary powers over what you can and cannot do on a piece of land that you nominally own; in effect there is a level of "state ownership" over each and every building plot which supersedes individual ownership and you must fulfil the conditions placed on you before you can begin to put your own ideas in place.

Time Lapses

One potential problem for the unwary is the fact that planning permission has a time limit on it. Normally this lasts for five years from the date the permission is granted, but there is one kind of planning permission, known as outline permission, which basically expires after just three years. As many small or selfbuilders will be buying a plot which has only outline permission to build, please note that you have to get detailed permission before the end of the three-year period or you have a very expensive field on your hands.

Once the work has begun, you no longer have to apply for planning permission. Exactly what the definition is of "work having been started" is a grey area, but it is universally accepted that if you have laid the footings then you have started. So if time is running short and you don't have the wherewithal to complete the building work, you can ensure your planning permission is permanent by undertaking just the foundation and footings work.

Planning Concerns

The planners are concerned with far more than whether a particular plot can be zoned for building. Some of the major areas they will look at will be:

- size of the house : is it "too big for the plot?"
- site of the house : don't assume you can build anywhere on the plot
- neighbours' privacy and right to light
- style of the house: design and materials "must be in keeping"
- vehicular access and turning heads: a particular problem on narrow fronted plots, less than 12m wide. The highways department insists that not only will adequate visibility splays be provided, but that there must be adequate room on site for cars to turn around or, as they say in planning speak, "enter and leave in a forward gear."
- trees and hedges: often have to be retained or replanted. Sometimes this can become a real hot potato and Tree Preservation Orders can be slapped on inconvenient trees just to make life difficult for you. It all calls for tactful negotiation, which is another way of saying that they will usually insist on you planting (native species only) around three times as many trees as you uproot. For builders, trees are a mixed blessing.

Conservation Areas

These are areas defined by the planners as being especially sensitive and on which they maintain a whole raft of extra controls over what you can and can't do — for instance you need to fill out a three page application in order to fell a tree. Conservation areas are typically the older parts of a town or the core area of a village, perhaps surrounding the village green, and the fact that you are buying in such an area should be apparent when you purchase — after all it is usually used as an additional sales bullet in the blurb and passes as an excuse to hoick the price. It affects new builders less than renovators because new build is already subject to stringent planning controls. But be aware that you will be unlikely to get permission for anything unusual in a conservation area.

Logically the issue of conservation areas ought to be dealt with by regular planning controls but logic and local government make uneasy bedfellows and conservation area issues are not dealt with by regular planners. There is of course a trap in here waiting to catch the unwary: if, for instance, you apply to build an extension to an existing house in a conservation area which involved the removal of some existing structure, you could find that your permission to build the extension gets approved by planning but your permission to demolish what already exists is turned down by the Conservation department. This is known, technically, as being kyboshed.

Listing

The other great wedge of planning control concerns the listing of buildings thought to be of merit and which, therefore, need extra protection from unscrupulous owners and developers. The complexities of repairing and altering listed buildings really lie beyond the scope of this book. Yet it is important to realise that many of the current crop of potential barn conversions are already listed by virtue of the fact that the adjacent farmhouse has been listed. There are, amazingly, nearly half a million listed buildings in Britain so most villages have one or two and some places have whole rafts of them. In principle, you are allowed to develop listed sites but you need to obtain listed building consent as well as planning permission; this is almost always a very slow and painstaking process and the outcome is that you will almost always have to spend rather more on the building than you would if it wasn't listed. Listed building officers are attached to each planning department and this is the person to head for in order to glean more information.

Unpleasant Surprises

When considering the problem from a perspective of hidden costs, it is the planners' interest in the design and materials of the house which is of most concern. Sometimes these concerns are easily predictable: if, for instance, you are building in one of the stone belts where there is a uniform vernacular style (as in the Cotswolds or the Yorkshire Dales), you will not be surprised to learn that you must build with similar materials. Expensive but not unexpected. However, most of Britain does not have a uniform building style and lowland England in particular is characterised by its great variety of building styles and materials. Despite this diversity, the planners can insist on any number of design details, examples of which now follow.

Slate Roofs

Even in East Anglia, home of the (cheap) pantile, planners are frequently known to insist on slate roofs despite the fact that most roofing slate comes from North Wales and wouldn't have been known in England before the railway age. You may be able to argue that reconstituted slate will be adequate but it will still cost you about £6-£10/m² more.

Dislike of Rooflights

They sometimes insist on dormer roof windows. A small dormer will add at least £400-£500 to construction costs; in comparison, a flat opening rooflight (a Velux) would cost no more than £250. Paradoxically, on barn conversions the reverse is true: planners hate dormers on barns.

Altering Roof Pitches

A common planners' ruse. A steeper roof pitch is more expensive because it increases the roof area. A 45° pitched roof covers an area 16% bigger than one at 35° and can only add around this much to roofing costs.

Altering Windows

If they insist on a window radically different from a standard casement this could easily double joinery costs, possibly adding £1000 to construction costs on a four-bedroom house.

Changing External Materials

Unless they insist on an expensive stone facing, the materials costs of differing wall constructions is not that large. And the brick market is such that insistence on a different kind of brick is unlikely to have a huge effect on price.

For more detail on the mechanics of planning permission, see Chapter 4, Design.

Only when a house has detailed planning consent without any reserve matters is it possible to accurately budget the above ground costs of construction. However, below ground, we come up against another set of unpredictable variable costs, determined to make a mockery of your budget.

Physical Problems

The development costs of any new home can expand considerably because of problems encountered on site. These potential pitfalls fall into two main areas: problems encountered with the site itself and difficulties encountered in getting access and supplying services to the site.

Problem Sites

There are three basic causes of alarming cost expansion:
- slopes
- bad ground
- trees.

Straightforward excavation and foundation work can be relatively cheap. A detached house built on a problem-free site with good bearing ground, both flat and treeless, could have oversite and foundation trenches excavated, foundation concrete poured and footings built for as little as £3000. However, any of the above problems could have increased foundation costs by up to another £5000, and if you have more than one of these problems in combination, expect your costs to increase by up to £10,000. My benchmark house was built on clay soil and the foundation work cost around £6000.

For more detail on these problems and how they are overcome, read Chapter 6, Groundworks.

Visual Inspection
The first step in assessing any building plot is to take a walk over the site and the surrounding area. Be on the look out for clues as to what may have gone on in the past. Some points to watch out for are:
- Foundations of former buildings on site
- Evidence of drains, old water courses or wells
- Subsidence cracks in neighbouring buildings
- Overhead cables
- Springy ground — suggests high water table
- Slopes greater than 1:25
- Trees within 30m of your proposed foundations — species, size and girth should be noted
- Any evidence of ground having been disturbed or used as a dump.

Background Detection
Investigations with local council, service companies, etc. should reveal more historical and geographical data on which to assess likely problems. Talk to neighbours, local builders or building inspectors who may well know the lie of the land.

Trial Pits and Borings
Many builders now dig trial holes as a matter of course, whatever the history or geology of the ground. The normal practice is for the pits to be dug to a depth of 3m (close to but not under the foundations) in the presence of a structural engineer and then filled in. The engineer then decides whether the house foundations can proceed as normal or whether a more complicated foundation so-

lution is needed. Expect to pay an engineer between £70 and £150 for this service, though their fees will be much higher if special foundation designs are needed; a JCB for an hour should cost an additional £20-£50 (depending on travel time). Augered boreholes are another alternative — likely to be more expensive but a better option where access to JCBs is not possible.

Contaminated Land
Where the problems with the site are caused by the natural characteristics of the land, the solutions are usually fairly straightforward, if expensive. However, there is now a trend towards recycling building land and an increasing number of new homes are being built on sites which have had buildings on before — these sites are sometimes known as *brownfield sites*. If the previous building was a house or a barn, then a pollution problem is unlikely but if the site has been used as a tip or as an industrial plant then it is quite likely that the ground may contain a whole cocktail of nasties such as heavy metals, toxic chemicals or methane gas. Now local authorities up and down the land are currently preparing registers of contaminated land and they will be empowered to issue *Remediation Notices* which will require the landowner to make the site safe, which usually means either excavating and dumping the pollutants elsewhere (the Brent Spa option) or encasing them in concrete or clay (the Chernobyl option). Sometimes the solution may be relatively cheap — for instance specifying sulphur resistant cement — but it will be some time before housebuilders are able to accurately budget for contamination problems.

Radon
Radon is a naturally occurring radioactive gas which is present in a few areas of the UK, most notably parts of Devon and Cornwall. It's a relatively low risk hazard but there is

Typical backland site development. Note the 100m driveway stretching away to the road beyond the bungalow: this will add at least £10,000 to development costs.

increasing concern about the long term effects of radon build-up in new homes which are built to much higher standards of air tightness and which, therefore, may act as potential radon traps. The good news for new housebuilders is that it is relatively easy and cheap to incorporate the recommended membrane beneath the ground floor which acts as a barrier through which radon cannot pass; however, renovators of existing properties should be aware that remedial work is much more difficult.

Access Problems

When assessing a plot or a barn, you should take note of the distance you think you will have to take the services and the access you will have to build. Many backland developments come onto the market these days — typically the rear of someone's garden — and the prices asked for these sites are often little different to the prices asked for somewhere with a road frontage. Yet the budget cost of laying private driveways, drains, water and electricity combined with providing fencing is upwards of £100/metre; that means that a plot set 50 metres back from a road is going to cost £5,000 more to develop than one with a road frontage. Whereas the layout of vehicle access arrangements are usually easy to work out, finding out about the services requires detective work.

Driveways

The basic cost of laying a drive can be budgeted at around £50/lin.m., rather more if it is required to be fenced off as well. Often there is extra work involved in connecting to the public highway: typically you may have to construct a dropped kerb if you are crossing a raised pavement, at the very least you will have to provide a small apron of asphalt or tarmac so that there is no unsightly gap between your drive and the public highway. In some situations you may be required to create a visibility splay which may involve removing existing obstructions and rebuilding them further back from the road. On the other hand, you may have to construct a bridge over a ditch or even make an opening through an existing building. There are, in fact, so many potential access problems that it is almost pointless trying to summarise them — you will, in all probability, be all too aware of them when you first visit the site. Just be aware that whilst a straightforward highway junction will cost a couple of hundred quid, complicated access arrangements may well set you back several thousand.

Drain Connections

Many isolated plots are too far from mains drainage to make connection feasible. To find out what the position is on any given plot you must contact your local council and/or your local water or sewage company. The detail and accuracy of records varies from area to area but they will have some idea of the location of your nearest drain.

If the mains sewer is reasonably adjacent and it's not obviously uphill from your plot, then the omens are fairly good. Excavation and drain connections are, however, fiddly and expensive on even short runs, and if your drain is, say, 50m away from your house it is worth talking to a groundwork/drainage contractor about the other possibilities.

Disposal Options

Sewage disposal via a nonstandard route is going to add significantly to costs. A reasonable budget on a no-problem single site, draining straight into a main drain, would be £2500. If you have to do something other than make a straightforward sewer connection, then you would be wise to budget these amounts in addition:

- Septic tank — add £1500
- Mini-treatment works — add £2500
- Cesspool — add £2500
- Pumping station — add £3000
- Foul drain runs longer than 50m — add £20/m
- Rainwater drain runs longer than 50m — add £15/m
- Rainwater that won't soakaway — add £300.

One frequently met problem is the development of a site that is located on backland or down a lane. Main drains are present under the main road but your site is maybe 150m or more away. How do you assess the situation? Probably the best solution is to get a groundwork contractor to have a look and give an estimate on how much a connection would be. If the figure goes up much over £2500 then you would do well to think of using some of the alternative solutions. This is something else that is touched on in greater depth in Chapter 6.

Service Connections

Water

Unlike drainage work, which is usually left to the housebuilder to organise, water connections have to be carried out by the powers that be. In England and Wales that means the private water companies and their fees are notoriously high, frequently higher than £500 for connections which need very little

excavation, involving perhaps just three hours work; if your connection needs a road to be dug up, then the connection fee will be in thousands. All new houses in England and Wales are now fitted with water meters and these are conventionally placed at the boundary of the property so that at least you can control the costs of laying pipe from the boundary to your house; but all work carried out under or next to a public highway must be carried out by the water companies and it will cost.

Fortunately, there is one ray of light in all this and this is that water companies will provide a free quotation for their work. They will need location and site plans, but there is no need for you to own the property, so it makes good sense to get this quotation before agreeing a plot price.

In Scotland and N. Ireland the situation couldn't be more different. Here it is beholden on the local authorities to provide water and, providing the property is a only a 'reasonable' distance from mains supply, then work is carried out at the council's expense.

There is always the possibility of drawing water from under the ground via a borehole; this is almost invariably a costly option and can only be recommended if you have a very remote site (or you have a particular desire not to connect to your local water company's supply). Costs depend largely on depth of groundwater and can vary from as little as £1500 to as much as £10,000; if you are interested, check out *Wellborers* in your Yellow Pages.

Electricity

Like water, installation to new sites is charged on a time and materials basis. Even a simple connection (say less than 25m from mains supply) is likely to cost in excess of £300 and charges rise in line with distance. However, RECs offer a similar quotation service to the water companies and you should avail yourself of this.

Other Services

It is unlikely that other service connections will result in budget busting costs. Gas supply to a new dwelling is either going to be reasonably cheap or it isn't going to happen at all. It all depends on how near the mains gas supply is. Very often supply is free if the mains is adjacent. Phone lines are costed on a flat rate; there is a maximum charge of £99 (+VAT) for new BT residential lines, whatever the distance. Cable charges are set by local companies but, like mains gas, will tend to be either low or not available.

Random Perils

Overhead Cables

Power cables running across your plot are bad news. They may intersect with your proposed building, in which case they will have to be moved; even if they don't they will detract from the resale value of the property. Burying them is the obvious solution but it can be horribly expensive; even a low voltage cable can cost over £20/m to bury, which can easily make a short diversion cost £2500 or more. Again, the trick is to get quotations for this before entering into any contract to buy.

Existing Drains

This is one real nightmare for rookies and professionals alike: existing drains running across your proposed building. Do what ever you can to find out if drains are present, but sometimes there are no records and no surface evidence. Drains vary in their importance; small runs connecting one or two households to a sewer may very easily be diverted — depending on the lie of the land — but sewers and pumped drains cannot readily be moved and discovering one of these in your footings is a Grade A disaster, though thankfully this doesn't happen too often. Again the key is to find out as much as possible about the plot before you exchange contracts to purchase. Instigate a thorough site survey and dig trial holes where you want to build. If there is any doubt in your mind,

The tell tale signs of an overspecified house: note the garage in the foreground hard on the highway boundary and neighbouring houses in the background look to be worth much less.

then try and place a retention in the sale contract which is only payable should nothing untoward be found under the ground.

Conversions

Don't assume that any building that has once been occupied by humans will automatically qualify for residential planning permission. Councils take widely differing attitudes to what constitutes abandonment and the most telling factor is whether or not an old building can be converted into a new home is usually the quality of the building, not it's previous usage. Always check on the status of a derelict property in the local plan to see whether redevelopment is likely to be controversial. Often the planners will allow the conversion of a particularly fine old barn just to stop it from disintegrating and sometimes this permission is dependent on the structure being maintained, even when this is a costly and relatively dangerous course to take. There have been cases of planning permission being withdrawn from barn conversions after the builder has undertaken demolition of a few select walls, sometimes on the advice of the building inspector.

Borrowing Money

I have already touched on the perils of property developing on borrowed money but it would be amiss not to touch on them once more because borrowing money, large dol-

lops of the stuff, is perhaps the most dangerous peril of all. Against this, it must be said that the borrowing climate has changed out of all recognition since the boom of the 1980s when developers were only having to put up 10% of the total costs and lenders were quite happy to see the loans repaid from the sale values. Nowadays you are very unlikely to be offered building money unless the lender believes you have the wherewithal to service the debt. If you already have a large mortgage and feel comfortable that you can meet the repayments, then the fact that you transfer this mortgage to an unbuilt or partially built property should not make very much difference to you. But never forget that there are many things that can come between you and the large paper profit which you start out with. Don't assume that this profit will flow effortlessly to you as you complete your building programme and always be prepared for a situation where you cannot sell the finished house at the price you hoped for, or indeed at any price at all.

Over-specifying

It is said that the three most important factors in property development are location, location and location. Like many other jokes, there is a pearl of wisdom here and one which rookie housebuilders would do well to heed. Building plots, just like existing houses, have to be assessed in relation to the neighbourhood they are located in and what goes on around them. If you are interested in maximising the return on your investment, then

Look out for evidence like this. PM stands for Pumped Main, the type of thing you really cannot divert.

don't fall into the trap of specifying a luxury house on a plot which is surrounded by houses of a much lower quality. Rich people like to live in quiet secluded neighbourhoods, well away from the noise and grime of traffic and industry, and close by other rich people; poor people don't get the choice and have to make do.

If you have no intention of moving for many years to come and really don't give a hoot that your house is next to a council estate or a rubbish tip or a chicken farm, then go ahead and build your mansion on that nice cheap plot you found. However, if you are hoping to maximise your profit, it pays to take careful heed of the location you are building in and to specify a house in keeping with the neighbourhood. This is not hard to do, just look around and see who your would-be neighbours are and, more importantly, how much their houses are worth. A well-built new house will tend to attract a premium price, perhaps as much as 15-20% more than second-hand stock nearby but it is vital that you realise that however much money you pour into your house, you will not improve much on this premium.

This is a particular problem for selfbuilders in SE England who have recently been competing with each other and chasing up the prices paid for quite humble plots of land.

Naturally enough, they want to build the best house they can afford because they want to live in it but this often means ignoring the time honoured rules about the importance of location. The general inexperience of self-build purchasers also means that the lessons contained in this chapter are often ignored or, more likely, just not known about so that there is often precious little difference in price between an A plus plot and a C minus. Most estate agents have only the dimmest ideas about building costs and tend to value properties and plots almost entirely by amenity and location. It is up to the buyers to assess the development costs and the likely resale value.

Pitfalls Checklist

Before buying a plot of land, you should check the following points. None of them is a reason for not buying, but all of them present potential extra costs which you need to be aware of and, perhaps, this knowledge may even enable you to negotiate a lower price.
* *Are the described boundaries accurate?*
* *Are there any restrictive covenants on the plot?*
* *Are there rights of way crossing the plot?*
* *Would you own all the land necessary for access and services? If not, are wayleaves readily obtainable?*
* *Are there any tree preservation orders?*
* *Are there any other "legal encumbrances" which might hinder you in anyway?*
* *Is access adequate for cars? Are there stipulations from Highways that could be difficult to meet?*
* *Is the plot wide enough? Plots narrower than 12m can present problems for turning vehicles.*
* *Are there any planning conditions in effect?*
* *When does planning permission run out?*
* *Is there a slope steeper than 1:25?*
* *What are ground conditions like?*
* *Is there evidence of existing drains on site?*
* *Are there any large trees within 30m?*
* *Are there any overhead cables to be moved?*
* *Are there likely problems with service connections?*
Many of these potential administrative snags should be unearthed by your solicitor. The more technical ones are normally dealt with by building professionals — i.e. architects and structural engineers. If the plot looks dodgy in anyway, don't hesitate to get help. Consider commissioning a feasibility study from your designer before contracts are exchanged — because this should unearth most of the bugs. At the end of the day though, it's caveat emptor — buyer beware — because you are where the buck stops and it'll be down to you to sort out any dodos.

Chapter 4
Design

House design is undoubtedly the trickiest issue faced by every potential builder. The central point that shouldn't be forgotten is that you want to build the best possible house for a price you can afford. Easily written, but how the hell do you do it? What is the "best possible house?" And how do you go about designing it?

Questions abound. Is an architect necessarily an expensive option? What about using a designer who is not a qualified architect? Isn't it cheaper to use a package build design? Won't the planners force me to redesign the whole thing in any event?

Well steady on, I'll cover these issues in due course. But first let's take a look at the design process because...well, it's a good place to start. The design process can be subdivided into a number of parts, some fixed points with known costs and others elastic in the extreme. Below is a list of the stages that you need to go through. You don't have to do it in this order (you could for instance apply for building regulations approval before you have planning permission) but it would be frankly very strange not to do it this way. It would be a bit like driving from London to Manchester via Scotland.

- Site Survey and Feasibility Study
- Design Process leading to Sketches of Options
- Commission drawings for Planning Permission
- Submit Plans for Planning Permission (fee)
- Try and Negotiate Positive Outcome to Planning Application
- Do this Over and Over Again till outcome is positive
- Detailed designs and specifications
- Submit detailed designs for Building Regs Approval (fee)
- Negotiate Positive Outcome.

Site Survey

Unless you are very confident of your surveying and drafting abilities, you should have a professional carry out an accurate site survey to measure and plot all the existing buildings, boundaries, levels, access arrangements, trees, drains, neighbouring buildings and any other information thought to be relevant. On simple sites this might cost £100-£200. If by chance you've read the previous chapter (Pitfalls), then you'll realise that a smart plot buyer will have carried out much of this work before signing any contracts. Don't rely on professionals to sort these problems out for you after the event.

Feasibility Study/Sketches

Assuming you have a plot and a budget, the most important questions are what can you build on it and how much will it cost? It may seem very early in the whole mysterious design process but you have already reached crunch point. This is usually the key moment when you start to commission the whole building process and your decisions at this point will have costly implications on down the line. I have distinguished between a stage called *Feasibility Study* and another called *Sketches of Options*; this is helpful in understanding how one grows out of the other but in reality there is no hard and fast dividing line between them, and how you and your designer get from an empty page to a full planning application will vary enormously from case to case.

Nevertheless there tends to be a clear path which leads from the site survey stage into a feasibility stage (which, if you like, is about eliminating impractical options) and then into outlining practical solutions and from there, plumping for your best choice at which point the designer changes gear and starts to look at the nitty-gritty decisions which spring from the choice you have made. A professional at £15-£25/hr may seem a luxury, but they will (or at least should) understand the issues and concentrate your thinking on the relevant areas. There may or may not be any consultation with local planners at this stage, depending on how confident you or your agent feels. If doing it yourself, then a visit to the planners would be advisable. Use books of house plans for inspiration (despite the fact that they're mostly anything but), but do not expect to fit an existing plan on to your plot; the chances of it working without amendment are small and amending existing plans can be almost as expensive as starting from scratch.

The cost of this stage is naturally very open-ended: some short-of-work designers will undertake the early parts of this process for free on the understanding that more work will follow. For many independent designers and architects, the early part of the process is the most challenging and the most interesting and they would anticipate spending around a third of their time on this stage. The biggest variable is you, the client. The more sussed out you are, the better your brief, and the shorter and cheaper this process will be. Even if you are planning to build a kit house or use an off-the-shelf design, it is still worthwhile getting a professional designer to undertake some sort of study if only to sort out practicalities like drain runs (though note that many kit suppliers have their own designers who will undertake this work).

Planning Drawings

A good designer with a thorough working knowledge of local practices and trends will be able to help you marry your ideas with the views of the planners, hopefully pre-empting any potential areas of conflict. Planning departments are surprisingly diverse in their ideas, often reflecting the individual tastes of the chief planning officer, and knowing the whys and wherefores of local planning decisions is one way in which local knowledge scores heavily over nationwide services.

Whoever you choose, they will have to produce a set (in fact several sets) of planning permission drawings to present to the local planning department. Budget anything from £200 for pre-drawn plans through to £1500 for architect one-offs.

For a detailed look at the mechanics of applying for planning permission, and the likely fees, see the following section. There are a number of plans and drawings that the planners require and your chosen designer/agent should know this rigmarole backwards — indeed if they don't I would be tend to be rather suspicious.

Working Details

If designing from scratch, it is conventional not to decide on all the construction details until planning constraints are established. This is simply to make sure that work does not have to be done twice in case of later amendments. However, construction details on conventional houses are remarkably similar and often the details can be lifted from previous jobs. On simple projects, the plans, construction details and specification (known as the *spec* with a soft 'c') can all be contained on two sheets of A1 (840x592mm) plans which would detail:

- Floor plans
- Foundation plan
- Drainage plan
- First floor joist layout
- Roof truss/rafter layout
- N,E,S and W elevations (or views)
- Section or sections through the middle of the house, showing room heights, floor levels, wall constructions, joist depths, staircase dimensions.
- Window and door schedule (list of joinery manufacturers codes)
- Text explaining construction standards (lots of BS numbers here).

On more complicated jobs, there may be extra plans perhaps running to many pages, showing various complicated details like eaves or dormer windows. Upmarket jobs tend to have the specification written separately from the drawings and a serious architectural practice may write a specification running to fifty pages or more. How much of this is necessary depends on a) the complexity of the work and b) the attitude of the client. Rookie builders would be well advised not to attempt anything too unusual first time around, in which case the standard two-sheet plans are probably adequate. Many experienced subcontractors never look at plans in any event — quite a few can't read — and complex plans could be wasted on many.

I know of a number of small builders who basically dispense with the working drawings stage. They work from little more than the planning drawings, littered with notes like "To be confirmed onsite" or "To Building Inspector's Satisfaction"; they are on site everyday and they prefer to work out these details as they go along. Once you've done it a

few times, it works fine provided you stick to fairly standard solutions (they do). But if you are new to this game and/or you can't be there on site a good deal, then you would do well not to skimp on working drawings as these form, in effect, your detailed instructions to your builder. Much of this detailed work and, in particular, the writing of the specification, forms the very heart of any forthcoming building contract. If you want an element of protection from the perils of badly executed building work, then a professionally written specification is worth far more than any off-the-peg contract that you might be tempted to sign.

In budget terms, these design details are the area with the most variance. If purchasing a set of predetermined house plans (typically for £300-£500), then all this detailed work will be included with the plans so the effective cost is zero. If using a package build, then again these details will come integrated with the package. But be wary of assuming that pre-drawn plans are necessarily the cheapest option, because 90% of the time they require significant amendments and sometimes it proves to be just as expensive as starting with a blank sheet of paper. However, even a one-off design may cost no more than a few hundred pounds if it sticks to tried and tested solutions; on the other hand, this part of the design work can also very easily cost £2000-£4000 for unusual houses as unusual features take time to design — and build. Here you would expect workshop joinery, arched openings, fancy staircases, patterned brickwork — generally expensive features which are also expensive to design. If you are building to a tight budget and are happy with conventional solutions, then make it clear that you do not want unusual detailing and, as a result, a) your working details should not cost too much, b) your house isn't likely to be expensive to build and c) it is much less likely to run over budget.

The danger in trying to put a price to all this is that you may lose sight of the fact that, as with so many things in life, you get what you pay for; if someone knocks up a set of plans for you over a couple of weekends for a few hundred quid, the chances are that your finished house will reflect the fact. On the other hand, if you are interested in creating a wonderful home you'd be daft to skimp on the design stages. If you want to save money, you'd probably do better to build a smaller house.

Structural Engineer

Having been called in during the digging of the trial hole, the structural engineer may have to make another appearance if the designs take on any non-standard features. All beams, lintels, roofs and foundations (the so-called structural elements) of a building require proof that they are sufficient to do the job asked of them. Standard solutions to standard problems are regarded as tried and tested, but anything out of the ordinary will require "proving" to the satisfaction of the building inspector. A structural engineer will calculate the forces applied to beams or foundations and come up with adequate solutions. If the ground you plan to build on is at all dodgy, then an engineer will be required to prove your foundation design; also many very ordinary situations like using steel beams or opening up a loft space require structural proving. If you want to build in timber frame without going via a specialist supplier, you need to get the design proved by a specialist engineer qualified to issue an HB353 certificate. This would normally cost between £300 and £500 per dwelling.

Detailed drawings and structural calculations (if needed) are presented to the local council's building control department for examination.

Sub-designs
Design and specification of finishes is often left to the client or builder to sort out and this is more often than not passed down the line to the tradesmen involved on the job. Therefore, the plumber designs the central heating system, the electrician designs the lighting, a kitchen specialist will take over design of the kitchen. This sort of arrangement obviously works as it is what happens in 90% of homes built, but arguably it could be much better coordinated by a single designer.

On large, commercial contracts these areas are all dealt with separately by specialist professionals who draw up a specification and arrange quotes from it. One-off housing is really too small to justify the expense of all these extra professionals, and much of the work, designed and installed by the various tradesmen, is consequently very unimaginative. The degree of competence varies enormously: many act as much as salesmen as designers: most make no charge provided you buy their product, which is all very well but it makes you very vulnerable to uncompetitive practices.

It's really a very difficult area to negotiate, even for hard bitten professionals. Many architects are not qualified to give advice on, say, lighting design or interior decorating. If you are happy with tried and tested solutions to problems then you will be well advised to keep it simple and deal directly with your chosen contractor; if, however, you want to explore the many and varied options open to you, then you could do worse than read the rest of this book which is peppered with contact names and numbers.

In Conclusion
Design and professional expenses are the hardest areas to budget for because they are so variable. To a large extent, they are dependent on the brief that you, as a client, present to the designers. An off-the-peg house plan can be purchased for a few hundred pounds but will very probably require a great deal of alteration to fit both the site and your ideas. In contrast, an architect would charge over £5000 for designing something like our benchmark house; however, it does not follow that the off-the-peg plans are necessarily better value. The resulting house might be £5000 more expensive to build but might also be worth £10,000 less when finished! Here you must use your own judgement and intuition.

Planning Permission

Planning permission and building regulations are two big hurdles that every would-be housebuilder will have to jump. They are complex and not easily mastered, and many building professionals have bald patches on their heads where they have torn their hair out from negotiating paths through or around the maze of regulations and precedents that govern our construction activities. For a rookie builder this can seem all rather daunting, especially when you're not even clear what's the difference between planning permission and building regulations — or *regs* as they are known in the trade, as in "God, there's been another bloody change in the regs." The regs are dealt with overleaf — first planning permission.

What Exactly Is It?
Various Acts of Parliament (notably the Town and Country Planning Acts), mostly introduced since 1945, require that local authorities should control what can be built where and how buildings (and land) should or should not be used. Planning permission is not concerned with how you build (that's the building regs), nor with who owns the land on which you wish to build. There are many small construction projects that do not require planning permission but something of the size of a new house invariably does.

The power-that-bees in this respect is your local council. Not your County or Metropolitan Council, but your District or City council. In Scotland the system works slightly differently, as it does in National Parks, but then they wouldn't want to make it too straightforward, would they? It gets worse. Officially, the licence to build is granted by the elected councillors, but every council has a full-time planning department which consists of civil servants known as planning officers, and these are the people who actually deal with planning applications. Indeed, the chief planning officer has powers to make certain decisions off his or her own bat. Even when they choose not to exercise these powers they make "Recommendations" to the committee of councillors as to whether an application should be accepted or refused. The planning committee rarely goes against the recommendations of its planning officers.

Foreplay
You don't have to have any contact at all with the planners before submitting your application, but it is commonplace to do so. Tactics are involved here and there is no such thing as a correct way of going about it — every case stands on its own. On the one hand, you don't want to be faced with the expense of drawing up plans only for the planners to fall about laughing at the very thought that anyone could build on that piece of land; on the other hand, if you wander into the planning department with questions like "What sort of house could I build on this spot?", then you are inviting the planners to design the house for you. This they won't do, but what will happen is that they will get in their minds all kinds of constraints that will severely limit your options: "You must do..." and "You can't have..." Like our legal system and our parliament, our planning system is adversarial; you may not get exactly what you want out of it

Guide to Planning Speak

Outline

Often used by landowners who are trying to find out whether development would be acceptable in principle without going through the hassle of having detailed plans drawn up. Outline permission to build is what turns a garden or a field into a building plot; getting it makes you seriously rich but it doesn't, on its own, allow you to build. Outline permission lasts for five years, but a detailed application must be agreed within three years or else the permission lapses.

Full Application

As its name suggests, a full planning application seeks to approve both the principle and the details of development. It lasts for five years.

Approval of Reserved Matters

This is used to convert outline permission to detailed.

Renewal

Planning permission can be renewed, but only if consent has not expired so this route is used to get an extension to an existing permission. If the permission has lapsed, then a new application has to be made.

Relaxation

Sometimes planning permission comes with a load of irksome conditions. You can apply to have these lifted at a later date but don't hold out too much hope.

Amendments

If you purchase a plot with detailed permission for a house that you don't actually want to build, you may be able to amend the plans without submitting a whole new application. There is no charge for amendment but if your changes are substantial the planners may not accept them as amendments and you'll be back to square one.

Extensions/Conversions

*If your building project involves work to an existing structure, you may not need planning permission. Phone your local council's planning department and ask their advice. They issue a free 22 page booklet called **Planning – A Guide for Householders** which makes a fair stab at explaining the rudiments.*

— most planning decisions are the result of compromise — but you stand a far better chance of getting more of what you want if you choose the battleground on which to fight; i.e. submit plans with minimal reference to the planners. Getting the planners too closely involved before submitting your application can be seen as ceding this battleground.

Now it may be that your planning application is not terribly controversial and that the planners will be delighted with your ideas. In which case you may think I am a paranoid old nutter. But don't forget that it's your money and that they have the right to make you shell out for things which you think are completely unnecessary. Adopting a "lie down and think of England" pose may earn you brownie points at City Hall but may also fire off alarm bells around the corner at the bank or building society.

Submitting an Application

The mechanics of submitting an application are straightforward, if time- and tree-consuming. There are, however, several different types of planning permission that can be granted and these are summarised in the adjacent box.

Application Forms

The actual application consists of a number of forms which you have to fill out, together with your plans and your cheque. Exact requirements vary from council to council but are not likely to be less than six copies of each of the following:

- Location plan (taken off OS map at a scale of 1:1250)
- Existing site plan (boundaries outlined in red) at 1:500
- Proposed site plan — showing position of house, garage, driveway, access
- Layout plans and elevations of any existing structures on site
- Layout plans and elevations of proposed dwelling at 1:100 or 1:50
- Details of materials to be used
- Details of trees to be felled — even though your application arrives in a wheelbarrow, they won't see the irony.

In addition to these, it sometimes helps to have three-dimensional bird's-eye view drawings *(isometric projections)* which show how the house fits with its neighbours.

Ownership Certificate

You also have to fill out a form stating ownership of the land in question. You don't actually have to own land in order to apply for planning permission over it but you are required to notify the owner of your intentions.

Fees

For many years, planning costs have been subsidised by local councils; in the current economic climate this is all changing, which is bad new for the applicant. Currently, planning fees are set nationally, but legislation is underway to enable local authorities to set their own fees. At time of writing, outline fees are £190 for each 0.1 hectare (=1000m^2 = small plot) of site area applied for. Detailed permission for one dwelling is also £190 and if you apply for outline and then move on to a detailed application it will cost you twice £190 (my calculator makes that £380 but it could be playing up). The only way to avoid this double fee is to go straight for detailed permission which involves more costly drawings: in some situations this is a risk worth taking but if the application is likely to be controversial, just go for the outline. There are no fees for consultation with planners or for making amendments to plans to satisfy planners' concerns.

Chances of Success

After submitting your application, the planners then go to work on assessing it. These days they all seem to work in teams, and this makes it even harder to get any sense out of them as to how they think the application is progressing. They are meant to take eight weeks to reach a determination, but in practice it depends on how busy they are—it can all take much longer. Keep ringing them to find out what's happening to your application; sooner or later they will reach some sort of provisional verdict and this is the point at which negotiations start. If they are completely hostile, then you may do better to withdraw the application and start anew; if they express some reservations (they usually do), then you must be prepared to compromise hard. Eventually, the planning officials will either grant planning permission (unlikely on a new house) or refer it to the planning committee of the local council who, typically, meet once a month. This referral will come with a recommendation either way — which the committee usually accepts. Planning permission is often granted with conditions attached; if you are Sainsburys wanting to build a supermarket, these conditions may be something big, but for a one-off housebuilder they are not likely to be terribly onerous.

Reasons for Refusal

There can be any number of reasons why planners take a negative view of your proposals. In rural districts the land is zoned (via the "structure plans" which you can inspect at your library), and if you are applying to build in a non-building zone then you've got your work cut out trying to get anywhere.

Assuming they accept that the site is suitable for development, here are several reasons why they may still not play ball:

- Lack of adequate parking
- Can't turn a car around on the hard standing
- Overlooking neighbours
- Roof too high
- House too big for plot
- Not enough garden
- Development out of keeping with neighbourhood
- Wrong position on the plot
- Don't like your choice of materials or overall design.

I could go on. Suffice it to say that many of these reasons are perfectly justifiable and if you weren't so greedy and pig-headed you would be able to see the sense in them. But applicants are apt to feel aggrieved whenever the outcome goes against them.

Lobbying

You don't have to take the views of the planning officials lying down. Many people have taken to lobbying their councillors to overrule the recommendation for refusal. This is real grass roots politics and in many parts of the world sums of money would change hands in order to get planning permissions through on the nod, but in Britain, of course, we don't do that. I don't wish to sound too sarcastic because by and large this is true — people tend not to go into local politics for money, but they do have a tendency to self-importance and many are not averse to a little bit of flattery. This is the network at work: it all depends on personalities and who you do or do not know. Even if you don't get very far with councillors, you should at least consider lobbying your neighbours. A couple of letters from neighbours saying positive things about your plans is worth a lot at a planning committee meeting. However, there is every chance that your neighbours may not feel as enthusiastic about your plans as you do and this tactic can backfire.

Appeals v New Applications

If you shoot your bolt and, despite all your lobbying, your application is refused you are faced with three choices:

- Give up
- Submit a new application
- Appeal.

The first is the cheapest but it doesn't get you very far. If you want to persist, then there is no reason why you can't go to appeal on your first application whilst simultaneously submitting a new one. Surprisingly, there is no charge for making an appeal but it does take time, around six months, and many people can't wait that long, especially if there's borrowed money riding on it. Appeals are presided over by an independent inspector, often a QC, sometimes an architect, and on small projects like individual housebuilding the usual way of going about it is to produce written evidence. Basically you must write your side of the story and explain to the inspector why you think you should have been granted planning permission in the first place. On the due date the inspector will visit the site and shortly afterwards they will make their ruling known. That's it. There are alternative methods of appeal, notably using the informal hearing method which gathers all the interested parties together to discuss the issue at hand, but the written representation is the simplest and least time consuming (and cheapest, if you are paying a professional to act for you).

Only one in three appeals succeed and from my limited experience it is difficult to predict the outcome in advance, so you are taking a big gamble in going to appeal. You can hire a professional to make the appeal for you, but this will be expensive and may not add to your chances. As there is no further drawing work to be undertaken — you can't amend your plans between first refusal and appeal — the appeal process can easily be undertaken by any lay person capable of using pen and paper, although a thorough understanding of planning issues will obviously stand you in good stead.

For many people, it will be cheaper and much quicker to submit a new planning application. When an application is refused, the planners have to state grounds for refusal. In an ideal world these issues could have been sorted out before the application ever came before the committee, but sometimes it takes a refusal to actually bring the problems out into the open. Armed with refusal reasons, you can make suitable amendments in your next application and, provided you can genuinely sort out the issues, you should have a much better chance of gaining planning permission, although the outcome is likely to be someway from your original ideas.

It is worth pointing out that this section was revised during the first months of the new Labour administration and it describes the process as it has evolved under the Tories. At time of writing there are rumours afoot of further changes in the planning process—such as third party right of appeal—and it is quite likely that things will change substantially during the lifetime of this edition.

Building Regs

As mentioned at the beginning of the previous section, the building regs are a different matter altogether from planning permission. As with planning permission, there are a number of small works that are excepted from having building regulations applied to them, but again a project as large as a house will invariably fall inside building control.

Each local council has a building control department which employs building inspectors, who both assess plans submitted to them and visit sites to ensure that the plans are actually put into practice. The plans submitted to building control are more detailed than those used for gaining planning permission and so this work is usually commissioned as an additional service after a successful planning application. Note, however, that much of the detail needed to satisfy building regulations is to do with written specifications rather than drawings and that much of this is standard to all housing. Phrases peppered with BS numbers and sentences finishing with "to the satisfaction of the building inspector" are commonly placed in specifications precisely to meet the regs. Furthermore, what is often the most important part of an inspector's job, checking that the foundations are adequate, can really only be done on site.

Getting approval for building regulations is not a political matter and there are no committees to go before or councillors to lobby. You just have to reach agreement with your appointed building inspector — which, by and large, means doing as he (occasionally she) says. If you stick to conventional methods of construction this is generally not too difficult. However, expect problems if you are inclined to unusual techniques.

What are they?

The building regulations actually consist of a number of separate booklets known as *Approved Documents*, generally referred to as *Parts*. Each part is given a letter and currently these run from Part A (which deals with Structure) to Part N (Glazing). You can buy the complete pack of 14 parts for £60.00 or for about £10 less you can get J.Stephenson's excellent *Building Regulations Explained* (both available from the Building Bookshop, 0171 637 3151.)

As you can judge from these prices, these are technical publications and most builders have never clapped eyes on them; instead they rely on their designer to have satisfied the regs in the drawings and their building inspector to put them straight if the situation on site requires it.

From time to time, the regs are amended and recently there have been changes to Parts F (Ventilation) and L (Conservation of Fuel and Power) which are intended to make our housing stock more energy efficient. These changes are actually quite profound and many time honoured techniques such as building with empty cavities and solid ground floors have been laid to rest (almost).

Building Control Fees
Local authority fees are set nationally and currently they specify that a new house (up to 250m^2 with a maximum of three storeys including basements) should pay £260 + VAT. VAT is charged on building control fees for new dwellings (unlike planning application fees), but it is reclaimable on new housebuilding provided the fees are not paid by your architect or designer and charged on to you. Independent design is one of the areas not zero-rated for VAT purposes.

NHBC
Whilst planning is exclusively the domain of the local councils, building control has been "privatised." For many years there was only one other option and that was the National House Builders Council (the NHBC), who run a building control scheme for their members side by side with their 10-year warranty. The NHBC is a force to be reckoned with in new housebuilding and it publishes its own standards which are, in general, slightly higher than the government's regulations. Professional housebuilders are mostly members because the 10-year warranty scheme is seen as essential to secure sales; besides this fact, the NHBC's fees for administering building control are a little lower than those charged by local councils. The NHBC is aimed at professional builders and charges a one-off joining fee of £520 plus an annual membership of at least £220 (dependent on how many houses you build) which is meant to deter the casual builder.

Warranties
I have already touched on the NHBC's 10-year warranty but it is important to realise that this is something quite distinct from the building regulations. Both are enforced by a series of on-site inspections; building control inspections occur at several pre-defined stages whilst warranty inspections occur unannounced so as to inspect other aspects of the work. Whereas it is mandatory to obtain building regulations for a major building project like a new house, the requirement for a warranty comes largely from mortgage providers who like it to be in place before advancing money on a finished property.

Now if a house is built to satisfy the building regs, then it should be good for ten years so in many ways the whole warranty scheme is a bit of an expensive red herring. The NHBC's warranty scheme (known as *Buildmark*) does provide some (arguably rather limited) protection for new housebuyers, particularly useful when your original builder goes bust, but it is nothing like a fully comprehensive guarantee and many new housebuyers are dismayed to find that after just two years the guarantee limits itself to "major damage caused by a defect in the structure" and just what that means is up to the NHBC alone to decide. Having said that, the NHBC accepts around 4,000 claims annually against its member firms (that's roughly one in every forty homes built) so it can hardly be accused of not facing up to its responsibilities. The *Buildmark* scheme has had a hammering in the press recently mostly as a result of aggrieved new home owners learning too late just how little is covered by this warranty.

The question facing many selfbuilders is whether it is worth having this extra insurance offered by the NHBC warranty which costs the builders between 0.3 and 0.8% of the selling price of the house, dependent on size of house and the builder's previous claims record. Well, there are alternatives. There is another warranty scheme from Zurich Municipal called *Custom Build* which is similar in many ways to the NHBC scheme but is tailored more to one-off builders who don't want to join the NHBC. There is a low registration fee of £50 but the policy itself is not cheap—expect to pay over £1000 for a one-off four or five bedroomed house. There is also the possibility of having your work certified by an architect which is a realistic option only if you have employed an architect to design and oversee your build: it's not quite the same as a warranty as any later claim you might have would be against your architect rather than an insurance company but most mortgage lenders are happy to accept architect certification. Your fee for this

would be negotiated independently with your architect, but bear in mind that many architects don't like certifying work (understandably — it's quite a risk and it has to be backed by expensive professional indemnity insurance) and will try and steer you towards using Zurich or the NHBC. Also bear in mind that if you are financing your housebuilding by other means than a regular mortgage, then a warranty is not needed at all, although absence of one could make resale within ten years more difficult.

Finally a note for barn converters. Both the NHBC and Zurich Municipal offer a warranty scheme for conversions, though these are both costlier and of shorter duration than their new build equivalents.

Which Route?

There are two distinct approaches to house design. One is to hire a designer (be they architect or not) and to let them get on with the task of melding your ideas with their expertise; the other is to approach a package build company who specialise in selling standard houses which can be adapted to particular needs. In some ways the differences are not that great — after all both involve building houses — but conceptually it's the difference between painting from scratch and painting by numbers.

Package Build

Whilst the creative types would probably be appalled at the idea that you could buy an off-the-peg kit house, package build does have one big advantage going for it and that is WYSIWYG. For those not up in computing circles, WYSIWYG (pronounced *Whizz-Ee-Wig*) stands for What You See Is What You Get, and it describes perfectly the attraction of the package build philosophy in that you know in advance what your home will look like. Furthermore, you know you'll have a conventional, resaleable property because it wouldn't be on offer if it wasn't. This is a very comforting and reassuring selling factor for selfbuilders, who are terrified of losing their construction virginity to some way out weirdo architect with ideas.

Package builds will almost certainly not be the cheapest route to a finished house: in fact, as reference to the next section of this chapter will show, they are usually considerably more expensive than the route taken by volume developers. However, they do offer the novice housebuilder something which few architects ever do and that is a price in advance — though I should add that in reality they only offer a price for the parts of the house they actually supply and erect, which is often no more than a quarter or a third of the total building costs.

Take a hill-trekking holiday in the Himalayas as a comparison. Many people would want to go on such a holiday first time with a package deal, but having done it once, would realise that it was not so difficult to organise and that if they ever went again they would go on their own, have more independence and save money. Housebuilding is not so dissimilar; the comfort of having a professional organisation behind you in your first venture and a feeling that you know what the final bill will be is worth a lot more than the vague hope that you just might be saving money.

No Free Lunches

What buyers of package building services should realise is that they are not getting free design. Rather, the design work is being paid for within the package price. The package build companies all employ architects or designers and these people get paid just like their freelance cousins, and who do you think pays their salaries? Now the logic of using predrawn house plans is that the whole design process is reduced to a matter of a bit of photocopying which should be much cheaper for all concerned. However, British planning restrictions being what they are today, there are virtually no uncomplicated building plots on which you can plonk an off-the-peg house: the houses all require "adaptation" which is tantamount to admitting that the brochure designs are just sales hooks to entice you, and that the actual house you have built will have had a fair amount of additional design work done to it in order to get it to fit both your ideas and the limitations of the plot. This extra work is invariably charged and you may well end up having a package build company designing your home from scratch.

Freelance?

Which begs the question "Why start with an off-the-peg design at all?" In theory, a freelance architect or architectural designer should be able to provide a similar service as a package build designer and really shouldn't cost any more. But, for many people, the prospect of hiring a freelance is off-putting and not just because they think it will be expensive.

If you happen to know somebody in the trade, then there is every chance that you'll appoint them (however inappropriate) just because it takes away the difficult task of finding a compatible stranger. Many people without any contacts will, however, be lured into the package build option just because it's there (coupled with the fear of the unknown). Eyeing up package build companies is like visiting Amsterdam's red light district: you can trawl up and down all night looking at the wares on offer but you don't have to consummate any deals if you don't like what's on offer. However, involving freelance architects and designers is much more personal: if you don't know them then it is akin to going on a blind date. You may or may not end up in bed together but you have to go through a courting stage just to find out where you want it to end up. It's a time-consuming and involved process and the outcome is just as likely to hinge on personal — not to say sexual —

chemistry as it is on the designer's suitability and competence to carry off your briefs (shouldn't that read "carry out your brief"? Ed.).

Of course it doesn't have to be thus. If you're the professional, organised type, there is absolutely nothing to prevent you having a sort of beauty contest between three or four designers, in which you interview them and ask to see photographs of their previous work, ask for references and even ask them to prepare a quotation for design work, and possibly building work as well. The fact that architects hate this sort of thing is bye-the-bye: you'll be paying their bills and there is no reason at all why you shouldn't organise a parade of talents so that you can make an informed judgement.

Red light districts, blind dates, beauty contests — it's all getting a bit far away from building houses. So who are all these people?

What's in a Name?

Architect

To be qualified to call yourself an architect you must have completed seven years training; an architect will regard him or herself as the natural choice for a commission such as designing an individual house and most architects love to take on such projects; trouble is, they may be rather high falutin' for your simple project and — worse fears — expensive. Just how expensive an architect is depends on how desperate they are for work but what can't be denied is that only a small fraction of new homes in this country are designed by architects. Traditionally, architects worked on a percentage fee basis, so that if they were just supplying plans and specifications they might charge around 5% over and above the value of the building contract, but if they were overseeing the work as well, this figure would rise to around 10%. However, the recession has knocked this particular tradition out of the window and now architects work for what they can get. Designers and architects have even been known to give quotations in advance for their work so they are showing every sign of rushing headlong into the 20th century. A newly qualified rookie might cost less than an a technician — say £120/day — whereas a top-notch, in-demand architect could go out at that much per hour. Hourly rate is, furthermore, a misleading figure to base your judgements on because some will produce far more in an hour than others; this is particularly true now that computer aided design (CAD) systems are becoming more widely used.

Most (but not all) chartered architects are members of the Royal Institute of British Architecture (RIBA) and they run a nationwide Client's Advisory Service (0171 580 5533) which will supply a list of suitable local practices who are actively looking for your sort of business. Another recent development is the formation of the Association of Selfbuild Architects (0800 387310), a group of around 45 architects who have combined in a sort of cooperative marketing exercise aimed at looking after the needs of novice builders. This group has been particularly innovative in its *marketing* (something architects as a whole have rarely dirtied their hands with previously) and have even gone so far as to quote their design fees in £ per square foot — incidentally, usually between £2.50 and £3.00/ft^2 (in metric that's equivalent to around £30/m^2) which is very similar to the cost of laying a reasonable carpet throughout the completed house; now there's a thought. Incidentally, there is a body called the Architects' Registration Council (0171 580 5861), who you can call to check whether someone calling themselves an architect is fully qualified.

Technician

An architectural technician is somebody trained in draughting and who may have wide experience of designing houses. They, too, have a qualification, a BIAT (the British Institute of Architectural Technologists) and there is a professional body which oversees and publishes a Directory of Practices — contact 0171 278 2206 for a regional list of self-employed members interested in taking on new work.

Many Others

There is in fact no requirement for anyone to have any qualifications to design houses. The country is stuffed full of unqualified but nevertheless competent designers. Some may have undertaken some architectural studies but never qualified, some may have qualifications in other related fields, notably structural engineers, quantity surveyors and building inspectors. And there are whole rafts of individuals who are "qualified by experience" — often designer builders — who do perfectly good work, some of it every bit as good as professional architects turn out. Obviously these designers are not regulated in the way that architects and architectural technicians are and you should be aware that if you hire an unqualified designer they are unlikely to carry professional indemnity insurance; on the other hand, unqualified designers are likely to steer you down a route where insurance is handled by third parties, such as the NHBC, so this is not actually as big a risk as you might imagine. You pays your money, you takes your choice.

Design and Build

This is a method of building that straddles the traditional distinction between designers and builders. In some ways it is similar to package build in that you are faced with an all-in-one solution but, unlike package build, there are usually no predrawn plans on the table, so in other respects, design and build is more akin to hiring a freelance designer. In fact many design and build businesses are based around the skills of a designer who also happens to run a construction business. It is hard to generalise because individual businesses will go about things in markedly different ways and, indeed, may rarely have two similar contracts. I have been involved in design and build since 1986 and if anything characterises our business it is the wide variety of projects taken on; some clients use us just as designers, some as just as builders, most as both. Some clients subject us to beauty contests, some to competitive tendering, some to both of these and some to neither, preferring to work in an atmosphere of trust all the way from initial contact to completion of building work.

Unqualified designers will tend to be a little cheaper and will also tend to be a little less imaginative, which can be a good thing if you want to build cheaply. Engineers and surveyors in particular have a reputation for designing to a cost, something which has been known to elude more upmarket architects.

You can, of course, design your own home. Indeed if you are building for your own occupation it would be surprising if you didn't do some sketching out of your ideas regarding room layouts and the like. However, there is a large chasm of knowledge between doing outline sketches and filling in all the construction details, a chasm which can only realistically be filled by training and/or experience (preferably both). There are currently being advertised several relatively cheap Computer Aided Design (CAD) programs which you can run on your home computer; they can be fun to learn and use but don't fall into the trap of thinking that mastering one of these will turn you into a house designer. They tend to come in two flavours, 2D and 3D. The 2D ones are glorified drawing packages which may well help you layouts and elevations whilst the 3D ones are to aid visualisation—they allow you to simulate walking around a house. The more expensive professional packages allow you to switch between 2D and 3D.

Selecting a Designer

For many people there is no selection procedure, they just happen upon someone. Perhaps the chap plays golf with you or you went out with his sister when you were students or maybe she's an old friend of your mother-in-law — the network. Logically, this a daft way to pick on a designer, but it doesn't half take away the difficult decisions of how to choose, and it does provide some limited protection from hiring a real bozo. Building is one of the ultimate network businesses, there being very little formal long-term work around (no wonder the original Freemasons were builders), so it is not surprising that your designer should arrive on your (yet to be) doorstep by word of mouth. But bear in mind that all designers have tastes and quirks that are individual to them and even the simplest house commission is likely to receive radically different treatments. Make sure that you can at least live with your chosen designer's ideas by taking a look at their previous stuff. If you have very particular ideas yourself, then you would be well advised to seek out a like minded soul.

Don't be Afraid

The key to hiring an architect or designer and not paying through the nose is to be very upfront about money from the first meeting. Ask for an estimate to undertake design of your house and don't be afraid to specify that your project should cost no more than £XX,000 and that it has to be designed to a budget. Most architects/designers would actually appreciate such specific requests from their clients — a lot get very tired of the polite to-ing and fro-ing that goes on around issues like this. The more specific your brief, the better you will be pleased with the results.

If it's a safe, packaged product that you are looking for then the package build route may well be your best choice. Package build also wins out if speed of construction is paramount. There is much going for the package build route but it won't get you a unique home nor will it get you a cheap home. Whilst you would expect to turn to a freelance designer for a one-off house, surprising as it may seem, I think they are also the route to use if you want to build very cheaply, though I doubt very much if it would be the same designer.

Kit Homes

We seem to have an ever growing appetite for the concept of kit homes and a recent review in *Build It* magazine uncovered around 70 businesses currently active in this field, often referred to as *package builds*. Some are now well established brand names, many more are distributors for Scandinavian businesses where the concept is far more widespread. And there does seem to be quite a high turnover of businesses: many of the smaller outfits that I analysed in 1994 are no longer around and you would do well to bear that in mind if they ask you for large dollops of money upfront. The great bulk of these firms are offering timber frame kit homes but there are now one or two venturing into steel framing and just one, *Design and Materials*, who supply masonry homes (or at least the materials you need to build one).

Potton are now the country's leading supplier of kit homes. This is fairly typical of their product. It went up in a matter of weeks in 1997.

Comparing Costs

When comparing costs between suppliers, be warned that many suppliers quote floor areas which are larger than accepted UK norms (which means internal living space only and excludes specifically perimeter walls and garaging). The Scandinavian suppliers in particular work to a different standard — which they refer to as "Gross" area — which means they quote floor areas 10-20% higher than British equivalents (see *Beware Building Costs* in Chapter 1). To get true cost comparisons, you must be prepared to measure actual floor areas off-the-plan. This is tedious to say the least but until an industry standard is adopted and policed, you are at the mercy of the supplier's sales literature.

Another pitfall to beware of is that no two kit companies provide the same features as standard, so that comparing like with like is a complex and time-consuming business. In addition, if you want to compare timber frame with brick and block, then you must be aware that timber frame kits involve a great deal of off-site fabrication which effectively adds to materials costs, whilst reducing on-site labour costs: a meaningful comparison can only be had by adding materials and labour costs together for all the relevant sections.

Having said all that, this is exactly what I've done to a handful of kit homes. Here is a summary of some of the systems currently available based on the kit costs indicated in their sales literature. The following chapters deal at length with the actual building costs of one particular brick and block house and I've used these costs — which are examined in detail in Chapter 2, The Benchmark — to fill in the parts of the kit houses not supplied by their manufacturers. *Raw Costs* is a phrase used for just basic materials and subcontract labour costs — i.e. what a builder would pay, not necessarily what he would charge. The letters *M* and *L* stand for Materials and Labour respectively, and these abbreviations are used frequently throughout the rest of the book.

Medina Gimson

Based in Kent but assembled in Leicester, their floor areas are "Net and Do Not include garages". They produce a range of English style homes ranging from very simple cottages to elaborate "Tudorbethan" mansions. Their kits include all the standard timber components plus all external and internal joinery pre-glazed and insulation, but exclude plasterboard. Their *Valiant* is a four-bedroom 152m² house which bears close comparison with the benchmark house. It is not one of their elaborate *Yeoman Cottage* range for which they are best known but is one of their simpler *Village Houses*. Supplied and erected, the *Valiant* kit would cost £21,500; in comparison, the raw costs on the benchmark house for the equivalent works as are included in the Medina Gimson kit are £17,100.

Potton

The first and largest producer of reproduction English cottage homes. They are best known for their *Heritage* range which is built around a post and beam system: the heavy timbers are "distressed" and stained, and re-main exposed inside the house after completion. Although they too produce a range of much cheaper homes, here I chose to look at one of their upmarket *Heritage* range (pictured above) and chose the *Caxton Showhouse* because it is almost the same size as the benchmark house. Its 162m² net floor area, supplied and erected by Potton, would cost £27,500; my 3 bedroom benchmark house for the same work would have been £16,300.

Potton's floor areas are accurate, as are most of the UK suppliers, but I do have cause to quibble with the "Guide Build Costs" indicated in their brochure, which take a very cavalier approach to the other building costs which Potton don't supply. Absolute minimal figures are put in for finishing the house whilst garaging, landscaping and service connections are left out. Potton produce an excellent product but you would be wise to base your budget on a figure somewhat larger than the £40/ft² which they claim will be enough to finish the job. Potton's "Extras" list (i.e. the parts of the house not supplied and erected by themselves) comes to just £37,300 on the 138m² *Caxton D*, highlighted in their guide; on my slightly larger benchmark house, I calculate that actual cost of all the bits which a Potton kit would not have supplied would have been around £60,000.

Potton's prices don't appear to have changed since my last edition compiled in 1995: timber importers have benefited from a strong pound. To their credit, the Potton package now includes a Zurich CustomBuild warranty

4a: Comparison Costs of Benchmark House and Kit Homes

SUPPLIER	HOUSE TYPE	NET SIZE in M^2	KIT COST	BENCHMARK HOUSE COST	LIKELY FINAL COST	LIKELY FINISHING COST/M^2	LIKELY FINISHING COST/ft^2
	Benchmark	166			£89,100	£540	£50
Medina Gimson	Valiant	152	£21,500	£17,100	£102,700	£680	£63
Potton	Caxton	162	£27,500	£16,300	£103,000	£640	£59
Border Oak	Meadowsweet	166	£92,000	£28,000	£153,400	£920	£86
Scandia-Hus	Dalsland	173	£53,000	£23,000	£114,500	£660	£61

which would set you back around £1000 if you were to buy it direct. They are a very proactive company, usually hiring the biggest display areas at the many selfbuild exhibitions that take place and they have a show-home site at St. Neots, Cambs, which is well worth a visit.

Border Oak

They take the Potton idea one stage further and produce oak-framed houses (Potton use construction grade softwoods), which are structurally identical to how mediaeval manor houses were built. Their 166m² *Meadowsweet Farmhouse* is nearest in size to the benchmark house and the supply and erection of its shell, wall coverings, plastering elements and external joinery would cost £92,000 — equivalent work on the benchmark house cost £28,000. This makes it among the most expensive of the kit producers, though they are by no means the only producers of oak-framed houses. Oak framing is very pricey in comparison with softwood construction, partly because of the cost of oak but also partly because of the extra work involved in jointing it. Whilst oak framing is an authentic mediaeval craft, its use in a modern house doesn't make much sense unless this attention to detail is carried right the way through the building — i.e. handmade kitchens, windows and doors.

Scandia Hus

Like most of the Scandinavian kit home makers, Scandia Hus use gross floor areas in their sales literature though, to their credit, they do at least make this fairly clear. Their *Dalsland,* which they claim to be 194m², is actually around 173m² when measured net. Like all their homes, it is beautifully specified to include built-in cupboards, and ventilation system. The erected kit price is £53,000; the comparable stages on our benchmark house cost £23,000. Scandia Hus themselves suggest a total supply and erection cost of £126,000 including sums for a

detached garage, driveway and service connections, items typically ignored by package build suppliers.

Comment

Timber frame kit homes are not the cheapest way to build a house, but they do have many things going for them, not least that they are much easier for the non-builder to comprehend and that the shells go up with amazing speed. This route is particularly suitable when speed is of the essence. In comparing costs with our benchmark house, the kit producers will no doubt feel aggrieved that I'm not comparing like with like and that their specifications and detailing in particular are far superior — after all you can't buy a bottle of *Chateau La Tour* for £2.99.

To an extent, this is a fair criticism but the consumer has to decide how much extra it is worth paying for intricate styling or superior detailing and, in particular, to ask if it might not be possible to achieve similar finishes by cheaper routes. In this respect, it is the Scandinavian kit home producers who have most to fear, because they are charging very high prices for houses with utilitarian styling and justifying these prices largely on the back of energy efficiency. It may be necessary to build to this standard inside the Arctic Circle, but in England and Wales it amounts to overkill. Similar levels of energy efficiency can be achieved at a fraction of the cost by building in more conventional British styles. The benchmark house, which is used here by way of comparison, scored a SAP rating of 97 (out of 100) which makes it highly energy efficient as is and any further energy saving measures built into it will tend to have only marginal effect.

Summary Table

Table 4a summarises the costs of constructing the four kit homes discussed in this section and compares these costs with our 166m² benchmark house. No allowances are put in for extra design work or supervision

of construction, which it is assumed the individual builder would be providing. What I have done in this table is to add in all the bits that the kit suppliers don't supply such as groundworks, roofing covers, services, fixtures and fittings, as well as an allowance for building an external garage and providing some limited paving and turfing. All these are absolutely standard for a new development of detached housing and yet are usually overlooked in the kit suppliers sales publicity. The costings for these items are all taken from the table in Chapter 2, The Benchmark. The column entitled "Developer's Equivalent Cost" shows what it cost Complete Fabrications to design and build the parts of their Eltisley house that would have been supplied and erected by the kit home suppliers — had it been a kit home. As the table makes abundantly clear, there are no bargains to be had in the world of package build homes. Bear in mind that the benchmark house is itself considerably more expensive to build than a bog standard developer's home where the build cost tends to come in at well under £40/ft² (£403/m²) and yet it still proves to be cheaper than any of the kits examined.

Two Freelancers

Whilst it is relatively straightforward to analyse the ins and outs of using package build systems, it is very much harder to pin down what you get from using a freelance designer. The service varies, as you would expect, from the excellent to the incompetent. As with the rest of the building trade, freelancers usually find work by word of mouth — the old network at work again — but there are more formal routes through which you can contact designers — see section Which *Route?* earlier in this chapter.

Rather than list a load of old tripe about how much money an architect will save you or how you'd be crazy not to use one, I thought it would be more interesting to look at the work of a couple of designers who work in this area and to examine just what it is that you get for your money. Neither of these guys is cheap and you'd be most likely to end up with a building cost of £600/m² or even more. But then Mercedes cost more than Fords and this doesn't make Mercedes poor value. Both men are exceptional designers and provide a very specialised service some way removed from the average jobbing architect.

A Traditionalist

Steve Mattick is a designer — not a qualified architect — who works from an office in the Essex village of Newport and who has a nationwide reputation for building houses in the old styles. And I'm talking old styles, not the Olde Worlde styles of the showhouses at the Ideal Home Exhibition with their timbered beams and leaded double-glazed sealed units. A new Mattick house will look almost indistinguishable from a 200-year-old one; the walls may not be perfectly perpendicular, the windows may not be exactly level and the roof will almost certainly sag (or "have movement"). The materials he uses are almost always natural and are often salvaged, and windows and doors are always made locally in a joiner's shop. Much attention is given to getting details right and many of these are worked out on site by Mattick and his crew for, above all, he is a designer builder.

Now going to the trouble of building roofs which gently undulate along the ridge is expensive. Carpenters are taught to erect roof trusses by hauling them up off the back of a lorry and arranging them all like a pack of cards, stringing lines along the ridge to ensure perfect alignment. In contrast, Mattick's roofs will all be hand cut on site and will actually be packed out in certain spots to ensure that they do not align along a string line.

Builders working for him tend to have to re-learn the old craft skills, long since abandoned in the rush towards mass production and streamlined products which are more and more made off-site. Coupled with his insistence on detailing workshop joinery, handmade tiles and cast iron guttering, Mattick's building costs are 50-80% higher than the standard fare of the big developers, though note that this does not make them appreciably higher than many kit homes.

Alone of the designers I've met, Mattick has few if any problems from planners (who by and large drool over his work) and yet is often in conflict with building inspectors. Many of the techniques he employs are no longer considered adequate though, as he points out, they have stood the test of time. He particularly dislikes the current mania for double glazing, which makes it that much harder to build good-looking, traditional windows. One of his trademarks is the sideways sliding sash window, once common in East Anglia but now all but abandoned. You can't really draughtproof such a window; you can't even stop water penetration when it is lashed by gales and so it has been relegated to the status of a vernacular has-been. Mattick is quite aware of the problems but reckons it's a price worth paying to achieve an authentic reproduction. As well as being well-heeled, Mattick's clients need to be enthusiasts capable of living with minor inconveniences like this.

Somehow, we assume that because a house is a new product it must perform to the same standards as a new camcorder or a new car; but if we bought an old wreck to do up we would expect to have a few wonky things going wrong with it from time to time, even after we'd shovelled a fortune into it. To some extent, an authentic new/old house is bound to perform in the same way. The current trick of aping old styles with modern materials and techniques comes at a price; it reduces art to artlessness, style becomes pastiche. As a na-

Top: dating from 1989, this house in Suffolk, is typical of what Mattick builds.
Below: the sideways sliding sash — a "vernacular bygone."

tion we know this intuitively because we flock to National Trust properties and to villages like Castle Coombe and Lavenham to see beautiful buildings, but as a nation of house buyers we seem to be happy with imitations which are usually executed rather poorly.

A Modernist

Which all rather begs the question why — if we want to live in smoothly functioning machines which never break down—don't we design houses that look like cars or computers? Well, why not? There are many architects working in the machine tradition but most of their work goes into commercial developments. Jonathan Ellis-Miller is one of the very few who are interested in housing.

He designs in the modern style, has been much written up in the architectural press but has been completely ignored by all the selfbuild organisations and magazines (unlike Mattick). This is a shame because his approach has much to offer the selfbuilder who wants something out of the ordinary.

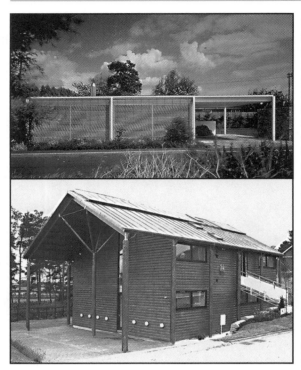

Above: Ellis-Miller's uncompromising selfbuilt home in Cambridgeshire.

Below: the house he designed for the FutureWorld exhibition at Milton Keynes in 1994

Ellis-Miller's most widely seen house is a timber frame built by Stewart Log Homes at the FutureWorld exhibition held in Milton Keynes in 1994, which attracted rave reviews from most visitors, but here I will describe the glass and steel home he selfbuilt on a plot at Prickwillow in the Fens near Ely. The plot was bought for £20,000 in 1987, the price being that low because the ground was poor and the foundation work was complex. He chose to build using a raft foundation rather than the more conventional pile. Either way it proves expensive and for a floor area of 110m^2 (not all of which is built on) he had to pour 60m^3 of concrete. In all, substructural works came to £10,000. In areas like the Cambridgeshire Fens where ground conditions are difficult, most plot buyers are aware of the problems involved and the plot prices tend to be cheaper to reflect the excess works needed.

The total building costs were £45,000 for a building which measures 70m^2. Apart from the £10,000 substructural works, another £6000 went on made-to-order patio doors, £1000 on blinds by Hunter Douglas. Parquet flooring from the local salvage yard was cheap, granite worktops in the kitchen were not. The kitchen doors came from IKEA (cheap) though the handles and door furniture throughout is by Modric (expensive). In-

ternally, the house is thus fitted with a mixture of cheap, off-the-shelf items intermingled with some pricey architectural fittings. The style is unashamedly modern (in the old-fashioned sense of the word) and Ellis-Miller is striving for that simple, uncluttered look which characterises the style. The quiet, slightly monastic feel to the house would suit anyone with a lifestyle to fit; children, I suspect, would not fit in so easily.

His building cost is around £645/m^2, though had he been building on good ground this figure would have fallen to £540/m^2. Had he not used expensive patio doors and spent money on fancy fittings, then he might have got the price down to near £430/m^2, but then he would have lost a lot of the style he was striving for. Other expensive detailing includes galvanised steel box guttering which drains to a soakaway via the centre of the house, bespoke aluminium windows at the back of the house, floor lighting and underfloor heating.

This style would be unlikely to appeal to more than a few aficionados of modern architecture, but it is by no means as avant-garde as you might think. If you have a site with a good view where single-storey development is preferable, this solution could provide a stunning house. In the case of his own house, the views out through the west facing glazed wall looking over Ely Cathedral is a fenman's delight, and despite the cool, semi-industrial look of the building it sits remarkably well in a side road in a fen village. Some people's immediate response to the thought of living in a glass-walled home is "What! No privacy?" but this problem is reasonably overcome with the use of external louvre blinds which are adjusted to suit conditions. Ellis-Miller's glass wall faces on to the road in order to get the view he wanted and there would probably be few people who would be happy with such a degree of overlooking. However, if the orientation had been more conventional (so that privacy could be maintained) then I think there would be few people who would not be bowled over by the effectiveness of the idea.

If you want to build in an unconventional style, you will likely have problems obtaining planning permission. Only estate agents are more conservative than planning offic-

ers and Ellis-Miller had a planning officer who was implacably opposed to such a dwelling. No way is Prickwillow a sensitive, conservation type area (quite the reverse) and no way does his plot impact on the casual visitor. Yet when he approached his local council planning department, he met with stares of disbelief and what can only be described as prejudice against his submitted plans. However, despite a recommendation of refusal from the planning officers (which 90% of the time carries the day), the councillors on the planning committee saw otherwise and let him build.

Without some support from more enlightened planning officers, any plans to build in any but the tamest vernacular styles will be stillborn. If you're interested in building in an unusual style, then first check with your local authority to get their views about your favoured site. Obviously, if the area is a conservation area or next to a listed building or the church, then you will expect to have to stick to a prescribed style. On the other hand, most building plots are not in such sensitive positions and arguably it's really none of the planners business what style of building goes up. Needless to say, planning officers do not see it thus. To them, everywhere is sensitive, which unfortunately translates as "If you want planning permission you'd better conform." Ellis-Miller's tale indicates that there is still room for innovation.

Renovate or Rebuild?

As virgin, greenfield building sites become more and more difficult to obtain, increasing numbers of people are looking to purchase dilapidated dwellings which they then seek to demolish and to build afresh. These are basically recycled building sites, sometimes referred to as brownfield sites. Planning permission is usually much easier to obtain on a site with established residential usage and there are also usually considerable savings to be made because the service connections are already in place. A few sites will have problems with contaminated ground but mostly the requirements of today's foundations to go much deeper than was previously thought necessary means that any existing foundations will be excavated and disposed of, just as if it was regular subsoil. In addition to buying a serviced plot, you have an existing structure from which you may well be able to salvage some useful materials.

So far so good. The decision to demolish, however, is often not as clear cut as this. For a start, few people care to sell their existing properties at building plot prices. To do so is to admit that your home is worthless which can be a bitter pill to swallow, even if it's true. In any event it's usually the case that the house is not worthless, it's just old and dilapidated and with a little bit of tender loving care and a whole lot of money it could continue to make a very serviceable home. So problem No 1 is the extra expense of buying such a site. In my locality, single building plots tend to sell for upwards of £50,000: in contrast, tumbledown houses ready for demolition, are rarely available for much less than £80,000. You have to be very keen on the location to pay that much over the odds for a plot.

Problem No 2 is best illustrated by the accompanying diagram. Whether to knock down and start again or whether to work with what is already there. Now here things start to get complicated because the chances are that it is not a clear cut issue, most renovation opportunities fall somewhere between the two extremes. Added to which it is a fiendishly difficult exercise to compare costs between the two approaches because this major decision has to be made at a pre-plan stage and you will have to work with ballpark figures. Whether the building is worth saving at all is an issue that only you (and the planners) can decide — each case will be argued on its merits and there is no point trying to make any broad generalisa-

The complete renovation and modernisation of this house cost £400/m², very similar to the unit cost of building from new

tions. However, I will now attempt to summarise the cost implications of the various routes.

Demolish and Rebuild

Budgeting for this is comparatively simple. The new build aspect of the work will probably cost upwards of £400/m² (£37/ft²), if you build to a fairly basic standard. The demolition side of the equation is less predictable but is not, as a rule, very costly. If there are valuable materials in the existing structure, then you can either reuse them yourself or you can sell them on. Some contractors will even pay you for the right to demolish and keep the materials. Watch out, however, for asbestos materials which are an expensive and dangerous pain to dispose of.

Renovate and Extend

Obviously this all depends on the condition of the existing structure but, to give you an example, my business recently undertook the refit of a 120-year old detached brick house near Newmarket. All the old plaster was hacked of, all the floors lifted and the timbers were repaired or renewed and treated, the slate roof was replaced, the windows were

all replaced with double glazed timber replicas of the originals. The house had a new staircase fitted, and bathrooms, plumbing and wiring were installed for the first time and a small 15m² extension was constructed to house a modern kitchen. The only underground work to go on was the installation of drains to the street. In other words, the house was stripped to little more than it's brick shell, which was actually in good condition and needed no repair work. By the time the job was completed, there was a four-bedroom house with all the amenities of a brand new one but with the charm and style of a Victorian cottage.

And the cost of all this? £47,000 for a 120m² house. Of which the last £7000 is VAT. Ouch. Renovating existing dwellings does not qualify for zero-rating of VAT and this can itself sometimes tilt the balance towards new build (which for these purposes is defined as the demolition of everything above ground except one side wall). On the other hand, in this particular case, the clients were able to obtain a £19,000 grant from the local coun-

Knock me
down and
start again

I'm listed. You be careful
how you treat me

Foundation work like this goes some way towards explaining why converting barns is often more expensive than building houses from scratch

cil because the house was sited in a conservation area; it's not all stacked in favour of the zero-rated new builders.

Comparison Costs

How does this major renovating compare in cost with building from scratch. Ignoring the grant, the cost per square metre is surprisingly almost identical to building from scratch. Despite the fact that much of the shell of the original house remains in place, this saving is all but cancelled out by the requirements to use more expensive fittings such as bespoke joinery and real slate on the roof plus the clients understandable desire to refashion some of the internal walls to make new rooms. Had there been considerable structural repairs to make as well (there often are), then the complete renovation of this building would have worked out to be as much as 25% more expensive than the demolish and rebuilding option.

Barn Conversions

The situation with the conversion of redundant agricultural buildings into homes is subtly different. For starters, the structure is most unlikely to have ever been a home (at least for humans) and is therefore likely to need considerable structural alterations in order to bring it up to the standards expected in modern housing. This is now accepted by Customs & Excise who allow such work to be zero-rated for VAT purposes. How-

ever, the very fact that the structure has obtained planning permission for conversion into a home usually indicates that the planners regard the building itself to be of some merit and that demolition is therefore virtually never an option. Barn conversions, good barn conversions, are almost always more expensive to build than new houses because they not only require all the fittings of a new home but almost always require major structural alterations as well. In my experience a minimum budget for a barn conversion is £500/m^2 (£46/ft^2) and a more realistic budget is perhaps £600/m^2 (£55/ft^2). If the building is listed or in a conservation area then this £600/m^2 figure becomes an effective minimum development cost.

Unlike existing homes, redundant barns rarely enjoy the luxury of having services connected or of having access arrangements in place. Indeed by their very nature, access is often rather laboured and therefore expensive to achieve, often requiring long driveways. Also note that the new building regulations have had a heavy impact on the cost of conversions; they have to be built to the same thermal standards as a new house and this can be much harder to achieve in an existing structure.

Shape and Size

Before you even approach a designer or a package company, you would do well to take on board a few home truths about the cost implications of your design decisions. If you are after cheap space, then you need to build your house in a simple shape, preferably a simple box with a simple roof. This doesn't have to look cheap — indeed it doesn't have to be cheap — but the point is that it is almost always going to be the simplest (and therefore cheapest) form of construction available to you. Many traditional house forms take this form and they are not all peasants' cottages.

So why should a rectangular box shape be cheaper than say two rectangular box shapes stuck together? In a word, junctions. You are introducing junctions at every stage of the building process and junctions involve head scratching and sometimes even expensive detailing. Your brickwork will take just that little bit longer to build, your carpentry will become just that little bit more complicated, your roofing will become *much* more complicated. However, it is important not to exaggerate the cost implications of building complex shapes: I estimate that the cost effect of these junctions is probably of the order of between 0.5 and 1%

on your total building budget per junction. Therefore if you were to build in an L shape, for instance, you would scarcely notice the extra cost. However, wherever you interrupt the basic shell shape of a house you are adding junction costs and if you choose a complex form with extensions, dormers, porches and the like then you can take it that the overall cost will increase by much more than the unit cost per square metre at which you build the main shell.

Circulation Space

There is another hidden cost brought about by using non standard shapes in house design and this is to do with having adequate circulation space — i.e. hallways, stairwells and landings. This is virtually impossible to quantify because no two situations are the same, but the basic tenet holds that the more complex your form, the more difficult it becomes to provide adequate circulation space or, put another way, the more space you end up using just to get around from A to B. For instance, in our lean, box-design benchmark house, circulation space occupies just over 25m^2, which is 16% of the internal floor area. That's a pretty tight ratio. Reconfigure the

house in a 'T' shape and you'll probably be looking at circulation space taking up 25% or more of your internal floor area. Now you may not mind that, you might even want a minstrel's gallery set under a glass atrium in your entrance hallway, but do be aware of the constraints you put on your space by choosing more complex designs.

It's worth bearing in mind that the amount of space you need to actually live in is surprisingly small: a bed, a loo and a comfy armchair does for most people. Arguably everything else is either storage or circulation space. The past century has seen us becoming progressively richer and we own more and more possessions which, of course, require more and more storage which in turn requires more and more circulation space. And this I believe is the main motor behind our desire for more and bigger homes. Enough of this cod philosophy. How do you get a bigger home?

Extra Space

The quest for extra space is on. Where is it going to go? Conventionally people have chosen to build larger houses but this is becoming an increasingly difficult option because of planning restrictions. Going up into the loft space is cheap but is not always an option. Could one of the solutions be underground? Maybe...

I have compared the cost of creating extra space using five different methods. There are some assumptions which need further commentary. Firstly I have assumed that we are faced with a situation where someone has plans to build a detached four or five bedroom house say of 150m²: they are then hit by the desire to have more space, another 40m² in fact (equivalent to three good sized bedrooms or a very generous double garage. I have looked at five different ways of achieving this extra space which are:
- Build a 40m² basement
- Build a 40m² single storey extension
- Add 20m² to the ground floor and 20m² upstairs
- Convert the loft space into usable space
- Build a large double garage

I looked at just the structural costs and ignored the fitting out costs as I figured these would be pretty much the same whichever option you chose. If the overall prices look low, this is why — the structure often costs under 50% of the total.

Lofts

The cheapest option for our space hungry builders is to convert the loft space: it involves re-jigging the roof carpentry and building in studwork walls and a new stairwell but otherwise much less in the way of structural changes than all the other options. It comes in at around £5,000-£6,000 (£140/m²). However it is not an option on all houses; you need a headroom of at least 2m to make lofts usable for anything other than storage and many house designs start with the upper storey already built into the roof—in these situations you can't borrow any more space from the loft. And if your fancy is to open out the roof so that your headroom is not confined to the existing roof line, then you are adding significantly to your costs.

There are a number of niggly little problems that come with loft conversions. When there is living space more than 4.5m off ground level, a whole raft of fire regulations come into effect. Chief amongst these is a requirement to have a fireproofed stairwell which exits close to the front door: in itself it's not that expensive to construct, but you may have to redesign your internal layouts to accommodate it. If designing a new house, this doesn't have to be a big problem but in existing houses it can be surprisingly disruptive. In fact the whole subject of building loft conversions in existing houses can be surprisingly complicated and it really lies beyond the scope of this book.

Two storey extension

The other option which looks cheap is to expand both the ground floor and the upper floor of your house, the two storey extension option. Adding 3m to the length of a typical four bedroom house will probably be enough to create an extra 40m² of space and because this can be spread between two floors you are effectively halving the costs of extra foundations and roofing, though not, of course, ex-

4b: Options for Space Hungry Builders

5 options for increasing size of structure by 40m²	40m² Basement	Two storey extension	Single storey extension	Add 40m² in Loft	40m² Garage
Oversite Excavation	£ 2,800	£ 300	£ 100		£ 300
Foundation Excavation		£ 300	£ 100		£ 400
Landfill Tax	£ 784	£ 168	£ 56		£ 196
Concrete Foundations		£ 1,000	£ 500		£ 800
Masonry Footings		£ 400	£ 150		£ 300
Concrete Slab/Floor	£ 2,800	£ 1,000	£ 800		£ 1,000
External Walls	£ 2,800	£ 2,400	£ 2,400	£ 900	£ 1,600
Waterproof Tanking	£ 780				
Rainwater drainage	£ 1,200	£ 200	£ 100		£ 200
Joinery		£ 600	£ 600	£ 800	£ 600
Insulation	£ 300	£ 400	£ 250	£ 200	
Steel	£ 400	£ 400		£ 400	£ 180
Stairs	£ 600			£ 600	
Roof Covers		£ 1,200	£ 800	£ 500	£ 1,400
Add Roof Carpentry		£ 1,400	£ 800	£ 2,000	£ 1,400
Less Foundation Work	(£ 2,168)				
TOTALS	£ 10,300	£ 9,800	£ 6,700	£ 5,400	£ 8,400
Cost/m²	£ 260	£ 250	£ 170	£ 140	£ 210

Note that there is a saving on many basements because the existing foundations are being replaced

ternal walls. I cost this option at between £6,000 and £7,000 (£160/m^2). In many ways it remains the most flexible option but, and it's a big but, its not always feasible to just add 3m to the length of a house: plot boundaries and/or planning consents may very well prohibit this course of action. You will also end up with two extra decent sized rooms but if you want a really large space, a two storey extension will only get you halfway there.

The other three options all come in between £8,400 and £10,300 (say £210-£260/m^2).

Garage

By and large, most new housing gets built with garage space whether its needed or not. The radical thing is to axe the garage from the spec, not to build a second one. I take a closer look at garages at the end of Chapter 7.

Single Storey Extension

Single-storey houses are about 15% more expensive to build than two-storey houses. There are some savings, notably in having no staircase, but the extra foundations and roofing more than cancel these out. Incidentally the same cost penalty applies to single-storey house designs, better known as bungalows. Bear in mind that it's the structure that's 15% more expensive to build and that the structure makes up around half the overall building costs. Other costs being equal (they ought to be), this makes bungalows about 7-8% more expensive to build overall than the same floor area built on two floors. Yes, the price difference continues up into the loft space so that a three storey house should be a little bit cheaper to build than the equivalent size on two storeys.

The bungalow has rather gone out of fashion in recent years and tends now to be built to satisfy a particular requirement. This requirement, more likely than not, emanates from the planning department and relates to the fact that the plot overlooks other houses and that only single-storey development is felt to be appropriate. Alternatively, they are commissioned by clients who wish to avoid staircases. When starting from scratch with a two storey house, a single storey extension would seem to be a strange addition unless it is a solution to a specific problem such as a sloping site.

Basements

What price a basement? The basement works would actually cost around £12,000 and is the most expensive option. At first this might seem to be illogical: after all there are no roofing costs and much of the expense that goes to make up kerb appeal in a new house — fancy brickwork, nice joinery — is, of course,

One of the few hundred new homes to be built each year with a basement

absent from a basement. The added costs come with the hole excavation, the extra strength required by the walls, the waterproofing details and the addition of another staircase. However to get a fair comparison you must subtract the cost of providing regular foundations which normally work out at around £30/m^2 and can cost two or even three times as much on difficult sites. Taking this into account, the basement is comparable with in costs to a single storey extension or a garage. If you have a problem site requiring such elaborate techniques as piles or rafts, then the addition of a basement makes even more sense as the increase in your foundation work will be proportionally much less.

Space Savers

Of the five options I've looked at, only the basement and the loft conversion satisfy the demand for extra space without increasing the footprint of the house. And the footprint of the house — that is the area of ground that is actually built on — is crucial in determining the density of housing. A 60m^2 footprint will give you 120m^2 living space on two floors and up to 180m^2 on three floors. By utilising basements and/or lofts, you should be able to build 50% more houses on the same area. Although this line of argument ignores the requirements of vehicle access and the desire for decent sized gardens, it cannot but help the situation we are facing where we apparently require space for four million new homes in the next 20 years and no one, but no one, has a clue where to build them.

Approved Document

One of the chief reason for this lack of basements in the UK is that the skills and knowledge that went into basement construction have largely vanished. The building trade are generally a pretty conservative lot and if you were to ask a builder or an architect for a basement, the chances are you would be met by a wall of tut-tutting and head shaking as they explained the problems would far outweigh the benefits. It is easy to mock but to be fair they have a good point as the ramifications if it all goes wrong are probably worse underground than anywhere else and most experienced architects and builders are wary of courting trouble. In an attempt to relaunch the basement in Britain, a group of interested parties including the British Cement Association and the NHBC have recently an published an amendment to the Building Regulations entitled *Basements for Dwellings*. This draws together all the relevant building regulations with some best practice notes so that for the first time there is an easily accessible reference source for design and construction professionals. There is much to understand that is beyond the ken of regular house designers: water tables, hydrostatic pressure, retaining walls, tanking details, reinforcement. Also it contains a complete reworking of the U value requirements to take into account the different thermal conductivity of materials below ground. The technical information is all in here so there is no excuse to be fobbed off by ignorance. The Approved Document on Basements is available from the British Cement Association (01344 762676, price £15.50 plus £1.00 P+P): if you get it now, you will be in danger of knowing more than your building inspector! There are not many specialist contractors who know much about basements: one who does is Godfrey Rawlings of Basement Construction (01908 366246).

Chapter 5
Project Management

What exactly is project management? It's become a buzz word among builders who assume that it's the be-all and end-all of running a building site. There are now professional project managers who apparently keep building sites going armed only with a mobile phone and a fast car, the yuppies of the building trade. It's all about networking and contacts, being at the very centre of a huge web of information.

Well, yes, there is this aspect, but don't get carried away. Really, project management is nothing new; it's what contractors have always done, which is to organise building work. There is power here and, if you've never employed anyone other than a baby-sitter, that is an undoubted attraction to many of us frustrated prefects. But, as the old saw goes, with that power comes a responsibility and, in the case of the contractor, that responsibility is considerable, because whilst you are hopefully making a bit on everybody's labour you also have to pick up the tabs for everybody's cock-ups. You are where the buck stops.

So, project management goes on at every building site, even out-of-the-way ones where they've never even heard of it. It's really rather a holdall term that covers just about every non-manual aspect of running a building site. And there are no rules as to who can and who can't be a project manager; it could be the selfbuilding client, or their architect or quantity surveyor, or it could be the main contractor or their foreman. And of course it doesn't all have to be carried out by one individual — the various functions may be split between people, though when this happens you can expect even more cock-ups than usual.

Raising Finance

The first step in the management of a project such as building a house is to have the finance organised to pay for it. For the majority of selfbuilders and small developers, that translates as how much you are able to borrow. Well how do you go about borrowing on a property that doesn't even exist? You will find it a lot easier to borrow money if you have a) substantial assets and b) substantial income, preferably both. If you don't fall into either of these categories then you are by no means ruled out of the game; you'll just have to work harder at impressing the mortgage lender. In fact, people of quite modest means are now regularly becoming D-I-Y property developers.

There are currently around 30 institutions actively seeking selfbuild borrowers; most of these are prepared to lend up to 75% of the finished value of the property and several will lend rather more than this including such big names as Halifax, Bradford & Bingley and First Direct — though most will expect you to come up with a hefty deposit for land purchase. The number of active lenders is now larger than ever but many of them just dip their toes in the selfbuild market only to withdraw a year or two later (often when they are taken over by a bank or some such). There aren't that many institutions who really understand this specialised market and the ones that do are generally pretty active with the advertising and exhibition appearances. Judges by these standards alone, the Norwich & Peterborough Building Society (0800 883322) is currently the pick of the bunch, actively courting the selfbuild market by offering to lend up to 80% of a plot's value provided it has outline planning permission and up to 95% of the value of the completed house.

If your fortune is modest and your income small, you don't necessarily have to give up any idea of building your own home, especially if you are prepared to rough it for a while by living on site in a caravan. It means that a house such as our benchmark house, with a market value of £150,000, would be within the reach of a young couple with joint income of around £35,000/annum and equity or savings of no more than £20,000.

If you are self-employed or you are actively wanting to sell on the finished property for a profit, then the regular avenues may well be closed to you but there are still a number of specialists who it is worth approaching. Check out Delta Finance (01323 417666) for more specialised selfbuild deals. Another very useful contact is the Ecology Building Society (01535 635933) who are particularly helpful in lending to those undertaking unusual constructions and renovations which mainstream lenders shy away from. The selfbuild magazines now run regular features on who is lending how much to whom and if you are in the market for specialised loans then check out one of these sources. Professional developers have traditionally borrowed from the major clearing banks but there are a number of finance boutiques catering for them as well such as Alban Marshall (0171 255 2585): again many advertise in trade journals such as the NHBC's *Housebuilder*.

One thing that almost all lenders are now very wary of is of borrowers continuing to live in one (mortgaged) property whilst borrowing to build a new one. Many people have come unstuck on this one in the past and now that we no longer live in an era where house prices go on rising effortlessly, it is hardly surprising that such arrangements are almost unheard of. On the other hand, the revival of the rented sector means that it is now much easier to live in rented accommodation whilst building a new home for your occupation.

Also bear in mind that most lenders are wary of lending against building plots alone. Some are fussier than others: some insist on you having detailed planning permission in place before they will lend you a bean — and seeing detailed planning permission for the house you want to build can take months to organise, this can itself be a significant hurdle. It really does help to have cash available to buy the plot (or barn or whatever) because you will be competing with other buyers who are in that fortunate position and many a good looking bid fails because the mortgage provider is not as keen as you are.

Your Presentation

Many lenders recommend that you contact them early, when you are still at the dreaming stage. If you have an existing mortgage, start by talking to this source and trying to gauge their attitude to your ideas. Talk in broad sweeps about what you are trying to achieve and try and winkle out of them how far they will be prepared to come along with you. Together you may be able to shape up a budget to work to. If you feel they are being unduly negative, then start looking at other lenders. The lenders themselves are tending towards centralised decision making which can make things more transparent but also rather less flexible: however they are not yet entirely monolithic—the Woolwich for instance still grants an unusual degree of leeway to the individual branch managers and a sympathetic Woolwich manager may be able to do rather more for you than a sympathetic Bradford & Bingley manager. It all rather depends on the individuals involved.

When the time comes to act, you will in all probability have to act quickly and you will need whatever ammunition you can get hold of — agent's details of the proposed purchase, copy of planning permission, your salary details, a building budget. If you've no plans, then show them a copy of this book and say you've read it from cover to cover — that'll impress them, may even swing it in your favour. You shouldn't have to show any plans at this stage because it is ludicrous to expect there to be any at this stage but this is one area where the timber frame package companies tend to win out because you can actually present a plan AND a budget, even if the house you end up building is nothing like this.

Scheduling

Unlike conventional mortgage lending, development loans and selfbuild mortgages are released in stages as the work progresses. For someone new to this, it can be a daunting process, especially if they are having to borrow to complete the plot purchase for a house that's not even designed, let alone built. The key to doing this is to prepare a schedule of works, the sort of thing that is outlined in the diagram opposite. This shows how a typical British house is built, taking around 8 months to complete. The costings are for something very similar to the benchmark house, which cost £85,000 to build at a slightly upmarket cost of £525/m² (that's £50/ft²). It's interesting to note that the rate of spending is surprisingly constant — it's actually very close to one pound per square foot per week. Eight months is generally a good time to set to build a simple house, especially if you've never built a house before. As you can see from the timeline, there are over twenty major tasks to accomplish, all needing coordinating and timetabling so that they occur in the right order at the right time. At this speed, you are actually paying the wages of three men to be on site continually and if that's how houses got built there really wouldn't be any problems trying to schedule a workforce. But in reality each house is built by upwards of 30 people, each with different skills and each of with their own schedules

Time and Cost: Schedule for Construction of a 4 bedroom House

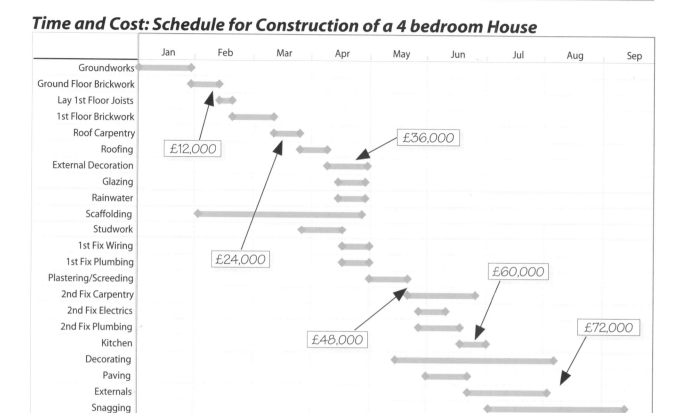

to work to; you can't expect everyone to turn up at the drop of a hat so you have to program some slack into the schedule to allow for this.

Bear in mind also that the economic background in the construction industry is now very different to what we have been used to in the early 90s: a greatly reduced workforce is now in great demand and this leads to not only much higher labour costs but also makes it much harder to get hold of good labour at the times you want it.

Speedy Builds

Now some houses do get built in much less time than eight months. Refer back to the opening of the book and look at the quick-cheap-good triangle; even though we're now in Chapter 5, I'm afraid that this rule still holds good. If you want to build quick, then either be prepared to spend good money on professional supervision of the whole construction process or to have a half-finished house with lots of snags which will probably never get sorted out. It's quite feasible to build a house from scratch in just three months but in order to do so you have to concertina all the events and, realistically, this means planning the whole process months in advance so that everybody involved in the construction knows exactly what they are required to do and when they are required to do it, just

the sort of intricate project planning for which British builders are famous! It also requires that the correct materials are delivered to site on the appropriate day (ditto British builder's merchants).

Speedy builds? It can be done, but...be prepared to spend the time you saved in the building process planning the whole thing instead.

Stage Payments

Almost all development loans and selfbuild mortgages are made in stages. That is to say that there are certain points in the construction process which, when completed, trigger the release of the next tranche of the loan. Each lender seems to use slightly different criteria to define when each stage is completed but a typical regime would involve three or four stage payments coinciding with

• Groundworks complete
• Structure watertight
• Plastered out
• Finished.

Normally the lender will insist on a surveyor making a site visit to check that the work has progressed as far as you claim, although some of the more intrepid bank managers will do this checking themselves.

Managing Cashflow

One critical point to take note of is that the lenders only ever release stage payments after a stage is completed, so that you have to be able to float the works between the payments. This fact has undone many a small builder in the past and will doubtless continue to do so in future; typically, the builder runs out of cash towards the end of the job and gets stuck in a Catch-22 where they can't get the final (largest) instalment of the loan because they haven't finished building and they can't finish building because they haven't got the final stage of the loan. A tricky little pitfall made all the worse because builders (and surveyors) habitually underestimate the cost of finishing building works off, and the time that the finishing soaks up. One of the major advantages of building reasonably quickly is that the strain on cashflow is minimised because the subcontractors may well be happy for you to withhold payment for a couple of weeks until the next stage payment is authorised; if that couple of weeks becomes a few months, then this option is effectively removed.

There is another little pitfall here awaiting the slower-than-average self builder: the VAT reclaim procedure. The *what*? Check out the last two paragraphs of this chapter (headed *End of the Party*).

Hiring a Main Contractor

If you are choosing to build with a main contractor, then the joys and perils of project management *should* pass you by because the contractor will take it all on. Indeed, you can probably skip most of the following sections because it goes through some of the things you won't need to know. Your problems begin and, hopefully, end with choosing the right contractor. However, this in itself is a major challenge.

Eight and a Half Tips

1. Try and start with a sensible shortlist. Get one or two of the bigger local builders on board who you suspect will do a good job even though you expect they might be expensive. Try and choose the smaller ones from recommendations rather than pins in the Yellow Pages.

2. Don't waste everybody's time by selecting fifteen or twenty contractors. It's much better to have three of four who you contact (even visit) personally beforehand to see if they have the time or the inclination to do your job. If the response is lukewarm, don't bother to send documents for quotation, look elsewhere.

2a. If you want to check on financial standing and/or membership of trade organisations now is the time to do it. Don't get someone to quote for your work if you are going to reject them later because they don't meet your standards. And whilst we're on it, there is really only one organisation which carries any clout in the world of new housebuilding and that's the NHBC (the National House Builders Council). You will want your contractor to be a member in order to get a 10-year warranty on your home unless the job is being certified by an architect.

3. The more detailed your plans, the more meaningful will be the quotations. Ideally, you should send drawings already approved by the building inspector. If you have a separate written specification, the process of quotation becomes much more straightforward (and therefore tends to increase accuracy).

4. Ask what the day work rates are and what mark-ups will be applied to materials supplied which were specifically excluded from the quotation — usually done to allow you to make up your mind nearer the time.

5. Be suspicious of very low quotations. Often you may find that most of the replies cluster around a figure (say £70,000) but one comes in way below (say £45,000). Without revealing your hand, try and elicit how this quotation was arrived at: what does this guy do that the others don't know about? Why is he so desperate for the work?

6. If there is no clear winner on price, then have a second informal round of interviews (probably by phone) to elicit more information. Are they busy? Are they very busy? If you haven't got a contract specifying completion dates, find out when could they start and how long would they take? Who would actually be running the job? Could you meet this person on their current site (good chance for a snoop)? Do they have a mobile number? Are they contactable out of hours?

7. If all still equal, then go for the best communicator. The one who you understand best, or just get on with best, will also be the one who will understand you best. It's that old chemistry at work again. If you've got to this stage and still haven't made up your mind, then trust *your instinct.*

8. Some of the very best of our small builders are extremely unambitious and don't go out chasing work. They keep a gang of three, four or five guys going and will turn work away rather than take on twice their normal workload. They don't advertise and you won't find them in the Yellow Pages. Often they don't even do quotations. Clients willingly wait months, even years, to get hold of these builders and work is almost always carried out in a spirit of trust and cooperation, usually with very few subcontractors involved at all. If you value quality above price and informality above deadlines then this may be the route for you. If there are any of these mediaeval craft gangs in your neck of the woods, chances are your architect or building inspector will know of them.

What Makes a Good Builder?

Hugely successful contractors (or project managers if you prefer) are a rare breed. Though they almost invariably have their roots in one of the building trades, the skills that are required for *managing* building work are quite different. Good, clear communication is perhaps the most important and, if you are weighing up potential contractors, it is probably the aspect to which you should give the most careful consideration. After all if you can understand what they are on about then chances are that they will understand what you are on about and anyone working for them will understand their instructions. 90% of the things that go wrong on building sites go wrong because of misunderstandings or plain bad instructions.

In some ways this is good news, because if you meet someone face to face then you do at least get an immediate impression. If you can't understand them it doesn't mean they don't do a good job but there is a much higher chance that they won't do the job you want them to do. For instance, you get a lot of Scotsmen and Irishmen in the building trade and, although most come from the same sort of background, some of them are almost completely unintelligible whilst others come through to English ears as clear as a bell. You only have to listen to two of our most successful soccer managers talk to know what I mean. Alex Ferguson and Kenny Dalglish are both from Glasgow, both about the same age and both conspicuously good at what they do, but whilst Ferguson speaks in a straightforward, uncluttered manner, Dalglish has retained that thick Glaswegian accent which is virtually impenetrable to anyone from Edinburgh let alone the English Home Counties. Whatever Kenny's virtues, he wouldn't be my ideal choice as a project manager.

Hiring Subbies

If you've chosen to dispense with the main contractor then you'll almost certainly be in the business of hiring subcontractors. Project management — piece of piss, mate. Subcontractors — no problem — there's simple ground rules aren't there! I mean.

Well there are. They go something like this.

What Should Happen
- Never hire anybody who hasn't been personally recommended to you
- Always check on their previous work
- Always get three quotations in writing
- Never hire anybody on an hourly rate; get all work priced before hand
- Check to see if they are members of a reputable trade organisation
- Check to see what guarantee they offer
- Never pay up front
- Always get "extras" priced and put in writing before they are carried out
- Impose a time schedule with penalties for late completion.

All sounds good, sensible stuff.

What Actually Happens
- Never hire anyone who hasn't been personally recommended to you
You might have to wait a long time.

- Always check on their previous work
Has anyone seriously got time to do this? Self-builders are normally incredibly stretched, and chasing up old working contacts for subcontractors who may only be on site for a day or two doesn't feature highly on most "To Do" lists.

- Always get three quotations in writing
You must be joking. You may have to approach about ten to get three to respond in writing and even then you may have to wait (and chase) for two months.

- Never hire anybody on an hourly rate; get all work priced before hand
Fine for most trades, but sometimes this is totally impractical. You have to have a detailed specification ready and chances are, if you are trying to save money, that you won't have.

- Check to see if they are members of a reputable trade organisation
They'll probably be more expensive if they are.

- Check to see what guarantee they offer
Worth checking on for kitchens and plumbing but a bit meaningless for most subbies. They've either done it right or they haven't and it'll be down to you to check.

A common site on British building sites—the vanishing subbie

- Never pay up front
Good advice for anybody anytime. Sometimes it's very hard to keep.

- Always get "extras" put in writing before they are carried out
Alright in principle but, again, sometimes totally impractical if you are in a hurry (you will be). Get a site diary instead. If you want it to go down in writing be prepared to do the writing yourself.

- Impose a time schedule with penalties for late completion
Risk losing your subbies.

What is a Subcontractor?
Legally a subcontractor (or subbie) is a worker who gets hired and paid by a main contractor. If a subcontractor works directly for you then they are, strictly speaking, not subcontractors at all but ordinary (or main) contractors. The difference is crucial because if you become a main contractor you also become responsible for policing your subcontractors' tax affairs (lots of unpaid admin.). However, if you are the client, this all flows over your head — i.e. you don't have to know anything about it. Even though your subbies won't be subbies at all when they are working for you, everybody still refers to them as subbies.

Generally speaking, when we say "subbies" we are referring to tradesmen providing a specific skill, like a plumber or a brickie. Sometimes subbies will be one-man bands. Sometimes they will be small firms employing several people. The one-man bands will tend to

work for a cheaper hourly rate but may well be just as expensive when it comes to quoted works.

Essential Subbies
Generally, you will be able to build a house by hiring the following characters:
- Groundworkers. Someone with a JCB and access to a lorry.
- Brickwork (brickies). Often overlaps with groundworkers — one of the two (or you) will have to lay the drains. Often work in gangs of three (two brickies/one labourer). Don't usually supply materials.
- Carpenters (chippies). Often work in twos (no labourer). Don't usually supply materials.
- Roofers. Most often hired in small gangs who supply and fix, sometimes doing the scaffolding as well.
- Plasterers/dry liners. Mixture of one-man bands and small firms.
- Plumbers. Same mixture of one-man bands and small firms.
- Electricians. Same mixture.
- Decorators. Most selfbuilders do this themselves but there are plenty of "professionals" around.

There are a number of other specialist subbies who you may want to use: glaziers, garage door fitters, kitchen specialists, pavers and drive layers, landscapers, scaffolders. Refer to Chapter 11, Shopping for more details.

Choosing a Good Subbie?
I'd like to come up with an easy rule for picking good subbies but I don't know what it is. If you've found one perhaps you would let me know. Obviously, you can go to great lengths

to see that you appoint a master, but this can be very time-consuming and if the guy is only going to be on site for a few days it seems like a big case of overkill. Generally, contractors and subbies know the going rates for various trades and they can usually work out an amicable agreement over a cup of tea and a ten minute chat and this is how 99% of subbies get hired. It's easy come, easy go and if someone is useless they usually get asked to move on. However, if you want to ensure high standards from the start then you have to do a great deal more work, taking up references and talking to other contacts.

NB Don't forget the builder's dilemma. High standards don't tend to go with cheap prices. You gets one or you gets the other.

Labour Only v Supply + Fix
Subbies tend to come in two distinct flavours. The *labour-only* subbies are usually hired singly (or in small informal gangs) and often hired on an hourly rate or a day rate. They tend to be concentrated on the heavy building side (brickworkers, carpenters, plasterers). Many of the later trades — i.e. those concerned with finishes — are more often organised by small businesses, which prefer to sell a package whereby they supply the materials and the labour to fix the materials: typically, roofers, plumbers, electricians, glaziers and kitchen fitters. These *supply and fix* subbies will tend to be more organised — you'll be able to get quotes out of them — and possibly a little more expensive, particularly as they are in the business of marking-up materials they buy on your behalf. In effect, you are introducing an extra layer of management which has to be paid for. From a small builder's point of view, the big advantage of hiring small firms rather than singletons, is that cost control becomes much clearer. If someone is quoting to supply and fit a kitchen into your new house for £5000 then you know in advance what the damage is. However, if you rely on your own buying power plus Jim's joinery skills (paid for on an hourly rate) then you will just have to hope that it'll be less than £5000; logic says it should be, but finishing jobs like this have a habit of running over budget. You could ask Jim to quote to install your kitchen but Jim might well be reluctant to do so, especially if you are supplying the kitchen fittings. And what about co-ordinating with the plumber, the electrician and the tiler? Who will do this? If it's to be you and they end up keeping Jim waiting (they will) then it's you who is taking advantage of Jim's fixed price and he'd have every right to cry foul. This sort of finishing work involves so much intricate planning that it is unrealistic to expect every part

of it to be quoted separately, so it tends to be either subbed out in its entirety or done on a time and materials basis.

Daywork v Price Work
Daywork is the term commonly used to describe payments by the hour (or day) and it contrasts with *price work,* where payments are related to specific works having been completed. For example, a brickie on daywork might hope to get paid, say, £70 per day: if he was on a price he would hope to get paid something like £140 for every 1000 bricks laid. All things being equal, you would hope that he would lay about 500 bricks per day whichever system was being used to pay him, but human nature being what it is, it is widely assumed that the person paying the brickie will get better value from priced work. Many advisors say you should only ever hire builders on a price work basis but there are many situations where a daywork arrangement is both easier and more flexible.

If you are building to a tight budget, price work is almost certainly the route to take. For a rookie builder this is perhaps doubly important because you don't know what's in a day's work. Ask yourself how many doors a chippie should be able to hang in a day; if you haven't got a clue then you qualify as a rookie builder.

The main problem with always insisting on price work stems from the fact that it is, contractually, a much tighter type of agreement and that, for it to work, you need to be able to describe the work accurately before you can readily ask for it to be quoted. So really you need to have a professionally written specification for it all to make sense to subcontractors. It's not enough to say "Here is a set of plans. How much will you charge to put the brickwork and blockwork up?", because there are any number of little incidentals that increase the size of this work and make a mockery of your attempts to limit the damage.

Measured Rates
Another problem is that many subbies find plans about as easy to read as you do. This is less of a problem with the finishing trades where they can come and give the house a once over and don't have to resort to plans, but often the hardest parts of a job to quote are the first parts when no house shell yet exists. Here a common ruse is to agree a rate for each section of work (say £200/1000 bricks laid) and then to total up when the work is completed. This is a perfectly sensible way of going about it and protects the subbie from any dispute about differences between what's on the plan and what actually got built: however, there is a great scope here

for disagreements over the quantities actually built. Even qualified quantity surveyors will disagree by 2 or 3% and they work to an agreed set of measuring rules: a contractor and a subcontractor may end up 10% apart.

PAYE v subcontract
Until 1997 almost every subbie you would meet on a small building project would have been technically a subcontractor as opposed to an employee. Many of them worked for the same gaffer week in, week out, year in, year out and yet were still subcontractors for tax purposes. The Inland Revenue and the Contributions Agency have seen fit to reclassify these workers as employees which is a very different kettle of fish for everyone concerned. From a client's point of view, the major change will be that many small building operations will have to charge labour out at about 10% more than they used to in order to cover the extra tax burden placed on them. In theory. In practice the market decides, as it always has done, and the true effect of these tax changes will take a year or two to filter through to market rates.

Not all workers have been reclassified. There are still many genuine self-employed building workers who negotiate their own contracts on a job by job basis. However they will have to work as individuals (or small partnerships) to remain self-employed, and it may be that, in time, they start to gain market share because of the tax changes.

Cash Payments
One of the big advantages of organising your own building work is the ability to negotiate discounts with tradesmen in return for paying them in cash. This is, of course, illegal and any serious publication such as this cannot, naturally, condone such behaviour. But cash payments for casual work are not going to stop because I start being self-righteous. The normal builder's scam is to take off VAT in exchange for payments in cash, but this does not make much sense in new housebuilding because almost all the work is zero-rated so you can reclaim this tax in any case. Unlike the professional contractor, a selfbuilder is not required to police subcontractors' tax arrangements and if you choose to pay them in cash then that is a matter between you and them — it is not illegal simply to pay cash. Should the subcontractor then fail to declare this income it is they who are committing an offence, though subsequent inquiries might get back to you to uncover these payments. Cash payments actually do very little to benefit the new housebuilder unless they are used to negotiate lower prices from subcontractors, something most subbies are reluctant to do.

Contracts

"Do I need one?"
You've already got one. It's a principle of contract law that every time you buy something or hire someone (or something) you enter into a contract. Any item you purchase should perform adequately, any person you hire should carry out the work described competently and you, in turn, should pay them the agreed amount. In essence, it's that simple and this basic principle holds whether you are hiring a baby-sitter or building the Channel Tunnel.

All building work is covered by these principles — after all it's why builders are referred to as contractors — and don't think that just because you haven't got a written contract then you have no redress should things go wrong. However, it is also true to say that if things do go wrong, the more written evidence you can produce to show how and why, the stronger your case will be. If you can produce a written contract, signed by the builder, to say that he should have been finished by the end of August, and it's now November and you still haven't got any glazing in, then you've got a pretty good case for withholding payment. Without something written down it's your word against his and — well there might just be two sides to the story: you're not in a completely hopeless position, but your case is much weaker.

"So a written contract is essential?"
Not at all. It's actually one of the most overrated of safety features devised by professionals largely to justify their fat fees. Take the aforementioned Channel Tunnel, the largest construction project undertaken in these parts in recent times. Teams of lawyers will have been draughted in by both sides to negotiate contracts as watertight as they hope the tunnel will be. Did it get the tunnel built on time and to budget? Of course not. Re-enter those same teams of lawyers to argue about compensation, etc. Who benefits out of all this? The contractors, Eurotunnel and its shareholders — or the lawyers?

"It's all down to a handshake?"
Not at all. That's throwing the baby out with the bath water. The basis of a building contract is that the client contracts to pay a specified sum in return for completion of a list of specified tasks. The more detailed this list, the stronger the contract becomes. If you have a professionally drawn up specification of works, then you already have about as good a contract as you can get. Signing a formal written contract for work that is only specified in the loosest terms is, in comparison, a complete waste of time and money.

"So you think that acceptance of a quotation is enough?"
Yes. If a builder has seen whatever plans and specifications you have, by quoting for them he is committing himself to carry out the work competently. If there are further conditions you wish to set (such as time limits), then you should add these to your specifications. Should it later prove that your specifications are inadequate then so be it; the situation would be no better had you signed a written contract.

"Is the spec. that came with my off-the-peg plans OK?"
You've missed the point. No contract is ever completely watertight. The more detail you put into a contract, the tighter it gets. There isn't a point at which it suddenly becomes OK; rather you get what you pay for. It's like asking how much life insurance is enough when you know that there's a 99% chance that you won't need any and a 1% chance that £2million would be very useful. Very detailed specifications are time-consuming to produce and are, therefore, expensive; only you can decide whether you need one.

"But I'm planning to organise the building work myself."
It's very unusual to sign contracts with labour-only subcontractors or indeed to put anything down in writing. Normally, the work is described verbally or with reference to any plans and specifications to hand. However, the contractual principles involved in hiring subcontractors are no different and neither are your chances of redress, should things go wrong. One of the penalties of building on the cheap is that you are more exposed to bad practice, but hopefully you can compensate to some extent by your frequent site presence. In the absence of any written undertakings, keep a site diary to record the comings and goings and at least you'll have some written evidence in case of trouble. Even to be able to say "Gary and Pete were there just two days in that week and no-one else turned up till the 27th" puts you in a much stronger position than saying "They were hardly ever there."

"I say, I say, I say."
This section (till now) appeared verbatim in the original edition of the Housebuilder's Bible and its assertion that you don't need a written contract for work that is only specified in the loosest terms is, in comparison, a complete waste of time and money.

contract has caused one or two people to hop up and down with indignation. Perhaps they have a point. The fact that I've never built with contracts doesn't necessarily prove that they are a waste of time. Julian Owen, one of the bright young movers behind the Association of Selfbuild Architects, pointed out that he was required professionally to work with a contract and that they didn't have to be expensive or difficult to understand. He particularly favours the simple 16-page JCT Minor Works Contract which is written in clear English and helps all sides to understand their responsibilities. I won't argue against this but I stand by my original line that a contract is no substitute for a detailed written specification of work.

"Anything else to sort out?"
There are somethings which you need to be clear about which are not to do with the technical specifics of building. The formal way of dealing with them would be to enclose the terms along with the plans and specs you send for quotation; by putting in a quotation, the contractor implicitly accepts your terms. However, you could choose to sort these terms out more informally after acceptance of quotation; if you are confident that the terms are not too onerous on the builder, he should be happy to accept and, if he isn't, then you've just been given the clearest indication you'll ever get that this marriage was not made in heaven. Reconsider. Sorting out these matters is in the interest of both parties and very often the first move will come from the builder.

Insurance
For terms and rates, see section on Insurance. Whoever is organising the building work should have cover. Make sure it's in place.

Payments
Agree payment terms. If your money is being advanced by a lender in stages, be open with the builder about when and what these stages are. Generally it's the builder who is advancing you credit and this makes him even more vulnerable than you are.

Retention
It is quite common to withhold a little money (between 2 and 5%) until snags are adequately sorted out. However, don't try and spring this on a builder halfway through a job as if it was a matter of course. It's not. Furthermore, it's always a delicate issue — it reeks of a lack of trust — and some perfectly good builders find it all rather insulting and

often choose to steer clear of such contracts. After all, how would you feel to be told you were having 5% of your pay withheld until such time as your employers saw fit. If you want a *retention clause* included, it's one to get into the open very early on.

Time penalties

Usually, these take the form of damages which are to be deducted from the overall contract value if the work is not completed to an agreed schedule. Again, it's one to sort out right at the outset and it's a very adversarial condition to place on a builder. You have to be prepared to keep your side of the bargain, which means no delays in agreed payments along the route and no changes to the specification of works. This still leaves the messy grey area of unavoidable delays (weather, strikes, illness, disputes with architects) which could keep an impartial referee busy for weeks. You need a very tight specification to be able to argue your side effectively; time penalties really only make sense when you yourself will suffer financial hardship because of a delay.

These added conditions are really nothing more than specialised forms of insurance and, if you load a contract with retention clauses and time clauses, you can expect to pay more overall for the works described.

Extras

The biggest single contractual nightmare any builder faces is how to adequately negotiate what the trade calls *variations* but what everyone else refers to as *extras*. People call them extras because, like Topsy, they seem to grow and grow. Some do shrink (hence variations being a more accurate term) but for every one that shrinks or even disappears there must be a dozen that expand. It's a particularly critical problem with renovations and smaller works (where often 20% of the final bill is made up of items not originally quoted for), but the new housebuilder is not immune from catching these particular bugs. If you've got plenty of time and money and like a nice loose specification where you can make up your mind as you go along then you'll be wondering what all the fuss is about, but if you belong to the 95% of builders who break out into a sweat everytime a bank statement arrives you will want to know how to avoid these nightmares.

The good news is that you can inoculate yourself against most of them. The bad news is that immunisation is itself expensive and time-consuming. Many extras can be avoided by having a professionally written specification, but people wanting to save money will probably have avoided paying for one in the first place and these are usually the same people who can least afford extras.

As if the fact that extras occur at all isn't bad enough, when they do occur you, the client, are negotiating with a gun to your head; you can hardly hire another builder just to do the extras. If you've gone in a bit hard at the beginning — including onerous time penalties and retentions, you can be sure that the builders will have their revenge here. Not only can they potentially stitch you up pricewise, but they have a cast-iron excuse for blowing your time penalty clauses out of the water. Even if things haven't descended to this sabre rattling, adversarial level there is still ample scope to misunderstand and to misconstrue — "Oh I didn't realise that meant the glass had to be toughened as well." "Well that's an extra £80." If you are the kind of client who expects your builder to give you fully costed options for free throughout the job, as in "How much extra would it be if we had a bidet in the kitchen?", you probably deserve to pay over the odds in any event.

Each little decision forms a mini-contract in itself and accounting them can take up over half the total admin. time spent on a job. The golden rules are 1) make it clear that extras need to be authorised by you before work starts on them 2) always negotiate extras direct with the main contractor — that is the person you placed the initial contract, not with anyone working for them, with 3) write down what you've agreed — even if it's just in the site diary.

The reasons for extras are many and various. Sometimes it is down to unquantifiable works discovered after the building work has begun — in new building this type of problem usually occurs underground. Most often it is down to the client adding to the original specification of works as the job progresses or, as it's known in the trade, "changing their bloody minds again." There are two specialised forms of extras, or variables, which deserve closer attention.

PC Sums

PC Sums are not a new form of anti-sexist arithmetic but a good old builder's routine for dealing with loose specifications. *Prime Cost Sums* are put into contracts to allow you, the client, the freedom to select a particular product at a later date. For instance, you might put a PC Sum of £300 for a bathroom suite into a specification. The contractor will have included this amount in the quotation but the actual figure you pay will be down to which bathroom suite you choose.

There is a nasty little problem here because things like bathroom suites have list prices and they have trade prices — indeed the trade price is a matter for negotiation. Don't bulldoze in and buy the kit yourself, because the builder (or perhaps plumber in this case) is expecting to make a profit on this deal and they would have every right to expect you to reimburse them for their lost profit. The normal arrangement is that the builder buys what you specify and that you get to pay list price and the builder pockets the difference between list price and his trade price, but this can work out very expensive, particularly if you up the spec. There is no reason why you shouldn't negotiate a radically different deal whereby you pay trade prices, but make damn sure that you negotiate it beforehand — preferably right at the beginning. Again, the sure way to avoid these sorts of problems is to have a tight specification and that mean ones without PC Sums. This means deciding on things like kitchen and bathroom finishes before the job starts.

Provisional Sums

Like their cousins, the PC sums, the provisional sums are placed in contracts where there is an element of doubt about the amount of work to be carried out. They are much more common in renovations than in new building but there are nevertheless areas — notably underground works — which most builders will only estimate rather than enter into a fixed price quotation. Understandably so. It's a buck-passing device, a way of saying that if there's more work to do than can reasonably be anticipated, then you, dear client, will be the one who has to pay. Well, you knew it was a risky game. Provisional sums are just one of the things that makes building work such a gamble. You can try to force contractors to take on the risk themselves but their understandable response is to hoick prices through the roof; more realistically you can establish guidelines for how provisional works will be charged: a labour rate, a mark-up applied to materials, that sort of thing.

Running a SIte

Plan your site as if you were Wellington planning the downfall of Napoleon, or Montgomery about to attack Rommel. Think of it as a military campaign. Montgomery defeated Rommel because he realised that a battlefield was like a building site and that the best building sites were well organised with things happening when and where you wanted them to happen.

Don't just order 14,000 bricks and think how clever you are to have got them so cheaply. Think about how much space 14,000 bricks will take up, where that space is to be found, who or what will put them there, whether they will stay there when you dig a trench in front of them and whether your hod carriers will be able to get to them if there are 200m^2 of concrete blocks stacked in front. Build the house in your head before you pick up a shovel in anger and you will be some way towards having a strategy for negotiating the obstacles that you will encounter along the way.

Always assume the worst. Plan for rain, lots of it; plan for sub-zero temperatures in which your tap freezes and your bricklaying sand sets hard like rock; plan for delays as your subbies slip off to finish another job. Don't be gobsmacked if materials turn up damaged or if the wrong materials get delivered or if nothing gets delivered at all. Keep calm when your mortgage advance fails to come through on time and four large roofers move threateningly towards you demanding payment.

It'll be alright. It won't be that bad.

Who? When? What With?

I cannot stress how much it is worth sitting down with a blank sheet of paper before you start building. In my experience, builders actually find this incredibly hard; they are, by nature it would seem, always wanting to "push on" or "get ahead" and they think admin is for accountants and blank sheets of paper are for poets. It's almost as if the child in us can't resist the lure of the sandcastle whereby you start digging and piling and gradually the structure appears as if by magic, because everyone is digging and piling. Perhaps it is the natural way to build— after all how many children do you see designing sandcastles before going onto the beach. Natural or not, building this way is a luxury which only the rich and frivolous can afford. Your preparation doesn't have to look incredibly professional — it may indeed look like nothing so much as a glorified shopping list — but it does need to identify who is going to do what, when and what with. As a rule of thumb, every hour spent planning the job beforehand saves between three and four hours tying up the loose ends at the end of the job.

Some of these *whos?* and *what withs?* will be blank at the beginning of the job — for instance, you may not know your plumber or your plasterers at that stage — but the key point to take on here is that you need to identify a time by which you should make a decision, otherwise you will loose the so-called critical path and the whole building program will slide gently off the rails.

How to Finish

Following on from this thread, there is another identifiable problem which you need to address from the word go and that is to do with the finishing details, the key ones listed below:

- Kitchen
- Bathroom furniture
- Light fittings
- Socket placement
- Decorating schemes
- Wall tiles
- Floor finishes
- Shelving, cupboards
- Pavings, driveway finishes.

Very often, and quite understandably, people don't want to make decisions about these features until the structure is finished and they can walk around it and visualise everything. Architect's drawings (and 3D computer walk-throughs) are no substitute for being there anymore than watching the Travel Show is a substitute for going on holiday. The ability to successfully visualise completed building projects when they are still on plan is something that is generally only picked up after years of experience. If you feel unhappy about making these crucial buying decisions before you have a building you can walk around, then be realistic about the scheduling of these delayed purchases.

Refer back to the eight month building schedule which appears at the beginning of this chapter. Notice that your first fix wiring and plumbing are taking place whilst the roofing is being completed, in Month 4. Well first fix wiring and plumbing can't actually take place until there has been some decision making taking place about what is being wired and plumbed in and this effectively means that you will have had to plan both the kitchen and the bathroom layouts, even if you have yet to decide on what the fittings are to be.

Usually these layout options will have been drawn in on the initial plans but note also that the socket outlet and lighting positions will also have to be inked in at this stage and this will effect your positioning of beds and desks and TVs, which is normally left off the plans.

Plan for a Pause

If you refer back to the timeline diagram and the beginning of this chapter, you will note that the finishes are booked in to Month 6. Note also that the plastering stage isn't booked to be completed before the middle of Month 5 and realistically this is the point at which the visually challenged can at last see what their schemings have produced. Most people are surprised to find that some rooms seem larger than they had imagined, some seem smaller, some lighter, some darker. If you are of the sandcastle persuasion of builder, you've reached the natural point at which decision making about finishes should take place — you know, a dark oak kitchen would look just so, or perhaps you feel like stretching to those sensational Provencal tiles you saw in the Fired Earth catalogue which would look a wow behind the bath. Now phone up your chosen supplier, be they MFI or Smallbone kitchens. "Yes, madam, we'd be pleased to supply you with these items. They will be shipped to you in six weeks time." "Six weeks! But I've only got ten days!" "Well perhaps madam would like to choose from our Salmon Slash range which can be delivered to you in three working days." "But I don't like any of those."

I could go on but my point is made. If you want the time to step back and think and then seek out obscure items, and you don't want to do it before your house is plastered out, then plan a quiet period in the building program so that you can engage on a second stage of the planning. If you are working to stage payments, then try and arrange it so that there is a stage payment coinciding with the completion of the plastering stage so that the financial pressure is taken off.

Site Tidy

A clean site is a happy site. It is also a more productive site and a safer site. However, keeping a site tidy takes time and some people regard this as wasted time. It's not. Take time out each day to clear away the crap and to return tools to the spot where they should be kept and it will repay dividends in time saved later on.

Subcontractors tend to be very messy; if someone is working for you on a price then they will tend to think that clearing up after them is your business. Typically, the issue doesn't even get discussed when the subbies are being hired but as a general rule if the subbies are supplying materials then they should be responsible for seeing that they clean their waste away after they've finished — afterall, in this instance they own the waste materials. On the other hand if you are supplying materials then they are yours and it's down to you to decide what to do with them. If you demand that your subbies spend half an hour at the end of each day clearing up their own mess they may well turn around and demand extra money for work which would normally be done by an apprentice (whatever happened to them?). Clean subbies are a blessing, but if yours aren't don't just stand there and moan, get on with it yourself.

Rubbish Disposal

Often the reason a site degenerates into something resembling the aftermath of a small bomb is that there is no coherent way of disposing of all the rubbish. Indeed, many builders are a) loathed to spend money on keeping a site clean and b) loathed to throw anything away because it might come in handy later on the job, or on another job. There is a balance to be struck here between a sensible amount of recycling of waste materials and a stubborn refusal to admit that 98% of what is not used the first time will never get used anywhere else. What this invariably hides is the refusal to admit to an earlier buying mistake.

The easiest option for most small sites is to have a skip on site all the time. It costs around £4/week to keep a skip in an off-the-road location which I reckon is very good value. The expense comes when skips are exchanged — expect an exchange to cost £50-£80, depending on your location, but don't forget that you can have sand and aggregates delivered economically in the new skip which can make a considerable saving. Many builders are tempted to economise on the rubbish and let the pile grow bigger and bigger, thinking that they'll sort it out later on. Just piling rubbish up in one corner can cause more problems than it solves — a windy day may send it all out over the site again, and into your neighbours' gardens as well. Another solution is to dig a pit on site which you will cover on completion — this sounds attractive but it is usually rather a dodgy way of going about things because you'll find that covering it over is easier said than done and you'll be unlikely to use the resulting land for anything useful because it will keep subsiding. Bonfires are OK for disposing of timber offcuts but most building waste is either inert (which won't burn) or is plastic (which shouldn't be burnt). Whatever you do, do plan to do something. Building work produces copious quantities of all kinds of waste and it won't just go away.

Security

Theft is a problem on building sites the world over. It's usually on a small scale and it's typically tools that get nicked, often by casual ne'er-do-wells rather than organised gangs. Fortunately, the way most sites work, the early stages of the work involve a large amount of largely low value commodities like concrete and blocks which are not easily stolen. Only after the shell is watertight (and hopefully lockable) do the expensive fittings arrive on site. If you want to beat the threat of any potential theft, then don't provide any tempting morsels for light fingers:

- Have valuable materials (joinery, sanitaryware, kitchen goods) on site for as short a time as possible before fixing.
- If you have nowhere to lock up kit like cement mixers, barrows and handtools then at least hide them so that the casual visitor does not see them from the road.
- Take small tools (especially power tools) home with you.
- Get the windows glazed and the external doors hung as soon as is practically possible.

- If your site is particularly vulnerable, consider building the detached garage first (if you have one) to use as a strong room. Alternatively, do what many of the professionals do and hire a container for the duration.
- Temporary fencing off is expensive and usually unjustified on small sites. However it may be worth considering if you are in a particularly high crime area or if your site is particularly hazardous and it is likely that people may be wandering around after hours. You can hire 2m high steel fencing such as SGB's *Heras Readifence* for around 50p/m/week—less for longer periods. If you need security fencing for more than five months it will probably repay you to buy it and resell when you have finished.

Safety

Building sites are by their very nature dangerous places. We demand finished buildings which are themselves structurally sound, weatherproof and safe to live-in but in order to create them we have to go through a series of steps which are inherently unsafe. Anyone managing small building sites is legally required to be aware of these risks and to take measures to minimise their impact. New housebuilding is actually one of the safer sectors of the construction industry — a fact borne out by lower insurance premiums — but there are still a large number of potential hazards to be negotiated.

Excavations

Trench work is usually fairly safe at levels down to about 1m (waist height), but thereafter the dangers of trench collapse become very much greater. There are well proven techniques for shoring up trenches and if you are not sure what you are doing then for God's sake get hold of someone who is. Deep foundations are potentially very dangerous and you need to guard against not just trench collapse but also materials and people falling down into them. If you are working close to or underpinning an existing structure there is the additional problem that you could undermine it and cause a potentially catastrophic collapse.

Another problem to always be aware of is encountering buried cables and pipes, something that is common when you are opening roads to make service connections. You can reduce this risk by doing your homework and trying to establish just where cables are likely to be buried.

Plant

Control machinery. Heavy plant can kill or maim if not properly controlled. If you get behind the wheel of a dumper truck don't

Isolated barns provide rich pickings for ne'er do wells. With slates fetching nearly £1 each, its a bit like leaving your car unlocked with the keys in the ignition.

play silly buggers, be very wary. They are not difficult to drive but they can be difficult to control, particularly if it's wet and muddy. They can easily end up crushing someone. Dumpers are often used to pour concrete into foundations and this frequently leads to accidents. Also, ensure cement mixers are properly seated before you start loading.

Ladders

Don't be tempted to be macho — anchor the top end on to something secure. Don't make do with funky old ladders with broken rungs. And wonky step ladders are a nightmare you can live without.

Scaffolding

Don't be afraid to spend money on extra scaffolding. If you are uneasy about doing some task off a ladder (or a scaffold tower) then get proper scaffolding erected. It's surprisingly cheap and you'll get the job done in half the time. Also be very wary about "rearranging" scaffolding. Usually, this means nicking boards off the scaffolding to use elsewhere. Think who might be going to use the scaffolding in the near future and make sure they know what's been going on.

Power Tools

If you don't already have a kit of power tools but are planning to buy some, then buy 110v ones rather than 240v. You'll need a transformer to get them to work but they are far safer. When you hire power tools you should be offered a choice of 110 or 240v. If you are committed to using 240v power tools then ensure that your temporary electricity supply is protected with RCDs (Residual Current Devices).

Electric Cables

Long extension leads are a menace (though sometimes unavoidable). Try and avoid trailing them across site where vehicles may drive over them. Get a portable screwdriver — they are brilliant and you won't need all those extension leads. Cables on building sites tend to get gashed and generally bashed about and it's not unusual for bare wires to get exposed. Keep your eyes open for this sort of thing and if you come across badly frayed cable then replace it, don't bodge it with insulating tape.

Steel Toe Caps

Bruised and broken toes are still one of the commonest of accidents. Yet you still see subbies wearing trainers on site. If you are buying purpose made shoes, get some with steel toe caps (from most builder's merchants from around £30). If you manage to acquire a pair with *Doctor Martens* written on them you'll have a valuable fashion accessory to boot. Most builder's merchants also do a line of steel toe capped wellies.

Head Injuries

Most "serious" sites insist on hard hats being worn at all times, yet you won't even find a hard hat on most small sites — which is a shame because small sites are no less dangerous and, when people are working above you, a hard hat makes good sense. Yet, because they have an image of being "for the big boys only," the small builders and their subbies tend to shun them at all times. At least make an effort. Have at least a couple of hard hats on site and wear them when people are working on scaffolding above you.

Sharps

Remove nails from loose timber lying around site. Common sense really but it usually gets overlooked. If you keep a clean and tidy site, this will be no extra work. If you don't then chances are the only way you'll even know that nails are lying in wait for you is when you tread on them. Ouch.

Lifting

Back injuries are far the commonest cause of lost time for builders. They can usually be easily avoided by asking for some help when lifting heavy objects like bags of cement. Again, don't feel you have to be macho just because you're on a building site. Ask for help.

Minor Accidents

Have a small first aid kit on site. Most injuries are minor and can readily be treated with TCP and a bandage.

CDM Regs

In 1995, there was a significant upgrade to the health and safety regulations in respect to building sites when the Construction (Design and Management) Regulations came into effect. The key point in the new regulations is that building work should be organised in accordance with a Health and Safety Plan which should be written by the designer and administered by the main contractor. If you are deemed to be a Domestic Client — definition = a client for whom a project is carried out, not being a project carried out in connection with the carrying on by the client of a trade, business or other undertaking (whether for profit or not) — your job does not come under the CDM umbrella but professional developers will have to begin by appointing a *Planning Supervisor* who will be responsible for seeing that the design is safe to build and then later a *Principal Contractor*, responsible for seeing that the health and safety plan is put into effect on site. The new regs are statute law and that failure to comply with them can result in criminal prosecution. The risks encountered on a building site haven't changed: the management of those risks has. Its a fair amount of extra work and red tape for

builders and unfortunately there is no evidence as yet that it has done anything to improve safety on building sites. It's a technical subject and there's not room to cover it all here; the Health & Safety Executive (HSE) publish several booklets and I recommend one called *Health and Safety in Construction,* price £7.95 inc P+P, available from HSE Books, POBox 1999, Sudbury, Suffolk CO10 6FS (01787 881165). Local authority building regs departments and the NHBC now offer a Planning Supervision service for professional developers: on our benchmark house, the NHBC charged £225 for this acting as Planning Supervisors.

Now selfbuilders and other domestic clients may not have to comply with the letter of the CDM regs, but you should be aware that all other construction jobs lasting longer than 30 days are required to be notified to the HSE, though technically this is the responsibility of the contractor not the client. Note that if you are managing your own build then you are regarded as the contractor.

Notes for Converters

As if it wasn't complicated enough already, there are a number of grey areas connected with the application of the CDM regs. One of these is the issue of demolition: demolition is the *bete noir* of the construction industry with alarmingly high accident rates and such is the concern of the HSE that the preamble to the regulations suggests that any building work involving demolition should automatically come under CDM legislation. Alright in theory but the policing of the new regulations is already so thin as to be verging on the nonexistent and it would now appear that the HSE have softened their line to exclude demolition of anything less than whole structures: it would be impractical to go through the CDM rigmarole every time you wanted to knock a wall down.

However, it is as well to be aware of the increased dangers of conversion work. In addition to all the regular safety hazards encountered in new build, conversion work introduces another tier of problems to be sorted through. Falling masonry and roofing timbers, support of temporary openings, removal of materials such as asbestos, application of noxious chemicals for timber treatment, to name just four that readily spring to mind. The principles of assessing and managing these risks are identical whatever the work, but the potential for accidents in conversion work will always be much higher than on new build.

Insurance

There are only a handful of insurance companies active in the construction market and most of them are now very open to the needs of selfbuilders as well as the professionals. Norwich Union were the pioneers in this area but now they are tending to be undercut by the Johnny-Come-Latelys. Quotation for construction projects is a complex area and you would do well to seek out the advice of an insurance broker before parting with cash, but expect to pay around 0.66% of the total project value to get all the cover you really need to build with a safety net. That translates at around £400-500 for a house such as our benchmark, four- bedroom detached house. Small builders pay much the same rate on their overall turnover. This would cover you for all the main areas that professional builders are supposed to cover, being employer's liability, public liability and all risks insurance, all of which are explained below. It ceases to have any validity once you have moved in.

Employer's Liability

If you employ any subcontractors — and if you undertake your own project management you are deemed to be an employer, at least from an insurance angle — and any of these subcontractors then has an accident which might in any way be deemed to be your fault, then they can sue you. If this is a serious accident the sums of money at stake will be large. Most policies now cover you for £10million.

Public Liability

This covers people (or objects) who you are not employing but might, nevertheless, still have cause to regret your building site ever existed. Maybe the mud from your site led to an accident, maybe your scaffolding fell down on someone's car, maybe some kids were playing in your foundation trenches when... This is "what if" insurance with a vengeance, but though the chances of a claim are small, any such claim is often extraordinarily large. Some local authorities are now insisting on public liability cover for up to £2million just to do a road opening for a main drain connection; most standard policies cover you for £1million damage.

Contract Works Insurance

Rather vague term used to cover theft of plant and materials from site (usually with a hefty excess) together with fire or structural damage to any structures that you may be working on. Your lender will probably insist that you have all risks cover — though chances are they won't be familiar with the term — just as a conventional mortgage lender will insist that buildings insurance is in place on any property they mortgage. If you are employing a builder to erect your house, then check to see that they have current all risks insurance large enough to cover the value of your completed house.

One important point to note is that contract works insurance does not cover any existing structure you may be altering, converting or extending. You would be expected to have this covered by a regular buildings insurance policy.

Guarantees

These are a different form of insurance which covers the workmanship of a new house. It is not mandatory but it is often very difficult to obtain mortgage finance without it. The NHBC operates the best known system (with a 10-year guarantee) but this is aimed exclusively at professional builder members. Zurich Custom Build operate a similar scheme aimed at the selfbuilder; it covers your new home against structural damage and ground movement for fifteen years and passes automatically on to subsequent purchasers. Expect to pay around £1000 for a house between 150 and 225m^2. Alternatively, most architects are able to issue completion certificates which lenders should be happy to accept; note, however, that an architect will have expected to have overseen the work in progress and this usually adds about another 30% to their fees for just designing and detailing your project.

Bookkeeping

Site Diary

Even if you loathe the thought of record keeping, do try and keep a site diary and write down a summary of every day's action:

- Weather
- What work was done
- Who was on site and how many hours they worked
- Quotations, orders, deliveries, shopping trips
- Payments made
- Contacts made, phone numbers
- Site visits by building inspectors, surveyors, etc.
- Comments, feedback from casual visitors, neighbours
- Accidents (however small), breakages, theft.

Not only does this provide a fascinating historical record, but a site diary has a more immediate benefit if a dispute arises; you have a written record of transactions as they occur. Whether you choose to work with or without a formal contract, a site diary will provide you with loads of unexpected ammunition should things ever turn nasty.

Basic Accounts

What level of accounts you keep on a project like a selfbuilt house is very much up to you. Because you are able to reclaim VAT on most purchases going into a newly built house, it is a must to keep every VAT receipt that comes your way (I recommend a lever-arch file and a hole puncher for filing). When the time comes to make your claim, you will have to total all the figures, but whether it's worth keeping a running total of costs going whilst the job is in progress is doubtful. Running trading accounts with builder's merchants and plant hire shops can be a big help; not only is buying more convenient (and often cheaper) but just the fact that tax invoices get sent by post to your home address makes it much easier to keep tabs on paperwork. Trading accounts is a subject dealt with in greater length in Chapter 11 on shopping.

Management Accounts

If money is tight then you should consider putting a lot more effort into job accounting. You need an early warning system in place to warn you when costs start to overshoot. The key to doing this is to split your whole project down into a number of little joblets such as Groundworks, External Masonry, Roofing, etc. Prepare a detailed budget for your house showing how much you expect to spend on each joblet and prepare a job schedule sheet showing how long each stage of the job should take. Analyse costs as they occur and use your site diary to estimate how much of each stage is completed each week.

You don't go into a project like building a new home without some sort of a budget. Sticking to the budget is obviously crucial to the success of the project, but in my experience you are more likely to come adrift through making an unrealistic budget in the first place rather than overspending on budgeted items. The other great budget breaker is the unavoidable extras (often to do with extra foundations or drains). There is only one safe way around this and that is to make a largish — say 5% — contingency sum available for such eventualities. If your budget doesn't stretch to this, then how about building a smaller house? The more loosely organised your management of the job is, the higher the chance there is of encountering unavoidable extras. No amount of clever management accounting will make up for an incomplete specification.

Correspondence
Keep handy copies of all correspondence to do with your house from plot purchase to suppliers terms. A lever-arch file with about ten subdividers should be sufficient. Don't forget that correspondence means keeping copies of your letters as well as ones received, so work out some system of making and keeping copies of your side.

When you express any kind of an interest in building, you soon find yourself getting snowed under with mailshots for this, that or the other. Some of this is junk, some of it is incredibly useful, but you will need to be on the ball about organising it or you'll never be able to retrieve the useful bits when you need them. Again a subdivided lever-arch file is a real winner here, though you may need to invest in a heavy duty hole puncher (round about £25) to pierce the thicker tomes. In addition, get a pack of cardboard magazine files which you can use to hold really thick literature like you get from kit home suppliers and certain kitchen manufacturers.

VAT

New housebuilding enjoys a privileged position in the VAT world. It's *zero-rated*. This means, in layman's terms, that you can reclaim all VAT charged to you in making purchases for your new house. This is something of an anomaly. Since 1983, almost all other building work has been *standard-rated,* which means that you cannot reclaim the VAT. The reason new build survives VAT free is that VAT cannot be levied on second-hand house sales since almost all sales are private, and that it would be regarded as inequitable for new housebuilders to have to charge VAT on their product when 85% of all house sales escape it.

This argument is bunkum. This VAT subsidy doesn't really save selfbuilders or professional housebuilders any money at all, it just makes building plots very expensive. As already discussed, building plots tend to be valued by subtracting building costs from sale values, and if building costs went up then plot prices would have to come down by an equal amount to compensate. Putting VAT on new house sales would not put up the price of new housing — the market simply wouldn't bear it — but it would cause the underlying land values to fall, possibly by as much as 20%. If VAT was charged on new housebuilding (as it is on most of the continent), then no one would be complaining; but it is not easy for the government to make the transition from a *zero-rated* to a *standard-rated* new housebuilding market. There would be real losers — those left holding building land at the changeover — and for them the pain would be very great if the transition was made overnight. On the other hand, if the introduction of VAT on new housebuilding was flagged someway in advance, it would cause a speculative flood of zero-rated VAT housebuilding which would in itself be very unsettling. As usual, the government has got itself in a corner and is losing £2billion/annum in revenue to a tax loophole of its own making.

The imposition of VAT on new housebuilding is a possibility that all new housebuilders must face. It's probably not so much a question of if but when, and one can only hope that the transition is handled sensitively — but it could be very bloody indeed. Having said that, recent moves by the government have actually widened the net of zero-rating to include a broader definition of what a new house is and also to include extra fittings, so it may well be that my thinking is way off beam — it wouldn't be the first time.

Reclaiming VAT
So much for politics. What you need to know is what to do to reclaim your VAT. Here the position varies depending on how you organise your construction.

Architect-run Job
If you appoint an architect or an independent designer to administer the job, they will normally select a main contractor to undertake all the building work. You will not be able to reclaim VAT on the architect/designer's fees but the bills payable to the main contractor should exclude VAT wherever possible. Note, however, that many smaller design practises will not be registered for VAT and therefore you would not be paying it in any event.

Design and Build
This form of contract differs from a conventional architect/designer-run job in that you start by appointing the contractor, and the contractor then decides who will do the design work. To put it another way, the designer is subcontracting to the main contractor. As such, the design fees are *usually* regarded by the VAT office as being part of the overall building costs and therefore to be zero-rated. Again you, the client, shouldn't really have to do anything because the bills presented to you should exclude VAT.

Self-managed/Selfbuild
In this situation you are on your own. You don't have to be a VAT registered business to reclaim VAT on new housebuilding because Customs & Excise runs a special scheme for selfbuilders. They also publish a booklet (No 719) entitled *Refunds of VAT to D-I-Y Home Builders*. Ring your nearest Customs & Excise department and ask them for a D-I-Y housebuilders VAT Claim Pack. Get hold of it and read it, twice, marking the good bits with a felt tip. The key points are:
- You can't reclaim VAT from subcontractors for their labour. Make sure they don't charge VAT in the first place.
- You can only make one claim and this must be within 3 months of completion. Completion is not the same thing as occupation: they expect you may well occupy before technical completion but if the delay between the two is longer than six months then they become suspicious and will demand explanation. Tread cautiously here.
- All purchases you wish to reclaim the VAT on must be supported by valid VAT receipts, made out to you. A VAT receipt is one that includes the supplier's VAT No. (but doesn't necessarily separate out the VAT). Credit card slips, cheque stubs, delivery notes are *not* VAT receipts. Also Customs & Excise want to see the originals; they don't accept photocopies. Note also that if some of your material supplies are purchased through a subcontractor who is not VAT registered, you will not be able to reclaim VAT — the original invoice must be made out to you.

What is Zero-rated?

You will not be surprised to hear that there are a number of grey areas when it comes to arguing what should and what shouldn't have VAT applied to it. In terms of new housebuilding these grey areas fall into two broad camps. The first deals with whether a project actually classifies as a new building at all and the second area concerns which of the various fixtures and fittings should be eligible for a VAT refund.

New Build or Not?

Since the introduction (in 1983) of VAT to most forms of construction there has grown up a set of ground rules for defining the differences between a new house and the conversion of an old one. This used to be one of the biggest minefields in the property developers battlefield but in 1994 the government changed the rules and widened the net of zero-rating to include the conversion of any nonresidential building to form a new dwelling. This should greatly simplify matters in future, though doubtless there will be arguments about just what "nonresidential" means; anticipating these disputes, the legislators have specified that to qualify as such, a building should have been unoccupied since 1973. Generally new housebuilders — and barn converters in particular — will welcome the changes; it will also put a stop to needless demolition work carried out solely in order to qualify for VAT zero-rating. Note however that there are technical differences between reclaiming VAT on new builds and on conversions and you would do well to seek further advice on this from your local VAT office.

Is it? Isn't it?

Provided you can establish that your project is a new build, almost all the construction costs are eligible for zero-rating of VAT. That is to say, that suppliers who are knowingly supplying a zero-rated project should not add VAT to their invoices and if VAT is applied (currently at 17.5%) you should be able to reclaim it. However, as your house nears completion, you will find a number of items which Customs & Excise, in their wisdom, regard as fittings which lie outside the zero-rating net. If there is any ground rule at all it is that if the items are fixed into the building then they are zero-rated but if they are removable then you must pay the VAT. However, there are so many exceptions to this rule that it is necessary to run through the list. Again this whole area was reviewed in 1994 and many fixtures and fittings previously excluded from zero-rating are now allowed. I present this list for general guidance only; your VAT office may view things differently to mine and please don't jump down my throat if you find you are unable to reclaim VAT on something I've said you can. It's your VAT office you should be arguing with and, if you're canny, you will do this before you start construction. VAT Notice 719 includes a similar list which you should refer to for the latest views from the VAT office.

Having tried to get myself off this particular hook, let's look at the current state of play. Personally, I find this catalogue of what's in and what's out ridiculous, and I'd be tempted to laugh at it if there wasn't so much damn money riding on it. Don't keep telling your VAT official that "This is crazy!"; they know it and they've heard it a thousand times before.

- KITCHENS: Fitted kitchens are zero-rated but white goods (cookers, laundry, dishwashers, etc.) are not. There is no distinction made between integrated and free-standing equipment — you must pay VAT on them. However, waste disposal units and rubbish compactors are zero-rated; water softeners are not.
- AGAS: standard-rated except when they have an integral boiler; then they are regarded as part of the heating system and you can reclaim the VAT.
- FITTED CUPBOARDS: At present the ruling seems to be this — if you build the cupboards (i.e. fitting doors across alcoves formed in the walls) then it seems that you can reclaim the VAT on all the materials, but if you buy in fitted cupboards then you can't. If that's not clear then ask your VAT office.
- FLOORING: All forms of carpeting are standard-rated. Everything else is zero-rated.
- HEATING/PLUMBING/SANITARYWARE: All zero-rated except water treatment units. Fireplaces are also zero-rated. Solar panels, heat recovery systems and air conditioning should also qualify for zero-rating, but air conditioning is standard-rated.
- ELECTRICS: All zero-rated. Light fittings should be OK provided they are fitted, but a zealous inspector may disagree.
- ALARMS: Both smoke alarms and burglar alarms are zero-rated. Also fire safety equipment is now zero-rated.
- FURNISHINGS: Movable furniture is invariably standard-rated. The status of fitted shelves is unclear. Curtains and blinds are standard-rated but you can reclaim VAT on curtain rails.
- DECORATING: Paint is zero-rated and you shouldn't have any problem with wallpaper. Also, if you want to have decorative finishes (like pine matchboarding) you should be able to reclaim the VAT.
- GARAGES and DRIVEWAYS: Zero-rated.
- LANDSCAPING: They will generally accept a limited amount of turfing and paving as zero-rated. However, trees, shrubs and plants will all be VATable.
- SWIMMING POOLS: A grey area if ever there was one. It seems that if the plans for a swimming pool are included with the original plans then the pool will be regarded as zero-rated. One to get a ruling on before hand.
- OUTBUILDINGS/CONSERVATORIES: Detached outbuildings (except garages) are standard-rated. However, attached extensions like conservatories are zero-rated.
- PLANT HIRE, SCAFFOLDING: These are standard rated items which you cannot reclaim, although note that scaffolding erection and dismantling is technically zero-rated whilst the hire is not. Therefore you can save money by getting your scaffolder to invoice separately for the two services.

End of the Party

A selfbuilder can only make one reclaim from the VAT office and so when it's done, it's done. This presents a major cashflow problem to many as there is usually several thousand pounds waiting to be reclaimed, several thousand pounds which most selfbuilders could well use to finish off their project; many end up forgoing further VAT reclaims in order to get their hands on this money before the house is complete. If you employ a VAT registered builder to construct your house this reclaim problem does not occur as the builder's invoices are zero-rated for all but the exempt items though note that you can still use the D-I-Y reclaim scheme if you buy just the odd can of paint and a few curtain rails on your own account.

VAT refunds for 'do-it-yourself' builders

Notice 719

Chapter 6
Groundworks

Groundworks is the term most often used to describe all the things that builders do beneath ground level. It's actually a hotch potch of different activities — excavation, drainage, service connections, concreting, some brickwork. It also conventionally includes the laying of the ground floor but I have analysed costs and techniques in the next chapter where ground floors can be more easily compared with upper floors. The advent of JCBs, readymix concrete and plastic drainware has taken a lot of the graft out of this part of building, but it still remains an exacting and potentially hazardous task. It is also incredibly messy, especially when there's rain about. Whilst neighbours will look on in horror as you recreate the battlefield of the Somme, you must shrug your shoulders and utter asinine comments like "You can't make an omelette without breaking eggs."

Groundworks is really a question of getting from A to B as cheaply and easily as possible. There are many reasons for using something other than the bog-standard solutions for your underground work, but all of them involve sorting out or avoiding problems, not increasing amenity value. This is not to say that the housebuilder does not face choices of how best to get the groundworks completed, but these choices are for the most part to do with ease, speed and cost of installation. This chapter concentrates on these issues as well as

taking a closer look at how some of the problems, outlined in Chapter 3, Pitfalls, are solved.

Given a straightforward site and a straightforward house design, the groundworks can progress with remarkable speed. However, a problem site with problem service connections could easily result in a figure of double or even treble this amount, so I cannot emphasise enough just how important it is to thoroughly analyse the costs involved in just getting your house out of the ground.

Groundworks are also one of the areas of housebuilding most prone to mistakes being made. The setting out of foundations and levels and the correct siting of drain terminals is not a job to be undertaken lightly; add a slope into the equation and you have a job to tax the most skilled surveyor. Yet the supervision of groundworking is often left to harassed digger drivers who "want to get on with it" and often barely refer to any plans that may have been drawn up. The horror stories that you occasionally see of completed houses having to be taken down because they were put up in the wrong place are a testament to the consequences of rushed excavations. If you've never been involved in setting out foundations, you can sit back and laugh at the incompetence; not until it's just you and a stroppy JCB driver do you begin to realise just how difficult it is and how easy it is to go badly wrong.

Of all the areas of housebuilding, groundworks is the one that needs the most management and the best management. If you are a D-I-Y project manager, this is the big one. Crack this and you will have no problems on down the line.

Most builders choose to subcontract all the groundworks but, whilst this makes it very much easier to navigate this stage, it is still vital to check that you are getting exactly what you asked for. You must check that the foundations are in the right place, that they are square, that they are at the right height (this last can be very difficult to measure). You must check that the access arrangements have been properly constructed, with falls going the right way. You must check that the drains and the services have been installed correctly. Your building inspector will provide some guidance and will be able to pinpoint errors and bad practise but building inspectors are not paid to be surveyors and they will have no idea if your trenches are off square or in the wrong position. It is much harder to ferret out mistakes on groundworking than on later parts of the build but it is also usually much more expensive to rectify at a later date.

Excavations

A flat site is a cheap site; clearing debris off the oversite will not take long and digging normal depth foundations will take a JCB no more than a day on a four-bedroom house. Note, however, that the crucial task of setting out the foundations on the ground has to be carried out after the undergrowth is stripped away. It's not a job to rush, especially if you are new to the game, and so you ideally want to leave a couple of days between site clearance and the start of excavation. The consequences of setting out in completely the wrong place are often disastrous — see cautionary tale opposite.

Unless you are working in a confined area where mechanical plant cannot reach, then you will want to get hold of a JCB or some similar digger. Some builders have diggers and digger drivers in their armoury, but most just have contacts with guys who are self-employed and own their own machine. They tend to charge for travelling time so it's worth getting someone local and — depending on how busy they are — they often charge for a minimum of half a day even when they're only around for a couple of hours. But at around £100-£120/day for driver plus JCB, they can do the work of around ten to twenty men and therefore represent a bargain not to be sniffed at. They can also do a lot of damage. The one-man band digger drivers tend to be the most helpful, but they do like to get

on with it. If you're not 100% on top of what's to be done then chances are that you'll get rushed into mistakes. Trench excavations happen remarkably quickly (at around 50m/day, enough for a 120m² house) and inexperienced groundwork managers will have their work cut out to keep up.

Demolition Man?

If you've an existing structure to demolish, then you'll have a choice of taking it down slowly and salvaging materials or getting a machine to demolish it (which is not very green but it's far more exciting — one for the camcorder). I'd suggest that it is almost entirely dependent on the value of the salvaged materials. There are also health considerations whichever method you employ — watch out for asbestos, which was very common in much of the 20th century housing now being demolished.

Muck Away

Charming expression for getting rid of the spoil. The topsoil is stripped off and stored on site for later use, but the subsoil is usually dumped somewhere else. Many digger drivers operate in tandem with a 15- or 20-tonne lorry and will have local dumping contacts. Alternatively, it is worth chasing up local landowners to see if they have any holes to fill. Subsoil taken out of the ground "bulks up" at least 30% when piled in a heap (or on

a lorry). This means that just under 12m³ dug out of the ground will fill a 15m³ space on a 20-tonne lorry. Some ground conditions, notably clay, bulk up at much more than 30%: a 50% or even 60% bulk up rate can be expected. Make sure if you get a quote per cubic metre whether you are dealing with muck in the ground or bulked up.

Landfill Tax

Since 1996, a tax has been applied to excavation at a rate of £2/tonne if the spoil is classed as inert and a whopping £7/tonne is it has man-made detritus in it. It is paid when spoil is tipped at a licensed pit and it has had the effect of increasing the cost of a 20-tonne muck away lorry from around £60/load to £100/load. Our benchmark house with it's deeper than average clay foundations would have had to have paid over £500 in Landfill Tax, adding 30% to excavation costs.

Ouch.

All the more reason to find a friendly farmer with a hole to fill. Many builders are choosing to put all excavated spoil in the back garden, then compacting it with heavy machinery and placing topsoil back on top. It's an option to consider but it's just not possible on all sites.

Around and About

On many sites you will be unable to get heavy plant like JCBs to the back of the house once you have completed the trench excavations. If you have plans for landscaping or drainage or even plan to build a swimming pool or a summer house at a later date, this may be your only opportunity to get the groundwork done quickly and cheaply and a change of plan or an oversight can have costly ramifications on down the line. Another area to sort out on day one is the site access; it pays to get your drive levelled and hardcored as early as possible.

Summary

For more information about muck removal see Chapter 11, Hiring in Plant. In summary, look to pay between £8 and £12/m³ bulked up — equivalent to £10-£15/m³ in the ground — for excavation and removal of subsoil to a licenced tip.

The 20 tonne lorry is the natural partner to the digger

Pull down your home, couple told

A COUPLE have been told their £250,000 retirement home must be pulled down because it was built in the wrong place.

Ken and Doreen Walker, both 65, were looking forward to years of peace in the four-bedroom brick and timber mansion with views over the Downs.

However, neighbours at Lindfield, near Haywards Heath, West Sussex, complained when they discovered that it had been put up 20ft away from the spot which had been proposed and cast a shadow over their homes.

When the case went to a public inquiry the inspector found against former businessman Mr Walker, who served on Haywards Heath planning committee and in 1992 was deputy major.

Fighting back tears, his wife, a retired primary school teacher, said: 'We made a terrible mistake and it's going to cost thousands.

'We had planned this as our little project for when we retired. We put our savings into building a dream home that our four daughters and their children would want to visit. We put the house up but set it further back from the road than was shown on the plans.

'It was only after the roof had been put on and tiled that neighbours complained. It's almost complete and everything has to be taken apart piece by piece.'

Mr Walker said: 'We cannot believe people can be so miserable-spirited to exaggerate out of all proportion what the loss of amenity was.'

But neighbours in Lyoth Lane were celebrating.

Fireman Dave Harding, 39, said: 'The house casts a large shadow over our property and stops the sun for everyone.'

Richard Walker, deputy director of planning at Mid-Sussex District Council said: 'If anybody fails to build in accordance with the approved plans they will always run the risk of incurring abortive expenditure.'

Doomed: The £250,000 house

Daily Mail. August 1995

I am not sure whether this is a case of inaccurate groundworks or just good old opportunism, backfiring badly but it illustrates just how important it is to get the setting out and excavations spot on.

Foundations

Where there are no problem foundations to be negotiated, there are two main techniques for putting down foundations. One is to pour the minimum amount of concrete possible into the foundation trenches and then build upwards in brick or blockwork — known as *traditional footings*. The other system reverses this logic altogether and pours as much concrete as possible into the trench before starting on the bricklaying — this is usually called *trenchfill*. Note that when you are pouring concrete into clay soils, you will probably have to use the trenchfill method.

Which is Best?

Both methods have pros and cons. The traditional method, laying footings below ground level, is cheap on materials but heavy on labour; it is also slower.

Our benchmark house uses trenchfill. Most professional developers do. They value the speed and comparative ease with which trenchfilling is done. What really tends to swing it for the trenchfillers is that a high proportion of the labour element goes into setting levels for the concrete to be poured to and that this work is the same whatever the concrete level. Add to this the fact that much of the graft of foundation pouring has been taken away by the increasing use of concrete pumps which do away with the need for barrowing, and you can see why trenchfill is tending to win out.

The depth and length of the trenches are not in your control, but the trench width is largely down to which bucket the JCB uses to dig with (the general choices being 450mm and 600mm wide). Using a 450mm wide bucket is going to reduce the amount of readymix used by a quarter (as well as reducing exca-

Traditional Strip Footings

brick and block cavity wall

blockwork footings

trench dug 600mm wide

concrete min 250mm thick

external ground level

Trenchfill Foundations

ground floor

concrete fills trench

The width of the foundation trenches follows the size of the digger buckets

vation costs) but it is not to be recommended to rookie builders. Cavity walls—generally now 300mm wide—sit uncomfortably on such a narrow trench; single skin masonry (as used in the garage) is obviously less of a problem, but the key factor in all this is accurate *setting out* of trenches. Unless you are an experienced surveyor, you really want to play safe and set trenches at 600mm wide, because not to do so is to risk not having square footings. This will end up costing you far more money than the few hundred quid (maximum) you may save through having narrow foundation trenches.

So is there still a case for traditional footings? Well, yes there is, particularly for selfbuilders. It is still marginally cheaper to build this way, even when compared to a house being done with all its trenches at 450mm width.

Tip
Check out the section in Chapter 11 on Concrete as well.

Slopes, Bad Ground & Trees

If you have worked through the book to this point from Pitfalls you will have twigged that, though groundworks can work out to be very cheap, they can also turn into a budget crippling nightmare. Whether you have or haven't, the crucial groundworky bits went as follows: *There are three basic causes of alarming cost expansion:*

- *slopes*
- *bad ground*
- *trees.*

Slopes

Obviously, it all depends on how much it slopes, but even quite gentle slopes can create havoc with a tight budget. Brinkley's Slope Law, pictured below, states that, no matter how you deal with it, each 1° of slope will add £1000 to your development costs. Obviously this represents an enormous over-simplification of different situations but you will be disappointed to discover that it rarely works

out less than this and sometimes it can be a whole lot more, especially if you are constructing a mansion larger than 200m². You just can't get away with building a sloping house and so adjustments have to be made between the lie of the land and the lie of your house and these adjustments are expensive. It's not just excavating out the ground so you can build on the level; there are complications with access roads and pavings, drains, and landscaping where any site with a slope of more than 5° is going to require retaining walls and possibly even safety railing. Faced with a sloping site, there are basically three options for the new housebuilder.

Excavate and Cart Away

Here you dig out large house-sized hole out of your slope, dispose of all the excavations and fit the house into the hole. This is perhaps the simplest and the one that the planners are likely to prefer as it will keep your roof line low. There will be the cost of excavation and carting away (estimate £8-£12/m³) which, depending on the lie of the ground, could easily cost £1000-£4000. Add to this the cost of any retaining walls that might have to be built: budget £90/lin.m for a 1m high retaining wall.

Build Out From High Point

Here you substitute the cost of excavating with the cost of building supporting walls. There may not be much to choose between the two in cost terms, but this method is likely to leave you with expensive steps to build up

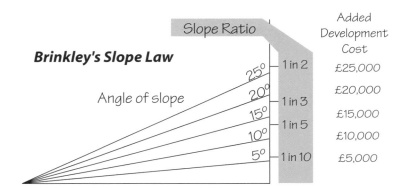

Brinkley's Slope Law

Angle of slope

Slope Ratio		Added Development Cost
25°	1 in 2	£25,000
20°	1 in 3	£20,000
15°	1 in 5	£15,000
10°	1 in 5	£10,000
5°	1 in 10	£5,000

to the back/front of the house. The overall structure is also likely to be far more imposing and, consequently, much less likely to pass muster with the planners.

Fit House To Slope.
Arrange the house as a series of steps, running up the slope. Building basements and/or mezzanine split levels may well be architecturally the most pleasing but it is also the most expensive. Split levels have cost implications at almost every stage of the building works: stepped foundations, shuttering for floor slabs, special stair joinery, complex service routes, complex roof details. Split level building adds 20% to your overall building costs.

Whichever method you choose to overcome the problems set by a sloping site, you will be faced with extra landscaping expenses — steps, turfed banks, rockeries. Although these costs can generally be deferred over a number of years, they will add significantly (£1000+) to the overall development costs. The extra thousands might well be better spent on building a semi-submerged basement — see Chapter 4.

Bad Ground
A variety of problems are dealt with under the category of bad ground. The commonest are clay soils and the presence of tree roots, but also you must be prepared for bog conditions, mining subsidence, wells, water courses, old factory workings, disused refuse tips, even problems when ancient remains are discovered. It's worth carrying out any amount of detective work to ascertain exactly what has happened on your site because the ramifications can be expensive. A fairly recent new menace (or, rather, newly described menace) is radon, a naturally occurring radioactive gas, which is being found in more and more parts of the country.

A site appraisal is likely (but not definitely) going to uncover the problems you will meet below ground and your foundation design is almost definitely going to be in the hands of an engineer. There are three likely solutions to bad ground:
- Deeper foundations (sometimes reinforced with steel)
- Raft foundations
- Piling.

Deeper Foundations
You will have to excavate to good bearing ground (if it's there). If it's just a question of going down to 2.5m, you may get away with the regular trenchfill foundation. But this will be expensive; on a four-bedroom house it will add around £300 for every extra 100mm depth you have to dig down. If the ground is soft or wet (which is likely), then extra will have to be spent on shuttering and shoring. Deeper than 2.5m, it usually becomes cheaper (and/or easier) to specify one of the alternative foundation systems — i.e. rafts or piles.

Clayboard
Increasingly commonly used in clay areas, *Clayboard* is a polystyrene sheet, very similar to the insulation sheets which you may later be laying under your ground floor, which you fix to the sides of your foundation trenches before filling them with concrete, rather like lining paper in a cake tin. The idea is that clayboard is inert, yet flexible enough to allow the clay to heave without moving the enclosed concrete foundations.

Rafts
On a problem free site, the floor slab is laid a couple of stages further on than the foundations. However, with rafts, you pour the foundation concrete together with the floor slab concrete in one operation. With various cambered design profiles and a whole mass of steel reinforcement, you create a concrete raft which will move as one. If subsidence occurs, the raft will absorb the changes without imposing extra strains on the superstructure above.

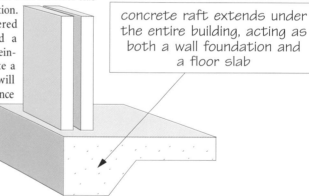

concrete raft extends under the entire building, acting as both a wall foundation and a floor slab

A raft foundation uses vast amounts of concrete and, if one had been specified for the benchmark house and garage, it would have cost as much as £10,000 but, unlike the alternatives, it would provide you with a floor slab to build off. In effect, it's similar in price to piling or digging foundations greater than 2.5m, that is to say around £5,000 more than the bog standard solution.

Piling
Reckoned to be cost effective in situations where foundations would otherwise have to be deeper than 2.5m. The number of piles and the depth of each pile can only be determined by a test pile being dug (budget £300), but a typical installation would place piles 2.5m apart under every load-bearing wall (including detached garages) and each pile would go down till solid ground was reached. All the piles are then filled with concrete and tied together with a concrete ground beam, which would be all that you would eventually see of the operation, and would look much like a regular trenchfill concrete foundation. Budget prices are £30/metre depth for individual piles (depth anywhere from 3-10m) and £60/lin.m for ground beams. A 5m depth piled foundation for the benchmark house and garage would cost around £8000, around £5,000 more than standard footings or trench fill on a non-problem site.

There are various other techniques which can be used as an alternative to concrete piling or reinforced rafts but these are really the province of the specialist engineer. If you have difficult ground you will in any event be having to employ a structural engineer to work out a solution acceptable to building control and you would probably be well advised to spend time looking for a good engineer rather than trying to tell your engineer how he should do his job.

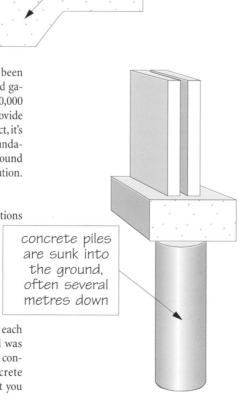

concrete piles are sunk into the ground, often several metres down

6a: The Tree Table
Effect of Tree Roots on Foundations

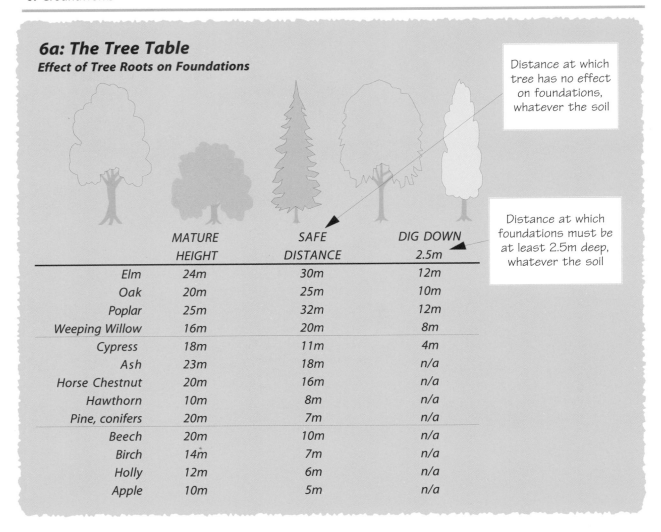

Distance at which tree has no effect on foundations, whatever the soil

Distance at which foundations must be at least 2.5m deep, whatever the soil

	MATURE HEIGHT	SAFE DISTANCE	DIG DOWN 2.5m
Elm	24m	30m	12m
Oak	20m	25m	10m
Poplar	25m	32m	12m
Weeping Willow	16m	20m	8m
Cypress	18m	11m	4m
Ash	23m	18m	n/a
Horse Chestnut	20m	16m	n/a
Hawthorn	10m	8m	n/a
Pine, conifers	20m	7m	n/a
Beech	20m	10m	n/a
Birch	14m	7m	n/a
Holly	12m	6m	n/a
Apple	10m	5m	n/a

Trees

There are two different ways in which trees may effect your development costs. One is visual; planners and neighbours may view the importance of your trees quite differently from you. The other is to do with the effect of tree roots on your foundations. A site with mature trees will tend to look immediately attractive but you should pay close attention to just where these trees are located in relation to your proposed foundations.

Tree Roots

Tree root systems can spread a very long way from the trunks and they can suck water from even greater distances causing movement and shrinkage in soils, which is bad news for house foundations. The solution to this problem is not to cut down the offending trees — this can actually make the situation worse for up to ten years afterwards — but to have deeper foundations. The NHBC publishes tables showing the foundation depth needed for different tree species at varying distances but this is too technical in scope for this humble work: the summary table is designed to let you roughly gauge the effect on construc-

tion costs. There are five variables which determine the foundation depth when tree roots are present; these are:

- Shrinkability of the soil — clay soils are bad news
- Water demand from tree species: some species such as poplar, willow and elm, are very thirsty whereas others, such as beech and birch, have much less impact on your foundations.
- Mature height of tree species
- Distance of tree from foundations
- Geographical location of site.

The worst case scenario would be to have a tall and thirsty tree, located 7m (or less) from your foundations which are in clay. God help you! The NHBC would want you to dig foundations over 3m deep which would mean you would have to employ an engineer to design them (over 2.5m) and you would expect to pay around £5000 extra to foundation costs on a house such as the benchmark house.

Action

If your plot has any of these problems it will pay dividends to seek advice at survey stage. The person who would normally deal with

such matters is a structural engineer, but if you are employing a designer to solve your problems, it would be as well not to engage another professional off your own bat; let the designer choose how (and who) best to overcome the difficulties. See Chapter 3, Pitfalls.

Services

The service connections are an administrative heavyweight. The actual amount of work is often relatively little but it will usually take many hours sorting out just what goes where. Most of the utility companies have something like a New Homes Division which is what you need to get hold of; this will arrange site surveys and quotations for installation and also offer advice about the dos and don'ts. It is quite possible to lay drains and services in the same trench and this is usually the cheapest option – providing of course that your connections are all in the same direction.

Water

New homes (and conversions of existing buildings) in England and Wales are almost always fitted with water meters which are themselves almost always fitted as near to the highway as possible – though there is a move afoot to start fitting internal water meters. The water company will usually put a temporary standpipe next to the meter which will enable you to have a water supply on site immediately and it is worth considering just where the meter is best located so as to avoid traffic.

You need to lay your water pipe at least 750mm below ground so as to avoid frost – and your water company will want to inspect this before you close the trench. If your main drain run goes more or less in the direction you want to go you can often lay it in the same trench. You don't have to duct it except where it comes through the foundations of the house; if you bring it up into the house against an outside wall or through a suspended floor, you need to lag the pipe with insulation as it comes up out of the ground (again to avoid frost damage). These days people tend to use alkathene (*aka* MDPE) for water mains and it will pay you to use a wide bore 25mm pipe (costs around £20/25m roll) if you are considering a mains pressure hot water system. Avoid underground joints at all cost — you are responsible for leaks on your side of the meter.

Electricity

Included in your quotation for electricity supply will be (hopefully) enough plastic ducting for you to get from the local supply to your meter. The route you take between these two points is up to you but the ducting should be buried 450mm below ground level. These days the local electricity companies prefer you to locate your meter in a white plastic box, recessed into your wall; whilst convenient (allowing for meter reading when you are

not at home), they are pretty ugly and if you haven't got anywhere you can hide them you can insist on an indoor meter.

It is very useful to have a temporary supply to site whilst construction is underway but you have to do a bit of construction work first to create a suitable housing for it. For more details, see section on Electrics in Chapter 8.

Gas

If you have a mains gas supply to lay, then you are usually best advised to install ducting (available free from British Gas) at the groundworks stage. You are conventionally aiming to get from the gas main to an external meter box which you can place pretty much where you please. British Gas supply a Semi-concealed meter box which is mostly buried in the ground and is much less obtrusive than the wall boxes. The incoming gas *service pipe,* which connects the gas main with your meter, should be buried at least 375mm below ground level.

Telecoms, Cable

Both BT and the cable companies will supply plastic ducting for free. BT supply may be overhead in which case don't trouble yourself. My local cable company (Cambridge Cable) will supply ducting for their service even in areas which may not receive a supply for many years to come. The routes and the depths of these runs are up to you though note that they prefer their lines to come out of the ground on the outside wall of the house, rather than inside.

Mains water, electricity, gas and telecoms are often laid in ducting which is laid across the site during the drain-laying excavations. The water company will want to inspect the ducting — it has to be laid at least 750mm below ground level to avoid freezing — but the other services will let you fend for yourself, so you need to know exactly where you want them to run. Industry standards are to set electricity and gas mains at least 450mm below ground level.

Infrastructure Charge

First introduced in England and Wales in 1990 to help pay for environmental improvements, these charges are raised by the local water companies and are additional to their already high connection fees. The infrastructure charge is nothing more or less than a tax on new building. It's applied to every new dwelling created — including flats converted

from existing houses — and it is applied at the same level regardless of the size of the dwelling. Until 1994, water companies were free to set their own charges and—surprise, surprise—they tended to charge the earth (often over £1500) but then OFWAT, the water regulator, stepped in and set a ceiling for the infrastructure charges, set to be around £215 for water and an additional £215 for main drainage connections in 1998. In Scotland and N Ireland the situation is very different; there the water industry is still publicly owned and infrastructure charges are unheard of.

Despite OFWAT's success in limiting the scale of these charges, this sort of backdoor tax (which loses few votes) is probably the coming thing and expect other similar charges to appear over the next few years. In America they are called *impact fees* and they get levied not just by utility companies but by the local councils as well to pay for roads, schools, etc. which the new development is deemed to need.

Two Parts

The infrastructure charge is made up of two parts, a charge for water provision and a charge for sewage disposal. Each water company sets its own rate; if you dispose of your sewage by other means than connecting to the main drains, then you will be exempted from the sewage charge. Normally the infrastructure charge is not levied until the house is finished but some water companies get around this by forcing you to pay an equivalent sum as a deposit before they will connect you up to the mains.

Drains

First things first; it is important to understand the difference between *foulwater* and *rainwater*.

- **FOULWATER** is the waste generated by normal household usage — flushing loos, emptying baths and sinks, washing machines, dishwashers, etc.
- **RAINWATER**, as its name suggests, is what falls out of the sky and flows down the gutters and downpipes from off the roof.

Generally our sewage systems are working at near capacity levels and therefore it is a standard requirement that rainwater is not added to the load. Hence it is normal to lay two separate drain systems to dispose of their respective wastes in different ways. In certain locations it may be possible to run rainwater into the main sewerage system (refer to your water company) but it would be unwise to assume that this is the case. You will need to prove that there is no alternative.

Drains for Drainbrains

Our benchmark house in Eltisley has its foul drains running into the village's main drains and its rainwater drains collecting in a couple of soakaways under the paved drive. You could say this is the bog standard arrangement for UK housing; it's certainly the most usual. The total cost of drainage on the benchmark house is a just under £2000. This is split between costs of laying two foul drain runs (£840), making a road connection (£200), and the cost of two rainwater drains to soakaways (£900). However, as has already been pointed out, the benchmark house is rather atypical of what a volume developer would try to build: savings could have been made by simplifying the drain layout. On the other hand, the runs were short and relatively straightforward and the road connection, whilst deep, was remarkably simple.

Rainwater drains typically cost more to install than foulwater drains. Bear in mind that not only are there downpipes at every corner of the house, but there is a detached garage which also has to have its rainwater disposed of and this contributes to some very long drain runs. When planning rainwater drains it is sometimes possible to replace a relatively expensive underground drain run with a relatively cheap gutter run overhead. Alternatively, you can sometimes use a larger size of guttering, which will enable you to cut down on the number of downpipes and therefore the length of rainwater drains. But I digress; this stuff really belong in the section on Rainwater — see Chapter 7, Superstructure.

Whereto?

In assessing the likely costs of any individual scheme there is one overriding question that must be answered at the outset. That is, "Where the hell am I going to dump all this crap?" There are other questions as well, notably, "How do I get it there?"; but "Whereto?" is the BIG ONE. So, though it may seem illogical to start at the end, we'll look at the drainage options this way around.

All these dumping options are extremely variable from case to case. The table indicates ballpark figures for many options but — I can't emphasise enough — you would be wise not to set too much store by these figures as they can often prove to be very much higher.

Running into the Main Drains

Fine if you've got them, but this isn't always the cheapest dumping option and, in England and Wales, you'll have to pay a £215 sewage infrastructure charge on top (whereas private disposal is exempt). Locating main drains can be a problem; what records exist are held by the water companies and, whilst access is open to all, accuracy is not guaranteed and it would be wise to allow £500 as a contingency sum to cover unforeseen complications. The amount of work in excavating and connecting to the main drain (usually referred to as "doing a road opening") can vary enormously according to depth of the drain, whether there are vacant junctions (known as *laterals*) already present to connect onto, the presence/absence of other utilities, and attitudes and charges of local authorities and water companies. Road opening is an administrative heavyweight. The council highways must be contacted and a road opening permit purchased (prices vary enormously from £10 to £300); to get such a permit, you need to show public liability insurance cover for up to £2million. Inspections of the opening and connection need to be carried out by 1) your water company, 2) the council highways department, 3) the council building inspector and 4) your own building inspector if different from 3). A busy road may require traffic lights and if your main drain runs under the other side of the road, the whole process becomes very much more complicated.

The sting in the tail here is the cost of reinstating the road after you've made your connection. This is very dependent on a) the classification of the road, b) the bearing of the ground and c) the attitude of the local authority — the highways department sometimes ask for a deposit of several hundred pounds to cover the cost of reinstating the road. Reinstatement can add anything between £100 and £1500 to your road opening costs.

Backdrop Manholes

It is much cheaper, easier and safer to lay house drains at depths of between 600 and 1200mm below ground level. Normally, drains are best laid at gentle falls (around 1:60) and sharp inclines are discouraged. If your main drain level is way beneath your optimum house drain level, you will probably find it easiest to construct a backdrop manhole near your boundary line (cost £150-£300). A backdrop manhole works a bit like a waterfall: it's a sudden drop from one level to another and it requires special construction methods and access arrangements. Our benchmark house used a plastic version called a marscar bowl (£80 to buy).

Pumps

If your main drain is higher than your house drain you have the option of pumping the waste up hill. This is done by building in a fibreglass (GRP) sump similar to a small septic tank (say, 2m deep and 1m in diameter) into which the house drains run, and fitting either a solid handling pump or a macerator pump. The macerator pump is the more expensive but allows the waste to be expelled in a 32 or 50mm pipe, which makes it a better bet for long distances. A control panel is placed somewhere indoors (garage?). Budget £2000 for supply of sump, pump and control panel, installation extra. Two useful contacts for pumps are T-T Pumps and Polycon.

Long Distance Pumping

Expensive though a pump is, it can be cost effective to install one when the main drain connection is further than 300m away even if it is downhill. This is because it can pump out into a 40mm pipe which can be laid in a flat trench, much reducing excavation costs. On the other hand, any system that works by gravity alone isn't going to break down.

On Site Treatment

Most selfbuilders choose to build in rural areas and many of these are inaccessible to mains drainage. There options are outlined below but before you go ahead specifying one or the other note that there are some more admin hoops to jump through and one in particular, gaining a Consent to Discharge, can take several months. I recommend that you contact your local office of the Environment Agency at an early stage to find out what you can and what you can't do on any given site.

Septic Tank

These days a septic tank is a large onion shaped vessel made of fibreglass. You bury it in the ground, usually encased in concrete. It digests the foulwaste — actually letting bacteria break down the shit — and releases the fragrant outpourings into a *leaching field* consisting of many (25-50) metres of perforated pipe, usually laid in shallow trenches under the back garden. A septic tank needs emptying once a year which costs around £60 — NB this compares favourably with paying sewage charges to your water company. To use a septic tank, you will have to satisfy the Environment Agency that you can discharge into the area without polluting nearby water courses, and you will also have to satisfy your building inspector that discharge will actually soak away. You do this by conducting a soil porosity test. If you can't meet these criteria, you may be able to use a mini-treatment works.

SEPTIC TANK COSTS
2700 lts (1-4 person)	£370
3750 lts (5-9 person)	£550
4500 lts (10-13 person)	£650

6b: Dumping Options

Foulwater

Road Opening to Main Drains	Budget min. £350
add for Deep Drains	extra £300
add for Situation Needing Pump	extra £3000
Septic Tank + Land Drains	Budget £2000+
Mini Treatment Works	Budget £3500 +
Cesspool	Budget £2500 +

Rainwater

Soakaway	Budget £50 per soakaway
Storm Drain Connection	Budget £200
To Main Foul Drains	Budget £200 for interceptor

These figures do not include the costs of drain runs between house and dumping ground, only the costs of final dumping

---

Budget an extra £2000 for septic tank installation. Against this however, there are some significant savings to be set; you won't have to make a mains sewer connection, you won't have to pay the sewage part of your infrastructure charge (saving £215 in England and Wales) and you'll be saving between £100 and £200/annum in water company charges. All in all, septic tanks are really not a bad option even when main drains are available. They suffer from an image problem more than anything: the pong is usually *just* noticeable on hot summer days, but is rarely offensive. Useful contacts, Klargester, Condor and Entec.

Mini-treatment Works

A sort of high-tech septic tank which uses macerators to speed the chemical digesting process and doesn't need an extensive drain run to leach away the outflow. Usually the Environment Agency will allow you to use one of these where an ordinary septic tank would be unacceptable or would not work because the ground conditions prohibit leaching; however you can't use one without that Consent to Discharge, as already mentioned. Like a septic tank, they will still need emptying annually to get rid of the solids but the liquid run-off is designed to be pure enough to discharge into a stream or water course. They are expensive (about £2000 more than an ordinary septic tank) and they need a power supply, but they are in almost every way preferable to a *cesspool*.

Cesspool

A cesspool differs from a septic tank and a mini-treatment works in having no outlet. Consequently, they tend to be much larger and, even so, still need emptying every few weeks. You could build one in concrete or you can buy proprietary ones made out of GRP. The minimum size allowed for by building

regs for a single dwelling is 18,200lts which, with lockable cover, costs just over £2000. The Klargester ones are 4.6x2.8m (sausage shape) and, if in wet ground, have to be concreted in. They would need emptying around ten times a year (for a four-bedroom house) costing around £600/annum, which makes a cesspool not only one of the most expensive options to install, but easily the most expensive to run.

Siting of Tanks

Septic tanks should be within 30m of vehicular access to permit emptying. In Scotland, tanks must be a minimum of 15m from house. No minimum exists in England and Wales but if you have a sensitive nose you would do well to stick to the Scottish standards.

Alternative Options

It would be amiss of me to pass on without mentioning a couple of alternative disposal systems that exist, dry composting toilets and reed bed treatment. The former requires a certain dedication, the latter a large garden at the very least. If you want to know more, contact the Centre for Alternative Technology (01654 702715) who run a consultancy service.

Rainwater Disposal

Soakaways

The normal destination of rainwater is a simple soakaway which is nothing more than a 1m deep hole in the ground, usually filled with free draining hardcore or brick rubble. They are conventionally sited 5m away from buildings, but the building inspector must be convinced that the water will percolate away. In heavy clay soils, for instance, a soakaway may not be appropriate and you may have to look at other ways of disposing of rainwater. Budget £50 if machine dug, £75 if hand dug.

Storm Drains

Common in urban areas, rare in the country, they are actually designed to stop the roads flooding, but can sometimes be used for house rainwater. Budget £200 to make a connection to a storm drain. Storm drains are often over 100 years old and in a poor state of repair, and locating them can be a hit and miss affair. Typically, they are managed by the highways department of the local council (rather than the local water company) and they often flatly refuse to accept any additional rainwater discharge, even when it is obviously the best option. If you have well-honed negotiating skills, here is a good place to put them into practice

Rainwater Into Main Drains

Attitudes to this vary from area to area, but nowhere is it encouraged. But when soaka-ways and storm drains are impracticable, this course will often be accepted as a last resort. There must be an interceptor between the two drain systems to prevent pongs coming back up the rainwater gullies.

Routes

This is the other major decision to be made when looking at drain runs. The idea is to get from the house to the final dumping point with as few bends as possible. Drains have a tendency to get blocked, so access is important at all but the gentlest bends and access is expensive.

Ballpark Drain Run Costs

Straight 110mm plastic drain runs can be machine excavated (to av. depths), laid and buried for around £10/lin.m. The building inspector may allow you to have a few gentle radius bends on your drain runs, provided he is satisfied that they will not prevent *rodding* — that is clearing future blockages with drain rods — but generally the accepted practice is to have access to the drains every time there is a bend. The addition of inspection chambers, gullies, rodding access, etc. ("fittings") more than doubles the basic metre rate for drain laying to between £20 and £25/lin.m — one manhole is equivalent to 10lin.m of straight drains. So the general idea is to plan your drain runs with as few bends as possible.

Eight Drain Tips

The Plans Need...

Drawings and specifications should include drain layout, invert levels (depths), junctions, inspection chambers and access (rodding) points.

Plastic or Clay?

Although the trade is still split between using clay and plastic (uPVC) drainage, someone new to the game would do well to use plastic. There is little to choose between the systems on price but the plastic systems are more user friendly. There are six major players in this field and, underground at least, there is little to choose between them on quality or price. Osma are the market leaders and their installation guide tells you much of what you need to know about laying drains. They do a free (but slow) design service but you must know your main drain invert (drain depth) levels for it to be worthwhile.

Buying Plastic Pipe

Plastic pipe is sold with heavy discounts off list price. A new house project should be able to get discounts of 30-40%. All the manufacturers produce guttering and internal waste fittings as well and, if you combine your order, you will have more muscle to negotiate better discounts.

Excavation of Trenches

Drain trenches are normally 450mm wide (the width of a digger's narrow bucket). If drains are to run parallel and close to wall foundation trenches, then you will be doing yourself a favour if you can set the drains higher than the concrete in the adjacent trench — NB this won't work with trench-filled foundations. Where this is not possible, drains will have to be concreted-in, whereas they are normally just bedded in pea shingle.

Drain Sizes and Depths

100mm drain (the standard) is going to be adequate for all situations where there are less than five loos. There is no set depth, but less than 600mm and you may have to cover the pipe with paving slabs, deeper than 1200mm and you will have problems working. The optimum fall is 1:80 which is equivalent to 250mm on a 20m run. If you have to cope with gradients much steeper than this then take specialist advice, don't assume that drains will work just because they are going downhill.

Pea Shingle

Plastic pipe should be bedded on pea shingle, which is a particularly fine grade of gravel. Allow one ton of pea shingle (cost £6 - £15/ton) for every 8lin.m of drain. When calculating excavation quantities, allow for 80% of excavated material to go back into the trenches once the pipes are laid.

Rodding Access

It is good practise to not have to rod from inside the house, so try to give every waste point a direct run to a manhole rather than joining drain runs together under the house in the assumption that they can be rodded from above.

Drains Under Driveways

Plastic drains less than 900mm deep under a driveway need a reinforced concrete capping. Note that clay drains only require capping when the depth is less than 450mm. Allow £5/lin.m extra for this, but note that it is a very useful place for excess readymix to be dumped, which can effectively reduce price to near zero.

Chapter 7
Superstructure

Superstructure is a long and pretentious word and I would like to use some funky Anglo-Saxon alternative, altogether more down-to-earth. Trouble is, I don't know one. Some use the term shell — as in "Putting up the Shell" — and perhaps this isn't bad, especially if you think of it in terms of sea shells, not egg shells. But, to confuse matters, the outer walls that make up the shell get referred to as skins or, sometimes, leaves; one suggests bodies, the other trees, neither eggs or sea creatures. It all

seems a bit of a mess; hence I'll stick with the term Superstructure.

Definition? Well you have hopefully figured it out by now — it's all the above ground bits of a house up to but excluding the finishes and the wiring and piping. Literally, the super (= above) structure as opposed to the sub (= below or under) structure. So in Superstructure we'll look at walls (as in inner and outer skins), doors and windows, roofs and all the fiddly bits that hold them together. Floors? As

mentioned earlier, ground floors are normally considered as part of the substructural works whilst upper floors are regarded as superstructural. I'm abandoning tradition here in favour of ease of comparison and you'll find the entire floors section buried in this chapter. If you buy a timber frame house kit, it's the superstructure that you are getting. Or at least part of the superstructure. The roof covers and the external wall finishes are left to you to sort out along with the substructural works and the finishes.

The Inner Skin

The *inner skin* refers to the structural, load-bearing part of the external walls. For many years that was just about all there was to it, but these days the requirements for insulation have made the decision of just how best to build the inner skin a complex and involved subject. Our benchmark house is built in brick and blockwork, the traditional and commonest form of house construction in England and Wales; it is well understood and relatively cheap to construct and its only serious challenge comes from timber frame.

Cavities

This was the preferred form of construction for the typical British housebuilder until 1995 when the building regs on thermal loss were last revised. Cavities became widespread in the first half of the century and were introduced to combat the problem of damp. The whole point of having a cavity was to keep it empty so that water could not cross between the outer and inner skin and the current requirement to start stuffing insulation in the cavity would seem to negate this. Indeed it does negate it. Yet bit by bit builders are learning that insulation and cavities are not an impossible marriage and many builders are now enthusiastically stuffing their cavities with all manner of insulants.

Having said all that, the changes to Part L of the building regs are nothing if not complicated and it is still be technically possible to build houses without any wall insulation, but possible only if many other considerably more expensive energy-saving measures are taken. The bog standard solution preferred by most developers since 1995 has been to reduce the wall U values from 0.6 to 0.45 and this means building insulation into the walls. How much insulation? Of the cheaper varieties, like expanded polystyrene or glass fibre, a minimum of 65mm thickness should suffice, depending on the construction of the rest of the wall. Alternatively, 38mm of polyurethane (or one of the new substitutes) should do the trick. Just how you build it into the wall is another problem altogether.

Cavity Fill Insulation

It is both cheap and easy to do — but you do loose your empty cavity. Full fill cavity batts are invariably made out of one of the woolly insulators such as glass fibre or mineral wool; these are "wicked" (rhymes with *licked*) to stay rigid and are cut to fit in around cavity ties. At around £1.80/m^2/75mm thickness and usually fixed at no extra cost, this was the insulation system employed on the benchmark house (at a cost of £330). An alternative would be to blow the insulation into the cavity after construction (known as *retro-fill*); this was costed at £400 for glass fibre or £520 for polystyrene beads. Cavity fill is becoming increasingly popular but the NHBC does not accept it anywhere in Scotland and also in a few other exposed locations outside Scotland.

Partial Fill

Most of the regular insulation materials are available in formats designed to partially fill the cavity. The empty part of the cavity should be as wide as 50mm and here is where the problem is with this method because, despite special "retaining" wall ties being available (which, at 24p each, actually cost more than the insulation), the wet Tuesday in February syndrome means that it is often extremely difficult for brickies to maintain a partially clear cavity. Also when you make a cavity wider than 75mm, which may be thought desirable from an insulation point of view, there are a number of extra costs (lintels, foundations) which start to appear elsewhere.

Insulated Dry Lining

This method involves using plasterboard laminated to expanded polystyrene and sticking the whole thing on the room side (i.e. inside) of the inner skin wall. British Gypsum's version is called *Thermal Board*. In theory this is a good solution, but in prac-

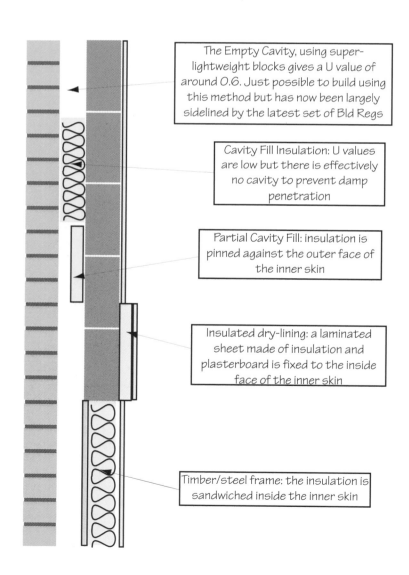

The Empty Cavity, using superlightweight blocks gives a U value of around 0.6. Just possible to build using this method but has now been largely sidelined by the latest set of Bld Regs

Cavity Fill Insulation: U values are low but there is effectively no cavity to prevent damp penetration

Partial Cavity Fill: insulation is pinned against the outer face of the inner skin

Insulated dry-lining: a laminated sheet made of insulation and plasterboard is fixed to the inside face of the inner skin

Timber/steel frame: the insulation is sandwiched inside the inner skin

tice it is rarely used because of a reluctance to "dot and dab" polystyrene to walls (some form of mechanical fixing system is needed, usually Nailable Plugs). This thickness of thermal board costs around £4.20/m², which makes it about £2/m² more expensive than setting insulation inside the cavity. Although it gets around the problem of having to partially fill the cavity wall (in practise, rarely successfully achieved), it leaves a number of cold bridges between floors and where internal walls meet external walls and, unless a super-lightweight block is used, it barely meets the 0.6 U value rating required for walls, let alone the new improved 0.45 U value rating. To get better insulation levels, you'd have to use a product like British Gypsum's Thermal Board *Super,* which uses a polyurethane substitute called phenolic foam: this however is very expensive at around £8.50/m².

Super-lightweight Blocks

The block manufacturers responded to the previous increase in the thermal regulations (in 1990) by introducing super-lightweight insulating blocks which can be used on their own to get U values of 0.6. Each manufacturer has different names for them — Thermalite's *Turbo,* Durox's *Superblock,* Celcon's *Solar* — but the idea remains to do for concrete what Aero did for chocolate. By introducing more and more air into the manufacturing process, the insulation capacity of the blocks increases until — hey presto — it's light enough to satisfy the old 0.6 U value figure required of external walls. Whilst this may not be enough to satisfy the current standards, super-lightweight blocks will only have to be combined with fairly minimal insulation materials to get the U values down to 0.45. These blocks are not without their critics; some question the strength and durability of these blocks (only time will tell) and others claim that the cold bridging effects of the mortar joints mean that the real U value of walls made from super-lightweight blocks is actually nearer 0.8 than 0.6. Nevertheless, they have been accepted by the powers that be and they are — or were —widely used by empty cavity lovers. One of the main drawbacks to using these blocks is their price, which is around £6.50/m² as compared to £4.50/m² for conventional concrete blocks. Using these instead of regular blocks would have added £800 to the cost of the benchmark house.

Timber Frame

Switching to timber frame requires a much greater leap of the imagination than just juggling figures. It doesn't have to be built offsite — but it usually is — and it involves different skills and expertise which tend to mark timber framers out as a race apart. Even the follow-on trades (plumbers, electricians, kitchen fitters, second-fix carpenters) have to rethink the way they go about things when the walls are made of studwork and the first floor is a structural element holding the whole building together. Lintel and wall ties change, and allowances for differential movement between brickwork outer skins and timber frames have to be built-in. In North America, timber framing is the standard form of construction and everyone is geared up to working with it, but in Britain it remains the province of the specialist.

Whilst timber frame internal walls are cheaper to build than blockwork ones (£7/m² v £11/m²), when these walls become external and structural, as required for timber framing, they become more expensive because they have to have plywood structural sheathing, breather paper and vapour barriers added; these combined more than double the cost of the basic studwork. The benchmark house has an external wall area of around 166m² and an internal wall area of around 170m² (of which 120m² — the upstairs — is built out of timber studwork), and the cost penalty for switching to on-site timber frame construction would normally be in the order of £500 to £1000.

However, the benchmark house is an interesting case in point. As discussed in Chapter 2, this benchmark house is unusual in having great deal of timber clapboarding fixed to a double masonry skin block wall: with a minimal amount of redesigning, the house could have been built for less in timber frame. Instead of having two skins of masonry coming in at around £22/m², it could have had one skin of timber frame for £15/m², for a saving of £750 or so. In this case, the client expressed a preference for a blockwall construction so blockwall it is but it does illustrate that timber frame can sometimes be a more cost effective solution.

Timber Frame Specialists

Another approach is to use a specialist timber frame company to manufacture the timber structural components off-site and to erect the product as it comes off the lorry, as

The benchmark house was built from two skins of Tarmac Hemelite blocks sandwiching 75mm of fibreglass insulation. Note the Damcor insulated cavity closer between the window jamb and the wall return—this detail is now mandatory

the kit homes tend to. There are a number of companies that perform this service, converting plans for brick and block houses into plans for timber frame houses and then quoting for manufacture and erection. Factory prefabrication is, however, relatively expensive and you would expect to pay around £2000 to £3000 more for such a service. Check out Taylor Lane (01432 271912) .

Accessories

- Wall ties: Timber frame requires a different shape of wall tie (Catnic's are called *BT-2*) and slightly more of them (750>620). They are more expensive to buy than blockwork wall ties (£23 for 100 instead of £8 for 100). Cost penalty £80 or 50p/m².

- Brick/timber frame lintels are about 35% cheaper than brick/block lintels, saving around £150 on the benchmark house or £1/m² on walling costs.

- Perhaps the most significant extra cost comes from having to have the design proved by a structural engineer. Your building regs officer will require an HB353 certificate which may well set you back £350/house, unless you are buying an off-the-peg design.

7a: Cost Comparison of External Wall Systems

WALL SYSTEM	BRICKWORK	CAVITY TIES	INSULATION	INNER SKIN	INSULATION	PLASTER	TOTAL	COST ON TEST HOUSE
Cavity Fill	£24.20	£0.30	£1.70	£11.80		£5.20	£43.00	£6,800
Partial Fill	£24.20	0.80	2.20	11.80		5.20	£44.00	£7,000
Insulated Dry Lining	£24.20	0.30		11.80	8.60	3.90	£49.00	£7,700
Super-lightweight Blocks	£24.20	0.30		13.40		5.20	£43.00	£6,800
90mm Timber Frame	£24.20	0.70		14.40	2.40	5.90	£48.00	£7,600
140mm Timber Frame	£24.20	0.70		15.50	3.40	5.90	£50.00	£7,900

Other Techniques

Hollow Insulation Blocks

There is a German system, marketed in the UK by Beco Wallform, using hollow polystyrene blocks which are assembled dry and then have concrete poured into them to give a sort of moulded shell; it is nothing if not ingenious, reversing the normal logic of construction and making it more akin to making jelly rather than playing with Lego. The polystyrene can be covered on the outside with polymer (flexible) renders; inside, however, there are many unusual techniques to be mastered for fixing internal walls, frames and floor joists which would probably completely flummox the average British builder. Also, the cost of the hollow wall blocks is high: the Beco blocks are around £28/m^2 which is a lot to pay for what is basically insulation. One plus is that insulation levels are very high — the wall U values are claimed to be as low as 0.29, which is similar to the 140mm insulated studwork found in many Scandinavian houses — but the benefits of such high levels of insulation should not be overestimated. The annual reduction in heating bills would be in the order of £30 as compared with the house as built.

Steel

There is a sudden upsurge of interest in steel framing for housing and three manufacturers, British Steel, Knauf and Metframe, are attempting to establish it as a *bona fide* alternative to timber framing. Their timing is right, as the increasing insulation standards, required by the building regulations, are making it ever more expensive to build using masonry materials and yet many traditionalists still have reservations about using timber frame. Here is a lightweight building technique which is capable of lasting a thousand years and at a cost which should be similar to timber frame. However, note that I use the word "should" — because, as yet, these steel systems are really only working at the prototype level and they are not yet a serious option for individual house builders. In the last edition I wrote that "I would expect matters to change within the lifespan of this book" but they didn't. Steel framing remains at prototype level in 1997. Whilst steel framing may have a big future in mass production housing, it may well prove to be too inflexible for individual house designs.

Solid Walls

All the above methods (Beco Wallform excepted) are variations on the theme of cavity wall construction, which involves the expensive habit of building two separate walls around a house with an unseen cavity between them. It's use in housebuilding is relatively recent — you are unlikely to find it on anything pre-1920s — and largely British; the questionable logic behind it has been that it is so wet here that you need an extra skin to stop rain penetration. It would seem that in the 1920s builders were primarily concerned in constructing dry houses and a clear cavity surrounding the house was seen as an excellent way of achieving this goal. However, since the 1970s, the emphasis has been moving steadily towards building thermally efficient houses and, to this end, builders have been asked to introduce more and more insulation into houses. Many Jeremiahs (myself included) predicted all kinds of problems when these two seemingly contradictory aims came into conflict with one another and assumed that the cavity battleground would end up being a disaster area which would be full of soggy (ineffective) insulation and act as a causeway for every passing rainstorm to flood the house insides. In fact, it has really worked out much better than might have been expected; NHBC statistics are now showing that rain penetration through cavity walls is scarcely any more common with insulation filled cavities than it is through empty cavities.

The original problem of damp housing also turns out to be much more effectively dealt with by building insulated homes with efficient heating systems. The real enemy all along was condensation not rain penetration and today's building standards do at last bury this old spectre once and for all. Rain penetration, where it does occur, is usually a result of poor site standards rather than defective design.

So is it time to end our sixty year love affair with cavity wall construction altogether? It will surprise many that there has never been a single regulation that insisted we build with cavity walls so the dead hand of legislation can hardly be blamed for no one even trying something different. Celcon blocks now produce a *Solar* block at 250mm width which on its own will produce a U value of 0.45, low enough to satisfy current regulations without the addition of any insulation. It's been proving popular for extensions but as yet very few housebuilders have been tempted to use it, largely because it costs over £17/m^2 which wipes out any cost advantage you might expect by having just one skin. Besides this, most housebuilders are looking for a brick exterior and once you specify brick you are specifying some form of cavity again. Still, if you can live with a rendered exterior, then the Celcon *Solar* block is an interesting option.

The Outer Skin

Including an allowance for scaffolding and including the garage walls, Complete Fabrications spent a massive £9300 on the external walling of the benchmark house — that's over 10% of the total build cost. For the lower part of the house and the garage, they chose an Ibstock cream brick, costing just under £200/1000bricks: above this most of the house received a timber clapboarded finish whilst the single storey extension and the garage were treated to a painted rendered finish. Other houses on the small estate are mostly brick though the immediate neighbour is a barn conversion which gets a similar clapboarded exterior.

Although the amount of timber boarding on the benchmark house is unusually large for a spec house, what is more typical is the mix and match effect of its external finish, a habit which many developers happened upon in the 80s — note the example of a current Wimpey house (photo right) using brick and render. It's all to do with kerb appeal — making a house look better and therefore more saleable. Although the actual base cost of the finishes is remarkably similar, there is always an added cost in introducing different types of finish with different trades involved, and if you want to keep costs down you would do well to stick to one particular wall style.

Reference to Table 7b: Costed Options for External Walls shows that there is actually remarkably little difference between these various options. It's hard to build an outer skin for less than £20/m² though it's not difficult to vastly increase this figure if you specify expensive materials and finishes.

Wimpey Homes in 1997. The mixed brick and render exterior is typical of current spec. housing styles. Indeed, Wimpey's detailing (brick string course, frilly bargeboard, stone cills) is rather better than average.

Brick

In England it remains most people's first choice because it looks good — or at least it can look good — and it is the most durable of facings. There is an enormous choice and prices vary from as low as £150/1000 (for what I call factory bricks) up to £500/1000 for hand crafted gems. Most developers stick to the ranges costing less than £200/1000 where there is a good choice of simulated handmade ones (like Ibstock's *Bradgate* range) which house buyers appreciate.

Much of the trick with bricks is in getting the detailing right. A very ordinary brick can look stunning with the right windows and the right cill and coping details; equally, a beautiful brick can be rendered dull and flat in an uninspired elevation. Much of this depends on the skill of the designer but brick manufacturers are increasingly aware of this problem and now proffer advice on how to get the detailing looking good. The Victorians were masters at brick detailing and you only have to look closely at some of their buildings to realise what I am on about. It's an art which has been largely lost to us in this century but it is showing tentative signs of making a come back.

A basic facing brick can be purchased and delivered direct to site for around £180/1000. Laying costs are around £200/1000; allowing for cuts, wastage, ties and mortar makes a minimum price of around £25/m². By using a better quality brick — say at £300/1000, this price ups to £40/m².

Buying Tips

If brick is your chosen facing material, then you may already have ideas about which brick you want. Indeed, the planners are quite likely to have tried to make the choice for you. However far you have got down this road, you would do well not to get fixed on a specific brick before you start chasing best prices because, given the range of bricks available, there is more than likely a very similar brick to the one you like at a much better price. Don't try to describe a brick to someone on the phone, take photos of the brickwork you like and send copies to your potential suppliers. In my experience, there is usually one supplier who tries significantly harder than the others and they usually come up with the best price too. Your final choice may have to be approved by your planners.

Render

Rendering is the expression most commonly used for an external plastered finish, a treatment which has been enjoying something of a return to fashion in contemporary house designs. In Scotland, where it's known as harling, it's never gone out of fashion. Two alternative techniques are used to get a rendered finish — rendering directly on to blockwork or rendering on to metal lathing which is nailed on to battens. The first would normally be used on masonry-built houses, the second on timber frame. Pricewise there is little difference between the two systems; including painting, they both work out at shade over £25/m².

Decorative Render

A nearly lost art which is undergoing a small revival. The finish is rather like an upmarket artex applied to the face to enliven the outlook. In East Anglia it is known as *pargetting* and there are so few exponents that ballpark figures are meaningless.

Pebble Dash

Uncommon on new build nowadays, pebble dashing involves throwing (or sometimes spraying) small stones into wet render to make a rough cast finish. Now perceived as downmarket, it costs little more than conventional smooth finished render. *Rough Casting* and *Tyrolean* finishes are two other variations on this theme.

Shiplap

Half-timbering

Brick noggins

Flint

Pargetting

Timber

Plain timber boarding (sometimes known as *clapboarding*) is coming back into fashion with the increasing popularity of barn conversions. There are several different styles which you can use. Rough-sawn timber (*featheredge*) looks more rustic; planed timber (*shiplap*) can look a shade more sophisticated. Shiplap is about £3/m² more expensive to buy but saves a large amount on decorating costs — sawn timber drinks wood stains by the gallon. Coupled with the waste which is bound to occur, stained external timber panelling costs around £20/m², slightly less than cheap brick. This may seem a high figure when the basic material (featheredge boarding) costs no more than £5/m² but an inordinate amount of time goes into staining, though this cost can be kept down by D-I-Y.

Incidentally, with all external timber, it is good practice to put at least one coat of paint or stain on the boards on the ground before fixing. Timber shrinks, and if the whole board is not covered with a uniform colour you will end up with 1-2mm flesh-coloured strips wherever boards overlap.

Half-timbered Tudor Look

This is usually achieved by planting 50x100mm or 50x125mm timber on to either a block work or timber frame backing. A typical gable would have between six and twelve verticals and two or three horizontals, plus framing around any windows. A simple arrangement such as this with planed timber would add around £6/m² (Mats. £3 Lab £3). Complex patterns with distressed timber or oak could easily treble this figure. Further expense could be added by doing the infill panels in brick rather than cement render. This is a beautiful old technique (called *brick noggins*) and it can be carried out in several different ways. It is very time-consuming and it would only look good with interesting bricks and timber, so allow £50/m².

Vertical Tiles

Using vertical tiling is another Victorian building feature that is coming back into fashion, particularly in SE England. Costs are very similar to plain tiles laid on roofs, although vertical hanging tends to be a little more expensive because there is more work involved in cutting corners, angles and around openings. Generally it can only be done with plain tiles or slate and it is probably more important to select a good looking tile for a wall than it is for a roof.

Rubble Walls

If you know the right quarries this kind of walling material can be extremely cheap to buy, but it tends to be very time-consuming to lay. Traditionally rubble walling was independent of any backing materials, but now it is much cheaper to lay if it is set against a background of blockwork — which makes it a bit like very rough pebbledash. Each area of the country has its own local "rubble" stones and seaside locations often tend to find theirs on the nearby beaches.

Around East Anglia flint is the usual material and prices for flint vary enormously depending on how it is finished. Flint can be laid as wholestones — which gives a rough "agricultural" look — or it can be knapped, which involves breaking the stones open to reveal a shiny black inside which is then set as the facework. Wholestone is available for under £10/tonne, but knapped flint is three or four times this amount. Expect to pay around £6-10/m² for rough walling materials (inc. sand and cement) and around £40-50/m² for laying. As you can see from these prices, laying is slow. It is, however, not particularly difficult and it could well suit a D-I-Y builder who has more time than money.

Artificial Boards

There are many artificial materials which can be used to clad buildings although they tend to look a bit too industrial for most people's tastes. None of them cost under £20/m² and you'll be unlikely to gravitate towards them without the promptings of a keen designer. There are too many products to give anything like a comprehensive overview; here are details of three to give you a taste:

- uPVC is used as a substitute for timber cladding as well as fascias and soffits. It is sold in timber width strips but is usually available only in white. It has very little going for it except the promise of no maintenance.
- Eternit makes a glass fibre panelling called *Glasell* which is popular with some architects. It costs £25/m² to buy, including fixings, and is used as an alternative to cement rendering, often combined with the half-timbered look .
- Rockwool, the insulation people, produce a compressed mineral fibre board called *Rockclad* in either a semi-gloss or a matt finish. I've had a sample of this stuff on my desk for five years and I must admit to becoming quite attached to it, so much so that I'm tempted to build a house using it one day. But it's not cheap so the design will have to be just so.

7b: Costed Options for External Walls

All figures are £/m² except the last column which is the cost of using each wall finish on the benchmark house

	BASIC MATERIALS	ACCESSORIES	LABOUR	PAINTS or STAINS	LABOUR	TOTAL COST/M²	COST ON TEST HOUSE
Cheap Brick	£13.00	£1.70	£12.00			£27.00	£5,900
Expensive Brick	30.00	1.70	12.00			44.00	£9,700
Render on Blockwork	5.50	3.50	12.50	0.70	4.00	26.00	£5,700
Render on Lathing	7.80	4.20	11.00	0.70	4.00	27.00	£5,900
Half Timber/Render	8.50	6.70	15.50	1.10	6.00	37.00	£8,100
Clapboard on Timber Frame	5.70	3.20	7.00	3.00	4.00	20.00	£4,400
Clapboard on Blockwork	10.70	4.20	13.00	3.00	4.00	32.00	£7,000
Planed Shiplap on TF	9.80	3.20	7.00	2.40	2.40	22.00	£4,800
Plain Clay Tiles	15.60	7.00	12.00			35.00	£7,700
Expensive Clay Tiles	35.00	7.00	12.00			54.00	£11,900
Rubble Walling/Flint	8.00	14.00	55.00			77.00	£16,900
Synthetic Panelling	20.00	3.00	4.00			27.00	£5,900
Half Timber/Panels	23.00	4.50	8.00	0.40	2.00	38.00	£8,400
Natural Stone	30.00	2.50	30.00			63.00	£13,900
Reconstituted Stone	12.00	2.50	20.00			35.00	£7,700
Glazed Walls	95.00	-40.00		0.40	2.40	57.00	£12,500
Add for Reconstituted Stone Cills		Av. £40ea		17No. on Test House			£680
Add for Reconstituted Stone Lintels		Av. £40ea		15No. on Test House			£600

Stone

If you live in one of the so-called *stone belts* you may well have to build in stone to satisfy the local planners. You may actually want to build in stone — it's usually very attractive — but it's likely to be very much more expensive than the developer's standbys, brick and render.

There are basically three approaches: you can use real stone quarried out of some hillside, you can use reconstituted stone which is stone dust glued together with cement, or you can use stone cladding which gets stuck on the outside of cheaply erected blockwork.

Natural Stone

Building stone tends to be a very local affair. It was, after all, hewn from quarries and, in the days before cheap transportation, could only be carried the shortest of distances. Many of these old stone quarries survive and supply the demands of the local construction trade. In some areas there are thriving second-hand markets in stone walling materials, yet nowhere is natural stone a cheap material. You may be given brownie points for using natural stone in your house — more likely the local planners will insist on it — but you'll probably be adding £10,000 to the overall cost. Civil Engineering Developments

(01708 867237) are a major stone factor and have depots and contacts all over the country.

Reconstituted Stone

A cheaper alternative is to use a reconstituted stone. Marshalls and RMC Peakstone are two of the largest producers. Although, to the practised eye, reconstituted stone will never

look as good as the real thing, it will cost about half as much and, if done well, looks as good as many of the cheaper bricks.

Cladding

Stone cladding has got a reputation for being naff as hell, but this is because it's often associated with people who fix it to their brick terrace houses to "make a statement" (such

New stone house in Northamptonshire

as "I'm naff as hell"). Out of context like that it does look more than a touch ridiculous, but on a new house in a stone village chances are most casual passers-by would not even know it was stone cladding. However, artificial stone claddings are now virtually unobtainable and natural stone cladding is very expensive — it is unlikely to cost less than £50/m² — so if you are starting from scratch you might just as well use real stone.

Glass

Building regulations require that windows should not be less than 15% of wall areas but in certain designs you may want to have considerably more. Ballpark figures show that double-glazed sealed units cost around a minimum of £32/m² but that this figure increases substantially if energy efficient glass or safety glass is specified. Both these may be necessary in very large glazed areas and this would more than double overall costs to £60/m².

Furthermore, glass needs to be seated in some joinery. Volume joinery costs around £35/m², simple made-up joinery around £70/m². Add in decoration and you can see that glass walling is an expensive option liable to cost a minimum of £80/m², and possibly as much as double this amount for unusual designs. As a comparison, a bog standard aluminium patio door costs around £80/m².

Against this, it mustn't be overlooked that a glazed wall is complete in itself and does away with the need for an inner skin of walling. The cost of building and finishing a standard external cavity wall with a brick exterior and a plastered and painted interior is not less than £32/m²: this cost ought to be deducted from the glazing costs in order for a more reasonable comparison to be made. If you have a very expensive walling material chosen for your house, then large double-glazed areas set into it may not add greatly to the overall cost.

Porches and Bays

Thus far I've been looking at exterior finishes but there is, of course, much more to the external design of a house than just the materials used. Features like bay windows and porches have been coming right back into fashion despite the fact that they are expensive to build. It's quite hard to separate out how much extra these features cost because they tend to get lost in the whole job costings. A bay window, for instance, involves minor additions to almost every aspect of the construction — excavations, foundations, flooring, brickwork, joinery, roofing, guttering, carpentry and decorating (to name just nine). Individually these changes are not great but added together I estimate that a two-storey bay may add as much as 3% to the costs of erecting the house superstructure. For an area less than 3m² that's expensive — getting on for double the amount spent on ordinary living space.

Porches are easier to quantify, although bear in mind that the standard of construction varies enormously from something little more than a rain shelter to what amounts to a mini-extension. Being (usually) rectangular in shape, porches are not appreciably more expensive to construct than the main structure, but bear in mind that any complications that might ensue will end up taking a disproportionate amount of supervision time. One recent development is companies producing GRP bolt-on porches and bay window canopies; it's proved to be a big hit with developers. One company, Storm King, produce a whole range of architectural conceits such as pseudo-lead infill panels and clock towers. Their bolt-on porches start at just over £100.

Cills, Arches

One of the classiest effects you can get on external facades is to use feature lintels above and cills below your openings. There are a number of options for doing this. The cills and lintels can be formed from special bricks or made on site with a granite and cement mixture, which is fine if they get painted afterwards. Another variation is to have reconstituted stone ones made up in a workshop: this is the most expensive option (see Table 7b) but also probably the most attractive.

Insetting joinery into the facade is not a merely decorative process. By its very nature it helps to protect windows and doors from the worst of the weather, and the building regulations acknowledge this by making recessed joinery compulsory in Scotland and in many exposed parts of the rest of the country.

Don't Ruin It

Having gone to all that trouble to get good-looking materials correctly proportioned, it is worth taking on board a cautionary word about the effect of those little elements which can ruin the overall effect — like a wart on the face of a much loved friend (shouldn't that have been a carbuncle? Ed.). Whether you go for period charm or ultra-modernism really makes no difference, just think about the details — remember God is in the details (enough of this plagiarism). Here are a few style tips:
- Rainwater downpipes — the fewer the better
- Plastic meter boxes — hide them round the side
- Security floodlighting — don't point it straight at people walking towards it
- Alarm bells — potential burglars will still see them on a side wall
- Satellite dishes — they can go out in the garden.

Glass-walled house (by Jonathan Ellis-Miller) built at FutureWorld, Milton Keynes in 1995.

Insulation

Everyone expected the last batch of changes to the thermal building regs — which came into effect in 1995 — to greatly increase the standards of insulation in new housing. In the event, a change of emphasis on how heat loss was assessed has meant that it is possible to continue building with little or no dedicated insulation materials except in the roof space. All materials insulate to a greater or lesser extent — see section on U values in Chapter 10 — but only since the 1970s have we seen the widespread use of materials that do very little else except insulate. By and large, these materials are not prohibitively expensive and most will pay for themselves — in terms of reduced running costs — within a few years. So whilst you could design your home to avoid using insulation wherever possible, there would be very little point in doing so.

Material Choices

There are several materials available to insulate housing. All have pros and cons and not all are suitable in every application; mostly they are available in a number of different formats — often in combination with other materials like chipboard and plasterboard — which makes describing them all extremely complicated. The basics are as follows:

Fibreglass

Cheap, reasonably good insulator. Excellent when laid flat in lofts but when placed in walls it will sag. But help is at hand: it can be "wicked" which stiffens it up and allows it to be placed into wall cavities without risk of sagging or, as they say in insulation speak, to "perform well in the vertical." Here they tend to get referred to as batts as in cavity batts or timber frame batts. Although nearly double the price of unwicked quilts, they are still good value compared to other materials.

Mineral Wool

Production is dominated by a firm called Rockwool who make it from volcanic dust using a spinning process. In most ways it performs very similarly to fibreglass and can also be wicked to perform well in the vertical. Rockwool is noticeably superior to fibreglass (and almost all other insulation materials) in terms of fire resistance. It is usually priced to compete with fibreglass though sometimes it is 5-10% more. Laying up to 250mm of mineral wool or fibreglass in the loft is cost effective.

Polyurethane

The most efficient insulator on the market, it is usually sold in rigid sheet format, sometimes foil backed. However, it is pricey even if you buy second hand, where a company called Seconds & Co. is busy (01644 231140). The main market is dominated by Celotex and Coolag. The main problem with polyurethane has been that its production involved the use of CFCs, now implicated in the demise of the ozone layer and therefore environmentally incorrect. This has led manufacturers to produce a number of poly-urethane-like insulators with names like *polyisocyanurate-modified urethane foam* with "CFC-free" splattered all over them. In terms of performance they are very similar to the older polyurethanes. Despite their cost, polyurethane (and substitutes) are being increasingly specified because their superior performance as insulators means that they are space efficient — in that you can get the desired insulation levels from a thinner sheet — and that means there are sometimes reductions in other construction costs.

Expanded Polystyrene

It gets used in buildings in two formats. The first is as a vast amorphous mass of little white beads which get blown into cavity walls from lorries. The second is in rigid boards; two brands dominate, Jablite and Kaycell — it is often referred to by builders as *Jablite*. It performs very similarly to fibreglass and mineral wool in terms of insulation capabilities (but not fire protection) and is similarly cheaply priced. Used widely in cavity wall construction (in both formats) and underfloor insulation (where, despite the fact that it must be shielded from damp penetration, it is cost effective up to 75mm thick). It is much the cheapest material when you are having to build with a partial cavity fill.

7c: Insulation Guide Prices

MATERIAL	STANDARD THICKNESSES								
	25mm	38mm	50mm	65mm	75mm	90mm	100mm	140mm	150mm
Bog Standard Quilt							£1.20		£1.90
Full Fill Cavity Batts (Glass/Wool)	All prices/m²		£1.35	£1.60	£1.80				
Partial Cavity Fill (Exp. Polystyrene)			£2.20						
Blown Fibre			£2.50						
Warmcell						£2.80			
Timber Frame Batts						£2.30		£3.50	
Paper Faced + Flanged						£2.30	£2.50		
Jablite/Kaycell	£1.00	£1.50	£1.90				£3.80		
Styrofoam/Polyfoam		£5.30	£7.30						
Polyurethane/Celotex		£4.10	£6.00						
Micafil							£7.00		
Sound Deadening Quilt			£2.80						
Thermal Board	£8.50	£12.00							
Vapour Barrier	£0.20								
Damp Proof Membrane	£0.30								

supplied and fixed

S+F price is £1.00/m²

Extruded polystyrene

This is a different version of polystyrene which is much denser and much stronger — expanded polystyrene sheets are notoriously brittle. In terms of insulation capabilities it lies midway between polyurethane and the much cheaper alternatives, but its big selling point is that it is resistant to water penetration. The American business Dow Chemicals dominates this segment with its product *Styrofoam*—look out for green sheets. However there is a British competitor, Polyfoam (pink sheets), which usually sells for 5% less.

Warmcell

This a promoted as a green alternative to the other materials. For a start, it's made from recycled newspapers (so that's where they go) and it can also be used in timber frame walls without a vapour barrier which is reckoned — by some — to be an advantage. It has one major disadvantage in that it is not available in a sheet form so it has to be blown in by specialists. Phone Excel Industries (01495 350655).

Buying Tips

Generally the best place to buy insulation materials is from the insulation specialists. Sheffield Insulation (SIG) and Encon are the best known national distributors but there are numerous local ones listed in Yellow Pages under *Insulation Materials*. Some of the *Insulation Installers* are worth checking out for supply only.

The supply and fix services offered are often a good deal; it is hard to beat them on price (or speed) except where you are not paying for site labour.

Vapour Barriers

Insulation works by trapping air within its body. To continue to work well, the insulation needs to remain dry and, because of this, it has become a common practice in timber frame housing to fit a vapour barrier on the warm (room) side of the insulation layers. This vapour barrier (fancy title for polythene sheeting) stops condensation occurring within the insulation which would cause the insulation to hold water and thereby cease to be effective as an insulator. Vapour barriers were a technical hot potato back in 1984 when an infamous World In Action programme did for timber frame construction what BSE has done for beef sales; the programme claimed that badly installed vapour barriers were leading to "Big Problems" with timber frame building which was, at the time, catching on in a big way in England. Most leading developers immediately dropped timber frame construction methods because — even though at the time the veracity of the accusations was doubted — they couldn't afford to be selling a product which had a question mark over it. Fourteen years on, timber frame construction has never recovered its position in the English market and yet the debate about vapour barriers has long since died down. The fact that they are not always installed with the thoroughness they deserve is now seen as a bit of a red herring; indeed there are now some construction techniques (see Warmcell above) which specifically abandon any notion of a vapour barrier in walls.

Cold Bridging

There are a few specialist products designed to overcome the problem of cold bridging. Cold bridging is what is said to happen when parts of your insulated shell are interrupted by things that don't insulate very well. What on earth am I talking about? Well primarily we are talking about openings in walls and, specifically, the supporting walls built around openings. Cold bridging affects both timber frame and blockwork constructions but, because it is generally easier to insulate timber framed buildings to a higher standard, most of the products aimed at overcoming cold bridging are aimed at the blockwallers. Lintels, cills and jambs around windows and external doorways are the main offenders, but chimneys and meter boxes are other ones that are noted. There is a product called *Thermabate* (RMC Panel Products) that you can use to insulate the gap around windows and doorways, but it is quite pricey and you have to be a dedicated energy saver to justify fitting it. *Damcor* is a cheaper alternative — this is what was specified on the benchmark house.

7d: Cost Effectiveness of Insulation Materials

	INSULATING CAPABILITIES 0=best insulator	COST/M2 FOR 50mm THICKNESS	COST EFFECT-IVENESS
LAID FLAT IN LOFTS			
Fibreglass Quilt	40	£0.60	24
Mineral Wool Quilt	40	0.66	26
Warmcell	35	1.56	54
Micafil	75	3.50	263
VERTICALLY IN WALLS			
Full fill Cavity Batts	40	1.35	54
Timber Frame Batts	40	1.28	51
Paper Faced + Flanged	40	1.25	50
Jablite/Kaycell	38	1.90	72
Styrofoam/Polyfoam	30	7.30	219
Polyurethane	23	6.00	138
LAID UNDER FLOORS			
Jablite/Kaycell	38	1.90	72
Polyurethane	23	6.00	138
Styrofoam/Polyfoam	30	7.30	219
MISCELLANEOUS PRODUCTS			
Softwood	130	10.00	1300
Super-lightweight blocks	150	3.25	488

Low numbers are most cost effective

Windows

The benchmark house has softwood timber windows made by John Carr, the biggest timber window manufacturer in the country. These *Narrow Modules* windows are very much a mainstream developer's window and a look at the costings will show you why. All 18 windows were purchased for just over £1000 — an average of £57 per window, barely nudging 1% of total building costs.

These windows arrive on site in need of glazing and decorating. Many alternative window and door systems that are available come pre-glazed and pre-finished but the majority of developers still plump for the traditional built-in timber windows because it remains the cheapest option to install.

Detailing

The Victorians set their windows and doors back into the brickwork. Not only does this decrease the effects of weathering on joinery but it tends to look better as well. However, it is an expensive way of going about things, primarily because it requires a masonry projecting cill underneath and some form of arched lintel overhead, adding perhaps £100 per opening.

Today's volume joinery is made with integral cill sections and is designed to fit just 25mm back from the outside face of the brickwork. This is easy and cheap but it also looks cheap, especially in brick facades. Rendered and timbered exteriors normally feature cottagey windows perched on the external face, but traditionally brickwork was associated with recessed joinery. Consider recessing your joinery if you are building in brick or stone:

- It will be cheaper than specifying hardwood windows
- It will almost certainly look better
- A softwood window, set back, will probably perform better than an exposed hardwood one.

Look at the relative performance of Victorian sash windows and timber or steel casements on 20th century housing. By and large the old sash windows last about 100 years or four times as long as exposed casements.

If you live in an area rated severe weather exposure (and this includes all Scotland and N. Ireland), you will have no choice but to recess your windows into the walls.

Standard Options

There are several volume joinery manufacturers who are turning out enormous quantities of standard-sized timber joinery — Boulton & Paul, John Carr, Crosby, Dale, Magnet. Of these manufacturers, Magnet are alone in maintaining a substantial branch network of depots through which they sell exclusively. All the others sell through the established builder's merchants. There are numerous others in this business (like Howarth) who sell directly to housebuilders and the trade, but they are unlikely to beat the majors on price. In 1997, John Carr's parent company, Rugby Cement, took over Boulton & Paul and their future as independent trading names looks in doubt but currently the plan is for them both to continue with separate identities and separate catalogues.

Many so-called quality window producers complain of the low standards of the volume producers. They may have a point, but it is worth bearing in mind that these standards have improved substantially in recent years. All timber is now vacuum treated with preservatives, opening casements are draught stripped and window locks and ventilation are now fitted as standard. The depth of the glazing rebates in the windows has yet to come to terms with universal double-glazed units (i.e. they are still too narrow), but even this is beginning to change; Boulton & Paul now offer "Slimline" glazing beads (albeit charging 8% on top for specifying them) which can accommodate the wider (more efficient) glazed units now standard in uPVC windows. Much of what people used to demand from a so-called *High Performance* window is now available right throughout the ranges.

John Carr

John Carr is now the undisputed giant of the timber window brigade. In common with the other manufacturers, they produce a comprehensive, priced catalogue and getting hold of one of these is essential if you want to understand your way around this business. For house designers, a joinery catalogue is an essential tool. John Carr's current (Feb 97) edition is a 305-page mammoth covering their entire output — doors, windows, stairs, conservatories, kitchens and PVC-u products.

Understanding Frame Sizes

All the timber joinery manufacturers produce standard joinery to set sizes. The unit heights are easy to fathom: they are in 150mm steps, which represents two bricks courses — the height options are 450, 600, 750, 900, 1050, 1200, 1350, 1500. The width options — 488, 630, 915, 1200, 1770mm — would at first glance seem to be selected by a random number machine. It appears that the widths were changed in the early 80s after a directive from Brussels indicated that the 300mm brick was about to take over Europe and that they'd better have joinery to suit. The joinery manufacturers all obliged but bricks remain 225mm long! To add to the confusion, the sliding sash window styles are made with a different selection of widths. These are based on the rules of classical architecture and to find out more ask Prince Charles next time you see him.

It is by producing windows in this modular fashion that the likes of John Carr make their economies of scale which, in turn, makes their product so competitive. Pre-cutting all the component parts, combined with computer-aided assembly, takes most of the traditional skill out of the whole process (thus keeping down costs) but it also reduces flexibility. If you have to fill an opening that doesn't conform to one of the industry standards, expect to pay about 50% more than the nearest catalogue equivalent and expect to wait at least six weeks.

The Styles

The John Carr catalogue has 70 pages of standard windows. At first glance the choice can seem mind boggling, but growing familiarity shows that the choice is rather like the menu at an Indian restaurant, where every dish is available in every sauce and the length of the menu actually disguises a paucity of actual choices — i.e. it's really just a question of which sauce you want with your chicken, lamb or vegetables.

The backbone of their window production is the casement window, by which is meant any window that opens on hinges (as opposed to a sliding action). A window that cannot be opened is known as a fixed light, but most casement windows incorporate a fixed light or two and still get called casements. The hinging can be arranged either on the side of the casement (side-hung), from the top (top-hung) or pivoted in the middle (well-hung?), and many windows have a combination of these arrangements. Add in a varying number of glazing bars (supposedly to give a window more character) plus a swept top rail (oozes charm) and you can almost taste the poppadums.

7e: Guide Prices for John Carr Windows

	SMALL 630x1050	MEDIUM 1200x1200	LARGE 1770x1200
BASIC SOFTWOOD WINDOWS (to take 14mm Glazing)			
Side opening casement	£38	£53	£84
Cottage Plain	£42	£62	£97
Swept Sash Casement	£44	£79	£115
Cottage Swept	£53	£97	£141
Top Hung	£44	£67	£82
Edwardian Traditional	£83	£99	£178
Edwardian Bar Trad	£94	£110	£202
Georgian	£59	£112	£164
HIGH PERFORMANCE SOFTWOOD WINDOWS (to take 22mm Glazing)			
Side Opening Casement	£46	£63	£100
Cottage Plain	£51	£74	£116
Swept Sash Casement	£53	£95	£139
Cottage Swept	£64	£116	£169
"COMFORT IDEAL"- High Performance Softwood Windows with PVCu Exterior			
Side Opening Casement	£80	£144	£208
Cottage Plain	£97	£174	£252
PVC-u Range (preglazed, metal subframes included)			
Side Opening Casement	£106	£168	£254
Cottage Plain	£116	£188	£285

To compare the products I have produced a simplified summary table so you can see how small (630 wide), medium (1200 w) and large (1770w) windows compare in price through some of the major styles. I have assumed a discount off list price of 40% which should be within your negotiating powers if you are buying in whole house lots.

High Performance Windows

If you work through the John Carr catalogue thus far, you will notice that the first set of windows you come to are called the Comfort ES 14 range. What on earth does that mean? Time for some de-construction, I think. Comfort? It's a stupid name for a range of windows but then Chum is a stupid name for dog food and everyone knows what Chum is. We can forgive the marketing department this blemish, perhaps they were having an off day. ES? It stands for energy saving (I think). Not that these windows will save you any energy. 14? This is the interesting bit. It actually refers to something useful which is the depth of the glazing rebate. It tells you that it will accept a 14mm double glazed sealed unit. 14mm is the absolute minimum depth of a double glazed sealed unit (4mm glass/6mm gap/4mm glass) but it's an improvement on the days, not so long ago, when these windows were made to receive single glazing only — hence the ES. But if you follow through 35 pages or so of the window

section, you will find a Comfort ES 22 range which will — you've guessed it — take a 22mm, argon filled double glazed unit *aka* the bees knees. This is what used to be called a high performance window. Apart from this glazing depth rebate, there is precious little else to differentiate the two ranges.

Sliding Sash Windows

The modern version of the Victorian sliding sash, which worked with concealed weights, has adjustable spiral balances that are a bugger to adjust and, even when well adjusted, can be very stiff to open and shut, but are in other ways superior to the original. John Carr supply two styles, the *Traditional* which is intended for refurbishment work and won't take double glazed units and the *Slide & Tilt* range which will, and will also tilt inwards to make cleaning easier. (The fake sash windows which John Carr call *Edwardian* have to be cleaned from outside.) They are also neatly draught stripped. They are, however, expensive; widths are different to other window ranges so direct comparisons are not possible, but the nearest to our standard 1200x1200mm windows that I've been using as a yardstick is the Slide & Tilt 1085x1350mm and these cost (with 40% discount) £180, which is nearly twice the cost of the *Edwardian*. Add glazing bars and you add 8-10% to the price. They are a quality prod-

uct, but are not much cheaper than a local joiner would charge for making something similar.

Other Features

There is a range of other options you can specify. You might want Easy Clean Hinges (extra £10) which enable you to get at the outside from the inside; maybe coloured fittings (£7 extra) tickle your fancy. Most windows are available in either a stain basecoat or a white primed finish. The default is the stained basecoat because you can paint or stain on top of that but you will be saving yourself time and money to get the primed finish if you are going to paint over the top. Just remember that all these options will delay your delivery schedules by weeks so they are only an option if you are planning well ahead.

Oh, and there's trickle vents. If you want to know about trickle vents, delve into the Ventilation section in Chapter 8.

Substitutions

There really isn't a lot to choose between the quality of the joinery turned out by the volume timber manufacturers, though the finer detailing does vary a little. Occasionally, you will find that one is offering much better terms than the others and you may have

Seven Basic John Carr Window Styles

Standard Casement 212C £53

Swept Head style S212C £79

Top Hung 212A £67

Cottage plain C212C £62

Country Bar style CB212C £80

Georgian style G212C £112

Edwardian Bar style EB212T £110

cause to switch horses. This is usually possible because, despite the different naming systems they use, the sizes are standard and therefore interchangeable. However, not all manufacturers produce such a wide range as John Carr or Boulton & Paul and if your choice is exotic you might get stuck.

Other Options

Bespoke Timber

Although there are many types of timber suitable for manufacturing external joinery, if you choose to have your windows supplied cheaply from a volume manufacturer then they will almost certainly be made from European Redwood, probably from Scandinavia. Although it is not particularly durable, it can be readily treated with wood preservatives; more importantly it is the cheapest type of suitable timber. It machines well and generally looks good, which makes it suitable for translucent finishes like wood staining.

There are better woods to use for external joinery but they are all very much more expensive and won't necessarily result in better (or longer-lasting) windows. Most hardwoods are inherently more durable than softwoods — oak, teak and Brazilian mahogany are particularly suitable — and there are some N. American softwoods such as Douglas Fir which are nearly as durable as the better hardwoods — certainly durable enough not to require treatment with wood preservative. However, it must be realised that the design, installation and maintenance of the joinery is at least as important in determining how well the items perform over the long term. Specifying more durable timber will

probably double your joinery costs at a stroke. Most joinery manufacturers offer "hardwood" alternatives in most of their ranges but you don't get any choice as to which hardwood. If you particularly wanted something like Douglas Fir for your windows then you would have to search out a small joinery shop to make them for you; this route would probably treble the cost of using a bog standard casement from a volume producer.

uPVC

Though uPVC is now widely used in the building trade (in drainage and guttering), its use in joinery is still regarded with suspicion by many housebuilders. The purists love to hate uPVC windows and doors because they don't look right, and they have a point. However secure, warm and maintenance free they might be, the finer detailing on them remains very crude. However signs are that early resistance to uPVC joinery in new housebuilding is melting away and many of our biggest housebuilders have switched away from timber.

uPVC windows have a stranglehold on the replacement market. What sells them is the fact that they are usually replacing clapped out timber or steel windows which may have been in place for fifty years or more, and they are offering comfort and warmth together with the promise of being maintenance free. It's actually too early to say if uPVC windows will be trouble free (uPVC guttering certainly isn't), but the indications are that they are performing well. In their defence the sales teams will claim that though installation costs are undoubtedly high, the fact that re-painting and repair is not needed means that over a 20-30 year period the uPVC windows

work out much cheaper. Obviously you must judge the pros and cons for yourself, but they do need a certain type of house — and it's the sort of house that most would-be housebuilders are not attracted to.

Incidentally, an American company, Andersen, is making big strides into the UK housing market with its windows and doors, which are made of timber but have an external uPVC coating. For some this will combine the best of both worlds and their sash windows (which are pre-glazed and decorated) are very good value. This has proved to be such a popular idea that John Carr have copied it with their *Comfort Ideal* range, as outlined in table 7e.

Metal
Aluminium has never been popular for windows though it remains the most widespread framing material for patio doors. Steel windows were the height of fashion sixty years ago but now suffer from an image problem. Though the detailing is much finer than the average uPVC window, they do not perform very well thermally and are often associated with condensation problems. Crittal were the biggest name in steel windows and they are still making them in Braintree, Essex.

Finishes
Whilst non-timber materials invariably come pre-finished, with timber windows you have a number of choices. The current standard is to coat the joinery before it leaves the works with a honey-coloured woodstain which leaves you with the largest number of options. You can apply darker woodstains or you can apply paint. Left to itself, the woodstain provides limited (6-month) protection for the joinery. Some period windows, notably the sliding sash styles, are only available primed (unless by special request) as it is assumed that they are always painted on site.

Now the volume producers are offering pre-finished (either painted white or stained dark) timber windows which just require glazing and touching up on site — look for a *high build finish*. These tend to be around 40% more expensive than the standard. And there is a move to also supply a totally finished and glazed product as well — though here look to pay around three times the price of the raw timber joinery as described in the catalogues.

Comparison Costings
It may have occurred to you by now that it is really very difficult to compare one system with another because we're not really comparing like with like. A timber window in the

raw is naturally much cheaper than a plastic one which comes glazed and furnished; but a naked timber window requires a whole lotta work doing to it. Table 7g, which is coming up in a couple of pages, addresses these matters and gives a more realistic comparison of what timber joinery costs in relation to pre-finished types.

Design Objectives

Whatever your particular preferences in building styles might be, the openings in the building will to a large extent determine the look and feel of the whole structure. In modern designs the tendency has been to create large, simple openings; in that most extreme of modern designs, the glass-walled office block, we have a situation that is virtually all window. In contrast, 99.9% of British private housing is designed along the traditional lines with which we are all familiar.

"Good Fenestration"

Architects and planners talk loftily of something called "good fenestration." By this they mean that there are some ways of placing windows (and entrances) in walls that look good and others that look ugly. You'd think that what looks good and what doesn't would be a matter of individual taste, but in fact there is a surprising amount of consensus about it.

Until this century, virtually all buildings that we constructed had "good fenestration." Whether we are looking at the great country houses now presided over by the National Trust or at the humble peasant's cottage or indeed at spec. built Victorian terraces, there is a general consensus that they look right. Throughout the course of the 20th century we've gradually lost the art of fenestration, so that by the 60s we were mostly building in ways that look all wrong to us now. Quite why this should be so is still a subject of some controversy (i.e. is it just fashion or is there something more basic?), but most designers and customers are now aware of the mistakes that have been made and in the 80s there was a movement to build back in, what developers call, *kerb appeal,* which refers to the visual impact a house makes on passers-by — what advertisers would refer to as sexiness.

The movement to build in kerb appeal has not been an unqualified success. Visit any modern housing development and you can't fail to notice what the current fashions are. Half-timbering, ornamental leadwork, rustic pantiles and cottage style windows all suggest that developers are trying to recreate *ye olde English village* look and yet, and yet it still all seems so unconvincing. You *can* get a house to look convincingly old fashioned, but you have to avoid things like standard John Carr joinery which tends to be made out of comparatively heavy sections which rarely looks authentic. The art of fenestration is partly to do with getting the openings in the right place but also partly to do with making sure that these correctly placed openings are filled with good-looking joinery.

Barn Conversions

Conversions usually pose problems quite different from new builds. There may be existing windows to match but more often than not you will be punching new holes in an existing wall and hoping to fit something that looks in keeping with the period of the original building. Incidentally the expression "punching holes" is very hip in barn converting circles at the moment, used widely by both planners and architects, so much so that you might be forgiven for thinking that the decision on where exactly to punch those holes is the be-all and end-all of barn design. As you may have noted, made-to-order joinery tends to cost and arm and a leg and specifying it is one of the major factors which makes converting barns more expensive than building new. However, if you want to keep costs down there are a number of options that may be of interest to you (or your planners) which can be bought off the shelf. First, the oh-so-modern looking *Top Hung* window can actually look just so in a barn elevation; certainly less obtrusive than the cottage or swept head styles. Also note that the Narrow *Module* casement windows, as used in the benchmark house, tend to look better than standard width windows in barn-type buildings.

External Doors

Many of the things that I've written about windows apply equally to external doors. Furthermore, there is a polite convention that your choice of door should not clash with your choice of window — a convention that's well worth following whatever your chosen style. As with windows, the door manufacturers tend to stick to pretty conventional ideas and all produce variations on some remarkably similar themes. One of the more daring ideas is to put a little bit of stained glass in the pocket window on some of the designs. By and large, the best that can be said about the design of these doors is that "it blends in quite well" or "isn't that unobtrusive?" If you want a door that makes a statement about you — and, after all, the front door is the first thing visitors come into contact with — then you'll have to look to a bespoke joiner's shop or a salvage yard. And expect to pay.

Materials

Timber is the still most widely used material for external doors but whereas it once enjoyed a near monopoly it now has to share the field with other materials. As with windows, timber doors are the cheapest to buy off the shelf but they are not universally loved by developers because they are prone to twisting and warping, entailing unwelcome call backs.

Switching to hardwood doors is one option but, by all accounts, hardwood doors are almost as likely to move as softwood ones A reasonable compromise for those who want something better than a softwood door but are not keen on specifying tropical hardwood is to go for hemlock, a durable N. American softwood particularly well suited to doors.

As the External Door Options table 7f indicates, there are now several other materials in regular use for making doors. All are more expensive than softwood and all share the plus point that they are dimensionally stable — which no timber door will ever be. Steel is the cheapest alternative; widely used in N. America, it has

7f: External Door Options

FRONT DOORS COMPARED	FRAME	DOOR	GLAZING	FURNITURE	HANGING	DECORATING	TOTAL
Softwood	£90	£80	£40	£50	£30	£70	**£360**
Hardwood	200	110	40	£50	30	£70	**500**
Steel		490		£50	40		**580**
uPVC	150	370			40	10	**570**
Fibreglass	220	230		£50	30	20	**550**

Comparisons are for a part glazed single door and frame with a single sidelight

FRENCH DOORS and PATIO DOORS COMPARED (c. 1800w)	FRAME	DOOR	GLAZING	FURNITURE	HANGING	DECORATING	TOTAL
Softwood French Doors	£110	£100	£140	£60	£50	£120	**£580**
uPVC French Door Set	50	630			40	10	**730**
Softwood Patio		530			40	40	**610**
Hardwood Patio		800			40	40	**880**
Aluminium Patio		290			40	10	**340**
uPVC Patio		390			40	10	**440**

Comparisons are for 1800w frames, though French Doors are just 1500w
Most patio doors are sold pre-glazed and furnished, hence costs of zero

an aura of security about it which is perhaps unjustified, since a door is no stronger than its frame (which is usually softwood) or its locks (which are no different whatever the door). Steel paints well but is susceptible to bodywork damage like a car. The market leader for steel doors is the *IG Weatherbeater*. uPVC is widely used in the replacement market but suffers visually in comparison with its competitors. The most interesting of the alternative materials is GRP — that's *glass reinforced fibre* or good ol' fibreglass. It's well established in the garage door market but is now beginning to make inroads into house doors. The wood grained effect is far more realistic than anything uPVC can achieve and the material can be stained to match other joinery. Look out for Lindman's *Fiber-Classics*.

French v Patio Doors

The idea of opening up a largish hole in the house facing the garden is attractive to most of us; it's a sort of poor man's conservatory. You have a choice here between sliding patio doors and hinged french doors. The table shows that there is not an awful lot to choose between them pricewise, but the overall visual effect is very different. You see, the patio door is that rarity in new housebuilding, an essentially *modern* design feature, a sort of junior relative of the glass walled office block. If you are spending money (lots of it) on creating an Olde Worlde look, then a set of patio doors — even with leaded lights — is going to look out of place. In contrast, a pair

of french terrace doors tends to add a little bit of Brideshead to the elevation; they're nothing if not old-fashioned.

French doors may look the part but they are notoriously fickle in their behaviour and are a bugger to hang well. Too tight and you'll forever be planing bits off every time it rains; too loose and the wind will whistle through them as if they were wide open.

Both french doors and patio doors present security problems. French doors are relatively easy to force open; this can to some extent be countered by fitting sliding and locking bolts to both doors, not just the first to open. They are also unusual for external doors in that the tend to open outwards which leaves their hinge knuckles exposed and vulnerable to being cut off though there is a little gizmo called a hinge bolt which can counteract this. Patio doors present a different problem in that they have frequently been prized, frame and all, from their moorings; very often they are secured only by three screws at either end.

Handles

Whilst in theory there are innumerable materials that you could use to make door handles from, in practice the range is surprisingly limited: aluminium, wrought iron or brass (or rather brass effect). Aluminium has the reputation for being cheap (though there are some very expensive aluminium fittings available) and brass is the preferred material for most developers both inside and out. It's

styling is usually either Victorian (plain) or Georgian (fancy scrolled edges). Black wrought iron is favoured for the country cottage look but looks out of place on anything else. If you want something a bit different you can look out modern stainless steel designs (check out Modric) or plastic (Normbau).

Heat Loss

Dip into the Heat Loss table 10f and you'll see that the role of the door in all this is pretty negligible, largely because their overall area is small compared to other elements in the house. However, if you are wanting to specify an energy efficient house external doors are a detail worth paying attention to, because 44mm of timber, the standard thickness, does not perform wonderfully well as either an insulator or a draught sealer. Doors are particularly likely to be a source of unwanted ventilation; even if you fit effective draught strip around the edges, you still have the keyholes and the letter boxes to contend with. Timber doors, in particular, are always likely to perform poorly in this respect because wood expands and contracts as the moisture content changes, so draught sealing is always going to be a hit and miss affair. But, to put matters in perspective, the cost of replacing heat lost around draughty doors is likely to be in the order of £10-£15/annum, so don't get too worried about it.

7g: External Joinery Schedule for Benchmark House

Where	Width		Height	Softwood Windows	List	Net -40%	Glass	Decorating & Labour at £42/m²	Total	Hardwood Alternative	uPVC Alternative inc met frames
Kitchen	1770	x	1050	4N10CMC	£162	£97	£15	£78	£191	£347	£280
Living	1770	x	1200	4N12CMC	£169	£102	£16	£89	£207	£369	£307
Living	488	x	1200	N12C	£63	£38	£6	£25	£68	£129	£100
Living	488	x	1200	N12C	£63	£38	£6	£25	£68	£129	£100
Living	915	x	1200	2N12CC	£121	£72	£13	£46	£131	£247	£160
Living	488	x	1200	N12C	£63	£38	£5	£25	£67	£128	£100
WC	488	x	1200	N12C	£63	£38	£7	£25	£69	£130	£100
Dining	488	x	1200	N12C	£63	£38	£6	£25	£68	£129	£100
Dining	915	x	1200	2N12CC	£121	£72	£13	£46	£131	£247	£160
Dining	488	x	1200	N12C	£63	£38	£6	£25	£68	£129	£100
Meals	915	x	1200	2N12CC	£121	£72	£13	£46	£131	£247	£160
Meals	915	x	1200	2N12CC	£121	£72	£13	£46	£131	£247	£160
Garage	488	x	1200	N12C	£63	£38	£3	£25	£65	£126	£100
Garage	915	x	1200	2N12CC	£121	£72	£6	£46	£124	£240	£160
Dormer	1342	x	900	3N09CC	£125	£75	£15	£51	£140	£260	£205
Dormer	1342	x	900	3N09CC	£125	£75	£15	£51	£140	£260	£205
Ensuite	488	x	1050	N10C	£61	£36	£6	£22	£64	£122	£95
Bed 3	915	x	1200	2N12CC	£121	£72	£13	£46	£131	£247	£160
				Total	£1,807	£1,084	£177	£739	**£ 2,000**	**£ 3,734**	**£ 2,752**

Where	Width		Height	Rooflights	List	Net					
Landing	1400	x	780	Velux GGL308		£186					
Bathroom	1180	x	1140	Velux GGL606		£165					
				Total		**£ 351**					

Where	Width		Height	External Door Frames	List	Net	Glass			Hardwood	uPVC
Front	1430	x	2100	Front Special		£175	£25			£250	n/a
Utility	900	x	2100	Back	£67	£40				£70	n/a
				Ext Doors							
Front	807	x	2000	Lindsey softwood	£186	£112	£20			£170	£500
Utility	807	x	2000	Back	£186	£112	£18			£170	£340
				Total		£438	£63			**£ 660**	**£ 840**

Glazing

The benchmark house is double-glazed with standard sealed units, using 4mm float glass either side of a 6mm air gap. The glass is toughened only where safety regulations require. 40 pieces of glass altogether measuring 13m^2 of which just the door and door frame glass was toughened (2m^2) and just the three panes in the garage were single glazed (1m^2). The two rooflights are not included in this summary because they were bought ready-glazed. This work would have cost around £450 supplied and fitted which for a total glazed area of 13m^2 works out at around £34/m^2. Toughened glass is about 40% more expensive than regular float glass..

Single Glazing?

Until the 1995 amendments to the building regulations, it would have been possible to single glaze the windows on the benchmark house for around £270 (Mats £120, Lab £150). However, the recent changes to thermal standards have made double glazing virtually mandatory in new homes and in renovations. It is just technically possible to build using single glazing but you would have to make many more expensive changes elsewhere in your building and you would also be inviting problems with condensation. In effect, double glazing is now the rule.

Safety Glazing

Most glazing is 4mm thick float glass. Sealed unit double glazing, in its bog standard form, is 6mm of air sandwiched between two 4mm panes. However, regulations require stronger glass to be placed in:
- Any window less than 800mm off floor level
- Any window less than 300mm from a door
- All doors and sidelights where pane width is greater than 250mm
- Internal glazed doors with pane sizes more than 250mm must be fitted with at least 6mm glass.

There are two common forms of clear, strengthened glass:

Toughened

Baked hard to about five times the strength of float glass and, when broken, shatters into, hopefully, harmless lumps.

Laminated

Consists of two sheets of ordinary glass sandwiched around a plastic film: when hit it breaks but doesn't collapse.

Toughened glass is currently quite a bit cheaper than laminated glass and performs better from a safety angle, but laminated glass is preferable if you are worried about

security; it's harder to break through. Using laminated glass in all ground floor units would have added £250 to the overall costs.

Energy Saving Glass

Much the most exciting thing to happen to double glazing in recent times is the development of *low emissivity* or Low E glass. A wafer thin and almost completely invisible coat is applied to ordinary float glass which causes it to reflect heat back inside a room. It is fairly cheap to produce and it can be used in otherwise normal double-glazed units. In Britain it is produced by Pilkington — along with most of our other glass — and is sometimes known as *Pilkington K Glass* — or just K glass.

The glazing heat loss table gives an indication of how much better Low E glazing performs than ordinary double glazing, especially when it is combined with an argon filled cavity. It is notable that it performs rather better than triple glazing; as it is much cheaper to produce, it has effectively killed off the triple glazing industry in this country.

There is one further quality to Low E glass which isn't easily described in a table. U values are all very well when it comes to measuring heat loss through a wall or a roof, but

7h: Glazing Guide Prices

All prices are £/m²

	MATERIALS	LABOUR	SUPPLY + FIX
DOUBLE GLAZING PRICES			
Minimum charge per sealed unit		25% of m² price	
Fixing charges for sealed units		£12	
Standard clear 4-6-4 sealed units	£20	£12	**£32**
Obscure 4-6-4 sealed units	£24	£12	**£36**
Toughened 4-6-4 sealed units	£28	£12	**£40**
Laminated 4-6-4 sealed units	£50	£12	**£62**
Low E glass with argon filled cavity	£30	£12	**£42**
Low E glass available in all options		add £12/m²	
Imitation leaded lights		add £25/m²	
Swept head glazing		add 20%	
SINGLE GLAZING PRICES			
Fixing charge for single glazing		£2/pane	
Minimum charge		£25	
4mm Float	£12		**£15**
6mm Float	£18		**£20**
6mm Toughened	£20		**£24**

glass is unlike any other commonly used building material in that it is also capable of transferring heat into the house when the sun is shining. Low E glass is particularly good at this as it absorbs short wave solar heat just like other glass but acts as a reflective shield to the long wave heat emanating from inside the house. Consequently, south facing Low E glass units are estimated to be net gainers of heat over an entire heating season. If you've designed your house with solar heat gain in mind, the actual saving achieved from fitting Low E glass can be as much as double the amount suggested by the table. The most obvious effect of this is that your south facing rooms will not need to be heated during the day time on all but the very coldest and gloomiest winter days. By arranging your house so that the dayrooms all have a southerly aspect, Low E glass will enable you to reduce your overall heating bills by substantially more than the simple U value heat loss calculations would suggest.

Air Gaps

A look at the Heat Loss Table will show that double glazing performs very much better when there is a large air gap between the panes. Furthermore, most glaziers will manufacture double-glazed units with an air gap of up to 12mm before introducing any sort of cost penalty. So why doesn't everyone use double glazing with a 12mm air gap? Why the ubiquitous 6mm air gap in sealed units going into timber windows? The answer lies with the joinery manufacturers. At present most standard timber windows and doors are designed to take glazing units of 14mm thickness, which translates into a 6mm air gap. If you want to have thicker glazing units you will have to specify high performance joinery and this is likely to add 20% to your raw window costs. Note however that Boulton & Paul have introduced a thinner glazing bead (albeit with an 8% cost penalty) which allows you to fit wider glazed units into the same space.

There are moves afoot to widen the industry standard glazing rebate in windows to incorporate thicker glazed units but not everyone is delighted at these prospects. It might make for a more thermally efficient window, but it will also increase the amount of timber being used to make that window. It will also make it even harder to make a good-looking window. The plastic window brigade have been using 20mm-thick glazed units for some time, and whilst this makes for a good sales bullet it doesn't do anything for the look of the product. There are purists who decry the move away from single skin glazing on the grounds that it has done nothing to improve the look of a window; they will be even more appalled if 20mm units replace 14mm ones, making modern windows even heavier and more clumsy.

Argon

Filling the glass sandwich with argon costs very little extra and achieves a significant improvement in performance. If you are considering spending anything extra on glazing then argon filled units are well worth specifying. Using argon doesn't appear to effect performance in any mysterious ways but note that you can't inject argon into sealed units with air gaps of less than 12mm — the nozzles won't fit.

Decorative Effects

Leaded Lights

The addition of imitation leaded lights is popular in many Tudor style developments. It can be added either as squares or diamonds. It is a relatively expensive operation (costing around £25/m^2 — that's an extra £300 on the benchmark house) and it can often look awful. In fact it often does; it's another effect that rarely looks good with thick double glazed units. However, when the design is carefully handled (which usually means using it sparingly), the effect can be to simulate a much older style of window. The accompanying photos hopefully indicate just how fine the line is between getting it right and getting it wrong; maybe you disagree, afterall it's always a matter of taste.

7j: Heat Loss Through Double-Glazed Units

SEALED UNIT MAKE UP	AIR GAP BETWEEN PANES					
	6mm	8mm	10mm	12mm	14mm	16mm
4mm glass/air/4mm glass	3.1	3.0	2.8	2.7	2.6	2.6
4mm/argon/4mm	2.9	2.7	2.6	2.6	2.5	2.5
4mm/air/4mm Low E	2.5	2.2	2.0	1.9	1.7	1.7
4mm/argon/4mm Low E	2.1	1.9	1.7	1.6	1.5	1.4
4mm/air/4mm/air/4mm	2.2	2.0	1.9	1.8	1.8	1.7

Figures above are U values: the lower the more efficient

	HEAT LOSS THROUGH GLASS					
U Value of glazing	3.1	2.9	2.7	2.5	2.3	2.1
Extra Installation costs	£0	£250	£250	£250	£600	£600
kWh heat lost/annum	1800	1684	1568	1452	1335	1219
Annual cost of heat lost	£28	£26	£24	£23	£21	£19

Figures are for 13m^2 glazing on the test house

Georgian Look

Fitting sealed units into Georgian style windows and doors can be a very expensive business, because most glaziers have a minimum charge for each unit made and small units therefore get heavily penalised. For instance, Solaglas, one of the largest of the national glazing firms, set a minimum charge per unit of 25% of the square metre rate; this means that double-glazed units do not get any cheaper when the size falls below 500x500mm (or its equivalent area). Now, a typical Georgian style bedroom window has 16 small panes measuring 250x275mm; you don't have to be a financial genius to work out that that's going to be one hell of a lot more expensive to kit out with double glazed units. In fact it's likely to cost 16 x £9 or £144 as opposed to just £35 for a more conventional arrangement with just two units.

Small wonder that a number of manufacturers like Andersen Windows are offering imitation Georgian glazing bars, rather like imitation leaded lights. If your heart (or your planner) is set on Georgian style joinery then look out early on for glass suppliers who won't exact such a savage cost penalty.

Swept Heads

The Georgian look has been drifting out of fashion in the last decade — possibly because of the high glazing costs — but it has been replaced by the Country Cottage look and, from the developer's point of view, the quintessential part of the Cottage look is the curved head to the window. Again, there are knock-on effects to the glazing costs, but there is an important proviso here that the cost conscious should know. Whilst the real swept-head windows involve manufacturing curved glass units — adding around 20% to the cost — there is an alternative, which is to stick timber swept-head inserts over the top of rectangular glass units after they have been fitted. Almost every major joinery manufacturer offers this option and it makes both the glazing and the joinery cheaper. However it is an imitation swept head at best, and though you might not be able to tell the difference from the outside, from the inside you can actually see that the insert has been stuck on top of the glass.

Obscure

People generally only fit obscure glass in bathroom windows, the reason being that they are often N-N-N-Naked in the bathroom and they don't want the neighbours to have a gander. This arrangement may well suit 90% of UK households, but think about you and your bathroom before blithely specifying obscure glass. You may not need privacy in every bathroom or you may not need privacy

Two examples of the effect of adding leaded lights to modern double glazed windows. For me, the top one (Medina Gimson house, FutureWorld) looks fine and the less said about the bottom one the better.

all the time, in which case venetian blinds or curtains might serve you better. You might even enjoy lying in the bath looking out of your window, perhaps having a gander at your neighbour.

Obscure glass doesn't add much to a room from the inside and doesn't look that good from the outside. The plainer patterns tend to look least obtrusive but none of them look as good as a real window. So think whether you really need obscure before you specify it.

Daylight Quality

The primary function of glazing is to let light in. Keeping heat in and not breaking when hit (either intentionally or accidentally) are lesser but more frequently discussed properties, but before passing on let's consider this primary function for a moment. Generally,

the thicker the glass, the less light gets through. Low E glass (which saves heat) actually cuts out quite a lot of light: it acts rather like Polaroid sunglasses do in reducing glare. In rooms with lots of glazing this can be a positive benefit in itself. On the other hand, if your design keeps glazing to a minimum, remember that daylight quality is improved by having windows in two walls of a room so that daylight arrives from more than one direction: this may be worth considering in kitchen design.

Floors

The "industry standard" is to build a concrete or masonry ground floor and a timber first floor. This is how the benchmark house was built, and my costings confirm that this is indeed a sensible course and you should have good reason to vary from it. However, note that I used the phrase "concrete or masonry" for the ground floor industry standards; there is a choice here between solid concrete slabs and concrete beams with block infill.

Before we move on, a word about the table 7k on Sub-floor costs, because even I find it a bit confusing. Why *sub*-floor costs? To distinguish the costs from floor finishes (dealt with in Chapter 9). By and large, builders do not supply floor finishes and therefore here we are looking at the floor costs strictly from a builder's point of view. But note that I have labelled the last few rows *Covers;* this is to try to distinguish between the floor base and the base supports — if you like between the sub-floor and the sub-sub-floor. You see the problem is that you can lay either cement screeds or timber deckings over the floor supports and this makes direct comparison costings a minor nightmare. The two top sections *Ground Floors* and *First Floors* will give you a basic price for the floor support but neither group will give you a completed sub-floor until some form of cover has been laid over it.

Concrete beams laid ready for block infill

Solid Slabs

A solid concrete slab is usually laid 100mm thick over a layer of compacted hardcore. This is the most labour intensive system and, conversely, the cheapest on materials, which makes it suitable for D-I-Y builders with access to cheap or free labour. It also remains the best way of doing garage floors. Industrial buildings have power-floated floor slabs which do away with the need for expensive slab coverings, but this technique is little used in housebuilding.

Beam and Block

Beam and block floors are not economical below areas of 50m² but become increasingly cost-effective on larger areas, especially if you can supply your own blocks as part of a larger order. Beam and block is gaining in popularity with developers, largely because it's fast and dry. It is an option on upstairs flooring as well, but here it gets expensive because a crane is usually required on site. It has better sound-proofing qualities than timber and so is an excellent choice for multi-occupancy dwellings like flats. Another reason for specifying suspended beam floors upstairs is when you are interested in fitting a whole house underfloor heating system.

Beam and block floors are provided by specialists who work from drawings supplied by the client. A number of businesses cater for this market and many have links with builder's merchants who act as middlemen; if you want to go direct, I can recommend Earthspan and Rackhams. Note that the infill blocks that are laid between the concrete beams are the same in size and specification to the standard 100x225x450mm blocks used in wall construction, and you will usually be able to effect savings if you supply the blocks. These floors, in common with all suspended ground floors, need ventilation, which is usually done by providing airbricks in the external walls; indeed the presence or absence of airbricks around the damp-proof course is very often the only clue as to what sort of ground floor a new house has.

Understand also that masonry beam flooring is an engineered solution for each situation. There is very often more than one way

7k: Subfloor Guide Prices

	MATERIALS	LABOUR	TOTAL
GROUND FLOOR			
Concrete Slab	£8.40	£6.50	**£14.90**
Beam and Block	12.70	4.20	**16.90**
Marshalls Jetfloor	16.40	4.20	**20.60**
Timber Joists	7.90	4.00	**11.90**
FIRST FLOOR			
Beam and Block	£12.70	£8.40	**£21.10**
Timber Joists	7.90	4.00	**11.90**
COVERS			
Damp-Proof Membrane	£0.30	£0.50	**£0.80**
38mm Polyurethane Insulation	4.10	0.50	**4.60**
50mm Polystyrene Insulation	1.90	0.50	**2.40**
65mm Screed	3.40	4.00	**7.40**
Chipboard	3.80	2.00	**5.80**
Sterling Floor	4.60	2.00	**6.60**
Plywood	6.60	3.00	**9.60**

Looks cheap but decking must be added to this total

Includes £3.50/m² for sub-level concrete

Again, no decking

to run the beams and you may be able to take advantage of a system like Rackhams 225 beams which can span up to 8m and can sometimes enable you to do away with sleeper walls within the main floor area.

Marshalls Jet Floor

A unique variation on the standard beam and block floor that uses polystyrene infill blocks to fill the voids between the beams and is, therefore, thermally very efficient, with a U

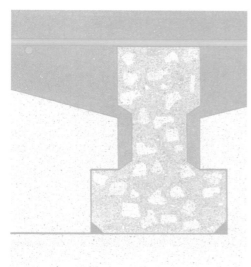

Marshalls Jet Floor wraps insulation — the lighter coloured bits — around the concrete beams. The top layer is a cement screed.

value of less than 0.3. Only an insulated timber ground floor could come close to this. However the insulation blocks are rather expensive and are unlikely to be as cost-effective as laying your own polystyrene sheeting on top of a more conventional sub-floor.

Timber

Timber ground floors are discriminated against by the NHBC, which insists on there being a concrete capping and damp-proof membrane laid over the oversite underneath the suspended floor, which effectively adds around £4/m² to the costs. Upstairs, of course, no such extra work applies and here timber joisting is clearly the cheapest option. However, it can also be a viable option when considering a timber-finished ground floor. Around £10/m² — 50% of the cost of a timber ground floor — goes into the sheeting (usually chipboard or plywood) that is laid over the joists and where a plank floor finish is desired this sheeting can be dispensed with. The problem with doing this is that either the planking will be exposed for the duration of the construction, which will almost certainly lead to damage, or some form of temporary sheeting will have to be installed, which will cancel out most of the perceived cost

advantages. However, the technique works well with reclaimed boards which need to be sanded and sealed in any event and can serve as both temporary and finished floor covering.

Chipboard

The lowest grade of timber floor covering in widespread use, chipboard is made out of tiny wood particles suspended in a sea of glue. At around £4/m², chipboard is nearly half the price of the much stronger plywood but is not nearly as durable. The NHBC now requires that all chipboard used in new housing should be *moisture resistant,* but this is far from being weatherproof and it is not recommended that chipboard is built into a house before the structure is watertight — nevertheless it regularly is. One mid-priced alternative is to use Sterling Floor, a waferboard now manufactured in 2400x600 T&G sheets like chipboard. Chipboard is now frequently laid as a floating floor: that is to say that it is laid — or rather wedged-in without any fixings at all — on top of polystyrene floor insulation sheets. This technique — sometimes known as a *polychip* floor (as in *poly*styrene and *chip*board) — is bound to become more common as floor insulation is now laid as standard. Whereas chipboard has for a long time been the standard material for covering upstairs timber floors, where it is nailed — using *ring shank* nails — to the timber joists, its use without any nails or screws at all is still in its infancy. Problems have been encountered with chipboard sheeting curling at the edges and with sheets getting wet and consequently expanding and cracking walls above. In theory, there is much to recommend floating chipboard floors, especially where a carpeted finish is required, and costs are no higher than the traditional cement screed topping given to ground floors. In practice it pays to use the technique with caution; lay timber battens underneath where extra support is needed such as underneath stud walls, at external doorways and at the foot of staircases.

Insulation

Even with the most recent changes in the building regs, underfloor insulation is not actually mandatory but the alternative ways of satisfying the energy efficiency requirements are all likely to prove to be more expensive. There are several methods of insulation available, the cheapest and most readily understood being to lay flooring grade expanded polystyrene at 50mm thickness over the sub-floor and under the screed or chipboard. It's not expensive (50mm *Jablite* or

Kaycell sheeting costs around £1.90/m²) and it is cost effective in terms of reduced heating bills up to a depth of 75mm. These techniques of underfloor insulation are relatively new and there are possibly problems building up in the future should the insulation not prove to be as rigid as expected: more cautious builders will use some form of reinforcement in their screeds to counteract any such failures. Alternatively use one of the denser insulating materials such as polyurethane or extruded polystyrenes such as *Polyfoam* or *Styrofoam*. Marley, makers of the *Turbo* super-lightweight range of insulating blocks, have been quick to point out that you can satisfy the new building regulations if you use only super-lightweight blocks in both a beam and block suspended floor *and* the supporting footings. This technique will be a balm to those who are resistant to using dedicated insulation materials underfloor, but the cost of super-lightweight blocks is such that it will be an expensive alternative. Another technique which may well come back into prominence is the use of timber joists on the ground floor: as with all other timber framing techniques, the use of timber joisting makes it relatively easy and cheap to obtain good insulation levels without having to compromise tried and tested construction techniques.

Aficionados of underfloor heating will wonder what all the fuss is about. Such systems only work well with very high levels of underfloor insulation — otherwise much of the heat would be lost — and, whatever problems there may have been with underfloor heating systems, laying insulation under heavy cement screeds does not appear to be one of them.

Trussed Floors

An interesting new system is now available in the UK from Trus Joist MacMillan; it involves building floors out of timber beams instead of masonry beams. On upper floors it is quick and lightweight to install and doesn't need any bridging: the board covering can be nailed directly into it. Using a Trus Joist system would have cost around £800 for the upstairs at the benchmark house, around 40% more than sawn carcassing but should enjoy similar speed advantages as beam and block floors do. It's a particularly useful system if you want to have floor spans wider than 4m but don't want to have to mess around with supporting beams. Contact 01527 854853 for stockists.

Internal Walls

The standard routine for internal partition walls is that which the benchmark house uses. That is to build blockwork walls downstairs and timber studwork upstairs. Internal studwork (at £6/m^2) is cheaper and quicker to build than blockwork (at £11/m^2) but it is felt by many developers to be a bit tacky. Timber framers will, of course, hotly dispute this, but it would be churlish to deny that a certain amount of prejudice still exists against timber stud partition walls. By the way, don't assume from this that timber frame houses are cheaper to build than block built ones: the costs of timber stud walls more than doubles when specified as the load bearing skin of your external wall, largely because of the essential addition of a layer of plywood bracing. And most houses have a larger area of external walling than internal.

There is another reason for favouring the block wall downstairs, and that is to do with the fact that many of the downstairs walls are load-bearing, whereas upstairs, with the widespread use of roof trusses which transfer all their loadings to the external walls, the walls serve no other purpose than room division. Now, timber stud walls are quite capable of bearing normal floor loadings but their construction needs to be more carefully designed, and this is a hassle that most builders could do without. Also, there is the problem that people automatically assume that any studwork wall is not load-bearing and that this may cause problems in years to come if alterations are undertaken.

Alternatives

Every year or so someone comes along with another system which will "completely revolutionise building techniques" and make "blockwork and studwork redundant." We've had *Stramit* straw partitions, *Paramount* plasterboard wall units, *Premaco* gypsum wall blocks, *Streamline* system walls. All promise great savings and yet none ever really catch on. Part of the problem is that you need to have a very large site going to start enjoying real savings since the amount of initial head scratching is large; I may be doing these manufacturers a great disservice, but I don't think the one-off house builder will be particularly interested. However, the steel frame systems like British Gypsum's Metal Stud Partitions and Knauf's *Diamond Dry Wall* system, have begun to make significant impact on the volume housebuilders and may well trickle down to smaller sites in time.

Steel Beams

Every designer will tell you that you can build rooms to any size that you want — "Your imagination is the limit" or some such nonsense. But they may not explain that once a room gets wider than the normal span for a floor joist you will run into extra costs because you have to fit a beam across the middle to split the loading. This width varies with the size and frequency of the floor joists, but once you get over 4m, your costs start to rise substantially. Steel beams themselves are not wildly expensive — a 102x178mm steel channel would cost less than £12/lin.m — but however they are fixed they take a lot of work. If they are set inside the floor void, the floor joists will all have to be hung off the steel; if the steel is put below the ceiling then

Steel partitioning is slowly gaining acceptance with housebuilders

it will have to be boxed in with plasterboard. Steel also needs looking after; it needs a coat of paint and it needs protecting from the threat of fire — usually this is achieved by fixing two thicknesses of plasterboard around it. Despite its inherent strength, steel is actually one of the first things to give in a serious fire so steel beams normally get extra fire protection.

Inserting a steel beam of around 5m length is likely to add around £200 (Mats £70, Lab £130) to construction costs. If you decide to make a feature of it and add an arch below it as well, this will add another £50-£100 to the total, depending on the complexity and size.

Other Beams

Timber framers tend to use specialised beams when they want to create wider than average rooms. If you are using a post and beam system of construction such as employed by some timber frame companies like Potton Timber or Border Oak, the solution comes complete with the house as they use the massive post and beam timbers to hang the rest of the house off. A more usual situation is to use a flitch beam which is a piece of steel sandwiched between timbers. Flitch beams can be made up on site and are subject to the same sort of cost provisos as regular steel beams. There are various other types and styles of timber beam available; one worthy of mention is the glulam (pronounced *glue-lam*) beam which is made up of hundreds of small timber sections *glue*d and *lam*inated together. Glulam beams are rather more expensive than steel on a strength for price basis but they have the big advantage that they look good, good enough to leave exposed even though they look a little too modern for some traditional tastes. Most specialist timber merchants will stock several sizes from around £15-£40/lin.m depending on girth.

Internal studwork in a timber frame house

Roof Carcassing

There are two major competing techniques for building roofs. Traditionally, roof timbers were measured, cut and assembled on site — a skilled job involving complex setting-out procedures and cutting lots of obscure angles and notches. Traditional roof carpentry is an art form in itself and it has its own rich jargon involving the likes of rafters, purlins, collars and birdsmouths. However, the rise of the prefabricated roof truss is slowly but surely putting an end to all this. With trussed roofs, the brainwork is done by computer, the cutting by machine and the jargon is reduced to *fink* and *fan*, the two commonest truss designs. Erecting a series of roof trusses is generally a straightforward matter — hoist them into place, straighten them up, nail it on and add diagonal bracing. On a simple rectangular box-shaped structure, roof trusses are about three times quicker to erect than traditional roofs and, because of the inherent strength of each individual truss, they use considerably less timber — usually about 30% less by volume. On a detached house with a simple roof shape, the roof carpentry using trusses would cost around £1200 (Materials £800 Labour £400) compared to £2000 (M £1000, L £1000) for a traditionally cut roof with purlins.

Whereas traditional cut roofs are built from sawn carcassing, readily purchased from any builder's merchant, trussed roofing tends to get fabricated by specialists. Not that this should present a problem to builders: provided you can present a set of dimensioned plans, you will get a quote back usually within a few days. You can contact specialists or you can take your plans to any builder's merchant who will do the donkey work for you.

If you choose to build using trusses, bear in mind that prefabricated roof trusses are sensitive things and they perform well only if they are treated well:
- Care should be taken not to put any twist or undue load on to them, both whilst being handled and when being stored before erection.
- They should be stored upright on bearers (not standing on their feet).
- They should never be altered on site. They can't be cut around chimneys and openings, so you must get the plan accurately built.

Another tip is to set the truss spacings as accurately as possible using a 600mm spacing. This will pay dividends when it comes to tacking the metric length plasterboard sheets to the ceilings formed by the trusses. Many older tradesmen still habitually use imperial measurements and will tend to work to imperial spacings; usually this is not critical but in this case the difference between 2ft and 600mm can be measured in pounds sterling!

So why doesn't everybody use roof trusses? Well mostly they do but there are some situations where the traditional cut roof holds sway:
- Roof truss manufacturers sometimes get very busy and cannot deliver for several weeks.
- Complicated roof shapes take longer to build whichever system you use and the difference in erection speeds — which is the trusses' big selling point — is much less marked.

Consequently, many builders specify trusses for their main roofs, but prefer to stick with the traditional methods when it comes to odd jobs like building dormer windows, porches or garages.

Attic trusses

There is another reason why many builders dislike the trussed roof; it effectively eliminates use of the loft space for anything other than storage. The cross members which make up each truss cannot be removed or altered in any way and this prevents the roof space being opened up at a later date. There is, however, the possibility of using specialised attic trusses which are designed to leave the main loft space open so that any future loft conversion can be arranged with a minimum of fuss and expense. However, whilst the speed of installation is maintained, attic trusses are between two and three times the price of regular ones and this means that they effectively lose their cost advantage over traditionally cut roofs.

Room in the roof designs

Where overall roof heights are restricted, it is common to build the upper storey of a house projecting partly into the roofspace, as is the case with our benchmark house. When added to an existing dwelling this is usually referred to as a loft conversion but in a new build the convention is to give the upper floor at least a metre of vertical wall before the sloping (or raked) ceiling cuts in. This type of design is sometimes known as a one-and-a-half storey house.

If you are going for a room in the roof design — and many timber frame companies specialise in this style of home — there are a number of knock-on effects which you should be aware of. The internal sloping ceilings on these houses greatly limit what goes on underneath them; beds are usually OK, cupboards are difficult and planning a bathroom in such a space is something you should consider very carefully. You can end up with a lot of expensive dead space; you may like the idea of under-eaves cupboards or a basin in a sloping alcove, but you'll probably live to regret it and end up wishing for convenience rather than character. When comparing floor space costs, consider space under raked ceilings to be worth just that little bit less than space with full-height ceilings.

This is what is meant by the term one-and-a-half storey house. This one has two dormer windows flanking a Velux rooflight, lighting the hallway.

ROOFING JARGON BUSTER

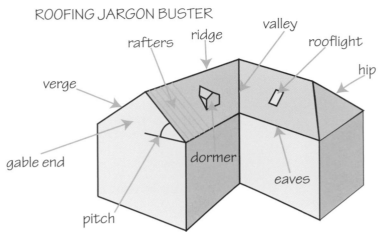

The prefabricated roof truss works most effectively when you are designing roofs that sit entirely above the upstairs room space. Then the horizontal section of the trusses can sit directly onto the wallplates at the top of the surrounding walls and form the ceiling joists for the upstairs rooms. When you introduce a raked ceiling you change the truss loadings and start having to use much wider rafter sections and if you have long sloping ceilings you will have to introduce a midway support beam known as a purlin: in effect you are back to constructing a traditional roof so again the supposed economies of prefabricated trusses largely disappear.

However there are roofing systems appearing now which address these problems. One such is a Dutch system called *Unidek* which is based on the idea of replacing rafters altogether with a series of insulated panels stretching from the ridge down to the eaves. It's a variation on the theme of using attic trusses to create an open space in the roof but its selling point is that it is lightweight and quick to install.

Vaulted ceilings

Some designs call for the room in the roof idea to be extended all the way up to the ridge beam at the apex of the roof. Here you have no flat ceiling area at all. This is a visually dramatic effect, often employed in barn conversions and new oak buildings where you have attractive timber rafters which are worth displaying in their own right. This is a world away from prefabricated roofing trusses, employing techniques of roof design similar to those used in mediaeval times.

Roof Windows

Once you have opted for a room in the roof design, you have to sort out how you will treat the windows for these rooms. When your natural window height coincides with a sloping ceiling you have two choices. You can "go with the roofline" and fit a sloping rooflight

window or you can "break through the roofline" and build a dormer. A dormer window is a fiddly construction. However they are formed, they involve building a sort of miniature house with walls, roofs and windows and then joining it seamlessly on to the main roof structure. Whilst this may appeal to the model makers amongst you, harassed builders in a hurry will not appreciate all this intricate detailing. People buying kit homes with dormers placed on the roof might think that they are avoiding all this hassle, but they will find that finishing dormer details is still a time-consuming business. The roofers have to form valleys and often stepped lead flashings, plasterers or bricklayers have to come back to fill in tiny wall spaces on the outside, and even tacking plasterboard on the inside calls for an ability to think three dimensionally. Another pitfall associated with some dormer designs occurs when they break the eaves gutter line of the main house, which results in extra rainwater downpipes; I have seen various ways people have tried to disguise this detail but none of them look particularly convincing.

Planners permitting, you can of course forget about dormers and fit opening roof lights. Velux is the big name in this field (though there are many others) and Velux rooflights

are very quick and easy to install; on a new building an opening rooflight will cost between £150 and £250 depending on size and will add virtually nothing to labour cost—it taking no longer to install than it does to fit the roof covering over the same space. In comparison, a simple dormer is likely to cost over £500. It may well be that your overall desired effect demands dormer windows in your roof and, if so, so be it. Just be aware that these types of windows (like bay windows) are not only expensive in themselves but are also heavy on management time. Unless very well planned out, they are more than likely to cause snags further on down the line.

If you are converting a barn you are likely to find that the planners will not allow dormer windows and will force you to use a rooflight. In response to this now well established pattern, Velux have produced a range of conservation rooflights which are designed to blend in with centuries-old buildings whilst still providing ease of opening and double glazing expected of modern roof windows. These conservation rooflights are however priced at a 30% premium to standard rooflights.

Open eaves (right) contrasts with the more common closed or boxed eaves detail (below)

Roof verge sits straight on top of the external wall

Here the roof verge rest on a timber barge board

Edge Details

One important detail to consider when thinking about roof designs is how to treat the roof edges. The ridges, hips and valleys will be sorted out by the roofing contractors, but the eaves and verge details are largely a matter of roof carpentry. Here, it makes no difference whether you've built a traditional cut roof or a trussed rafter one; you still have to sort out some sort of effective junction between the roof cover and the underlying structure.

Eaves

There are numerous variations on this theme, none of which is likely to cost less than about £12/lin.m (Mats £6, Labour £6) to fix (excluding decorating costs). If there is an industry standard detail it is the closed or boxed eaves. It would cost around £500 to surround a four bedroomed house and garage with this detail.

An alternative is to have open eaves. These are reckoned to look less modern and often more attractive. Some designs dispense with fascia boards altogether and allow guttering to be strapped on to the rafter feet — this is a particularly useful technique to employ with timber barn conversions where a fascia would look out of place — but the more usual method dispenses with just the soffit boards and leaves the rafter feet exposed. An open eaves detail is a little more expensive than boxed or soffitted eaves as you still have to provide a plywood plate (albeit above the rafter feet to catch the felt) and you are left with fiddly finishing details on the exposed underside.

More expensive still is to use the Georgian-style parapet. Here you build your external walls up above the eaves line and collect the rainwater draining off the roof in a hidden lead gutter behind the parapet. This technique was once common in inner-city housing terraces and large country houses, but nowadays tends to look a little bit pretentious — unless you happen to be building a large Georgian-style house.

Verges

Verges are only found over gable ends, so many houses without gables will have only eaves details. There are, again, two classic treatments of verge junction details. One is to lay the tiles or slates straight on to a bead of cement at the top of the supporting gable wall, the other is to oversail the wall and to finish the roof cover over a (usually timber) bargeboard. Each technique has its merits: the direct method can look horribly cheap but, equally well, is capable of being enhanced by using some fancy dog's-tooth brickwork: the bargeboard method is rather easier to install (it too can be enlivened by adding decorative effects).

Ventilation

It is surprising to many people that roof timbers do not need to be treated with preservatives (unless you live in a long horn beetle area, mostly south of London) but they do need good ventilation if they are to remain in peak condition. Where you have a conventional trussed roof where the upstairs living space does not project into the roofspace, the ventilation requirements are satisfied by the provision of a 10mm continuous air gap all the way around the eaves. You might think that this is a very straightforward matter but there is also concern that a ventilation gap shouldn't become an open doorway to birds and insects, and therefore there has grown up a whole industry making plastic roof vents which let air in and keep bugs out. There are several different types of vents; some are cut into the soffit boards, some are nailed on top of the fascia and some get fixed between the rafters. They range in price from £1-£3/lin.m. The roofing giants, Redland and Marley, both make proprietary ventilation systems but you will find better value from specialist producers like Glidevale and Rytons. Rytons, in particular, are geared to mail-order sales and produce a most helpful catalogue explaining the ins and outs of roof (and sub-floor) ventilation.

Ridge Ventilation

When you have a room in the roof design, roof ventilation becomes a more complex problem and care has to be taken to leave a airflow gap between the roofing felt and the insulation surrounding the living space. There is also a requirement for ventilation at the top of the roof, the ridge, and this can be expensive to achieve.

Plastic roof ventilation keeps bugs out but keeps the air flowing through the roof timbers

Building regulations for roof ventilation

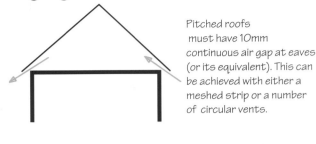

Pitched roofs
must have 10mm
continuous air gap at eaves
(or its equivalent). This can
be achieved with either a
meshed strip or a number
of circular vents.

If there is a "room in the
roof" design then this air
gap must be increased
to 25mm at the eaves
and you will be required
to supply some ridge
ventilation as well

Also here you must keep a
minimum air gap of 50mm
between the roof cover
and the insulation

50mm air gap

One way of achieving this is to fit a ventilated ridge, a plastic extrusion which fits under the ridge tiles: this has the advantage of being visually unobtrusive but it comes at a cost of around £18/lin.m, much more than the cost of the ridge tiles themselves. Alternatively there are several formats of ridge ventilation tiles now available: they are invariably expensive — expect to pay between £30 and £50 each — and unlike the dry ridge systems they are all too obvious from the ground.

Another reason to use roof or ridge vented tiles is when you have an internal soil pipe or an extract fan that are most conveniently ducted up through the roof space. Glidevale produce the most complete catalogue of roof ventilation and also some of the best solutions for these types of problems.

If you are working with a handmade tile, Tudor Roof Tiles produce an Invisible Venting System which uses the natural camber present on most handmade tiles to provide adequate ventilation space to take the foul air away from extractor fans and soil pipes.

RedBank (01530 270333) produce a vented ridge tile suitable for taking the exhaust from gas fired appliances: it's called a low resistance terminal and it costs around £55. Smoke from solid fuel fires has to be expelled via the more traditional chimney arrangements.

Roof Covers

There are many different materials you can use to cover your roof but before we go on to examine them consider first that virtually every housing estate in the country has a concrete tiled roof. Why? Simply a question of cost — concrete tiles are an amazingly cheap way to provide a roof cover and, designed well, they can look very effective. Yet more often the overall look is much more likely to be modern and featureless.

Another plus point for concrete interlocking tiles is that they can be laid at very shallow pitches, some at as little as 14°, whereas the more traditional tiles often demand roof pitches of 35°. Low-pitched roofs have two

advantages over steep-pitched roofs: their surface area is less — this makes for savings on roofing materials — and they are less visible, therefore the visual impact of any roof covering is diminished. Note however that if you are trying to recreate an older style of building, a low pitched roof will probably look out of place.

Concrete v Clay

In contrast to concrete a clay tile is seen as an upmarket product and people often enthuse about how much better they look but, ultimately, it's a question of personal taste. The most attractive tiles do tend to be made of clay — the colours seem to be that much

more vibrant — but an awful lot of clay tiles look no different to concrete and often only a roofer could tell you what you've got on your roof. Note that concrete tiles are usually what is known as *large format* which means that they are big — often measuring 330x270mm, the size of six plain tiles; you don't need very many and this fact alone makes them much quicker to lay. Large format concrete tiles start losing their cost advantage on complex roof shapes with lots of cuts, so you tend to see them on very simple roof designs.

Handmade clay tiles are something else and, like handmade bricks, they tend to lend a strong vernacular flavour to any building they are put on. However, handmade clay tiles are also amazingly expensive, costing around five times as much to supply and fix as the basic concrete interlocking tile.

The roof tile market is dominated by two giants, Redland and Marley. Redland set the standards to which others aspire and if you want to get a better understanding of the possibilities with tile coverings, you should get hold of their Roof Tile Product Selector (01737 242488 — should be free if you ask nicely); it's an incredibly useful 14 page booklet which will probably tell you more than you ever want to know about roof tiling (unless of course you are a roofer). Redland tend to be more expensive than the competition (at least on single site developments) and you may find better prices if you chase Marley roofing or one of the smaller manufacturers such as Sandtoft, Russell or Weatherwell. Most roofing contractors have cosy relationships with one particular manufacturer and you may well find that it pays you not to be too picky as to whose tile goes on your roof. Handmade tiles tend to be the province of smaller producers: if you have a deep wallet, look at Acme, Keymer and Tudor who produce visually stunning roof tiles that are brand new yet manage to look at least 200 years old.

If you crave the look of an traditionally tiled roof but your budget doesn't stretch that far, Forticrete produce a large format concrete tile called the *Gemini* which simulates the plain tile look.

Slate

Slate became the preferred roofing choice of the Victorians when the railways provided access to the cheap Welsh slate quarries. The slate is still there but it is no longer cheap; indeed it is up there with handmade tiles and thatch as one of the most expensive options for the pitched roof. In rural areas, slate is unlikely to be most people's first choice. However planners often insist on slate roofs for the flimsiest of reasons and it is as well to be aware of the possibilities

If you want slate but are reluctant to pay the going rate for new Welsh slate there are a number of other options. You can look to source your slate from Spain or South America: prices are much cheaper than Welsh slate but quality has been patchy and it's worth looking out for slate carrying a 30 year guarantee. Alternatively you can track down a supplier of second hand slate. Prices are similar to imported slate and quality is similarly variable but, if you know what to look for, it's relatively easy to assess the quality of a recycled slate and it can make a very good buy. There are also a number of slate substitutes on the market. The cheapest are the asbestos cement slates — surprisingly, this is one of the few applications in construction where asbestos is still used. At this end of the slate market you get something that looks wholly industrial and is liable to warp and discolour over time.

There are also a number of interesting slate products, usually made out of reconstituted slate dust. Redland produce the best known reconstituted slate called the *Cambrian* and Eternit are launching a similar product called the *Melbourn*: they are, in fact, not traditional slates at all but interlocking tiles. It is a mid-priced alternative to the natural slates and the unimpressive artificials. However many planning officers will insist on you using natural slates, even though they couldn't tell the difference when laid on a roof.

Stone Belt Roofing

Don't think that you can get away with just a stone facade if you live in an area where stone is the predominant building material. For

Above: Marley Mendips are one of the cheapest concrete roof coverings available. Almost every commercial developer uses something like this. In contrast (below left), handmade clay tiles will cost about five times as much whilst a reclaimed Welsh slate roof (below right) will be three times the price.

7I: Roof Coverings Guide Prices

> ACCESSORIES includes underfelt and battens together with an allowance for standard roofing fittings like ridge tiles, eaves tiles, valleys and hips, verge undercloaks, lead flashings around chimneys and at roof abutments. The benchmark house is a good example because it has all of these features: if you had an extremely complicated shaped roof your accessories figure could easily double up costs.

	COST per 1000	NO. NEEDED per m²	COST per m²	ACCESS-ORIES per m²	LABOUR per m²	SUPPLY + FIX RATE per m²	OVERALL COST ON TEST HOUSE 210 m²
TILES							
Concrete Interlocking	£500	10	£5.00	£5.00	£3.00	**£13.00**	£2,730
Clay Pantile	430	16	£6.90	7.00	5.50	**19.40**	£4,074
Concrete Plain	220	60	£13.20	7.00	8.00	**28.20**	£5,922
Clay Plain	260	60	£15.60	7.00	8.00	**30.60**	£6,426
Handmade Tile	700	50	£35.00	15.00	10.00	**60.00**	£12,600
ARTIFICIAL SLATES				0.00			£0
Asbestos Cement	620	13.3	8.20	5.00	5.00	**18.20**	£3,822
Asbestos-free	840	13.3	11.20	5.00	5.00	**21.20**	£4,452
Simulated Natural	1400	13.3	18.60	5.00	5.00	**28.60**	£6,006
Redland Richmond	600	11.1	6.70	5.00	5.00	**16.70**	£3,507
Redland Cambrian	1300	13.3	17.30	5.00	5.00	**27.30**	£5,733
NATURAL SLATE				0.00			£0
Spanish	950	20	19.00	5.00	8.50	**32.50**	£6,825
Reclaimed Welsh	950	20	20.00	5.00	8.50	**33.50**	£7,035
Welsh	2000	20	40.00	5.00	8.00	**53.00**	£11,130
Westmoreland	varies		40.00	7.00	12.00	**59.00**	£12,390
SLATE/TILES				0.00			£0
Mini Stonewold	550	9.9	5.40	6.00	5.00	**16.40**	£3,444
OTHERS							£0
Lead			20.00	5.00	30.00	**55.00**	£11,550
Felt						**15.00**	£3,150
Reed Thatch						**60.00**	£12,600
Cedar Shingles			24.00	6.00	10.00	**40.00**	£8,400

sure, you will be required to lay a stone tile roof to match your neighbours. Local material prices vary from quarry to quarry but are invariably high. I was quoted "a penny a square inch" (£16/m²) by one salvage yard for

Coursed stone tiling is another expensive option, but it almost always looks good

Westmoreland slate which puts it on a par with the other very expensive roof covers you could possibly choose. There are numerous cheaper, artificial alternatives around (e.g. Redland's *Stonewold* range) which will not look in the least bit convincing but using them may save you several thousand pounds. Again you face a tricky task reconciling your budget with the demands of your local planners.

Shingles

Another old vernacular stand-by is the cedar shingle. A shingle is a tile fashioned out of cedar wood and is usually supplied in random widths to give a broken up effect. It is a reasonably hard wearing material — though not as good as clay, slate or concrete — and it is used just as often to do vertical wall panels as it is pitched roofing. Cedar is a naturally durable timber which doesn't require any treatment or staining and, if you covet a genuine timber house then shingles will be your chosen roofing material.

Thatch

This is really one for enthusiasts. People do build new thatched houses — about one every year. Not only is it very expensive, but there are numerous regulations about where thatch can go on new building — for a start it has to be 12m from any neighbouring dwellings. Thatch is not something that can be added as an afterthought; if you are really serious about it you must design the roof around the thatch.

Sheet Roofing

Sheet roofing is often associated with flat roofing and there is very little flat roofing being built today. There is nothing intrinsically wrong with flat roofing, but too much cheap felt got stuck on too many cheap houses in the 60s and the bitter taste of continual roof repairs has yet to fade away.

You might, however, be considering flat roofing for, say, a roof garden or a balcony. Be aware that the durability of a flat roof is almost entirely dependent on how much you spend on it. Mineral felts are the cheapest covering (at around £10/m², supplied and fixed, but don't expect much more than about fifteen years lifespan); areas which are to get walked over really require something a bit stronger like asphalt (about £25/m²) or lead (around £50/m²).

Sheet metals such as lead and copper actually make very stylish coverings for pitched roofs but their expense means that they are rarely seen on new housing.

Tile Weight

Roofing materials vary enormously in weight. For example:

* Lightweight slate   20kg/m²
* Concrete interlocking tile 45kg/m²
* Plain tile   90kg/m²

Does this matter? Well it matters to the roof designer that the timbers holding up the roof should be strong enough to bear the imposed load but the effect on cost is surprisingly small, particularly if roof trusses are being used. The cost of using a roof truss system for a heavy roof covering will add about 10% to the truss cost — probably less than £100 for a detached house.

Felt and Battens

Building regulations require that whatever (pitched) roof covering you decide on there should be a layer of roofing felt underneath. At a cost of less than 50p/m² this is no great cost and it has the added advantage for quick builders of providing a temporary waterproof cover for work going on below. Felting takes place simultaneously with battening, which is necessary to provide fixings for the tiles or slates. On all but the largest houses, the whole process of felting and battening usually takes roofers no more than a day and costs around £2.00/m² (M £1.00, L £1.00). Don't make the mistake of felting and battening before choosing a roof covering: the spacing of the battens is set by the gauge of slate or tile and the gauges are very variable.

One interesting development is Tyvek, a roofing felt that breathes. Although its expensive to buy — two to three times the price of ordinary roofing felt — it has a distinct advantage in that in enables water vapour inside the roof space to permeate through the layer: thus using Tyvek eliminates the need for ventilation channels in certain roof designs.

Additional Fittings

As most roofing is carried out by specialist contractors, usually on a supply and fix basis, there is perhaps not the need to know so much about the intricacies of roofing. However, there is a lot more to a roof than its slates or tiles and on a typical detached house the

actual roof tile may make up no more than 50% of the overall roofing material costs. The most visible additional element is the ridge and/or hip tiles (usually around 20% of cost); the underfelt and battens (12%) are the other significant costs. Ventilation gear, which is often fitted by roofers, is another expensive item. Table 7m illustrates the extent of additional items on the roof of the benchmark house.

If you are planning to purchase your own materials then you can take advantage of one of the roofing suppliers own quantity estimating services. Redland's is contactable on 01525 850400: their shopping lists are usually very accurate.

Hip Treatments

The hip is the name given to an external angle in a roof — an internal angle is called a valley — and the standard way of finishing a hip is to use something very similar to a conventional ridge tile, although the hipped version is sometimes slightly differently shaped. This is a cheap and quick specification, costing no more than about £10/lin.m (M £4, L £6) and it is really the only practical way of finishing a concrete interlocking tiled roof. However, if you are planning on a plain tiled roof there is an alternative which is to fix bonnets which look very rural and vernacular. However, bonneted hips are way more expensive both in labour and materials (you'll need something like 10 bonnets/lin.m as opposed to 2 hip tiles) and the rate per linear meter works out at over £35 (M £25, L £10). An even more expensive option, which is most often seen on slate roofs, is to cut the tiles or slates to meet exactly over the hip. This is known as a close-mitred hip and it tends to be preferred by those going for neat, unfussy solutions. It is heavy on the old labour and it is relies on underlying lead soakers to be effective which makes it cost in excess of £40/lin.m.

Standard Hip Treatments

Hip tiles — £10/lin.m

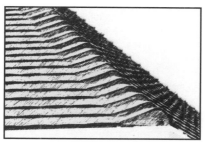

Bonnets — £35/lin.m

Close mitred hips — £40/lin.m

7m: The Roofer's Shopping List

WHAT WAS NEEDED	HOW MANY	HOW MUCH
Second hand Welsh Slates	4200	£ 4,200
Ridge and Hip Tiles	55	130
Marley's Ventilated Ridge	8 packs	230
Nails and Ironmongery		45
20x1m Felt Rolls @ £6.00ea	20	120
25x38 Battens @ 18p/m	900m	160
Verge Undercloak	27m	15
Lead slates	2No	30
Code 4 Chimney Flashing	3mx450mm	35
Code 4 Step Flashings	35mx150mm	95
Code 3 Lead for soakers	12mx150	30
TOTAL		**£ 5,090**

Bonnets and close-mitred hips may sound like unnecessary extravagances, but although they are way more expensive than hip tiles, the total length of hips to cover is often not that much and specifying something different here has a marked effect on kerb appeal.

Valleys

Another cost-sensitive area of roofing is the valley which is formed when two roof lines meet on an internal corner. The valley is not as visually prominent as the hip and this makes it a candidate for treating as cheaply as possible. The commonest way of doing this is by fitting a purpose-made valley gutter and cutting the tiles or slates around it. Here, fibreglass is tending to replace lead; it's quite a bit cheaper and much quicker to lay but labour costs are still significant. Valley gutters cost around £17/lin.m. when done in fibreglass, rising to £30/lin.m when finished in lead.

On plain tile roofs there is the alternative of using purpose-made valley tiles which are very similar to inverted bonnet hip tiles. Again, this is an expensive option — £35/lin.m (M £25, L £10) — but it is worth considering around features like dormer windows where the valleys are visible from the ground.

Verges

If you are roofing up to a gable wall, you will need to form some effective junction at the verge. The simplest method is to lay a mini-soffit board (known as an undercloak) on top of the brickwork (or timber bargeboard if one is specified), run the roof cover up to the edge of the undercloak and then fill the void between with cement. Such an arrangement costs no more than £3/lin.m to execute and is no different whether the roof cover is slate, tile or stone. There are alternatives; Redland make a concrete wrap over tile that can be used with certain tile covers and there is even a plastic verge system. However, these other methods all cost around double the cement undercloak technique and they add nothing to the look of your roof edge.

Decorative Accessories

Whilst most fittings are purely functional, occasionally a decorative touch can make a very plain roof exciting. Caught by the general trend for all things vernacular, roofing manufacturers have been busy reproducing Victorian embellishments like cockscomb ridge tiles and fleur-de-lys finials. Handle with care; in the right place these can look fantastic but on most roofs they look plain silly. Similarly, two-tone effect roofing (either with contrasting tile colours or accentuated ridge tiles) is invariably very striking — but

that doesn't always mean it works. If you see a roof you like, photograph it and show it to your roofer for quotation. Chances are it will be out of your price bracket!

Dry Tech Systems

The parts of the roof most vulnerable to weather damage are the perimeter areas like ridges, hips and verges. The traditional way of fixing ridge, hip and verge tiles is to bed them in cement. For some time now the tile manufacturers have been trying to persuade us to use dry systems, which clip together with a series of mechanical fixings, but there is a general reluctance to take up their offers partly because of the higher prices charged for these fittings and partly because the look is even more modern and nondescript than the conventional roof. Note that in Scotland, dry verges are the norm and that housebuilders seeking a low maintenance finish are also specifying them — cement fillets on roof edges are notoriously brittle.

Fires and Chimneys

Functionally, central heating has made the fireplace redundant yet the fireplace lives on in most new family homes. If you want to save money building your home and you want a "green", low-running cost style of house, then you will be doing yourself a great favour by cutting out all plans for room fires of whatever type. Trouble is — what do you put in the middle of the living room wall? Without a fireplace something is missing. It's like a church without an altar — it just doesn't look right. A living-room fire on a cold winter's night feels so good because it strikes a chord with the caveman or woman inside us all, whose control of fire was the very thing that separated us from the wild beasts roaming outside. In other words, we are in the land of the adman's "aspirational purchases." This particular aspiration is so strong that most housebuilders would not dare to challenge it, though an increasing number of new houses are getting built without traditional fireplaces.

The benchmark house is no exception to the general rule. There is a fireplace located centrally on the side wall of the living room. By most people's standards, it's quite a modest affair but, just by putting it there at all, it added £1200 to the cost of the house, of which 75% is down to the chimney building costs, 25% to the fire and fireplace.

Fire Options

Open Fires

Just about the simplest option available is what Complete Fabrications chose to do, and that is to form an opening using a fireback unit. Ventilation is provided by an airbrick opening somewhere in the vicinity of the fireplace, and the house is sold without a fire basket or grate of any description. For just over £100 more you can fit a purpose-made fire basket complete with ventilation and removable ashcan — the Baxi *Burnall* is the best known — and if you want a regular fire this is a worthwhile addition.

Stoves

Another approach is to take the fire out into the room space and contain it in a metal surround — the stove. This is a thermally much more efficient way of heating a room (though even the most efficient cast iron stoves are no match for a new oil- or gas-fired boiler) and is much favoured by hippies living in isolated cottages. However, in a new house it probably represents the worst of both worlds in that a) you don't actually need a stove for room heating and b) you loose the sexiness of having open fire in your living room. Most solid-fuel stoves are very traditional in appearance and they are not cheap.

A more detailed discussion of the merits of stoves appears in the section Alternative Heating in Chapter 8.

Gas Fires

For those who cannot be doing with the hassle of solid fuel but still want a focal point fire, then gas fires may be the answer. You can buy a student digs style gas fire such as Valor's *Firelite* for around £80, or you can get gas fires which can be inset into a fireplace (£200 upwards). Of more interest to new housebuilders will be the balanced-flue gas fires like the Canon *Coalridge* and the Valor *Flamenco* (£280 plus) which can be set on any outside wall and don't need a chimney at all, which makes for a very cheap way of getting a focal point fire into a living space. There is also a range of decorative effect gas fires — what I call *Loggy-Glows* — which heat up ceramic coal and logs. By the time you've fitted them with decorative fire baskets and decorative fire surrounds you won't have much change from £250 and you still have to fit a chimney to take away the exhaust gases.

Electric Fires

Ever keen to compete with gas, there are a number of electric *Living Flame* effect fires. As these are a poor imitation of a gas fire making a poor imitation of a coal fire I can't see them being hugely fancied by new housebuilders but, in this business, choice is king and it would be ungracious of me not to mention them in passing. Prices range from £70 for a free standing 2kW (bar) fire with plastic logs stuck on top to £300 for ones which have a flame effect glow going on in the background. Electricity showrooms are the place to view them.

Chimney Options

Masonry

The standard way of evacuating smoke from fires is via a brick- or block-built chimney, the higher the better. The standard way to do this is to use clay flue liners set into an insu-

The fireplace used in the benchmark house is a simple affair, mostly made out of MDF

lated cement screed, built up with the masonry work. It makes little difference to cost whether this chimney is built against an internal or an external wall — though there is a small cost penalty when building a masonry chimney in a timber frame house. In many traditionally styled homes, a large fireplace and chimney are designed to be the very heart of the house; for instance, Potton Homes, who specialise in creating Tudor style interiors, indicate that the construction costs of an inglenook fireplace and chimney suitable for one of their *Heritage* homes would cost around £4000, which is probably as much as would be spent on the kitchen in such a house; this figure could be quartered if you specified a simpler style of chimney but you would of course loose the splendour of the timber-beamed, brick-faced fireplace.

Feature chimneys, as opposed to feature fireplaces, are another money soaker. The old English (or Jacobean) chimney is enjoying something of a revival. On a steeply pitched roof with a handmade roof tile it can look fantastic, but it is likely to take three or four days to build and will add not less than £500 to the chimney costs. If your budget doesn't stretch to ornamental brickwork, you might be interested in just an ornamental chimney pot. Salvage yards usually have stacks of them and Redbank produce a wide range at costs between £10 and £700.

Stainless Steel

There are a number of outfits producing stainless steel flues which can be used instead of a conventional chimney. Check out Selkirk and Brefco. A stainless steel insulated flue is

7n: Benchmark House: Fire and Chimney Costs

	QUANTITY		RATE	TOTAL
Extra Brickwork	10	m²	£ 27.00	£270
Extra Blockwork	10	m²	12.00	£120
Extra for High Work	8	lm	40.00	£320
Form Lead Roof Flashings	1		40.00	£40
Redbank Fyrerite Chimney Units	1	No.	60.00	£60
Flue Liners 300hx225mm	27	No.	5.50	£150
Chimney Pot	1	No.	12.00	£12
Firebacks	1		45.00	£45
Extra for Fireplace Construction	1		150.00	£150
Fire Surround	1	No	24.00	£24
Tiled Hearth	1	m²	30.00	£30
Damper/airbrick	1		40.00	£40
TOTAL				**£1,300**

Stainless steel flue terminals can ruin a traditional roofline

Very popular in Scandinavia, the best known names in the UK are Isokern (01202 861650) and Anki (01926 842545). They produce a pumice stone chimney lining system which fits together like Lego and has the advantage of being pre-insulated. One of the problems with conventional, flue-lined chimneys is that the temperature of the escaping smoke drops substantially as it rises up the chimney, causing both condensation and tar deposition; this is a noted problem when relatively high temperature stoves are being used. Ideally the chimney linings should be insulated as constructed but this is frequently not done and specifying a pre-insulated lining such as Anki or Isokern (or one of the stainless steel ones) should alleviate the problem. On the benchmark house, a pumice stone chimney system would have added £300 to construction costs.

not cheap: it would cost more than £500 to purchase an 8m-long system for the benchmark house, which is about twice as much as the materials for a conventional chimney — but there are a number of plus points worth examining:
- They allow total flexibility as regards siting
- They are quick and easy to install
- They work rather better than regular chimneys.
- They need very little cleaning

- They are particularly well suited to timber frame construction.

The biggest downside to using these systems is the look of the flue terminals. Instead of a traditional brick chimney you get an industrial looking stainless steel flue terminal; this can look fine in modern designs of housing but if you aspire to the trad then it looks pretty awful.

Rainwater

For some time now plastic — uPVC in particular — has been the housebuilder's favourite material for removing water from both the inside and outside of the house. uPVC is cheap, it's light, it's easily cut and, most importantly, it's very easy to join up — with the aid of a few rubber gaskets. However, whilst the internal waste pipes and underground drain runs are hidden from view, the guttering and downpipes remain all too visible. Most designers reckon on trying to minimise the impact of these details and some will go to considerable lengths to make it look as if a house doesn't have any guttering or downpipes. Incidentally, our most famous architect, Sir Richard Rogers, has turned this assumption on its head and designs buildings (like the Lloyd's building in London) where all you can see is the service pipes, lift shafts and downpipes, which he then paints lurid colours. But then he doesn't design speculative housing.

Back in the Real Worlde, you will find that your main weapon in detailing guttering is disguise. The manufacturers produce plastic guttering in a choice of four colours — black, grey, white and brown — and these are reckoned to cover most of the regular fascia colours. In the old days, gutters were made of cast iron and were painted with the rest of the house, but plastic guttering is not designed for painting — indeed that's the whole point about it.

Technically, there's really very little to it and it's a job that's ideally suited to the D-I-Y housebuilder. Osma, the market leaders, produce a wonderfully concise Installation Guide which will tell you more than you would ever want to know about falls and flow capacities. Having said that it's quite easy to install incorrectly; one frequent error is putting in downpipe connectors the wrong way up, which you won't even notice — until it rains heavily.

Deeper Sections

Whilst the best you can really hope to do with plastic guttering is to get it to blend into the background, the idea with downpipes is to have as few of them as possible and to locate them where they have the least visual impact. One way of achieving this goal is to use deeper guttering sections which are capable of holding more water and, therefore, need

fewer outlets. Osma produce an *Amazon* gutter section which will drain over 100m² of roof area, as opposed to the 57m² maximum specified for their standard *RoundLine* section. Now, the *Amazon* is over twice the price of the *RoundLine*, but specifying it can sometimes actually save money by cutting down on both the number of downpipes and the length of underground drainage work.

Alternative Materials

There are two drawbacks to using plastic guttering. One is that, as discussed, it all looks rather naff; the other is that it isn't actually any good. uPVC guttering generally, and the rubber jointing gaskets in particular, seem to break down under the effects of bright sunlight and the effective lifespan of a uPVC rainwater system is probably only about 10 years. Expect to start replacing bits after this time. Manufacturing standards have increased somewhat over recent years and you can improve the overall performance of your guttering by choosing a plastic system with a high-gloss finish (Osma, Terrain) which is better at reflecting sunlight, but if you want a much better performance, then you should consider using different materials.

The trouble is the alternatives are all very much more expensive. Our benchmark house has 50m of guttering and 20m of downpipe: it cost on the benchmark house for £480 (Mats £260, Lab £220) which is just under £7/lin.m. There is really nothing else to touch this on price. Cast iron and aluminium are the most commonly specified alternatives for this job but expect to pay over £12/lin.m for either of them. Cast iron is heavy and needs painting but looks authentically traditional; best known manufacturer is Glynwed, the Aga makers. Aluminium in contrast looks high tech and can be erected without jointing (called *seamless guttering*); to find out more look in your Yellow Pages under "Guttering Services."

Conversions

It is worth noting that there are a number of different types of gutter bracket designed to cope with situations where you don't have a regular fascia board to attach to. Particularly useful is the *rafter arm* which attaches itself directly onto the feet of the rafters; also note that virtually all manufacturers produce a rise and fall extension arm which will allow you to build the gutter bracket into the masonry and then make the height adjustments after you have fitted the guttering.

House building inspired by the Richard Rogers school of architecture

Recycling

There is no reason to stop you putting some of this mildly acidic rainwater to good use before pouring it all away. Many people will be interested in building in rainwater butts and these can be made much more useful and more productive if they are designed in from the beginning. For around £10, you can add a *rain diverter* to your downpipes which will not only redirect your rain into a tank but is also intelligent enough to know when the tank is full and then redirect the rain back down the downpipe. If you want to use the rainwater for domestic purposes — and there's good money to be saved here — you are talking more serious underground storage tanks and pumps. May I refer you to the section called *Saving Water* in Chapter 10.

Conservatories

Adding a conservatory is big business in the home refurbishment market but comparatively small beer in the world of new building — only about 1% of new homes are built with conservatories. Why should that be? Well, for one thing, a conservatory is much more expensive to build than an ordinary extension. The substructural works are no different but both glass walls and glass roofing are more expensive than traditional building methods, and these combine to make the costs of conservatories range from around £500/m^2 to over £1000/m^2. In comparison, the basic cost of an extension would be less than £300/m^2. The reasons for this are not hard to fathom; whereas a developer might spend around £40/m^2 on external walling and £30/m^2 on roof carpentry and coverings combined, the cost of toughened double-glazed units alone is £40/m^2 and normally a conservatory's glazing costs are much less than the cost of the surrounding frames.

Conservatories also cost a lot to keep warm in winter and require specialised (i.e. expensive) blinds and fans if they are to be kept cool in summer. You can, of course, choose to not use your conservatory when it's either too hot or too cold or too dark, but that's an awful lot of times for a room that's so expensive to build and it makes little sense when you consider the size of the initial investment. Furthermore, conservatories add little if anything to house values — not everyone loves them.

Alternatives

Adding a conservatory onto a *new* house is usually a sign that the original design work is not what it might have been. Conservatories are expensive and problematical, and whereas they may make stunning and effective extensions to existing houses, their role in a new house is not at all clear. If you feel you need a conservatory to add that certain panache to your dream home, then you may just have under-designed the house in the first place. A rethink on the basic layout would probably save you money and give you a better house to boot.

If you want more living space, think of incorporating a south-side summer room (with lots of windows and a french/patio door) and a north-facing winter room designed for cosy dark nights around the fireside. If you really want glazed roofing, consider fitting two or more large Velux rooflights in a lean-to section. Veluxes are much easier to clean and are easily openable, making ventilation a doddle; this way you can achieve some of the benefits of a conservatory without the drawbacks.

Aspirations

Despite my reservations I must admit that there are certain situations where a conservatory comes into its own. Sunday lunch in April, reading the newspaper on a sunny winter's morn, sundowners on long summer evenings among the potted plants. Rather like an Aga, the conservatory forms part of many peoples dreams of stylish living and, however inappropriate in a new house, some people cannot be without them. In advertising jargon, conservatories are another "aspirational purchase" for romantics and who am I to decry their pleasures? Shame on my puritanical self.

Though not fundamentally different to any other types of building, conservatory construction has evolved into a specialist trade. Many glazing firms have branched out into designing and building conservatories, and many of them offer an all-in-one design and

Professional housebuilders are sometimes heard to refer to conservatories as "bolt-ons": contrast the integral "wrap around" sun room taking shape below with a Wimpey showhouse conservatory, bearing little relation to the adjacent house.

build service. Styles range from utilitarian greenhouse to ornate Victorian complete with fancy ridge pieces; structures are commonly built from timber, aluminium or uPVC. Budget conservatories can be picked up from the D-I-Y sheds and Wickes, whilst the more upmarket structures are dominated by the likes of Amdega and Portland who advertise heavily in the national press.

If you are interested in designing and building your own conservatory there are a number of specialists who produce the structural channel sections to order. Check Alcan Metal Centres or Conservatory Fittings.

SAP ratings

Note that conservatories are now included in the energy-loss calculations for new homes and that if you are planning to include one in your design, you may be in for a shock because glass doesn't perform well in the old-U value stakes. You may have to use special energy saving Low E glass and you may well have to take other (expensive) energy saving measures on board in order to qualify for an appropriate SAP rating.

Garages

In common with almost all new house developments built in the UK, the benchmark house has a garage. In this particular case it is an attached double garage, sharing a wall with the utility room and also housing the oil-fired boiler. It cost £9000 to build (£30/m^2) which makes it a very expensive garage for a development, probably about £2500 over the odds. The added cost comes about largely because of two factors. One is the clay soil which required a beam and block floor which itself requires a reinforced concrete slab to be laid on it because it has to be able to take a jack loading — this in effect doubles the floor costs. The other is the already noted effect of having to use a natural slate roof cover. Whichever way you look at it, a garage is deemed to be a necessity and it usually costs around 10% of the overall building budget to construct it.

Is a Garage Necessary?

Before you commit yourself to spending good money on garage space consider for a moment whether it is really necessary. Although current fashions in house styles tend towards the traditional, there is absolutely nothing traditional about a garage. Its nearest equivalent in pre-20th century housing is the stable or, perhaps, the cowshed; but the housing of cars is an altogether different affair. Furthermore, whilst thirty or forty years ago it was a good idea to keep vehicles undercover to facilitate winter starts and to stop rust, cars these days are made to very much higher standards and it is really not necessary to keep them undercover. Nowadays, security is often cited as a reason for building garages — but does this really justify spending as much on a garage as it costs to buy a small car? And for many practised car thieves, a locked garage doesn't really represent much

of an obstacle in any event, especially as people tend to be much less security conscious on outbuildings.

Other Functions

Of course, garages have many other uses besides providing undercover car parking, as is shown by the numbers of people who have them but never park their cars anywhere near them. Solid fuel, tools, lawnmowers, gardening equipment, bicycles, golf clubs, baby buggies, deep freezes, paddling pools, paint, you name it, it gets stored out there, and very useful it is too. But if you are designing a house from scratch, you may come to the conclusion that what you need is a larger utility room or a basement, not a garage. Garages are obviously valued by a great number of people otherwise speculative developments wouldn't include them as a matter of course, but don't just fall into the trap of assuming that a house must have a garage because it's not a proper house without one.

When To Build It?

You can, of course, decide to leave the construction of a garage until an unspecified later date. If it is included in on your planning permission drawings, then the right to build it cannot be taken away once you have started the main house. *NB This ruling goes for conservatories, swimming pools and any other fancy accoutrements that you aspire to but can't afford.* Therefore just drawing the plans in might represent a good compromise solution for those who don't really need a garage but worry that the house might be difficult to sell without one. Against this, you should be aware that any building work that takes place after you move into a house will not be exempt from VAT, so it will cost you 17.5% more to construct. Also, it is worth pointing out that many people find it very useful to build the garage *before* the rest of the house as it provides a useful and secure store-cum-site hut whilst the main construction work forges ahead. Indeed, with a little bit of adaptation, you could just about live in a garage for a few months — certainly not much worse than the average caravan.

Siting

By and large, house designers do not like garages. They are difficult. On most sites, access demands that they are located somewhere prominent near the frontage and yet, by their very nature, they are more akin to outbuildings and sheds. Now, polite architectural convention dictates that you don't put a humble shed in the front garden and so you are left with the problem of having to make the garage look good without costing too much.

Integral

One way around this conundrum is to have an integral garage, that is, one that is built into or at least attached to the main house.

For

- It makes for a more effective utility room type garage if that's what you have in mind
- You can use it to house boilers and freezers
- The arrangement fits better on narrow fronted sites (under 15m wide).

Against

It doesn't usually do much for the look of a house. Most garage doors are better suited to largely unseen parts of your estate — i.e. they are naff — and placing one prominently in your front elevation can be very ugly. The problem of the garage door is particularly acute when you are building in a traditional style. One way of alleviating it is to have an "L" shaped house and to tuck the garage into the bit of the L that projects forward towards the road. This softens the impact of the integral garage on the all important kerb appeal.

Detached

Given a site without space constraints, most builders will plump for a detached garage. The main attraction of this arrangement is that it maintains the integrity of the house design but, even so, this can still be overwhelmed by the siting of the garage. Ideally, this will be well away to one side but most plots these days are not large enough to make this a viable option and so very often the house is half-hidden by the detached garage in front of it. Effectively, this means that the garage plays a crucial role in people's initial views of a house, and developers have responded to this by spending more and more money on the external appearances of the detached garage, commonly including fancy roofing effects not seen on the main house.

7p: Benchmark House: Garage Costs

GROUNDWORKS		**£2760**
Clearing Oversite		200
Excavating Foundations		320
Concrete Foundations		800
Garage Floor		960
Rainwater Drains		480
MASONRY		**£1380**
Garage Blockwork		640
Garage Plinth Brickwork		560
Steel/Lintels		180
FIRST FIX CARPENTRY		**£1300**
Garage Roof Carpentry		1300
JOINERY/GLAZING		**£85**
Windows		55
Glazing		30
ROOFING/SCAFFOLD		**£1790**
Roofing		1470
Rainwater Goods		150
Scaffolding		170
PLASTERING		**£ 310**
External Render		310
GARAGE DOORS (Supply + Fix)		**£530**
PLUMBING/HEATING		**£ 0**
ELECTRICS		**£200**
Power Circuits		100
Lighting		100
DECORATING		**£470**
Staining Ext. Joinery		150
Painting Ext Render		290
Mastic		30
GARAGE BUILDING COSTS		**£8825**
INTERNAL FLOOR AREA		**28m²**
COSTS/M² of FLOOR AREA		**£315**
COSTS/FT² of FLOOR AREA		**£29**

The attached double garage on the benchmark house which absorbed more than 10% of the building costs

A traditional stable door approach suitable for a barn conversion

The Horman Open-for-infill doors allow you to improvise a little

Building Costs

Many of the costs of building a garage — whether integral or detached — are no different from the costs of building the main house. Garages do not have to meet the standard building regulations as regards insulation and damp penetration and this allows them to be constructed with thinner, single-skin walls. However, groundwork costs and roofing costs are basically identical, and despite the fact that garages are rarely fitted out with all the paraphernalia of a finished house, the construction costs of a garage are still as much as 60% of those of a finished house when compared on a floor area basis.

Alternatives

Car Ports

One alternative approach is to build just a lean-to car port or undercover car parking bay. You need some form of hard standing for the car and then the rest is up to you. The finished result could be anything from a flimsy timber construction which might look better as a garden pergola to a fully fledged garage without a door.

Prefabricated

There are several manufacturers who produce prefabricated garages at prices way below standard construction costs. Expect to pay less than £1000 for a single garage; though they will need a concrete hardstanding, they do not usually require foundation trenches and effectively they can be laid on a patch of drive. Check out DW Pound for timber structures, or Leofric for self-assembly concrete ones, but bear in mind that the overall effect is little different to a garden shed; they are very utilitarian and would probably be best sited away from the main house.

Underground

Budget costs for a fully submerged basement (shell only) are £250-300/m², about 50% more than an above ground structure. Consequently, an underground garage is unlikely to be a cost-effective option unless space is at a premium. Access ramps (budget £8000) and potential drainage problems make the totally underground garage an expensive luxury. However, the economics look far friendlier when sorting out sloping ground. There are instances where burying car parking below ground can actually free up ground elsewhere for more cost-effective uses (like building extra houses), but this is unlikely to be relevant to many single housebuilders.

Garage Doors

For many designers, the problem with garages begins and ends with the garage door. Until the 1970s garage doors were strictly functional and utilitarian, often made of steel with no attempts at embellishment. Since then, a large number of imitation traditional door styles have sprung up, aping the move back to other traditional forms. The trouble is, that whilst a window or a front door can be made in styles copied from old doors, there are no old garage doors to copy from. Hence a mock Georgian or mock Tudor garage door looks more than faintly ridiculous. Double doors, over 4m wide, look particularly strange and attempts to mould classical patterns on to them merely serve to emphasise how strange and out of place they look.

If there is a traditional British garage door it is the side opening style that you see on houses built in the 1920s and 30s, made from solid timbers and lit by small square frosted glass panels. Magnet still produce such a door and it is remarkably good value at around £125 for a pair large enough for a single garage (though these need glazing and painting). The current trend is to go for doors which open vertically — known as *up-and-overs* — and there are a number of manufacturers producing especially for this market, e.g. Cardale, Henderson, Wessex, Catnic and Horman. As with front entrance doors, there is a choice of different materials, the main ones being timber, steel and glass fibre (or *GRP* as it gets called in this business). Garage doors are large and therefore tend to get pricey. It's a specialist business and your best bet is to trawl through Yellow Pages to "Garage Doors" and seek quotations from there. Steel is much the cheapest material but also the least attractive. Timber and GRP are around twice the price. GRP doors are usually produced to look like timber and can be stained; their main advantage is that they are (hopefully) maintenance-free, yet many people will prefer to stick with timber.

If you don't like any of the commercially available doors yet still crave the convenience of an up-and-over door, then check out Horman's sub-frames which you can fill in with your own designs at your leisure. They are called *Open-for-Infill* doors

Remote Control Door Openers

An increasingly popular item which allows you to open and close your garage door from within the car. They are not cheap — coming in at around £250 which includes just one operator (extra ones cost £45ea) — but they do make a lot of sense when you consider the hassle involved in opening garage doors manually. Leading makes: Stanley and Slave-Dor.

If you are going to spend £6000 plus on a garage, then it's probably worthwhile spending the extra £350 on an operator so that you actually get to use the garage for its intended purpose.

Chapter 8
Services

Sandwiched between the two biggest chapters in the book, Superstructure and Finishes, comes this chapter Services, which deals with the work of the plumbers and electricians. This broadly follows the logic of the construction process but it is important to realise that both plumbing and wiring involve a first-fix and a second-fix element. The first-fix work involves all those parts which will be hidden from final view when the house is occupied — typically this includes pipe laying for plumbers and cable laying and fitting socket boxes for electricians. If you want an alarm system, it is best to get the cabling for this laid at this first-fix stage as well. When this part of the work is complete, the house is ready for plasterers and floor layers to come in and cover up all that is considered to be first-fix and only when their work is done are the plumbers and electricians welcomed back to site to finish their work. With electrics, bathroom fittings and burglar alarms, your choices are relatively straightforward; it's largely a matter of what you want and where you fix it. Home heating is, in comparison, a very much more complicated field and you will do well to consider the options in some detail before deciding what system to plump for. I begin by taking a look at the background.

On Heat

Deciding on a heating system is one of the biggest bugbears facing a builder. It's such a complex field and there are so many options available that it is terribly easy to get swamped by the sheer volume of information. It's all very well saying something smarmy like "You should choose the system that suits you best" but that doesn't actually make it any easier to know what that system might be. There's nothing for it but to start at the beginning. A little background on the physics of heat will improve your understanding of all the areas discussed. Here answered for you are seven questions that you'd never even think to ask.

What is Heat?

Heat is a by-product of "work" going on or, if you like, energy being spent: this usually involves one substance turning into another. Our bodies (like our houses) leak heat and this leaked heat must be replaced which we do by eating (calories are a measurement of energy). The colder it is outside our bodies and our houses, the more heat we leak and the more energy we have to take on board to stay warm.

What is "Feeling Warm?"

The rate at which we lose heat determines how hot or cold we feel. "Feeling cold" is a signal that we are losing high and potentially dangerous amounts of heat: "feeling warm" signals that all is OK.

What Determines How Warm We Feel?

- The insulating effect (U value) of our clothes (or duvets)
- The temperature of the surrounding air
- Wind speed (wind chill factor)
- Level of water vapour around
- Whether our skin is wet or dry
- How much heat is being "given off" (radiated) by surrounding objects (including the sun).

When assessing heating systems, we use air temperature as a shorthand indicator of background comfort but it is important to be aware that air temperature is just one of several factors at play. Anyone who has ever had a thermostatic control dial in their home will be well aware that what's warm on a dry day can be 2-3°C too cold on a wet or a windy day.

Is There an Optimum Comfort Level?

Not as such, but the general consensus is that you need to be dry and free from draughts, and that, of the two forms of heat, *radiant* heat is more pleasurable than *convected* heat.

Radiant v Convected Heat

Radiant heat is the glow you feel on your face when you are standing near a bonfire; the air temperature may be minus 10°C but you feel as warm as toast. Convected heat is warmed air: car heating is the ultimate form of convected air heating: when combined with the forced draught of the fan heater, it dries your throat, makes your eyes water and induces drowsiness.

Does it Have to be One or the Other?

No. In fact all heat sources are a cocktail of convected and radiant heat. Bonfires (and sunshine) will tend to heat the air and warm air will tend to heat the objects it comes into contact with. Convected (or warm air) heat is characterised by being very responsive — i.e. you feel warm very quickly: radiant heat can take a long time to get going (and a long time to cool down).

Having said that, a couple of readers have been at pains to point out that radiant heat is largely insignificant at low temperatures (say below 80°C) and that what is often referred to in manufacturer's blurb as radiant heat is no such thing. Rather it would seem that what is happening is that warm, draught-free air is being mistaken for radiant heat or, to put it another way, the pleasant effect of warm, draught-free air is being wrongly attributed to heat radiation when it may be nothing of the sort. I never said it was easy.

So What's the Perfect Heating System?

Hopefully you have just twigged that there is no such thing. Like most design decisions, you must make a series of compromises and your aim should be to make the least bad compromise overall.

Watts it All About?

Finally a word about how we measure power output, because I know everyone finds it confusing, not least because there are different systems of measurement in operation. Here I try to plump for one, the watt (W), and it's big brother the kilowatt (kW) which is, as you might hope, 1000 watts. British Thermal Units (BTU) get a look in on the boiler section because generally boilers are still rated in BTUs:

- 1W = 3.41 BTU
- 1kW = 3410 BTU.

These are all measurements of heat output. However, you will also be frequently coming across the kilowatt-hour (kWh) which is a measurement of heat actually consumed.

The simplest way to understand the difference is to think of a old-fashioned two-bar electric fire because it so happens that each bar puts out 1kW of heat. If you leave one bar on for one hour, it will have used 1kWh of energy: if you put both bars on it, it's output will obviously double and the kWh will be used up in half the time. So its output is measured in kilowatts but the power actually used is measured in kilowatt-hours — output through time. Thus when I am rabbiting on about boilers I'm mostly referring to kilowatts and BTUs, but in the sections on fuel costs it's all kilowatt-hours.

Standard Heating

All this theory is all very well but how well does a standard central heating system stack up? The "wet" central heating system described below is that which goes into 70% of new homes; it is also, incidentally, the usual route taken when central heating is put into an existing house.

Heat Loss Calculation

This is carried out, usually by the plumber, on a room by room basis, and the results are used to assess the size of the radiators needed in each room. The boiler itself is sized up by adding all the outputs of the various radiators and adding "a bit."

Boiler

The boiler is fitted against an outside wall and the exhaust gases are ducted horizontally outside by way of a *balanced flue*. The boiler heats water to 80°C and this water is then pumped through the *primaries* (large copper pipes) and thence to the *cylinder* and the *radiators*.

Cylinder

Placed in the airing cupboard, this acts like a giant (bath-sized) kettle for heating domestic hot water (DHW). It starts to empty every time a hot tap is turned on; it is simultaneously filled from a tank of cold water in the loft space which, in turn, is filled from the water main. The cylinder is *indirect* which means that the water inside never passes directly through the boiler but is heated at one stage removed by the boiler water passing through copper loops inside the cylinder.

Radiators

These are fitted and connected by two copper pipe circuits: one — the *flow* — takes the hot water from the boiler around the circuit, the other — the *return* — takes the cooler water coming out of the radiators back to the boiler. A small plastic tank (*feed and expansion tank*) is placed in the loft which gives the hot water in the circuit space to expand — which it does as it gets hotter.

Controls

The system is electrically pumped to supply even heat around the house. There is a programmer and a couple of thermostats which turn the system on/off and also switch motorised valves so that the hot water pumped from the boiler can be switched between heating the water in the cylinder or circulating around the radiators.

Labour Content

In a new four-bedroom house, the pipework and control cabling will be "first fixed" in 3-4 days; first fixing needs to take place after the structure is up but before the plastering starts. The "second fix" (including hanging radiators) will take 5-6 days. Conventionally, the heating engineer also fits the sanitaryware, kitchen plumbing and the above ground waste runs, and all this work tends to get lumped into one quotation and carried out together.

Cost Summary

The table on this page shows the costs for a 16kW, 13-radiator installation of the type that was fitted into our benchmark house. Materials are at prices which non-plumbers should be able to obtain at specialist merchants like Plumb Center. The grand total figure is derived from quotations and so includes an element of profit which a small plumbing firm would charge.

Open Fires

Most large family homes are still built with an open fire in the living room. Despite modern central heating being quite adequate to provide warmth in the most extreme winter conditions, housebuilders are still apparently happy to pay £1000 plus for an open fireplace with accompanying chimney. Whereas central heating is regarded in entirely functional terms (fuel efficiency, programmed control, water pressures, etc.), the open fire is altogether much more of a romantic dream — and a very potent one. So what if 70% of the heat goes up the chimney, so what if it has to be cleaned out daily? To the average British household, fire in the living room is as fundamental as sex in the bedroom.

Open fires are dealt with in their own section in the previous chapter and any heat given off by open fires will be treated as free background heating in the same way that we treat winter sunshine, heat from electrical appliances and, of course, body heat. Solid fuel stoves and kitchen ranges, together with other nonstandard forms of heating are looked at in a later section of this chapter, Alternative Heating.

8a: Benchmark House: Central Heating Costs

A mains pressure cylinder is an unusual option for a developer

	MATERIALS	LABOUR	TOTAL
1125lt Oil Tank + Tiger Loop	£280	£120	**£400**
16kW Oil Boiler + Flue	550	160	**£710**
150lt Mains Pressure Cylinder	450	240	**690**
Primaries/Valves/Pumps	160	160	**320**
13 Radiators + Pipework	650	440	**1090**
Heating Controls (inc TRVs)	200	120	**320**
Wiring and Commissioning	50	320	**370**
TOTALS	**£2,340**	**£1,560**	**£3,900**

Which Fuel?

When considering which fuel to use to provide space heating and domestic hot water (DHW) there are a number of considerations:

- Availability
- Installation and storage costs
- Capabilities of each fuel
- Fuel costs
- Environmental impact.

Availability

Piped gas from the North Sea reserves is currently available to over 70% of UK households, which includes almost all urban areas. However, large tracts of rural Britain (and all Ireland) are deemed too remote to justify laying gas mains and the majority will never have the option of a piped gas supply. If in doubt, a phone call to the local office of British Gas will illuminate the situation in your area. Sometimes an initial enquiry will trigger the offer to extend a gas main along a side road.

All the other fuels touched on here are available everywhere.

Installation

Electricity

Installation to a new site is charged on a time and materials basis. Even when it's straightforward it is unlikely to be less than £300. However, as its use in modern housing is universal, when considering electricity as a heat source it is effectively there for nothing. An Economy 7 (two-rate) meter can be installed at no extra cost and is generally well worth doing even if you don't plan to use electric heating — more information in Chapter 10, Kitchen and Laundry.

Gas

British Gas subsidises the installation costs because they want new customers. If gas supply is adjacent then connection is usually free. Longer distances are possible, subject to negotiation with British Gas new supplies. Beyond a distance of a couple of hundred metres or so, it becomes prohibitively expensive unless the costs can be borne with neighbours.

Oil

The costs are solely to do with on-site storage. Storage tanks are available in steel or plastic. Steel is much cheaper (£150 for a 2730lt tank compared to £230 for an equivalent in plastic) but plastic is guaranteed for ten years. Steel tanks have been known to start leaking after five years and are meant to be painted every year (nobody ever does). Add to this figure building up supporting piers (Mats £25, Lab £50), initial placement (L £50), measuring gauge (£40), filter (£40), fire check valve (£30) and microbore connection to boiler (M £10, L £30), and budget around £400 for a steel tank, £500 for a plastic one. The tank can be placed up to 2m below the boiler, but then a tiger loop will be needed as well (extra £40). Attention must be paid to placing oil tanks; they must be outside and they must be 1.8m from any openings. If there is a danger of leaking into watercourses, then a catch pit must be constructed. They are also extremely ugly and their careless siting can spoil an otherwise attractive elevation. They can be buried underground (like a petrol station) but the cost here soars to more than £2000. Camouflaging with trellis and climbers is a cheaper option but allow access for tank replacement.

Liquid Petroleum Gas (LPG)

Storage tank needs to be 3m from any buildings or boundaries so there are comparatively few sites that it is suited to. Calor Gas are the biggest supplier and they take on full responsibility for installation and maintenance of tanks. They usually charge around £300 to install a tank: this includes pipe laying to boiler. Occasionally they are prone to doing special offers at around £100. Bulk gas tanks are even more of an eyesore than oil tanks and their placing is a matter that the planners will want to consider — don't plump for an LPG supply as an afterthought, you may be letting yourself in for big problems. Note that, like oil tanks, LPG tanks can be buried underground but this is likely to cost £400 extra plus excavation costs.

Solid Fuel

This all-embracing term includes just about everything you can burn which isn't a liquid (oil) or a gas: housecoal, anthracite and the processed coals (coalite, fernicite, coke) wood, peat, you name it. Solid fuel can be stored anywhere under cover (the bath?) but purpose-built coal bunkers would cost a minimum of £200 (M £80, L £120). Plastic ones are available from £90. If you use wood, it is important to have somewhere dry to store it; this takes space but can be an attractive feature in it's own right.

Capabilities

Gas

Gas is the preferred fuel for most people and gas is at the leading edge of heating technology. Nearly 80% of central heating systems run on mains gas and, where it is available, it is the overwhelming choice in new developments. The market responds to this by making far more gas-burning products available — and at keener prices. Another plus for gas is that it is, arguably, the best fuel for cooking.

LPG

Despite having a tiny fraction of the market (around 2%), LPG versions of many gas boilers are available, though usually around 10-15% more expensive — LPG boilers can be converted to mains gas. Note that LPG can also be used for cooking.

Oil

Oil-fired systems account for around 10% of the market overall, and are much the most popular choice in rural areas where mains gas is not an option. There is a much smaller range of boilers available and prices are 20-50% more than gas equivalents, though this is partly because they use the more efficient pressure jet burner which reduces running costs. Oil cannot be used to cook with (unless using an oil-fired range).

Solid Fuel

Solid fuel heating systems are available as kitchen ranges, living room stoves or utility room boilers. Anything that the other fuels can do, solid fuel can do; however, compared to the other fuels though, solid fuel heating is unresponsive, inefficient and plain hard work. Wood-burning stoves do not generate enough heat for DHW and wet heating systems combined.

Electricity

Using electricity as a main heat source invariably means latching on to one of the off-peak tariffs. This, in turn, means restricted hours of use which is the biggest limitation. In other respects electricity is the most capable of all fuels because it can be used for just about every household function requiring power.

Solar

Solar power is, at best, a top-up energy source which can provide most of the hot water needs for a UK house in summer and less than 15% in winter. Using solar power is unlikely to save more than 10% of overall fuel bills, whichever system you use for your main heat source.

Fuel Costs

Prices in the Fuel Costs table 8b are for the Cambridgeshire area, where the benchmark house is located, for the period covering mid 1997. There is inevitably some regional variation in prices but these tend not to be greater than 10% up or down, and so these figures give a reasonable guideline to likely charges. Table 8b shows the apparent cost of each fuel and gives a method for converting these costs into kWh for easier comparison. I have only covered the main fuel choices and if the fuel you are planning to use is not listed get in touch with Sutherland Associates (01737 370077) who publish a very comprehensive guide to comparative fuel costs. The Effective Costs table, 8c, shows the cost of the heat after it has been converted from the raw fuel by your boiler; this effective cost is dependent on the efficiency of your appliance.

Electricity

Electricity is charged by the kWh and so price comparisons are straightforward. Also, electric heating is virtually 100% efficient so what you pay for is what you get. Since privatisation, *regional electricity companies* (RECs) have been free to set their own tariffs and there is now some variation between them. All of them have introduced, or are in the process of introducing, a tariff aimed specifically at electric home heating (Eastern Electricity calls it *Economy 10*) which has a facility to have three hours of daytime heating to boost the normal complement of seven hours cheap night time heating. To get prices contact *Bill Enquiries* at your local electricity supply company.

Note that electricity has always been the most expensive fuel you can buy but it now appears that we have long been overcharged for it. Since 1993, my REC has handed out seven rebates totalling £100 (6% of the total bill) whilst in 1997 both unit prices and tariffs have come down, quite apart from a cut in VAT from 8% to 5%. Pricing structures are becoming very much more complex with discounts given for heavy usage and also for prompt payment. Looking murkily into the next two or three years, I would say there are more cuts to come.

8b: Fuel: Raw Costs Compared

	STREET COST	CONVERSION	COST /kWh	ANNUAL TARIFFS
ELECTRICITY				
Standard Rate	7.0p/unit	none	7.0 p	£ 25
Economy 7 - daytime	7.0p/unit	none	7.0 p	£ 38
Economy 7 - nightime	3p/unit	none	2.5 p	
Economy 10 - daytime	8p/unit	none	7.0 p	£ 38
Economy 10 - nightime	3.3p/unit	none	3.2 p	
BRITISH GAS	1.6p/unit	none	1.5 p	£ 35
LPG (Calor Gas)	17.7p/lt	Divide by 7.1	2.5 p	£ 55
OIL (28-second)	12p/lt	Divide by 10.2	1.2 p	£ 0
House Coal	£150/tonne	Divide by 8300	1.8 p	£ 0
Anthracite	£220/tonne	Divide by 9370	2.2 p	£ 0

ALL FIGURES INCLUDE VAT at 5%

8c: Fuel: Effective Costs Compared

	Fuel Cost	Appliance or Boiler efficiency	Effective Cost
ELECTRICITY			
Daytime Peak Rate	7.0 p	100%	7.0 p
Off-peak Rates	3.2 p	100%	3.2 p
BRITISH GAS			
Elderly Cast Iron Boiler	1.5 p	60%	2.5 p
New Boiler	1.5 p	70%	2.1 p
Condensing Boiler	1.5 p	85%	1.8 p
LPG			
Elderly Cast Iron Boiler	2.5 p	60%	4.2 p
New Boiler	2.5 p	70%	3.6 p
Condensing Boiler	2.5 p	85%	2.9 p
OIL			
Elderly Cast Iron Boiler	1.2 p	65%	1.8 p
New Boiler	1.2 p	75%	1.6 p
Condensing Boiler	1.2 p	85%	1.4 p
COAL			
Open Fire	1.8 p	35%	5.0 p
Stove	1.8 p	65%	2.7 p
ANTHRACITE			
Open Fire	2.2 p	35%	6.3 p
Stove	2.2 p	65%	3.4 p

ALL FIGURES INCLUDE VAT at 5%

Mains Gas

Gas is also billed in kWhs which makes comparison with electricity easy — again, phone your *Bill Enquiries* for local rates. How much of the gas you consume actually ends up heating your house depends on the efficiency of your boiler, hence the variable efficiency ratios suggested in the accompanying table 8c. Note that British Gas also offers a favourable tariff to customers offering to pay monthly by direct debit; doing this should save you more than 5% on your gas bill. Also note that the chill wind of competition is blowing through the gas industry as well as electricity and during this edition's lifetime, there will be alternative gas suppliers on tap in most parts of the country. Unit prices look set to tumble here as well. By late 1996, the South West had no less than nine gas supply companies besides British Gas and the cheapest supplier was over 20% less than BG.

LPG

Although there is no tariff as such, Calor Gas — the main supplier — make a charge of £52/annum for tank maintenance. For local prices, check Yellow Pages under *Gas Suppliers* or *Bottled Gas*.

Oil

The most common fuel of this type is known as *28-second burning oil*. The modern generation of pressure jet oil boilers are more efficient than gas by up to 5% but only if regularly maintained (which means replacing the burner every year). Otherwise, the same general principles of boiler efficiency still operate — although note that oil-fired condensing boilers are very expensive.

For best local prices, check Yellow Pages under *Oil fuel distributors & suppliers*. Four suppliers I checked on one day (10/7/97) varied from 11.7 to 12.8p/lt There is also a significant seasonal fluctuation, and having a tank large enough to allow buying once a year — in summer — will lower your fuel bills.

Solid Fuel

More complex to price because of the variety of different types of fuel and the enormous variation in boiler/stove efficiencies. I have priced two of the most common solid fuels, household coal and anthracite, but there are numerous other processed, smokeless coals around. Their effective cost is unlikely to be less than anthracite.

For local prices, see Yellow Pages under *Coal and solid fuel merchants*. Charringtons have a free phone number (0800 585372) which is very helpful if you want to find out about the costs of other fuels.

Wood is altogether too variable to present any comparative costings: although it burns well and results in a garden-friendly ash waste, it is unlikely to be cost effective when compared to coal which burns very much hotter.

Environmental Impact

To get a better understanding of the environmental issues involved with home energy use, refer to Chapter 10, Green Issues. Here there a two particular areas where concern focuses; firstly how clean (or dirty) any particular fuel is and secondly how much carbon dioxide (CO_2) each fuel releases into the atmosphere. CO_2 is the gas readily associated with the greenhouse effect, which is reckoned to be causing long term global warming.

- **Solar power** is generally a very green power source. As yet its impact on the environment is limited because it's too expensive to install.
- **Gas** is the cleanest of the fossil fuels in that it produces very little sulphur dioxide or nitrous oxide (the acid rain gases). It's also efficient in that little is lost in transmission from source to end user and so its combustion produces comparatively little CO_2.
- **Oil** is a slightly dirtier fuel than gas (acid rain wise) but tends to produce even less CO_2 than gas. Transporting oil around the world is cheap but occasionally hazardous when tankers run aground.
- **Electricity** is a form of converted energy so it is much processed before it enters the home. It is generated in a number of ways — by burning coal, oil, gas and other fossil fuels, by hydroelectricity, by wind and solar power and, most controversially, by nuclear fission. Some of these are clean, some are not, whilst nuclear power is, paradoxically, both the cleanest major energy source available and potentially the most dangerous. Whatever the merits or demerits of electricity generation, much of its energy is lost in transmission along the national grid, which adds to its expense and reinforces its poor environmental rating.
- **Coal**, British Coal in particular, is a dirty fuel which contributes loads of sulphur to the atmosphere. Despite cutbacks in coal-mining, it remains the one British fossil fuel with long-term reserves. Anthracite and the smokeless fuels are much cleaner than housecoal, but do still not compare well with gas or oil.

And the winner is..

The big table 8d opposite summarises the comparative costs of using different fuels on the benchmark house. It's a photo finish. Mains gas and oil are about neck and neck and electricity is just a short head behind. If you are on mains gas, use it. Use it for cooking as well. And for tumble drying. Oil is actually cheaper to heat with but gas wins the contest because you can cook with it and gas cooking is way cheaper than using electricity.

If you are deemed to be too remote for mains gas, then oil is the best option, although, if you can penetrate the intricacies of the table, you may be surprised to see how well electricity shows. Electric heating is a much improved product and the new 10-hour cheap rates have improved it still further. Its running costs are way higher than oil, gas or even solid fuel, but its installation costs are way less and this stands it in good stead in the 10-year heating costs table. Furthermore, as electricity is going to be present in your new house there is not going to be any further charge for using it for heating — indeed some RECs will even offer incentives like zero or half-price connection if you fit electric heating as well. Also bear in mind that electricity prices look set to fall over the next few years.

Super Insulation

The effects of super insulating the benchmark house is to reduce the fuel bills by between £100 and £250/annum — depending on the choice of fuel and heating system. As the extra cost of super-insulation is going to be in the order of £1000-£1500, it is a worthwhile option. The net effect of super insulation is to reduce the heat demand by around 40%. Whichever heating system you choose, super insulation levels pay for themselves within five to ten years. Interestingly, on a super-insulated house, electric heating is still the cheapest after ten years despite having an annual heating and cooking bill of £480, nearly twice as high as gas and oil.

Condensing Boilers

These energy efficient boilers only just begin to pay for themselves after ten years. This is entirely down to the extra cost of fitting them. However, expect prices to fall over the coming years, making the condenser even more cost effective. Note that gas-fired condensers are much cheaper than oil-fired ones.

8d: Benchmark House: Fuel Cost Comparison

The First 10 Years

	CONVENTIONAL BOILER	CONDENSING BOILER	CONVENTIONAL BOILER	CONDENSING BOILER	CONVENTIONAL BOILER	CONDENSING BOILER	ELECTRIC HEATING	SOLID FUEL
SPACE HEATING								
Fuel Connection Fee	£150	£150	£0	£0	£0	£0	£0	£0
Storage Costs	£0	£0	£300	£300	£400	£400	£0	£100
System Installation	£3,300	£3,600	£3,400	£3,700	£3,500	£4,300	£1,500	£3,700
Annual Tariff	£35	£35	£55	£55	£0	£0	£13 *	£0
Annual Service	£25	£25	£25	£25	£45	£45	£0	£20
Basic Fuel Cost (p./kWh)	1.5 p	1.5 p	2.5 p	2.5 p	1.2 p	1.2 p	3.2 p	2.2 p
STANDARD HOUSE CONSTRUCTION								
Heat Required (kWh/annum)	14,800	14,800	14,800	14,800	14,800	14,800	14,800	14,800
System Efficiency	70%	85%	70%	85%	70%	85%	100%	65%
Fuel Used (kWh/annum)	21,143	17,412	21,143	17,412	21,143	17,412	14,800	22,769
Annual Heating Bill	£315	£259	£529	£435	£247	£204	£474	£501
10-Year Capital and Running costs	£7,200	£6,944	£9,786	£9,153	£6,824	£7,187	£6,366	£9,009
SUPER INSULATED HOUSE CONSTRUCTION								
Heat Required (kWh/annum)	7,400	7,400	7,400	7,400	7,400	7,400	7,400	7,400
System Efficiency	70%	85%	70%	85%	70%	85%	100%	65%
Fuel Used (kWh/annum)	10,571	8,706	10,571	8,706	10,571	8,706	7,400	11,385
Annual Fuel Bills	£158	£130	£264	£218	£124	£102	£237	£250
10-Year Capital and Running costs	£5,625	£5,647	£7,143	£6,976	£5,587	£6,169	£3,998	£6,505
DOMESTIC HOT WATER								
Heat Required (kWh/annum)	5000	5000	5000	5000	5000	5000	5000	5000
System Efficiency	70%	85%	70%	85%	70%	85%	100%	65%
Fuel Used (kWh/annum)	7143	5882	7143	5882	7143	5882	5000	7692
Annual Fuel Bills	£106	£88	£179	£147	£84	£69	£160	£169
COOKING								
Cheapest Fuel	BY GAS		BY LPG		BY ELECTRICITY		BY ELECTRICITY	
Fuel Used (kWh/annum)	1000	1000	1000	1000	1000	1000	1000	1000
Annual Fuel Bills	£15	£15	£25	£25	£70	£70	£70	£70
COMBINED 10-YEAR TOTALS FOR HEATING, HOT WATER and COOKING								
STANDARD HOUSE	**£8,414**	**£7,970**	**£11,821**	**£10,874**	**£8,354**	**£8,570**	**£8,661**	**£11,397**
SUPER INSULATED HOUSE	**£6,838**	**£6,673**	**£9,179**	**£8,697**	**£7,118**	**£7,552**	**£6,293**	**£8,892**

ALL FIGURES INCLUDE VAT on FUEL at 5%

* Standing charge is taken to be the extra paid for Economy 10.

About This Table

I have compared eight likely candidates for heating the 166m² benchmark house and two likely built standards of home building, standard and super-insulated. What I have not looked at is the cost difference between building to these two standards but you will find out more about this in other parts of the book. Figures for fuel consumption are taken from an NHER energy rating — see Chapter 10.

I haven't included anything for the extra finance costs involved in spending more on the installation. A genuine cost accountant would be appalled at my omission, but I think the table is confusing enough as it is and adding rows of amortisation is maybe going to sink it altogether. Anyway, there is not that much difference between the installation costs, except in the case of electric heating which is almost £2000 cheaper to install than the others. If you want to account this I suggest you subtract the interest you would get over 10 years by not spending this £2000 (which at 7% return is £1900). However, I bet you would spend it on something else so the whole subject is just piping into the wind in any event.

The accuracy of this table is subject to many variable factors. Perhaps the biggest of these is fuel costs. Who would have predicted in the 70s that oil would have been the cheapest fuel in the 80s and 90s? The table reflects 1997 prices; I'll leave it to you to guess what they'll be in 2017.

Why stop at ten years? After all, the average heating system should last at least twice as long. I chose ten years because it gives a good period to compare capital costs (which an accountant would probably write off before then) with running costs. These overall costs comprise both installation costs and running costs and the relative importance of each factor changes as you alter the time-frame over which you assess them; in other words, the longer the period you use to assess costs, the better the systems with the low running costs do, but remember that a central heating system does not last forever, and that it may be that by 2017 some other heating methods will be all the rage and we'll be ripping out our oh-so primitive condensing boilers and planting special heat absorbing grass on our roofs.

Boilers

Boilers are rated according to the power they can produce. Manufacturers still work in BTU (British Thermal Units); I'm trying to be metric, but in the section, for clarity's sake, I'll use both. Just remember:
• 1kW = 3410 BTU.

A small application — like a one bedroom flat — might use a 20,000 BTU boiler (6kW): a large Victorian vicarage would require something in excess of 100,000 BTU (30kW). A new four-bedroom house built to current thermal regulations will need — well read on, it's a bit controversial.

Conventionally boilers are sized by totalling the radiator output (worked out from the heat calculation) and adding a bit for heating domestic hot water (DHW), and then going to the nearest size above. This is a bit hit and miss, to say the least. For a more detailed explanation of heat calculations, see Chapter 10, Green Issues.

The *industry standard* is to design heating systems capable of keeping the house around 21^{0}C warmer than the temperature outside. Now in a new house, built to 1995 building regs, the amount of heat needed to keep the structure 21^{0}C warmer than outside is surprisingly small. As a rule of thumb, you actually need 20 watts per m^3 of living space. The benchmark house, with a floor area of 166m^2, has 410m^3 of living space and this means that the heating requirement is (20x410) 8200 watts or 8.2kW (28,000 BTU). However, the quotes that came in for this job all recommended a boiler of not less than 15kW (50,000 BTU). How come the discrepancy? Are U values (the basis of heat calculations) meaningless or is there some conspiracy to sell us bigger boilers and radiators than we really need?

One little known reason for apparent oversizing is that radiators are usually only 70% efficient: outputs claimed in manufacturers' brochures apply to radiators connected at the top corner on one side and at the bottom on the other: these days radiators are usually connected bottom to bottom and this dramatically lowers their output. *Mears* calculators and various rules of thumb, used by plumbers to carry out heat calculations, take account of this discrepancy without ever explaining it. However, whilst radiators should arguably be oversized by as much as 50%, boilers themselves do not have to be 50% larger to deliver the anticipated heat from each radiator.

Another factor to take into account is that a central heating system has to be *felt* to be working and that means that it must be able not only to keep a house warm, but to heat it up from cold within a reasonable (say one hour) time-scale. This obviously requires extra heat but not that much extra — the benchmark house requires just 1.4kW extra heat to raise the temperature 10ºC in one hour — and a 12kW (40,000 BTU) boiler really ought to handle background heating, boost heating and hot water needs. Such a boiler will be £100 cheaper to buy and cheaper to run. However, if you insisted on a 12kW boiler, your plumber would probably want you to sign a disclaimer in event of it being underpowered! I know of plumbers who have been sued by clients — albeit ones living in uninsulated old houses — because the system they installed didn't make the house warm enough, so perhaps it's not surprising that plumbers tend to view these things conservatively and to err on the side of caution.

How Size Effects Price

Typically, each model will be produced in six or seven sizes ranging from mini 15-30,000 BTU (4-8kW) up to 80-100,00 BTU (23-30kW). Plumber's merchants will regularly knock 30% off list for trade customers — more for regular clients. The accompanying table gives list prices minus 30% for the balanced-flue Baxi *Solo*, one of the most popular of UK gas boilers (and one of the most reliable).

The price difference between sizes is not great, however that difference increases with the boiler sizes. The difference between the smallest and the next smallest is just £40, whereas the difference between the largest shown and the next size down is £100. This weighting of charges is common to all the boiler manufacturers; sizing down is therefore more cost effective on larger installations.

Boiler Heat Exchangers

The older type of gas- and oil-fired boilers use cast iron heat exchangers and work by heating this cast iron, which holds heat well and, in turn, transfers the heat through to the hot water. They are characterised by being easy to install, reliable and inefficient. The cast iron takes a comparatively long time to heat up and a correspondingly long time to cool down — hence the inefficiency of heat transfer.

The more modern style of boilers — which includes the *combi* and *condensing* boilers — are made with copper or other lightweight metal heat exchangers and operate with a much lower water content. They are more efficient but have to be much more carefully commissioned, and it is vital that the correct corrosive inhibitors are present. They also need more servicing.

Combination Boilers

A combi has a second heat exchanger in the boiler which works as an instantaneous water heater, in the manner of the now defunct *Ascot* water heaters in that it is used to heat water bound directly for the hot tap. This second heat exchanger adds 50-80% to the price of the boiler but this cost penalty is clawed back by the elimination of hot water storage (in cylinders), and tanks and associated pipework in the loft. All in all, it is cheaper to install than a conventional system. Combi boilers are still relatively new in the UK and the market is dominated by continental manufacturers like Vaillant and Vokera. Low flow rates mean they are not that wonderful for applications such as showers but they are good choices for households with erratic life-

8e: Guide Prices: Baxi Gas Boilers

BAXI MODEL NO	OUTPUT		TRADE PRICE
	in BTU	*in kW*	
Solo 2 30 RS	30,000	9	£300
Solo 2 40 RS	40,000	12	£340
Solo 2 50 RS	50,000	15	£380
Solo 2 60 RS	60,000	18	£480

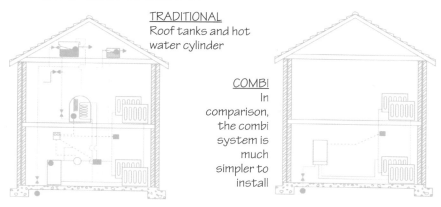

TRADITIONAL
Roof tanks and hot water cylinder

COMBI
In comparison, the combi system is much simpler to install

styles, coming and going at all hours; also the relatively low water content heat exchangers mean they need much more careful commissioning by the plumber and, even so, the heat exchangers scale up in hard water areas.

Condensing Boilers

Condensing boilers, also known as energy efficient boilers, work by having extra large heat exchangers which extract a much greater proportion of the usable energy from the fuel; the greatly reduced temperature of the exhaust fumes causes condensation (hence the name) which in all other boilers would spell disaster. The exhaust gas comes out at a surprisingly low temperature — the flue is plastic — and they also give off a mildly acid condensate which should be piped into the soil stack or to an outside gully. To cope with the condensation, the heat exchangers are made of aluminium — one of the main reasons for their extra expense. Under the new building regulations, their installation in a new dwelling will allow builders to lower insulation standards elsewhere, although most selfbuilders would be well advised to avoid such a tacky trade-off.

The sales of condensing boilers really took off in 1992 when the Energy Savings Trust (0345 023005) offered a £200 grant to private householders for installing one. Currently, this grant is only available for people replacing old systems but the situation could change again — check it out. Despite the grant and a tightening of thermal building regulations, the market share for condensers remains tiny (less than 3%) and the plumbing trade in general remains very reluctant to embrace this new technology. Ask a plumber to fit a condenser and he'll most likely advise you not to touch them as they are full of problems. Ask him how many he has fitted and he'll most likely say none.

Preliminary indications are that they are not full of problems but seem to work pretty well. There is a rapidly increasing choice in gas and

LPG but, as yet, there are only two suppliers of oil-fired condensers, Yorkpark and the Hellfire Combustion Company. British Gas claim that the Malvern is excellent and at around £600 is considerably cheaper and somewhat easier to install than many competitors. Gas-fired condensing combis are still relatively rare though now leading manufacturers like Potterton are going full swing into production, you should start to see them frequently specified in new houses.

Boiler Efficiency

This is now a key selling point, indeed it is the whole reason behind the move to condensing boilers. By all means, consider installing a condensing boiler but be aware that the quoted efficiency rates of 92-95% only apply when the boiler is in condensing mode, and how often a boiler works in condensing mode can vary enormously with a number of factors. When in non-condensing mode, these boilers are still capable of being very efficient but not significantly more than many of the latest conventional boilers (oil-fired boilers claim efficiency rates of 84%). For any boiler to work efficiently it must be correctly commissioned (often overlooked) and regularly serviced.

System Efficiency

Whilst the efficiency rates quoted by manufacturers (known as bench efficiency) may or may not be accurate, the delivery of hot water around the heating zones is also subject to a number of other inefficiencies — basically boilers providing hot water that's not required. This can further reduce *fuel in:usable heat out* ratios by as much again as the bench efficiency (or inefficiency) rates, so that actual heating efficiency rates achieved are often under 70% for boilers which claim 85% efficiency. The more oversized the boiler is, the worse the problem. There are a number of gadgets (boiler managers, anti-cycling devices) which claim to improve the situation, but these are no substitute for correctly sizing the installation in the first place. This inbuilt system inefficiency is another area where condensing boilers tend to win out, since they are — in effect — going to be about half as inefficient as conventional boilers; their effective efficiency may be reduced from 93% to 85% but that's still twice as good as from 85% to 70%.

Flue Choices

Where you have a boiler, you must also have some form of exhaust pipe to get rid of the fumes. The flue, as it is known, is actually quite an expensive part of the kit and selecting the right flue is an important step. There are currently three options.

Potterton's Envoy Flowsure is both a condensing boiler and a combi. Note the mini hot water tank which pre-heats enough water to get around the combi problem of feeble flow rates

Conventional Flues

This is the old-fashioned, low-tech solution and involves releasing the exhaust fumes into some sort of vertical chimney. However, conventional flues require an intake of air from the house. This presents no problem in an old draughty pile, but in a draught-proofed new house provision must be made for an air feed from outside or under the floor — which will add to the heat load of the boiler. Also, the possibility of these air vents becoming blocked at a later date presents a safety hazard.

Balanced Flue

This draws fresh, combustible air in from the same opening through which the exhaust fumes are expelled. Nowadays, the preferable option with gas and oil-fired boilers; some balanced flue versions (Glow Worm's *Fuelsaver*) are the same price as conventional flues but most manufacturers add a 15-20% premium. In a new dwelling however, this is almost always going to be much cheaper than building in a conventional flue.

Fan Flue

Popular in flats where boiler positioning is sometimes difficult. Specifying a fanned flue adds 20-30% to the cost of a conventionally flued boiler, but allows a far greater number of positioning possibilities because the fumes can be expelled a much greater distance. The remarkable Maxol *Turbo* boiler can be situated up to 8m from the flue terminal.

Flue Positioning

There are tightly enforced regulations about where you can and can't place boiler flue terminals in outside walls. For instance, they shouldn't be less than 300mm below an opening window or under the roof eaves and they shouldn't be less than 600mm from an internal or external corner. Your designer should be aware of these hurdles but every now and then someone gets caught out and has to reposition the boiler away from its preferred spot. Generally, the regulations are not as stringent for fan flue terminals and fitting a fanned flue boiler can sometimes be a useful (if expensive) way around an otherwise intractable siting problem.

Kitchen Ranges

This is an option that appeals to many because of the intrinsic style and feel. The *Aga* is the best known, but it is basically just a huge cast iron cooker not a whole house-heating boiler. There are a number of products (e.g. Rayburn, Stanley, Hergom, Wamsler) which will fit the bill and provide all three required functions — that is cooking, space heating and DHW — from one heat source. The Rayburn *GD80* (costs around £2700) is a gas-fired cooker which can provide 23kW (80,000 BTU) of space heating, but is also capable of running on a summer setting which reduces output to around 1kW. There are limitations in using ranges for all your heating requirements — no mains pressure tanks, relatively unresponsive — but the top models now have electronic time and thermostatic control. No way is this a cheap option but if you have your heart set on a cast-iron cooker (which is unlikely to cost less than £1700 in any event) it is worth considering upgrading to one that does space heating and DHW as well. Having said that, the space/DHW heating capabilities come at a price (£600-£800) for which you could purchase many more efficient gas- or oil-fired boilers as well as more sophisticated controls. It is also little understood that ranges are very expensive to run, whatever the fuel. The gas-fired *GD80* uses around 30,000kWh/annum (cost £400) for just normal cooking usage; this is rather more than the anticipated space heating costs for the benchmark house and nearly twenty times the cost of conventional gas cooking. The water boiler on the other hand has a bench efficiency of 80% which compares well with other gas boilers.

Emitters

"Emitters" is a convenient tag to use for the bits of space heating systems that deliver the heat. Go into Plumb Center and ask for an emitter and they'd most likely direct you to the local psychiatrist, but if I just call them radiators (*rads* in plumber-speak) then I am ignoring all the other weird and wonderful heat emitters that exist. More on those later. Conventional wet central heating systems use *rads*, so we'll start here.

Pressed Steel Radiators

These are what goes into most central heating systems today and most readers will be all too familiar with them. Functional rather than elegant, there are several well-known makes which tend to compete on price: e.g. Stelrad, Myson, Barlo, Brugman. Rather like windows they come in standard shapes and sizes, typically from 300mm to 700mm high and from 500mm to 3000mm wide. Most manufacturers produce three or four height options, each available in lengths which increase in 100mm steps. There are also double-panelled and finned versions which give off more heat. The Plumb Center catalogues give charts for two manufacturers' products, which enables you to plan with some degree of accuracy. Roughly speaking, they produce heat in proportion to their size: the smallest (300H x 500L) will give out 0.3kW, the largest, double-panelled type (700H x 3000L) will give out 7.8kW. Having carried out a heat calculation for each room, you will be faced with a choice of shapes and sizes as to how that heat load can be met and here thought can be given to radiator placing.

Pricing

List prices are, as ever, indicative of where the haggling starts. Discounts off radiators can be huge (60-70% is not uncommon with some manufacturers); look to pay around £30 for each kW of output — discount outlets like Harrison McCarthy can go as low as £25/kW. Merchants tend to have special offers going and so it pays not to be too fussy as to make. On the benchmark house, 13 rads with a total output of 15kW were priced between £400 and £450. Piping up the rads with 100mx15mm copper tube, fittings, valves would cost an additional £250 in materials. Using the "greener" heat loss calculations (see previous section on boilers), which estimate heat loss at less than 10kW for the whole house, would save around £150 solely on the cost of the radiators. Condensing boilers, which work at lower temperatures, would need rads about 15% larger to get the same effect.

Alternatives

High Efficiency Radiators

Faral are the market leaders with their aluminium rads. Their Italian styling is a wow — but perhaps too modern for many tastes — and they are designed to work at low temperatures which makes them very suitable for condensing boilers. Cost about £75/kW. Using Faral rads would add £600 to the standard radiator costs in our test house.

Low Water-Content Rads

Designed to work with tiny amounts of water (less than 1lt sometimes), they are very quick response and efficient, but tend to give out little radiant heat which is a *bad thing*, but there should be fuel savings because less water is being heated overall (*a good thing*). Thermalpanel are a noted producer. Cost around £56/kW output, which would add £300 to the overall price in the benchmark house.

Period Radiators

Traditional cast iron radiators are still available from Clyde Combustion. In period bathrooms and the like they are just the ticket but they do not come cheap. Expect to pay around £180-£200/kW output — and that's just for rads supplied in grey primer that need painting.

Skirting Radiators

Sometimes preferred because of their low visual impact. Myson's *Wallstrip* is market leader. It goes where you would normally fit skirting board — now there's a saving. Like skirting, it can go around bends and it tends to get priced by the metre and so it's a little difficult to compare with conventional rads. Look to pay around £30-£35/metre run (depending on the number of bends, ends, etc). Heat output depends very much on water temperature. A conventional 75°C would give off about 0.5kW/m; a condensing boiler, working at 55°C, about half that amount. However you look at it they are not going to be less than £70/kW, about twice the effective cost of bog standard rads.

Heated Towel Rails

These specialist radiators, usually hung in the vertical, are now becoming an item in the contemporary bathroom. Zehnder are the most elegant, complete with dinky little collapsible towel rails, but they cost between £140 and £250 (about £170/kW). Myson and Worcester are around half that price. All can be coloured to match your bathroom suite (add £40) and all are available with an electric immersion heater option for summer use (add £100 plus).

Underfloor Heating

Available as either water-based (wet) or electric, underfloor heating is becoming increasingly popular. With an underfloor heating system, the floor itself becomes the emitter and, so as you don't burn your tootsies, the wet systems need to work at lower temperatures than ordinary wall rads and they are often used in conjunction with condensing boilers (which are designed to work at lower temperatures), otherwise temperature reducing equipment is needed. They are mostly laid under a cement screed which is used as a heat

reservoir (like an electric storage heater); this means that the heat is released slowly throughout the day — it is pleasantly draught free and the heat stays close to the floor. Electric underfloor heating is touched on in a following section in this chapter (Alternative Heating). No two systems are the same and I have quotations from three companies providing wet underfloor systems which varied from £2000 (Mats £1400, Lab £600) to £3600 (materials only). However you arrange it, wet underfloor heating is going to be expensive to install; little details like the heating controls can work out to be over £50/room, rather more than the average panel radiator. Even though such a system is cheap to run, the payback period will be very long — I would estimate in excess of 20 years. One practical solution is to just fit underfloor heating downstairs and radiators upstairs — they've yet to develop an underfloor towel rail! A downstairs only installation could typically be done for about 60% of the whole house price. As you can't easily (if at all!) fit under-

floor heating retrospectively, the suppliers of these systems tend to concentrate heavily on new build and, in particular, the selfbuild market. Consequently you will always find a plethora of interested suppliers willing to quote for in the pages of the selfbuild magazines and at selfbuild exhibitions.

There is currently no satisfactory British Standard for underfloor heating: there is a BS 7291 used for testing plastic pipe but it its only partly applicable to underfloor application. You must, therefore, exercise caution when evaluating the claims of competing systems — in other words, heaven alone knows which is best. Underfloor heating is the No 1 topic on the *Individual Homes* internet forum and it's all claim and counter claim. The cheapest system seems to be one used by Nu-Heat and Kee which is based on a plastic cum rubber tube called Santoprene; most of the other systems use P-ex pipe which is considerably more costly and may (or may not) be much better suited to the task.

Above: classic look from Clyde Combustion. Below: a Wirsbo underfloor heating system

Domestic Hot Water

The *bog standard* system uses a copper cylinder, fed by a tank overhead or in the loft, and is heated by copper tubes inside. These tubes transfer heat from the boiler primary circuit to the water in the cylinder: the domestic hot water (DHW) never passes through the boiler at all and thus it is known as an *indirect system*. All cylinders these days come ready insulated (lagged).

Cost

Fitting a regular cylinder (inc. backup electric immersion heater) costs around £180 (Cylinder £80, Labour £100). *Quick recovery* cylinders (which heat cold water to 60°C within half an hour) cost around £50 extra.

Plus

Cheap, easy to install and well understood by the average plumber. Replacement is straightforward; facility for electric immersion heating if the boiler is out of action.

Minus

Having water tanks and pipework in the loft. Poor flow rates achieved from hot water taps due to inadequate head (or pressure) of water — this poor flow rate only really matters where a powerful shower is valued.

Loft Plumbing

In conventional systems, there are two tanks in the loft: one (usually 227lts) feeds the cylinder, the other (usually 18lts) supplies the central heating system. Having to put a tank in the loft — avoiding this is sold as a big plus for other systems — actually costs around £220 (Mats 100, Lab £120) for the water storage tank and around £80 (M £40, L £40) for the feed and expansion tank (aka the *Jockey Tank*). Therefore, any system that does away with all loft plumbing is going to save you around £300.

Instantaneous Hot Water

Small instantaneous hot water heaters are still sold but in a new house the normal way of achieving this is by fitting a Combination Boiler (or *combi*). Although combi boilers are 30-50% more expensive than conventional boilers, the savings in avoiding cylinders as well as loft plumbing combine to make this system as cheap and possibly cheaper to install than the standard DHW system.

Plus

No cylinder: no loft pipework or tanks: hot water on demand, 24hrs a day: simplified controls: no switching valves needed.

Minus

Poor flow rate remains the big problem — anything below 15lts/minute is not adequate for a family home and many combis produce as little as 10lts/minute. Also problems with scaling (in hard water areas) in the hot water heat exchanger which reduces flow rates still further. The heat exchangers can be *de-scaled* but this is costly and time consuming. Combis are reckoned to need more servicing.

Mains Pressure Hot Water

These systems use *unvented* (i.e. no loft pipework for expansion) hot water cylinders which are strong enough to withstand storing hot water under mains pressure. They answer the problem of low flow rates to showers but at a cost of around £500. To operate to full effect they need at least 2.5 bar of mains pressure and a mains flow rate of 35lts/minute. Unfortunately, UK water companies are only obliged to provide mains water at 1 bar pressure so many situations will not benefit at all. Phone your water company to determine your local pressure. Mains pressure systems are potentially dangerous and they have only recently been allowed in the UK; an installer must be competent and must have CITB certification.

Plus

No loft pipework: mains pressure hot water delivered to all parts of the house, particularly valued by shower users: a small saving on being able to use smaller bore pipework throughout.

Minus

Expensive (extra £200 on Bog Standard): need certified installers (also likely to be expensive). Don't buy a copper one, it won't last, and don't use with cheap taps. Leaks, when they do occur, are much worse when under mains pressure. No back up storage if supply is cut off. It's worth paying extra for a stainless steel or enamel version. Recommended: Megaflow, Grosvenor.

Variations

I have outlined three approaches to delivery of DHW. Needless to say there are a number of other options that sort of mix and match these three approaches.

Combis with Cylinders

The Worcester *Highflow* boiler has been around some time and it has an integral small hot water cylinder which improves the flow rate to around 16lts/minute, which will satisfy larger homes. At around £700 for boiler and instant hot water, it's one of the cheapest options available and it is also available oil-fired. It's also proving to be a popular approach to the problem, as witnessed by the increasing number of imitators, like the Potterton *Flowsure* which became available in 1996, complete with condensing boilers.

Thermal Stores

These systems work by reversing the logic of the bog standard setup and use a cylinder of hot water to heat cold water channelled through it at mains pressure; result? Hot water at up to 30lts/minute comes straight out of the hot taps. As hot water is not actually stored under mains pressure, it doesn't have to be installed by a qualified plumber. Thermal stores also usually work without the need for tanks in the loft; instead they come with integral feed and expansion tanks. For a four-bedroom house, expect installation costs of around £300 (including mixing valves), about midway between using the bog standard route and using mains pressure unvented systems. Because these systems work on keeping water at high temperatures, they are not well suited for using with condensing boilers. Look out for Gledhill's *Boilermate*, the Albion *Mainsflow* and the IMI *Powermax*.

Shower Pumps

A complex field in itself. There are *single impeller* pumps which boost the water after the mixing valve, and *double impellers* which boost both hot and cold before they enter the valve. There are also an increasing number of all-in-one pump and valve shower units like the Triton *Aquasensation* (£150). Which you choose is partly dependent on the layout you have. Prices are largely dependent on the power of the pump. They can be purchased for just over £100, but a pump delivering 30lts/minute (equivalent to a good mains pressure system) will cost £180 plus. Most work on a timed switch. Add the costs for extra wiring and fitting and you can see that a shower pump is not a very clever option in a new building, where you would be quids in by starting off with a better DHW system. Leading manufacturers: Mira, Aqualisa.

Background

- A bath takes about 70-80lts of hot water and so water storage needs to be above this level (or instantaneous) to be adequate.
- A typical household of four uses between 200 and 250lts of hot water a day, conventionally heated to 60°C. Just under

half of all water consumed is heated. The cost of this metered water will average around £180/annum.

- It takes 12kWh to heat 200lts of water through 50°C (the difference between the temperature of the cold water and the hot water). The cost of heating 250lts/day will average around £100/annum (inc. VAT).

Showers and Flow Rates

- A good power shower needs a flow rate of 25lts/minute. This will not be achieved by the bog standard system where the flow of hot water is determined by the height of the loft tank above the outlet. A pump will be required (or else feeble showers endured).
- In an unvented mains pressure system (or a thermal store), the flow rate is dependent on the mains pressure supplied by the local water company.
- With a combi boiler, which produces instantaneous hot water, the flow rate depends on the design of the boiler. It is unlikely to be better than 10lts/minute.

Recovery Rates

The time taken for cold water from the mains to get to 60°C inside the cylinder is referred to as the *recovery rate*. This rate is dependent on the size of the boiler *or* the cylinder heat exchanger, whichever is smaller. For instance, a typical cylinder for a four bedroomed house needs 8kWh of energy to heat its 140lts of water from 10°C to 60°C: an 8kW heater will accomplish this feat in one hour whereas a 16kW heater will take just half as long. In theory a 32kW heater would achieve the same feat in 15 minutes, but in practice this would not happen unless the boiler was also rated at 32kW, which is unlikely. Here the boiler size becomes the limiting factor in the recovery rate. Unlike boilers, cylinders are not advertised by the size of their heat exchangers; however, most manufacturers sell a "standard" version (Cost £80) which takes about one hour to heat up and a "quick recovery" version which takes 20 minutes (Cost £130). The latter simply have larger heat exchangers.

Efficiency/Heat Loss

All new cylinders are insulated to reduce heat loss to less than 3kW of heat during a 24 hour period. Effectively, this heat loss can be ignored for six months of the year as it is simply transferring heat from water to space heat; during the summer you might leak something like 500kWh of heat — value £10-£15. Many new cylinders (like the *Megaflow*) are encapsulated by 50mm of polyurethane which reduces heat lost over a 24hr period to under 1kW — nothing to all intents and purposes. Annual DHW costs using an average 225lts/day should be about 5000kWh or £100 for a gas or oil system. A super-lagged cylinder will save around £10/annum.

Dead Legs

The hot water piping running between the cylinder and the hot water taps is effectively an extension to the cylinder; water sitting there loses its heat very quickly. An efficiently designed installation would have around 5lts of water sitting in the hot pipes. This may sound insignificant, but bear in mind that every time a hot tap is opened some of this water is replaced and so if every hot tap is turned on just 3 times a day, then 15lts of extra hot water has to be heated (cost per annum 300kWh or £6-£10). An inefficient design with much longer *dead legs* — i.e. bathrooms and kitchen all at opposite ends of the house — might use four or five times the length of hot water pipe. Not only does the cost of supplying hot water to the dead legs then become significant (£30 plus/annum) but you start getting 20-30 second lags between opening the hot tap and getting hot water. Avoid long dead legs if possible.

There is a way around this problem which is to create a pumped hot water loop around the house so that there is always hot water at each hot tap. However you have the added cost of installing and running a circulation pump and, to be effective, you have to insulate the hot water pipes to a high standard otherwise you will gain very little.

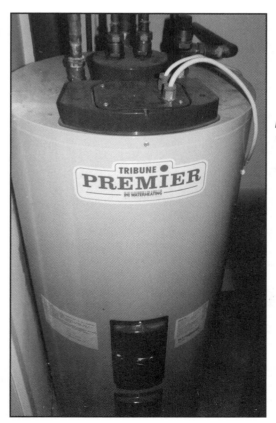

Left: this is the mains pressure hot water cylinder was fitted into the benchmark house. Right: inside a thermal store

Heating Controls

Before the days of central heating (c.1950), heating controls consisted of putting (or not putting) coal on the fire or, at best, an on/off switch on an electric heater. Here is an industry that has grown at a prodigious rate and there is now a bewildering range of options open to the householder. Yet the purpose of controls is quite simple:

- to increase comfort
- to decrease fuel consumption
- safety.

This section concentrates on wet heating systems; other heating systems (warm air, electric, solid fuel) tend to have different control systems which will be touched on in the following section, Alternative Heating.

Programmers

Timers to the layman. These are basically the on/off switch for the whole heating system and, as such, override all the other controls (except safety features like frost thermostats). Digital display has brought big improvements to programmers and now for little more than £30 you can get separate control for hot water heating and space heating which you can switch on and off 21 times a week. Changing the setting is about as easy as recording a film on the video — i.e. it helps to be young. Also, plumbers just love being called back to find out why the heating isn't coming on, only to find that you've been messing around with the programmer.

Look for ones with a boost (or "Extra Hour") facility which allows you to turn the system on at odd times (Potterton EP2001, Honeywell ST6400C, many others). A basic electronic programmer is now considered an absolutely essential component of a central heating system. Digital displays are now almost universal — although it hasn't made them easier to use or understand than the older ones with plastic knobs.

Thermostats

Known by plumbers as just *stats*, these provide a secondary level of on/off switching, controlled by temperature. So if the air or water temperature is higher than the thermostat setting, these controls will switch the heating system off, even though the programmer says "run."

- ROOM STATS: cost £12. Will cut off hot water to radiators when the set temperature is reached. Placing them requires care. To some extent being replaced by *TRVs* and *programmable thermostats*.
- CYLINDER STAT: cost £9. Does much the same for hot water cylinder. Some are integral with the cylinder, some are strapped onto the copper walls.
- BOILER STATS: Usually integral with the boiler, these set the temperature of water passing through the boiler, which is the hottest part of the system.
- FROST STAT: cost £20. A safety device which turns on heating if there is a danger of any components freezing — e.g. boilers in garages or other unheated spaces. It can of course take precedence over a timer which says the system should be off. Malfunctioning frost stats can be expensive to run and difficult to pinpoint.
- HIGH LIMIT STAT: cost £30. A safety device to stop sealed system boilers overheating (or boiling). Ask if your preferred boiler needs one.

Motorised Zone Valves

These are what the programmer operates; they are used to switch the flow of hot water around different parts (or zones) of the system. The cheapest systems use a 3-port valve (£40) but it is better to use two 2-port valves (2 x £30). The simplest valves switch all water either this way or that and therefore give rise to something called *hot water priority*, which means that the hot water stops being pumped around the radiators when the domestic hot water is being heated in the cylinder. There are more costly valves that are capable of opening in a middle position which allows a flow of hot water both ways.

A standard set of heating controls (excluding TRVs) for a four-bedroom house would cost around £200 (Mats £100, Lab £100). These controls are often sold in packages which usually include a pump, motorised valve, a programmer, a room stat and a cylinder stat. Note that wiring must be provided between all these components.

Further Controls

TRVs

Thermostatic radiator valves (TRVs) are apparently simple little gizmos fitted on to the bottom of the radiators that can sense the air temperature and switch off supply to the radiator when satisfied. They are cheap (£7); they increase comfort levels by stopping overheating and they reduce fuel bills. They are becoming almost standard — they are fitted in the benchmark house.

Minus

There have been problems with the operation of TRVs. Many people do not understand the principle of thermostatic control and, when feeling cold and seeing a dial, turn the TRVs on fully, thinking this will make the radiators hotter. It won't. Furthermore, because they require manual operation, there is no way of knowing (other than learning from experience) how high to set them to achieve comfortable space heating in any given room — though note that the latest versions (Danfoss) allow you to adjust the highest/lowest settings.

Another Minus

TRVs have been prone to sticking (usually in the off position) and many people have reported radiators not working at all at the beginning of the heating season. Drayton TRVs had a particularly poor record; I know of someone who took all their TRVs off because

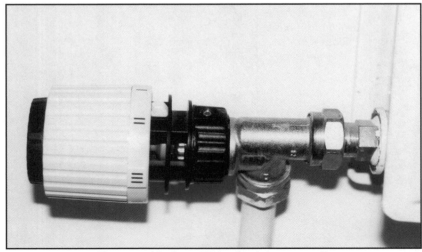

The near ubiquitous TRV — but is it any good?

they appeared to stop the radiators working at all. Manufacturing controls now appear to be better and this problem should be eliminated, but only time will tell. Honeywell TRVs are said to be among the more reliable.

Yet Another Minus

TRVs don't reduce fuel bills by as much as you might think — or that their manufacturers might claim. Although they can stop supply of hot water to the radiator to which they are fitted, they have no way of letting the boiler know this fact. In some systems which replace the room stat with TRVs, all radiators can be satisfied yet the boiler will continue to push hot water around the flow and return runs controlled only by the timer and the boiler thermostat. Don't be talked into doing away with the room stat just because you've fitted TRVs. They really only offer fine adjustments to the heating in each room.

Underfloor Systems

If you want underfloor heating controlled on a room-by-room basis, you have to use wall mounted room stats, which is an expensive option when compared with TRVs.

Programmable Thermostats

These combine the functions of the ordinary programmer (time switching) with that of the room stat (temperature switching). They also allow you to pre-select different temperature maximums for different times of day: very clever but even less user-friendly than the ordinary electronic programmers. A potential energy saver; a potential comfort increaser and no more expensive than a programmer and room stat separately. Whereas ordinary programmers can be placed anywhere that's convenient, once you introduce a thermostat you have to think very carefully about its location and which temperatures it will be measuring. Which? liked the Eberle Instat 2, cost £40.

Boiler Managers

(aka *optimisers* or *weather compensators*). Currently the most upmarket controls option available, the use of these is slowly filtering down from large industrial buildings to housing. The price reflects the variety and complexity of controls from relatively simple systems like the Honeywell AQ 6000 (costs around £150 — about double the bog standard controls) to multi-zoned systems like Landis & Gyr's RVP 75 (which starts at £270).

They aim to stabilise room temperatures whilst reducing the fuel consumption of boilers. You programme the manager to have your home heated to the temperatures you choose at the times you select and the manager decides the most efficient ways of

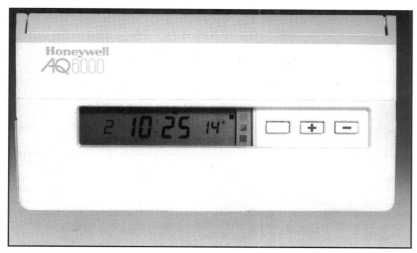

The Honeywell AQ6000 was the first boiler manager to be aimed at the home market

achieving this. A microprocessor is fed data monitoring outside air temperature and heating water temperature and it is able to independently switch the boiler and the pump on or off to maximise efficiency. Their use is particularly recommended with condensing boilers where they are able to maximise the length of time that the boilers can work in condensing mode (which increases fuel efficiency).

Minus

There have been problems to do with rusting heat exchangers when boiler managers have been coupled with a cast-iron boiler. Check with your boiler manufacturer to see if it is compatible with a boiler manager running a low temperature heating system.

Another Minus

The controls are even more difficult to understand than programmable thermostats; many people are likely to be flummoxed by them, which partly accounts for their slow uptake in domestic situations. This is particularly true of the more upmarket systems like the Landis & Gyr. If you lead an erratic lifestyle, in and out at all hours, the supposed efficiencies of a boiler manager will be wasted on you: but for homes with regular occupation patterns, a boiler manager should produce tangible savings.

Two Zone Heating Systems

An energy saving idea which splits the space heating into two heating zones — typically upstairs/downstairs — in addition to heating the hot water. It involves using a 3-zone programmer such as the Horstman *Channel Plus*. Again, the benefits very much depend on lifestyle — i.e. whether you really use your house in a predictable way. If, for instance, you hardly ever went upstairs before 9.00pm then you could have upstairs heating off all day which could conceivably save 10-15% of space heating bills. You could achieve similar results with TRVs but these would need daily manual adjustment. Zoning more complex than upstairs/downstairs is possible, but would probably involve longer and less efficient pipe runs which would tend to cancel out any advantage.

Are They Worth It?

The savings achieved by superior heating controls are extremely difficult to estimate because they depend to a large extent on how the house is lived in. Often manufacturers will claim 15% or 20% savings on running costs but these are usually comparisons with systems with no automatic controls, which are most unlikely to be fitted today.

A more reasonable assumption would be that any one of these extra levels of heating control might save 5% on fuel costs for heating. At the present time you cannot run a boiler manager covering more than one heating zone unless you pay around £370, so it's either/or but not both.

The oil-fired space heating system at the benchmark house should cost around £330/annum in oil, and so fitting a cocktail of sophisticated heating controls might save around £50/annum. However, had you already decided to spend extra money on super insulation and condensing boilers your prospective fuel bills would be halved, so your 15% saving would also be halved, down to something like £25/annum. Even so, the cost of more effective heating controls should not be more than £300 and so they are what you might call a moderately attractive investment.

Alternative Heating

Electric Heating

The electricity supply companies would be horrified to learn that they are an alternative heating supplier, but a scan of comparative fuel costs (see Which Fuel? earlier in this chapter) will show you why I have placed them in this category. The popularity of electric heating with developers is due almost entirely to its low installation costs. At peak rate it is a prohibitively expensive fuel to run (7p/kWh); off-peak is less than half this price (3.2p/kWh), but still twice the price of gas (1.5p/kWh). Off-peak night-storage heating is also about the most uncontrollable, unresponsive heating system ever designed, delivering the bulk of its heat when it's hardly needed.

To counteract these failings, the supply companies are now introducing tariffs with off-peak rates in the afternoon and evenings (ask for *Economy 10*). Also, they recognise that night-storage heaters are not everyone's idea of beauty and so they currently recommend underfloor heating topped up with ceiling heaters, which are designed to run on the new Economy 10 tariffs. These developments represent a big improvement in the outlook for electric heating — the pluses that apply to wet underfloor systems apply just as strongly to electric heating — yet as long as oil and gas remain half the price, electricity is unlikely to be many people's first choice. It will also remain a relatively uncontrollable heat source as long as the effective hours of use are limited to 10 per day.

Night storage heating for the benchmark house was quoted at £1800. This involved fitting 7 night storage heaters and providing convector radiators for the rest of the house. An electric underfloor/ceiling system was quoted at £1400 for underfloor heating just downstairs and ceiling heating to both downstairs and upstairs; adding an underfloor system upstairs (which would necessitate a beam and block first floor) adds just £200 to the whole system. Electric underfloor heating is now controlled automatically as standard in ways not dissimilar to how boiler managers work; both outside temperatures and screed temperatures are monitored to adjust the levels of heat input needed.

This *under and over* system, as it is known, is by some margin the cheapest form of central heating to install. Note, however, that quotes for these systems invariably anticipate a super-insulated house which would cost approximately £1000-£1500 more to construct; by super-insulating, you will have electric space heating bills similar to those of a bog standard house heated with gas or oil (i.e. around £350-400/annum for the benchmark house) — without taking these measures, your electric heating bill would leap to £720/annum. But also note that by super-insulating a gas- or oil-heated home, your heating bills will be reduced to around £200/annum. Over a 10-year period, it pays to super-insulate whichever heating system you choose. However, electric heating systems have come on leaps and bounds in the last few years and it is certainly worth considering as an option, particularly if you're interested in underfloor heating.

Your local electricity supply company will have a New Homes Dept. which will design and cost (and arrange installation of) a suitable system for your house. Other underfloor/overhead specialists are ESWA and Flexel. Also note that you can run a "wet" heating system with a GEC electric night storage boiler, but these are expensive to install (c. £2000 for just the boiler on the benchmark house) which rather destroys the main attraction of electric heating

Plus

No additional connection charges: available everywhere: cheap installation costs: low maintenance costs as the "boiler" is located at a distant power station: doesn't leak: no radiators with underfloor heating: underfloor heating coupled with convector booster heaters are actually a very good team, the first giving comfortable heat, the second giving quick response.

Minus

Expensive to run: generally unresponsive: underfloor heating concept does not work so well upstairs: not very green: when comparing quotations don't overlook the fact that electric heating makes no allowance for domestic hot water: Economy 7 cylinders are expensive and limited.

Warm Air

These heating systems are usually seen with gas boilers (or LPG). Oil-fired systems tend to be imported from the USA and are prohibitively expensive; electric systems are now rarely used on new installations. Johnson and Starley are market leaders with their conventional flued, floor-standing gas-fired warm-air boilers. The system must be installed by a CORGI registered installer and would cost around £3300 for the benchmark house. This would include a gas-fired boiler and all the ducting to push the hot air around the house, but domestic hot water (DHW) would have to be supplied by other means.

Plus

Very responsive — heat house quickly: no radiators: air can be filtered: easily and cheaply combined with a heat recovery system.

Minus

Warm air is the least comfortable form of heating: lacks any radiant heat and, despite air filtering, tends to throw up more dust particles: needs to be very carefully commissioned in order to distribute heat evenly: lacks the sophisticated controls available in wet systems. Not well understood in UK: poorly designed and installed they have been known to be noisy.

Heat Recovery

see next section on Ventilation

Underfloor Heating

see previous section on Emitters

Solar Power

A standard installation on a 166m² family house would cost over £2000 for the flat plate collector and about £3500 for a vacuum tube collector. The vacuum tubes are a considerable improvement; they are sensitive to light rather than sunshine and they are not as affected by wind chill. However, even when working at full whack the output is only going to be 3kW: this would easily be enough to provide DHW in the summer and provide some DHW in the winter. The problem is that the cost of DHW heating with a well insulated cylinder and a gas-or oil-fired boiler is remarkably small — just £100/annum in the benchmark house. Getting £40 or £50 of "free" hot water each year is paltry when compared to installation costs; the payback period is as much as 70 years. If you're still interested, make sure to find out how much additional plumbing you are getting for your money. Until someone does for solar collectors what Alan Sugar did for word processors (i.e. makes them v cheap), they will remain a green toy.

Having said that, there are signs that solar panels will become cheaper as they become much more widely installed in places with warmer, sunnier climes than ours. If you are interested in alternative energy production generally, you should point yourself towards the Centre for Alternative Technology in North Wales (01654 702400). They have carried out much excellent pioneering work in this field and they also have an excellent bookshop.

Plus
Very cheap to run: low maintenance.

Minus
Very expensive to install and unlikely to be cost effective for the foreseeable future: the collectors are often an eyesore: difficult to access for servicing.

Solid Fuel

Solid fuel stoves exist which can handle heating for the largest houses. This means that they can be harnessed to provide hot water to be pumped around radiators and through the hot water cylinder as well as giving off more than a pleasing glow in the room where they sit. They come in three basic styles, the decorative cast-iron finish to go in the living room, the kitchen range which adds cooking capabilities, or the utilitarian box to be hidden out of view, now rarely seen.

They are never going to win on the convenience stakes as in order to perform the task equivalent to a gas/oil boiler they will have to be kept going all through the winter, which means frequent stoking, riddling and emptying. Attempts by manufacturers like Charnwood to market automatically loading and emptying stoves have been abandoned because of high cost. And in the semi-cold seasons (September-November and March-May) you'll never be quite sure if or when to fire up and so you'll need some sort of backup system (probably electric), which rather defeats the purpose of spending all the money in the first place. There is still a place for them as whole house heat sources, but realistically only in homes permanently occupied. Many remote locations still suffer regular power cuts and the ability to heat the home without recourse to electrically controlled components remains important yet, like other wet central heating systems, solid fuel systems are nowadays designed with electric pumps and valves to distribute the hot water so even this potential advantage is largely lost.

Living Room Stoves

The *Coalbrookdale* range (made by Glynwed who also make Agas and Rayburns) are well known and readily available. There are four sizes and each size is available with or without a boiler. Without a boiler, the stoves are really just efficient room fires; the boiler (which absorbs around 60-70% of the stove's heat output) is essential if a wet whole house heating and DHW system is wanted. The benchmark house would require at least the second largest Coalbrookdale, the *Severn*, which belts out 10kW of hot water as well as 3kW of room heat. It weighs a quarter of a ton and costs around £900. There are a number of other manufactures, both British and European, who produce variations on the same theme some with highly individualist styling (Euroheat, Waterford's Erin, Morso) but prices are remarkably similar.

Kitchen Ranges

Another approach is to use a cast iron cooker as a centre piece in a kitchen. The *Aga* is the best known and, at around £3300 to buy, the most expensive. However the Aga only has a small boiler, capable of supplying DHW but not further space heating. There are a range of good-looking stoves which can cook, heat and do DHW — e.g. Rayburn, Stanley, Wamsler, Hergom. Strictly speaking, we're moving away from solid fuel because these cooker/heaters can be (and most frequently are) fired by gas or oil. In its solid fuel version the top of the range Rayburn would be just big enough (16kW) to provide for the benchmark house — but it would require refuelling every 2 hours! Overnight its output would drop to just 2kW, which would make those January mornings a bit too nippy and would necessitate electric backup heating. At around £2400 plus installation costs it's an expensive but stylish option. Wamsler produce a solid fuel central heating cooker that looks more basic (as you might see in a restaurant kitchen) which is about 25% less than Rayburns and Stanleys. All these ranges can be run in summer, thus doing away with the need for separate cookers, but then they belt out more heat than you'd really want.

To find out more, check out dealers in the Yellow Pages under *Heating Eqpt - solid fuel.*

Plus
Style: reliability: doesn't pack up during power cuts (although central heating at least is usually electrically pumped): many stoves are "multi-fuel" which means they can burn virtually anything, which may be an attraction if you own a wood or a peat bog.

Minus
Initial price is high: need back up heating: extra housework: fuel not especially cheap: inefficient (unlike gas or oil the boiler can't be turned off at the flick of a switch): unresponsive: fuel needs storage: need open flue (and probably chimney): room stoves get hot and are not child friendly.

Cooling

Air conditioning and cooling has always been thought of as being unnecessary in UK homes because our summer climate never got that hot. However the sweltering summer of '95 caused many people to wish that they had something more sophisticated than an electric fan installed in their home. There are home air conditioning systems available in the UK but whilst new housebuilders show increasing interest in more and more sophisticated ways of staying warm during the 20-odd week annual heating season, there remains approximately nil interest in staying cool during the 10-week high summer period.

Why? Well for a starter, it is expensive to install. A whole house air condition system for a detached house would set you back in the region of £5000, rather more than the most elaborate heating systems on the market. A one room system would cost around £1500. The existing models are all electrically powered and a whole house model would consume around 3-5kW of power when going at full blast — typically it would run for only 50% of the time, even on the hottest of days, providing you remember to keep the doors and windows shut. The units also tend to be noisy, though this problem can be reduced if the design of the installation is good. Like boilers, air conditioning needs to have exhaust ducting and this means that the system has to be built in permanently and is connected to an outdoor unit. To my knowledge, there are no portable air conditioners that you could move around the house with you. Most of the businesses selling air conditioning concentrate on commercial sites like shops and offices but one firm that is active (and would like to be even more active) in the residential market is Trane (01675 444000). If you want to find out more, they are a good place to start your inquiries.

Ventilation

Buildings need to breathe. Almost any space that becomes airtight sooner or later becomes a problem. Trapped water vapour in particular can be very damaging, causing condensation and encouraging mould growth and wet rot. It's a potential problem in both the external structure of a house — especially under ground floors and in roofs — and the enclosed living space.

The building regulations deal with the need for ventilation in both areas. Underfloor ventilation (only applicable with suspended ground floors) is by way of air bricks; roof ventilation is by eaves or soffit vents and occasionally air bricks too.

The building regs dealing with *internal* ventilation specify that habitable rooms must have opening windows fitted with trickle vents (more on these later) and that kitchens and bathrooms must have extractor fans (or "adequate means of extraction"). A cooker hood ducted to the outside is acceptable in a kitchen or else there must be an extractor fan capable of shifting 60 lts/s (litres/second); the bathroom fan must be capable of shifting 15 lts/s. A separate toilet can make do with an opening window or a small fan.

Standard Solutions
Fit trickle vents in the windows. Extractor fans in kitchens and bathrooms.

Trickle Vents
These slimline plastic inserts (also known as *headline vents*) have now become nearly universal on standard joinery — indeed Boulton & Paul no longer supply windows without them. Trickle vents, which can be open or closed from inside, are slotted into a hole drilled out of the head of the window. Some manufacturers still charge £6 extra for fitting them, some just supply windows with just the slots cut out and supply the vents separately at around £6/ea.

Cooker Hoods
Normally fitted as standard in kitchens, although they don't have to be ducted outside. It makes very good sense to make sure your cooker does duct directly outside as it works much better and saves the cost of a second, more powerful extractor fan. Cooker hoods are usually sold as part of a package with hobs and ovens. They cost around £50-60: automatic versions with humidity controlled switching are available at around £90-£100.

Bathroom Fans
A basic, 15 lts/s, fan (such as the Vent Axia 100L costing £25) can be controlled by a pull switch, or linked to a room light switch. Bathrooms without windows have to have models fitted with automatic overrun timers, and where ducting is required a centrifugal fan is recommended (Vent Axia Solo T: £45). At the top end of the range (Vent Axia Solo HP2: £87), the fans have humidistats which can automatically switch fans between off, low and high settings dependent on humidity in the bathroom.

Not included in the above prices for fans are exterior wall grilles (£4) or any ducting (£12/3lin.m). Fans can be ducted horizontally through external walls or vertically into the roof space and then out through the ridge via a ridge vent tile (£45) or through a roof vent tile (£35). Fitting is normally done by the electrician and budget charges will be around £20 for the switch (Mats £5, Lab £15) and around £25 labour for fitting the fan, more if there are complex ducting routes involved.

The total cost of these measures on the benchmark house was around £400, made up as follows:

- Trickle Vents   16@ £6   £96
- Cooker Hood and Ducting   £100
- Bathroom Fans 3 @ £100   £300

Whole House Systems
Mechanical Ventilation

The building regs allow for radically different approaches to ventilation. One is to do away with trickle vents and to provide both extract and inlet ventilation via a series of ducts controlled by electric fans. A number of manufacturers are extolling the virtue of recapturing some of the heat being thrown out of the house by extractor fans and mixing it with fresh air brought in through the loft. A house built to current building regs will lose as much as 25% of its heat by required ventilation — in the benchmark house, that would amount to £50-£70/annum. Worth saving. Unfortunately, a heat recovery system will cost at least £1500 to install and as much as £70/annum to run because it is powered by two electric fans on continuously; in addition there will be occasional servicing costs. In terms of power saved v power used (known as the efficiency ratio), heat recovery systems perform reasonably well, but when costed it turns out that the power saved usually costs about 2p/kWh, whereas the electricity to run the unit is costing around 7p/kWh. The evidence suggests that, in our temperate climate, airborne heat recovery systems are not good value.

When pressed, most manufacturers will admit that the economic return is negligible but will still insist that there are benefits in increased comfort levels. This may well be true but it will have to be taken as an act of faith because it is notoriously difficult to predict how an as yet unbuilt house will behave: most people find warm, well insulated housing remarkably comfortable and free of condensation without recourse to mechanical heat recovery systems.

To find out more, contact ABB, Indux, Rega Metal Products who are prominent among the many who advertise regularly in the self-build magazines.

Passive Stack Ventilation
This is another option that can be used if you are interested in whole house ventilation. Passive stack ventilation also uses ducts to

Trickle vents are now placed above most windows to ensure adequate background ventilation

Diagram of how Willan's passive stack ventilation system works

extract stale air from the house but there the similarity ends. Trickle vents are fitted in all the dry rooms (i.e. living rooms, bedrooms) whilst ducts run from the wet areas (bathrooms, kitchens) up to a vented ridge tile; air pressure does the rest, drawing air in through the house and away through the roof. A simple concept, essentially no different to a chimney stack (hence the name). Each extract duct has to be connected to its own vented ridge tile via an insulated flexible pipe and will cost £120-£150; in certain situations (bathrooms with no external walls) this will be cheaper than using a centrifugal fan with ducting. A whole house system (with four passive stacks) would cost around £555 (Mats £430, Lab £125). Add a cooker hood (which is recommended) and the overall cost will be around 60% more than the bog standard route.

Willan, who are currently the sole distributors of PSV systems, produce a superior version called *Passivent* which introduces humidistats on both the inlets (trickle vents) and the extract grilles. This effectively cuts down excessive air-changes as the vents close below a certain level of humidity. Strictly speaking this would seem to be contrary to the building regs standard that half an air-change per hour should take place throughout the house, but humidity levels are a good indicator of the level of use a room is getting (people produce water vapour) and no one seems to be complaining. The "intelligent system" with humidistats costs around £225 more than the ordinary stack system, and nearly double the bog standard route — though still half the price of mechanical heat recovery. For around £400 above the standard solution, you get a system that works without anything mechanical to go wrong and introduces an element of heat saving. Passive stack systems are still relatively new and many architects and designers are unaware of their existence: if you want to find out more contact Willan.

Comment

The subject of ventilation is intriguing because it is as yet very poorly understood. There is a general consensus that ventilation needs to be planned into modern buildings but there is no agreement on how much ventilation is really needed. If it were a question of just replacing oxygen used by the inhabitants, the ventilation rate would have to be no more than 1lt/s/person: some authorities think a minimum figure should be about 2.5 times this level, others think it should be no less than 40 times this level. Our current building regulations suggest that 0.5 air-changes/hr is sufficient — this equates to around 50lts/s in our 410m³ benchmark house which puts it bang in the middle of the range of assumptions.

Both mechanical and passive stack ventilation systems work on the assumption that, without their intervention, houses would be inadequately ventilated and would suffer from:

- excess water vapour
- condensation
- smells
- stuffiness
- general lack of oxygen
- build-up of toxic gases like radon, formaldehyde or Volatile Organic Compounds given off by synthetic carpet and the like.

However, it is worth emphasising that before spending good money on fancy ventilation systems, you should ensure that you have a reasonably airtight structure. The "air-leakiness" of your house may make the installation of such fancy ventilation schemes quite redundant. Even with trickle vents all sealed, it would appear that many UK homes will "self-ventilate" at a level of around two air-changes per hour just through leaks in the structure — for instance, where there is imperfect draught sealing around doors, windows, skirting boards, pipe holes and loft hatches; an unsealed chimney alone extracts 20lts of air/s.

A cursory glance at heat-loss calculations for the benchmark house (see Chapter 10) will show what a large part heating air-changes plays in the overall heating costs. At half an air-change/hr (50lts/s), the benchmark house would loose just over £50 of heat per annum; however, if the house is built "leaky" — at say two air-changes/hr — then this heat-loss figure will multiply fourfold to around £200 per year. In comparison, the so-called building fabric (walls, roof, ground floor, windows) ships no more than £130 of heat during the course of a year, so you can see what an important place ventilation has in the scheme of things.

So if you are interested in installing something more advanced than the bog standard ventilation requirements, you should pay careful attention to draught proofing beforehand. To this effect, you should fit a damper on your chimney to shut it off when not in use, you should seal all cracks, holes and joints with a flexible silicone sealer — dry-lined plasterboard walls have a particularly bad reputation in this respect — and you should consider fitting a proprietary sealed loft hatch (like Marley's, cost £50). Pay attention to door furniture so that you do not have open keyholes and note that french doors and stable doors are particularly difficult to draught proof.

Pressure Tests

If you want to take this process to it's logical conclusion, then you can have a pressure test carried out on your house for around £150. They attach a giant vacuum cleaning-type device which puts the house under pressure and then measure the leakage rate. The UK average for new build is just under one air change/hr. This may seem an expensive and unnecessary test to put your house through, but if you are about to pay out a great deal more than this for a whole house ventilation system not to mention an elaborate heating system, it's possibly worth ensuring that it's at least going to work as planned. Contact Wimtec Environmental (01753 737744).

Standard Electrics

Market Standards

The housebuilding industry's standard for electrical provision is someway in advance of the minimum requirements listed in the left side column. This will surprise many who automatically assume that professional developers always try and get away with the bare minimum, but in fact the NHBC standards for power supply to any new house are absolutely basic and most house buyers and selfbuilders will want around double that number of outlets. As the table 8f opposite shows, power and lighting specifications for the benchmark house are way above these standards — you could hardly have less than one light per room. The benchmark house has a rather superior lighting specification and, without going over the top, the builders have spent rather more than many developers would.

Complete Fabrications specified a reasonably generous number of power points together with four outside lights, a fluorescent light in the garage, lights in the airing cupboard and loft. The living room is fitted with uplighters but elsewhere lighting is by central pendant. It's not an elaborate spec for a reasonably upmarket house but even so it's well in advance of the NHBC minimum. It's worth bearing in mind that even if you chose the NHBC minimum standard for lighting, you would probably spend a lot more money on lampshades, table lamps and fittings, all of which would attract VAT at 17.5%, whereas built-in light fittings are zero rated in a new house. It's probably a fair estimate to assume that you won't be leaving naked bulbs hanging for more than about five years and that in the long run you'll spend an additional £500 on shades and separate table lamps.

You may feel that the NHBC minimum requirements are a red herring but, be warned, that costs derived from these standards are widely used by businesses selling the bits of houses that don't include the wiring, to illustrate how much (or how little) it will cost to finish off the house. So it is as well to be aware that by current market standards the minimum requirements are unrealistically low — possibly by as much as 50%.

The accompanying table 8f shows just how each element of an electrician's quotation would be made up and how this translates into a whole house quotation — in this case the one used on our benchmark house. It is compared with the NHBC minimum standards.

Quality

More than most aspects of construction, electrical fittings vary enormously in quality. For many years, the market has been dominated by two British businesses, MK and Crabtree: indeed many specifiers indicate that fittings should be by either of these two firms. But there is a huge gulf between MK/Crabtree prices and some very cheap imported gear that you can get hold of. The current QVS catalogue has MK Logic Plus 13amp sockets at £6.10 each; however they also have unbadged versions of the same line "to British Standard" going out at £1.62 each. I may be wrong but common sense tells me that MK and Crabtree aren't making £4.48 surplus profit on every double socket they sell, so there must be something they do that makes for a better socket. If you want a mid-priced alternative, I can recommend MEM (0161 652 111 for catalogue). Somewhere about the £3-£4 mark.

The electrician begins marking up positions for lights and sockets. For many housebuilders this is the only time they pay any attention to lighting design and it's all too often a rushed and ill-thought out process

8f: Guide Prices for Wiring and Lighting

ITEM	MATS	LABOUR	TOTAL	BENCHMARK HOUSE		NHBC MINIMUM	
				NO.	COST	NO.	COST
POWER CIRCUITS/CONSUMER UNIT							
Double Socket	£8.50	£12.00	£20.50	25	£510	11	£226
Single Socket	7.00	12.00	19.00	3	£60	3	£57
Fused Spur	7.50	12.00	19.50	4	£80	1	£20
5-amp Socket	7.50	12.00	19.50				
Cooker Switch	12.50	15.00	27.50	1	£30	1	£28
Cooker Outlet	5.00	10.00	15.00	2	£30	1	£15
Shaver Point	25.00	20.00	45.00				
Immersion Point	8.00	20.00	28.00	1	£30	1	£28
External Sockets	15.00	30.00	45.00	1	£50		
Consumer Unit	30.00	10.00	40.00	1	£40	1	£40
RCDs	40.00	4.00	44.00	1	£40		
Each Fuse	4.00	2.00	6.00	10	£60	8	£48
TV/TELECOM WIRING							
Coaxial Point	7.00	12.00	19.00	2	£40	1	£19
Telephone Point	4.00	12.00	16.00	3	£50	1	£16
Loft Aerial	20.00	20.00	40.00	1	£40		
Door Bell	5.00	20.00	25.00	1	£30		
SAFETY							
Smoke Detectors	30.00	15.00	45.00	2	£90	2	£90
LIGHTING							
1-gang Switch	4.00	10.00	14.00	9	£130	13	£182
2-gang Switch	6.00	15.00	21.00	4	£80		
3-gang Switch	8.00	20.00	28.00				
Pull switch	6.00	10.00	16.00	3	£50	2	£32
2-way Switching	2.00	5.00	7.00	2	£10	1	£7
3-way Switching	4.00	8.00	12.00	1	£10		
Central Pendant	4.00	10.00	14.00	17	£240	12	£168
Fixed Ceiling Light	3.00	10.00	13.00	2	£30	2	£26
Down Light	2.00	10.00	12.00				
Wall Light	2.00	15.00	17.00	7	£120		
Extra for Light Fittings	25.00	20.00	45.00	7	£320		
External Light Points	5.00	20.00	25.00	3	£80		
FANS							
Bathroom Fans	50.00	50.00	100.00	3	£300	3	£300
Kitchen Fan		30.00	30.00	1	£30		
			TOTALS		£2580		£1300

House Wiring

Connection Fees

Regional electricity companies (RECs) are free to set their own connection fees and, being monopoly suppliers of an indispensable power source, they tend to charge a lot. There is no minimum charge, but even a straightforward connection is likely to cost in the region of £300; if you are considering electric heating in your house, you may find that the REC offers to halve or even waive the entire connection fee as a sweetener. Long cable runs (say in excess of 50m) can be prohibitively expensive, costing thousands, and should be carefully costed when assessing the plot. Each REC has a new supplies department, which is where you should look for quotations; you don't need to own the plot before getting a quotation.

Temporary Supplies

Some builders manage without temporary electricity supplies, relying on generators and diesel powered mixers; indeed most of the house superstructure can be easily erected without power tools. However, plumbers, electricians and second-fix carpenters are big users of power tools and you can't have your permanent supply turned on until they're finished so, for most builders, a temporary supply makes good sense. Current regs insist that the temporary supply board is adequately housed; on most sites this means building a blockwork box with at least a paving slab roof and a lockable door. Budget a day's work and £100 materials to build an adequate shed with consumer unit and sockets on a backing board inside. Care should be given to locating the temporary supply so that long cables are not left trailing over the site where they could be run over by diggers, dumpers or lorries. Discuss your requirements with the REC's new supplies estimator; there will be an extra charge for temporary supply but it's usually not large, provided there are no major cable detours.

Meter Boxes

The industry standard is to install white plastic boxes built into the external wall. The RECs like them because they can access the meter without entering the house; builders like them because the RECs supply them free (as they do lengths of underground ducting) and they can be built into the outer skin brick wall without a lintel. Only problem is that they are ugly, ugly enough to ruin a fancy period facade. If this bothers you then either look to locate the plastic meter box where it won't detract from your kerb appeal or insist that the company supply comes into the house where it can be concealed in a cupboard. British Gas supplies have the same problem but they offer an alternative meter box concealed in the ground; however, this is felt to be unsafe for an electrical supply. Water meters are always concealed in the ground.

Consumer Units and RCDs

The consumer unit — what used to be known as the *fuse box* — is the place where the REC's supply is split into a number of separate circuits for distribution around the house. There are conventions on how these circuits should be arranged, although the exact design will depend on each particular layout. A 10-gang unit will suffice for all but the largest houses and it is recommended not to economise too much on this item. Miniature circuit breakers (MCBs) have now all but replaced the traditional fuses; instead of fusewire blowing, a little button pops out and reconnection is never more complicated than pressing the button in again.

Another recent development is the advent of Residual Circuit-Breaking Devices (RCDs) — now mandatory — which provide increased protection against electrocution in event of contact with live wires. One drawback of RCDs is that they are very sensitive and that they can be triggered by thunderstorms or faulty equipment. Another problem is with gadgets that must not have their power supply cut off — chiefly freezers. An RCD-inspired power cut out could have very messy consequences if it occurred during your two weeks in the Algarve, and for this reason it is recommended that freezers are run off separate circuits not protected by an RCD. The net result of all this is that you'll be spending around £100 on your consumer unit whereas in the bad old days it might have cost only £20.

Sockets

If you've got deep pockets, fit lots of sockets — but at £20-£25/outlet this can rapidly become a prohibitively expensive option. If you know how you are going to arrange beds and furniture in each room you can minimise the

A temporary supply box — waterproof and secure

Plastic meter boxes — convenient but ugly, even when painted

number of sockets needed; if you want to retain flexibility for each room then you'll probably need a minimum of three sockets per bedroom and four sockets in living rooms. Don't think that you are saving money by fitting single sockets instead of doubles. The work involved in installing them is identical; the materials price is only pennies different. You can step-up to brass fronted sockets for £3/outlet.

Safety Issues

Britain is one of the few countries that allows unqualified people to install wiring. A new installation is routinely checked over by the REC before final connection is made but the inspections are often rather cursory and often they only check that the earth bonding is in place . There are a number of areas where D-I-Y housewirers — and professional electricians come to that — are prone to make untraceable errors and you be well advised to steer clear of house wiring unless you have a thorough knowledge of the tasks in hand. Even if you are just supervising a subcontractor, you should be on your guard for the following errors.

Cables in Walls

Cables buried in walls must be set either vertically or horizontally from the outlets they supply. The idea is that the follow-on trades have some idea where not to drill holes. However, this requirement is frequently ignored in the rush to get jobs done and sometimes even to try and save money by using less cable. Even if you know where the cable is buried and, therefore, think it doesn't matter, don't forget that the cable will still be there long after you've moved on and some poor sucker thirty years hence could be in for a nasty surprise. Technically, you are allowed to run cables within 150mm of internal corners and wall/ceiling junctions, but this habit cannot be recommended.

Earth Bonding

It is a requirement that exposed metalwork should be earthed to prevent it becoming "live." This is normally done with 10mm Earthing Cable (it's green and yellow). What exactly needs to be bonded?

- Water and gas mains as they enter the house. Also oil tanks
- Any exposed structural steelwork and oil tanks
- All services must be bonded together
- All metal in bathrooms must be bonded together.

Circuit Lengths

Many electricians do not realise that there are prescribed maximum circuit lengths for any given cable size. For instance, a normal ring main run in 2.5mm^2 cable should not be longer than 66m. Further information is available from IEE, Savoy Place, London WC2R 0DL: ref. a booklet called the "On-Site Guide."

Electric Heating

If you are interested in electric heating — and it's a much improved product — then your best bet is to contact your REC's New Homes Department. They are rather more entrepreneurial than British Gas — their product is harder to sell — and they are keen to suggest and quote for different types of electric heating (cf. underfloor, night storage, electric boilers). These can be installed by specialists or by your own electrician. The power supply to your house is likely to be uprated — in some cases to three-phase — but you are unlikely to have to pay excess for this. Off-peak electricity is what it's all about and your off-peak usage will be metered separately and controlled by a separate consumer unit. For a more detailed assessment of electric heating, refer to the section, Alternative Heating, earlier in this chapter.

Off-peak Electricity

Even if you don't choose to install electric heating, you can still have an *Economy 7* meter fitted at no extra cost and enjoy the savings of using half-price, off-peak power at night. For a more detailed discussion see Chapter 10, Kitchen and Laundry.

Frequently Overlooked

When designing electricity supplies to a house there are a number of points to watch out for — and easily forgotten at the first-fix, cable burying stage. Many electricians are used to doing what they are told and no more and will be of little help in designing a better system. Here is a bulletted list of commonly forgotten wiring details:

- Loft lights, cupboard lights — do you want them?
- Separate freezer circuit — preferably not protected by RCD
- Separate garage supply if garage is external
- Outside power points, security lights, welcome lights
- Kitchen unit lighting — usually fixed below wall units
- Wiring for electric showers and power shower pumps
- Wiring and installation of fans in bathrooms and kitchen
- Separate circuit for immersion heater
- Outlets left for smoke detectors (now mandatory)
- Doorbell wiring
- Heating controls wiring: boiler, programmer, thermostats, pump and valves all need to be connected. This work is often undertaken by the plumber but the electrician must leave at least a fused spur to power the controls. If the plumber does this wiring, then a separate test certificate will be needed from him
- Fused spurs for waste disposal units and/or water softeners
- Wiring to sewage or waste pumps
- Wiring for electric garage door operators: needs an accurately placed single socket, not really a problem if power is in the garage
- Burglar alarm first-fix.

Off-peak meters are now switched remotely by the REC

On Light

The best light is natural sunlight. *Lux* is a measurement of light density and whereas 500 lux is the generally accepted level of electric light needed for reading, bright sunshine delivers 100,000 lux and even a cloudy overcast day will produce 5000 lux of light.

The older you get the more light you need. A 60-year-old requires ten times more light than a 10-year-old.

Apart from brightness, there are two qualities of light that are important.

Colour Rendering

Some light sources show colours close to their natural daylight colours and are said to have good colour render. Other sources — notably orange street lamps — are incapable of showing any colour variations at all. Fluorescent lighting (including low-energy light bulbs) tends to give a washed-out, faded look to colours. This bothers some people more than others, but before you install energy-saving lightbulbs everywhere in your house, make sure you can live with the light quality.

Colour Appearance

Or How White is Your Lamp? The bog standard tungsten lamp which we all know and love is said to be orange white — others say warm; halogen is, like Daz, a whiter white — or crisp white; fluorescents give off a milky, cool white, though there are now some warm-coloured fluorescents available.

This may seem all very technical and uninteresting but the quality of the light source is an important feature of how a room looks. Some lighting designers will actually recommend that a multipurpose room (say an office by day and a living room by night) has two different lighting schemes — fluorescent for business, tungsten or tungsten-halogen for pleasure. The feel of the room is then transformed at the flick of a switch.

Lights by Type

Central Pendant Lighting

This is the bog standard lighting scheme much loved by penny-pinching developers. It provides adequate ambient (background) lighting and it will always be the most efficient way of distributing light into a room but it is, generally, a very poor source for reading by or carrying out intricate manual operations because you will tend to be in the shade. It is really only a very good light source when the light is wanted directly beneath it — e.g.

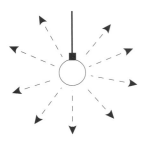

Central pendant

dining tables — but most other light sources require multiple outlets in each room to work well and so pendant lighting will remain a cheap and cheerless option.

Spotlights

Back in the 60s the appearance of spotlights on the scene was a breath of fresh air and they became the first popular form of directional lighting. They are still immensely popular but there are often better ways of achieving the required results. Because the entire fitting is fixed and visible, spotlights have the ability to completely ruin the look of a room, especially when mounted on tracks in the middle of ceilings.

Downlighters

Light sources concealed in the ceiling have the big advantage of being stylistically neutral — i.e. they can blend in with any type of decor. They have the disadvantage of only being able to light a rather limited area and a large room lit entirely with downlighters might need as many as ten — which is expensive. Despite their name, downlighters do not have to point straight down: there are "eyeball" versions which beam the light off at an angle — in effect sidelighters.

Low-voltage halogen downlighters, which supply a very bright, good quality light, are now the height of fashion and some lighting specialists specify them almost exclusively.

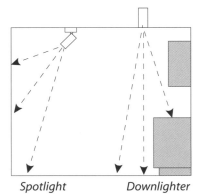

Spotlight   *Downlighter*

The low-voltage is achieved by the use of transformers and, whilst installation is not particularly difficult, incorrect wiring can be dangerous — there are many electricians who know nothing of low-voltage work. If you are fitting low-voltage, then make sure that yours does.

Uplighters

These work by reflecting light off another surface (usually the ceiling) and many people assume that the light quality will therefore be low. However — provided the room has white or near-white ceilings — they are actually a very efficient way of providing ambient light and the light cast down from the

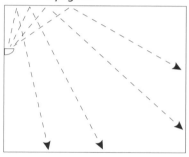

Uplighter

ceiling is usually very good for reading under. Uplighters are normally fixed slightly above eye level to conceal the light source and they come in many shapes and forms; one particularly popular one is to fit *unglazed* ceramic bowls (cost £15-£25) and then to paint them with the same emulsion used on the surrounding walls. This provides a stylistically neutral form of lighting that blends well with natural wood finishes and off-white walls.

Sidelights and Table Lamps

People habitually refer to their sidelights as "reading lights" which suggests that the central light is good for vacuum cleaning and not much else. There is an enormous variety of shapes and styles to suit every taste; table lamps from £5 upwards, floor (or standard) lamps from £30. The one big advantage of independent lights is that you retain the flexibility to arrange your room in any fashion you choose, as long as you've got a socket nearby.

5-amp Plugs

A handy idea for living rooms where you want to have a number of sidelights is to fit a series of 5-amp lighting sockets (usually with small round-pin holes to distinguish them from 13-amp mains sockets). These can be linked together and all switched from one point. It's convenient not only because it gives you a master switch to control all the sidelights plugged into the 5-amp sockets, but it

also gives you the ability to dim. By arranging the switching next to the door, it gives you the option of doing away with the central pendant lighting altogether. Budget £20-£30 per outlet plus a similar amount for the switch.

If you know nothing about the art of good lighting and you are in a hurry and don't want to waste a small fortune, you won't go wrong by specifying a handful of 5-amp sockets. You can create quite sophisticated lighting effects by using side lighting and, without spending a fortune on fittings, you can get pools of light wherever you want them whilst retaining a flexibility to change it all if you get bored and want something different.

Dimmers

Dimmer switches give you the ability to control the amount of light given off by a bulb and thus set the mood for a room. They are particularly useful in living rooms where you may want to relax in front of the tele, watching the fire, and don't want to do it under the glare of 100 watt bulbs. Furthermore, dimmed lights save energy, and if you use dimmers which *don't* have a push on/off capability, you increase the length of your bulb life by having a "soft start" — most bulbs blow when you turn them on. As regular dimmers can be bought for around £5 (as compared with £3 for an on/off switch), there is an argument for fitting them just about everywhere. You can dim just about any kind of light but the standard dimming switches will only work on the standard GLS tungsten lightbulbs; specialist bulbs (i.e. fluorescent, halogen, low-voltage) require specialist dimmers which cost £25-£30 for one gang switching. Contact Home Automation (01249 443422).

Alternative Lighting

If you wanted to improve on the basic developer's specification at the design stage, there are two other routes which you may be interested in.

The Green Approach

An energy-efficient lighting scheme is looked at in some detail in Chapter 10, Green Issues. I estimate this would add around £300-£400 to building costs (but would cut furnishing costs by perhaps £150-£200) and could easily save £50/annum on electricity bills.

The High-tech Approach

In this low-voltage light scheme, the emphasis is on quality using ultra-bright, tungsten-halogen downlighters. Because of the comparatively narrow light fields of low-voltage downlighters, a bedroom would require a minimum of four and a living room probably eight or more. Costs of lighting the benchmark house would be in the £3000-£4000 range. Perhaps more realistically, you could choose to light just one room with low voltage but budget at least £75/outlet. Low-voltage lighting is less power hungry than standard tungsten bulbs but low-voltage lighting schemes get used to provide more and better lighting and therefore don't imagine that such a scheme will save you on running costs, even when a scheme incorporates a number of compact fluorescent bulbs as well. There are many specialists in this area, though mostly working in the commercial field. Marlin (0181 894 5522) will undertake free designs and quotations on a whole house basis.

Central pendant lighting doesn't have to be a single bulb. Here Bovis strain for that Paris Metro look

Lighting Room by Room

Kitchens

Central pendant lighting is particularly inept at providing light for kitchen worksurfaces, and this is one area where task lighting is now considered essential. The conventional place for this is under the wall cupboard units, hidden from view by the decorative downstand known as the pelmet. There is a choice of tungsten or fluorescent fittings; tungsten gives better light rendering but gets hot and tends to "cook" the contents of the overhead cupboard; fluorescent stays cool and is generally preferable, particularly if you choose a warm, white type like Sylvania *Homelight de Luxe.* An alternative is to fit downlighters in the ceiling over the kitchen surfaces, but placement has to be extremely accurate and you risk getting unlit areas under the wall units. If you have an extractor hood, make sure it has a light as well. Lumiance have introduced a range of low voltage halogen downlighters which are only 20mm deep and are specifically designed to fit into a cupboard shelf. If your kitchen design doesn't want or need pelmets under your wall cupboards and you don't want exposed lights, then this is the answer for you.

Dining Tables

A pendant light hanging over a dining table works very well, but make sure that the bulb is well concealed by the shade or fitting. Lighting from the side is much more difficult because of the shadows cast by the diners. As an alternative to a hanging light, go for a cluster of low-voltage downlighters — the way they do it in fancy restaurants. Avoid fluorescent lighting if you are of the gourmet tendency and like to see what it is you're eating. And if you are the type who goes for candlelit dinner parties, it's very useful to be able to dim the ambient lighting.

Living Rooms

There are no set rules for lighting living areas. Chandeliers, spotlights, uplighters, wall lights, downlighters, table lamps, sidelights — all have a role to play and it's very much a question of taste. Most developers and selfbuilders will be planning fairly conservative interiors, particularly in their living rooms, and an awful lot of the high-tech lighting schemes would be completely inappropriate here. However, the use of concealed fittings, such as downlighters, is compatible with virtually all settings. Lighting a room with downlighters is generally pleasing to the eye but it is expensive because of the numbers needed. Pendant fittings and wall lights may be preferred but considerable time and expense may go in selecting the right fittings for the room; downlighters actually require less thought. Another option is to go for three or four uplighters or wall lights, which will generally be enough to provide all the lighting needs (including reading) for a largish room; this presents a stylish mid-priced alternative between the expense of downlighters and the poor light quality offered by a central light.

Feature mirrors need to be set where they do not directly reflect lights. A traditional effect like a mirror above an Adam style fireplace will be ruined by a chandelier directly in front of it. Picture lighting is another problem area which you can ruin if you don't get it right.

Bedrooms

For most people, bedroom lighting will be a mixture of an ambient central pendant and table lamps for reading. Although a central pendant light source will be cheaper to install, when the cost of task lighting is included, the alternative options of uplighters or downlighters look more pocket-friendly, though you must pay attention to switching from the bed as well as by the door.

Bathrooms

The regulations require that bathroom light fittings should be concealed to prevent direct contact with water. Conventionally, this is done by placing a central light inside some sort of glazed casing. There are some extremely naff bathroom light fittings around and finding a good one can be difficult. An alternative approach is to use sealed downlighters.

Task lighting is also very useful around bathroom mirrors. The standard method is to fit a tungsten strip light (combined with electric shaver socket) which is adequate but rarely beautiful. Mirrors with integral lights are a stylish solution but they are very expensive.

Hallways/Stairwells

- Don't be tempted to hang lights where you can't change the bulb without a ladder.
- Don't fit uplighters at the foot of stairwells where you can see the bulbs from above.

External Lighting

The bane of external lighting is the 500 watt halogen floodlight. In the last few years these have become very cheap (under £20) and very common, yet their effect is blindingly unpleasant, unless well concealed. Security lighting need not be unattractive. It is worth giving a bit of thought to external lighting; unless you are building next to a well-lit road, you will find that some form of external light is essential just to negotiate the front path. By all means arrange to switch it on a timed Passive Infra Red (PIR) detector, but that doesn't mean you have to blast people in the face with 500W bulbs. PIR switches can be purchased on their own for around £25 and can be adjusted to trip on at different light levels and for different lengths of time — from a few seconds to several minutes. As alternatives to tungsten halogen floodlights, consider wall-mounted lanterns (c. £30), outdoor spotlights spiked into the ground (c. £10), free standing bollards (c. £60) or even brick lights (which replace a standard brick in your external wall) (c. £30). A good source for mail order light fittings is QVS Electrical (0800 801733).

The bane of external lighting is the 500w halogen floodlight

TV and Telecoms

Telecoms

Whether your supply is from BT or one of the newer competitors, installation is usually relatively straightforward. Bear in mind that whereas you may be happy now with one or two phone outlets, in years to come it is likely that you may want extra lines and many extra outlets. Most cables coming into your house are now capable of carrying several separate lines which allows for future expansion, and installing extra outlets in the house is no problem but, if you want to conceal the wiring, it will have to be concealed during the first-fix wiring of the house.

Installation Charges

The cut and thrust of competition from cable operators — often offering free connection — has not yet forced BT to rethink its blanket connection charging policy which is £99 (+VAT)/line at the time of writing. If cable lines are available, you will save on connection charges as well as bills. Most cable companies will supply just phone lines; you don't *have* to take the downmarket satellite channels.

TV and FM Radio

The cheapest solution for terrestrial channels is to place an aerial (cost around £15) in the loft although reception may be a little better from an aerial placed on the chimney. FM reception requires a separate aerial; the signal can be combined into one cable by fitting a *diplexer* for which no power is needed, but if you want multiple outlets then you will probably need an amplifier (cost around £20) which can be wired into the lighting circuit.

Satellite TV

Installation costs around £240-£300 and the dish must be on a south-facing wall — or hidden out in the garden. Rentals from around £10-£30/month depending on how many channels are taken. It can be taken by two sets without amplification but you can only receive one channel at a time.

Cable TV

Much more flexible than satellite dishes, cable has the advantage that it carries strong signals — enough for around five TV sets — and you can pick up the terrestrial channels and FM radio without separate aerials — but it is costs upwards of £10/month on top of any licence fee. Remote districts will have to wait many years before cable comes on stream yet it seems likely that in years to come cable information services will be as ubiquitous as telephone wires so it is as well to plan ahead.

First Fixing TV

Conventional (terrestrial) TV signals and FM radio signals are transmitted down coaxial cable, which most electricians are quite familiar with. Satellite and cable TV use quite different cables; if you want to conceal these cables during the first-fix stage you will have to approach your local supplier directly who, in all likelihood, will supply cable free of charge in order to gain a customer.

Future Proofing

The more technically minded of you may be interested in building in a phone and/or computer network around the house. It's a complicated area and there are no set standards to work to. Computer networking can be achieved with regular phone cable but more sophisticated Ethernet systems use Cat 5 twisted pair cable which has to be carefully installed without kinks or sharp bends. Internal phone systems are slowly becoming available: Evolution Systems (01480 493655) produces a *Homenet* cable system which can handle up to four incoming lines as well as such tasks as door entry-phones, cable TV distribution, baby monitoring and voice mail. Alternatively look at wireless systems like Philips DECT (costs around £250) which can handle two outside lines and up to seven extensions.

Built-in Vacuums

There are a number of small manufacturers moving into this market. Most advertise heavily in the selfbuild press and can be regularly found making pitches at the selfbuild exhibitions. If you are interested, most will quote from floor plans you send them. They aim particularly at the new build market because the system is most conveniently fitted at the first-fix stage so that the ducting is easily concealed. Put another way, it's more trouble than it's worth to fit the pipes into an old house but building into a new home is relatively straightforward. Quotes for a built-in vacuum cleaner installed on the benchmark house came in around the £450 mark. The installation involves putting a power unit — in the cupboard under the stairs — which supplies the suck for two outlets (one upstairs, one downstairs). The hose is several metres long — which is fine when working at full stretch but could be cumbersome when coiled up and may well snag.

If you like gadgets, you'll probably love a built-in vacuum cleaner. They are expensive when compared to portable cleaners but actually cost no more than dishwashers or remote-controlled garage door operators: it's just a shame that they don't do the vacuuming as well — that would be real labour saving! The various systems available all promise much more suck and, consequently, a much cleaner house with benefits to asthma sufferers, etc. but, as yet, there is no British or European standard for these systems, no recommended trade associations and little come back for the customer should installation not live up to expectations. This is largely because the built-in vacuum cleaning market is still too small to be effectively regulated and doesn't imply that the products don't work.

Service Ducts

Now, it may surprise some of the cynics amongst you, but new housing, even spec. built new housing, is built to last. At a rough guess I would estimate between 100 and 200 years. But the services we put into these new houses are not expected to last longer than 20-30 years. Therefore it follows that we all design services so that they can be easily accessed, repaired and, when the time comes replaced. Hmmm, if only it were so.

Anyone who has ever had a house rewired will know what an almighty hassle it is. Old rubber cables buried in walls have to be ripped out and channels of plaster get cut out in every room to provide a passage for the new PVC cabling. The electrician will replaster these channels but afterwards you are faced with a complete redecoration as every room will have been disrupted. Installing central heating is usually a lot less damaging to the internal fabric of the house but even here there are often major redecorations needed afterwards.

Problems ahead?
What is often not realised is that it is very much harder (and messier) to replace services in modern housing. Floors used to be laid with square edged boarding, easily lifted: now they are commonly made of solid cement screeds or are overlaid with chipboard; walls used to be covered with lime plasters (easily hacked off): now they tend to get a much harder cement render or, worse still, covered with plasterboard. Yet we are still happily burying pipes and cables under solid floors and behind plasterboarded walls, storing up problems for the next generation. Doubtless they will be a resourceful bunch and they may well come up with all kinds of

clever gadgets for overcoming these problems but if we were a bit more thoughtful now (and a bit less penny pinching) we could fit all our services inside removable ducting.

Well actually that is easier said than done. You see it all depends on which services and what you've built your floors and walls out of. Let's start with the easy bits. In most houses, the loft space is accessible and doubles up as a superb wiring duct connecting all your ceiling lights. So no problem with upstairs lights. Also in most houses the upstairs floors have a chipboard (or sometimes plywood) covering. Chipboard can be cut and lifted though it never goes back down so neatly. Plywood usually the same though note that in certain applications—notably some timber frame designs—the plywood floor acts as a structural brace for the entire house and cutting long strips out of it is potentially hazardous. In both cases, though, you can, with a little foresight, arrange to build the floors with screwed down sections where you can get access to your pipes and cables, though you may be surprised to learn just how much of this floor ends up being screwed-down sections. Provided that your upstairs doesn't get finished with a bonded covering such as you might find with tiles, you should be able to carry out repairs and replacements without needing to redecorate.

Profiles
The areas that cause the most problems to people wanting to keep services reachable are the ground floor and the walls. You can fit ducting into your ground floor screed: check out Pendock Profiles (01952 580590) who produce a range of galvanised steel channels which can accommodate water pipes and

have a screwed plywood covering. They are designed to fit into either a 50mm or a 70mm screed: I estimate that fitting Pendock Profiles to the ground floor of the benchmark house would have cost around £200 in materials: this would have been enough to take all the radiator pipes around the seven radiators downstairs. There is nothing to stop you making your own profiles, as Complete Fabrications did on their benchmark house, but this can be surprisingly fiddly and time consuming. Whatever you do you should be aware that they are at their most useful when the ground floor gets a carpeting. Tiling of any description and tongued and grooved timber floors cannot be taken up without a good deal of disruption and it will be impossible to replace them as before.

Alternatives
So are there any other options? Well, these profiles do rather assume that you are going to use 15mm rigid copper tube to connect up your radiators. If, on the other hand, you switch to flexible microbore copper tube or to one of the new plastic systems, it becomes possible to thread the pipes inside larger plastic ducting so that (in theory at any rate) it becomes possible to remove and replace the pipe at a later date. If you are considering underfloor heating, then the lifespan of the installation is something to bear in mind. All the systems sold on the UK market are guaranteed for at least 10 years but you will be lucky if the best available system is going to last as long as the house will and replacing such a system will involve digging out the entire ground floor screed, a major repair which would require the house to be evacuated for a couple of weeks at least.

Another option is to arrange all downstairs tap and radiators to be fed from pipes which either drop from the ceiling or are clipped to the walls. This gives you accessibility but at a price — exposed pipework, not everybody's cup of tea. You can then go to great lengths to conceal this pipework in various ingenious boxings or over-large skirtings but you are then in danger of finding that you spend more on ducting than you do on plumbing. It may well end up as a compromise solution — you leave most of the pipework accessible but end up having a few runs which are completely concealed. Life being what it is, you can rest assured that it will always be these latter runs which will spring a leak.

One way around the problem is to feed radiators with surface mounted drops

Burying Cables

This ducting principle works much better with PVC electric cabling. Normally electric cables don't even get laid under the ground floor; electricians prefer to drop them down from the first floor void where (as discussed above) they are accessible (if not readily so). However, whilst it is industry practise to cover the cables with a metal sheathing, this is to protect the cables from being drilled through by the follow-on trades or the D-I-Y house-holder putting up shelves, not to enable them to be removed or replaced at a later date. Centaur make an oval plastic conduit which could act as a removable duct down which you could arrange your drops (but at £3/lin.m it is expensive, twice as much as regular sheathing). But before you embark on installing a totally removable wiring system do bear two things in mind. 1. PVC electric cable won't last forever but the signs are that it should be good for 50+ years, certainly much longer than the rubber cable that used to be fitted. 2. When the time comes to rewire, the strong chances are that you will be wanting different types of outlets in different positions so the advantage of being able to remove existing cabling is lost. Bear in mind also the pace of technological change in this area means that the wiring requirements of a house in, say, 2048 (when rewiring might naturally be taking place) will be very different to those today and that we frankly have only a vague idea what these requirements might be. Who, for instance, would have thought of providing outlets for TVs, microwaves or central heating programmers back in 1946? One change that does seem possible in the next few years is the remote light switch which turns lights on and off by sending a radio signal from wherever the switch is located. Could well be that all the switch cabling in your home will be completely redundant by the time you come to rewire so why bother to make these cables removable?

It is far more likely that you will find your existing wiring outlets inadequate for your needs long before you need to replace the whole system. The standard solution to this problem in offices is to provide bus bars around the walls which can handle power circuits, phone lines and computer network cabling and can have outlets added whenever and wherever needed. But this is unlikely to catch on in the home in a big way a) because they are expensive and b) because they are ugly. What is more, it seems that the emerging wiring standards will mean that our soon-to-be intelligent houses will not need vast networks of cables to work because just one wiring system will be able to carry all

Left: a Pendock Profile
Below: the designers of the benchmark house are unusual in insisting on floor ducting wherever possible. They construct their own, designed to sit flush with the top of the screed (bottom shot).

kinds of information; i.e. you may be able to plug your phone into the power circuit when you want an extension.

As mentioned in the section on TV and Telecoms, there are many emerging information technologies and you can already do a certain amount of future proofing in a new house. However as no one knows which technologies will come to dominate in years to come, the wisest form of future proofing currently available is to provide removable ducting and access panels around the house.

The Intelligent House

Much of this chapter called Services has been concerned with routing things around the house, things in this case being water, electric current, TV signals, telephone conversations and vacuumed dust. We haven't even touched on security devices, whole house surround sound systems or computer network cabling. These are all technologies which are with us now but which each exist in a little cocoon world of their own. Enter the intelligent house, a concept which attempts to link all these disparate threads together and to add some new ones as well.

Every year some new scheme is launched to get intelligently switched housing out into the consumer market: every year there are articles saying "It's just around the corner" or "The future is here today." Currently all attention in the UK is focused on the Integer Project (0181 876 7553) which has been put together by architect Nicholas Thompson and involves several big names from the world of plc housebuilding, mortgage lenders and housing associations — indeed Berkeley Homes is planning to build 200 intelligent homes in 1998, based on the Integer Project standards. Look out for news about it.

Will it catch on? Well it probably will, but I doubt very much that it will be just yet. At the present time there simply isn't enough logic in combining all these different technologies under one umbrella; whilst it's all quite feasible, there is little to be gained and there is no one out there to service the system when it all crashes (as it will). Take this quote from Honeywell's business development manager about the potential merits of their home automation system, *TotalHome*: "You just dial up your home from your mobile phone and have the oven switch your dinner on." Now think about it. Is that remotely useful? Would you have remembered to have put the dinner in the oven in the first place? What would that dinner consist of? Leftovers? More likely some dreadful TV Microwave dinner that only takes 3 minutes to cook in any event. Real men would be taking real women out for a meal at a restaurant, not piddling about with their mobile phones tapping in codes to get the microwave booted up. No, the whole concept is just too deeply nerdish to catch on with Joe and Joanna Public just yet.

On the other hand, we've been living quite happily with light switches for three or four generations now but when they were first introduced the idea that you could switch on a light in the middle of a room from a plate by the door was somewhat mind-boggling. Home automation is simply an extension of this switching idea and it's day will come because it'll make houses
- a) easier to run and
- b) cheaper to run.

Running around locking doors and turning lights off will become a thing of the past as will having to struggle with five to ten keys: you'll just have to turn one switch which puts the house onto "Gone Shopping" mode and all these things will be taken care of. And if you forget, locking it all up from your mobile phone will definitely be useful. When you are away on holiday, your home will be busy turning lights on and off, opening and closing curtains and making itself look occupied. Your appliances will automatically inform their servicers when they are about to break down and diagnose their own faults so that the parts are ready on site when the engineer calls.

Just don't get too excited. Don't rush out and cable up every nook and cranny in your home because it's not clear yet what sort of cables you will need — or indeed if you will even need cables. It seems likely that whatever standard prevails will be a multi-medium one. This means that it is capable of passing information along a number of different channels including the ordinary electric power cables and phone cables as well as using radio and infra-red transmissions needing no cabling at all. In effect, it will be able to piggyback onto what already exists in most houses and it will not be necessary to carry out extensive rewiring to take advantage of the systems on offer.

Total Home

Several businesses have nibbled at this market but none have been particularly successful yet, at least in the UK. Honeywell, the American controls company, are perhaps the biggest world player with their *TotalHome* system, yet they are reluctant to launch it in the UK. It would cost upwards of £2000 to install one in a new house which makes it about 50% more than independent burglar alarm and heating controls but it is capable of doing much more, including controlling the lighting and opening and closing curtains. It works on a series of easy-to-grasp modes — such as Sleeping, Breakfast, At Work, On Holiday — and resets the various controls accordingly. It is, if anything, slightly easier to use than a conventional burglar alarm system and, if you add the modem option, you are able to reset it all over the phone. It is certainly a good deal more flexible than an average alarm system: it not only allows you to alarm individual rooms separately but it will warn you when someone walks in the house unannounced. There is even a *Duress Setting* which can allow a quiet help message to be sent to your monitoring firm without setting off the alarm — very useful for those awkward moments when you are being held at gunpoint by uninvited guests.

What's Coming Next

The point about intelligent systems like Honeywell *TotalHome* is that it is virtually unlimited in what it can control. As more products come onto the market offering a remote switching facility, then *TotalHome* (or its competitors) will be able to switch them. For around £20-£30, you can buy addressable plugs and light switches which can be programmed to turn on and off or, alternatively, they can be operated remotely via a modem attached to the phone system. In years to come your appliances may be partly controlled by signals coming from the met office or your electricity company so that you are able to take advantage of cheap tariffs. Your morning paper (or just the bits you want) may well arrive down this same phone line; your weekly shopping list may well be automatically drawn up from a stocktake in the kitchen and sent down this same line to the supermarket for delivery at a time that is convenient to you; and of course your money will all live in here as well, debiting and crediting your accounts as you go about your business. Doubtless too, the brown goods (TVs, videos, CD players, PCs) so much revered by the burgling fraternity, will be programmed to only run on commands received from your home control system which would do far more for crime prevention than any amount of sophisticated alarm systems.

Of all the many profound changes that have taken place in the home during this century, the coming of the intelligent house could be the biggest of them all. This reads like a very grand closing sentence for this chapter: the trouble with it is that the coming of the intelligent house looks set to be something for the next century, not this one just passing.

Chapter 9
Finishes

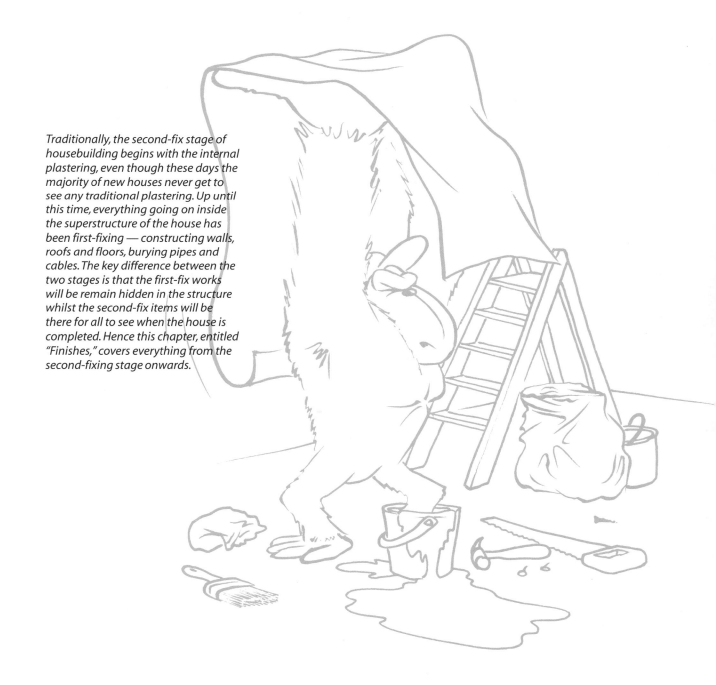

Traditionally, the second-fix stage of housebuilding begins with the internal plastering, even though these days the majority of new houses never get to see any traditional plastering. Up until this time, everything going on inside the superstructure of the house has been first-fixing — constructing walls, roofs and floors, burying pipes and cables. The key difference between the two stages is that the first-fix works will be remain hidden in the structure whilst the second-fix items will be there for all to see when the house is completed. Hence this chapter, entitled "Finishes," covers everything from the second-fixing stage onwards.

Internal Wall Finishes

Plastering is the cheapest way of providing good internal wall and ceiling coverings. There are different systems of "plastering" but they all come within spitting distance of £5-£6/m^2 in price. There are alternatives which can be used when you know exactly what you want — exposed brickwork, tongued and grooved matchboarding — but they are considerably more expensive than a plastered finish and are normally only built as features.

The big question facing house builders is whether to go for a wet or dry system of wall coverings. The wet techniques use wet-mixed cement renders and gypsum plasters: the dry systems use dry-lined plasterboards. The wet techniques are traditional British building — the dry techniques are imported from countries where timber frame is prevalent. Ceilings are almost invariably fixed with plasterboard, but here there remains a choice about whether to cover them with a wet *Thistle Finish* plaster, to dry-line or to comb on *Artex*. Pricewise, there is very little to choose between the systems — though I estimate that dry-lining is a little bit cheaper.

Wet Plastering

Plus

It is well understood by builders and favoured by most plasterers; a well-skimmed plaster finish looks fantastic — at least initially.

Minus

It's wet. Something like 1m^3 of water (=12 bathfulls) is being built into the fabric of the house if it is wet plastered and this must in time dry out, which will take a summer at least. This drying out results in movement which causes cracking in the top coat plaster which looks naff and gets builders called back on site to carry out cosmetic repairs. This problem is particularly bad when plasterboard ceilings are skimmed with a plaster finish; here the movement in timber behind the boards causes hairline cracks around all the plasterboard joints. None of this cracking is in the least bit dangerous — it doesn't mean subsidence is occurring — and many people live happily with it knowing that these bedding in problems can be filled in at the first redecoration. However, for many unsuspecting souls it is a source of genuine grievance and complaint.

Dry-lining

Plus

It's dry — see paragraph above for problems caused by being wet. It is relatively easy to correct out-of-plumb blockwork — you just adjust the thickness of the adhesive dabs. It also gives a comparatively soft wall with enough give for small children to bounce off unharmed, whereas a hard, plastered wall would bring forth tears.

Minus

Not that well understood by the trade, it tends to be the preserve of specialists. Dry-lining is not particularly difficult to learn — the plasterboard manufacturers all run cheap two- or three-day training courses — but it can be badly applied, leaving a ridged effect on walls and ceilings. Plasterboard has to be fixed more carefully than is normal trade practice so as to keep the number of cuts to a minimum. The wall finish is similar to what you would get if painting on to lining paper (which is basically what you are doing) and this may not be glossy enough for some tastes. Plasterboard walls are not as damage-resistant as traditional plasters, though repairs can be easily effected.

Another problem with dry-lining is that it can be draughty. In theory the backing walls should be airtight — why do you have to put in all those expensive trickle vents in the windows? — but in practice air sneaks through the most unlikely joints. The solution to this problem is to seal all the joints between sheets and around openings prior to taping and jointing. However this is both expensive (Gyproc's sealer costs around £9/lt.) and time consuming. This air leakiness problem occurs with all forms of construction that use dry-lining, but its significance is greatly reduced when you build in timber-frame, incorporating a vapour barrier in the external walls.

Blockwork v Studwork

You can only apply wet render on to a masonry background and it is, therefore, not an option for timber framers. Those using studwork walls will have to fit a wallboard, usually plasterboard — though, as already noted, plasterboard *will* take a 3mm wet plaster finish. On the other hand, if a dry method is desired in a brick and block house, then the favoured method is to stick plasterboard on to the blockwork using the *dot and dab* technique which uses specialised gypsum plasters as adhesives. This is the method currently in favour with over 70% of professional house builders — just goes to show how much they value not being called back because "there's cracks in me walls."

Plasterboard

What is it? Gypsum plaster sandwiched between two layers of paper. It is characterised by being easy to cut, fairly easy to handle and it provides a good backing for paint and plaster. Note that wastage can be high when using plasterboard — up to 30% on small rooms and ceilings, between 10% and 15% on walls. It is available in several different formats: square edged (for wet plaster *skimming*) or tapered edge (for dry-lining); 12.5mm thick for 600mm spaced studwork and 9.5mm thick for 400mm spacings; foil-backed for providing an integral vapour barrier (it's cheaper to use a separate polythene sheet); small boards measuring 1800x900mm as well as the more normal, room-height, boards which are

9a: Plastering: Guide Prices

	MATS	LABOUR	TOTAL
Render and Skim	£1.50	£3.70	£5.20
Carlite Browning and Finish	2.00	4.00	6.00
Tacking (Nailing) Plasterboard	1.60	2.00	3.60
Dot and Dab (Sticking) Plasterboard	1.60	1.60	3.20
Skim Finish on Plasterboard	1.00	2.40	3.40
Dry Lined Finish to Plasterboard	0.80	1.50	2.30
Artex Finish on Plasterboard	0.80	1.50	2.30
Fixing External Renderlath	7.80	2.00	9.80
Two-coat External Render	2.50	6.50	9.00
Floor Screed, 65mm Thick	3.40	4.00	7.40
Floor Screed, 50mm Thick	2.60	3.70	6.30

All figures are £/m^2

1200x2400mm. There are also now a number of plasterboards which are laminated to insulation. Make sure you get the right format for the job and make sure that you've used metric spacings on your wall studs and ceiling joists as imperial-sized plasterboard is no longer made.

Plasterboard is a very competitive business with three companies (BPB or British Gypsum, Knauf and Lafarge) slugging it out for the European market. Its price is given to wild fluctuations and do not be surprised if you have to pay £4 for a full-sized 12.5mm thick board on occasion. BPB used to have a monopoly but the entry of the French and Germans into the market has caused a price war which tends to keep prices very low — at 1970s levels. There is little to choose between the rivals either on price or quality.

Plasterboard: tacking in a timber frame house

Alternatives

Fermacell

A new kind of building board now available, *Fermacell* is in some ways very similar to plasterboard and in others, rather superior. It has a much higher racking strength than plasterboard and is therefore particularly useful when you want to hang radiators and bathroom furniture off timber stud walls and you don't know where the studs are. *Fermacell* also makes for better soundproofing. However, it is pricey in comparison with plasterboard, costing over £3/m², nearly three times the price. Consequently, it is mostly being used in the UK as a backing board for kitchens and bathrooms. There is a big future for boards like this which, when used in timber frame construction, are strong enough to do away with the need for external plywood sheeting which is one of the major factors making timber frame more expensive than masonry constructions. However, note that at the present time, no one in the UK is doing anything more than experiment with such lean designs. Wickes have also introduced a similar product called *Fiberbond*.

Exposed Brickwork

Costing between £17 and £30/m² — depending largely on your choice of brick — using exposed brickwork internally can be surprisingly cheap. With block and stud walls costing between £6 and £9/m², plaster finishes costing around £5/m² and painting costs of around £1/m², exposed brickwork from £17/m² doesn't look an expensive option. On internal walls, with both sides exposed, the arithmetic looks even more favourable. However, please note that £17/m² buys a pretty basic "developers" brick and that a "charac-

ter" brick (i.e. second hand or handmade) will cost 50% more to lay. Also note that a masonry sealer (at around £4/lt) should be applied — and this is more expensive than emulsion work. More significant problems are encountered with fixtures like door and window lintels and electric cables which would normally be concealed behind the plaster. These problems mean that feature brickwork is most often seen in small areas such as fireplaces. Used adroitly, exposed brickwork can be an effective feature at a cost little more than conventional plastering.

Pine Matchboarding

Finishing walls and ceiling with timber matchboarded panels cost £16/m² (Mats £8, Lab £8). This price is made up of timber at £6/m², fixing at £5/m², sanding and filling at £2/m² and varnishing at £3/m². Pine panelling used to be very popular but is now rarely

seen over whole walls, though it's use as a stained boarding, fixed vertically between skirting and dado rail, is a currently fashionable effect. It is also an effective way of creating decorative service panels behind which can be run pipework and cabling, though this is a complex matter which ideally needs designing into the building from the beginning.

Plastered Fancies

Plain Coving

Often not seen as a fancy detail at all, bog standard coving can be a very useful way of covering up doubtful ceiling/wall joints. It's not particularly expensive — rather cheaper than skirting board at around 80p/lin.m and is fixed for around £1.10/lin.m. Providing coving throughout our benchmark house would have cost around £400; however, it's a

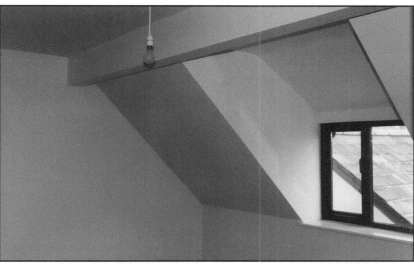

Internal detailing on the benchmark house: note how many angles are formed by the relatively simple dormer design

Family bathroom in the benchmark house was boxed using pine matchboarding,

detail which many builders dislike and the actual benchmark house is unadorned. Its wall to ceiling junctions are bare and square.

Fancy Covings

Artex produce a range of four classical styles which are widely available through builder's merchants. These cost around £3/lin.m and are harder to fix than standard coving but do add a certain grandeur to a room that you might like. They can be combined with fancy ceiling roses (at around £6). There are a number of other specialist companies producing all kinds of plaster mouldings — arches, dado rails, corner details, wall plaques. Check Yellow Pages under *Plaster Ware* or phone Original Plaster Mouldings (01733 351022).

Decorative Panelling

British Gypsum produce a number of decorative fielded panels out of a material called *Glasroc* which, as its name suggests, is gypsum plaster reinforced with glass fibre. They can be combined to provide a very smart looking interior wall detailing that would, in truth, look better in a shop or a restaurant than a home. They would be normally fixed on top of a wall finish (instead of replacing it) so the cost, at around £9/m² to buy, makes it similar to pine matchboarding.

Ceramic Tiling

Tiling is not strictly speaking an alternative to plastering because it is usually applied on top so "addition" might be a better word. Its use is often entirely functional when applied as a splashback behind sinks, basins and baths, but visit Italy or Portugal and you'll be amazed to see ceramic tiling in living rooms and bedrooms as well. In the UK wall tiling is seen in more functional terms; our benchmark house is unusual in this respect in that

there is 25m² of ceramic tiling, far more wall tiling than you would normally expect in a house of this quality.

Whether you pay under £5/m² for some unadorned and unnamed import or £80/m² for some top of the range, handpainted tile out of the Fired Earth catalogue, the fixing costs remain remarkably similar. The adhesives which you use to stick the tiles down with and the grouts which you spread between the tiles tend to work out together at between £3 and £4/m² depending on the thickness and specification. The laying costs depend on the intricacies of the task in hand, but on fairly straightforward work, it takes a tiler around one hour to fix a m² of tiles and about 15 minutes to grout them up later. Big straight runs will be faster than this but most tiling work in new housing involves a fair amount of cutting and this takes the time.

Buying Tips

Ceramic tiles vary enormously in style and quality from the cheap, mass-produced output of large factories to the exotic and individual handmade styles, often produced in the third world. The UK market is dominated by two big names, Pilkington (the glass makers) and Cristal. Their ranges are widely available at all kinds of outlets — D-I-Y sheds, builder's merchants and tiling specialists — and their ranges are also largely complementary; at their simplest they have several earthy and pastelly coloured floor and wall tiles priced below the £10/m² mark. They both

have acres of largely nondescript kitchen and bathroom *motif* tiles either with inoffensive patterns or odd adornments like wheatsheaves or dolphins. Very homely but not going to win any design awards. However, both Pilks and Cristal have some much more interesting designs that you might have to visit a tiling centre to gen up on. And, of course, there are any number of lesser known producers — check out Marlborough, Sphinx or any of the Italian imports.

The revived interest in all things handmade has produced a rash of simulated handmade tiles like Cristal's *Linda Beard* collection. Though nothing like the authentic ones, these tiles do represent a reasonable compromise between looks and price. For the real thing, you can do no better than phone Fired Earth for a catalogue.

The revival of old English styles means there is now a wide choice of Victorian tiles available

Floor Finishes

Nowhere else in building is there such a great variety of materials at such a huge variation in price. You could carpet a four-bedroom house for less than £1000 (inc. VAT); equally you could spend over £5000 and not risk being accused of extravagance. Normally, floor finishes are not included in building budgets unless they are an integral part of the construction; developers rarely fit floor finishes although they occasionally offer to carpet houses as a sweetener to encourage a sale.

Carpet

Even when glued down, carpet is regarded by Customs & Excise as a movable item and therefore subject to VAT as a furnishing — all other types of floor finish are zero-rated and therefore effectively exempt from VAT when built into a new house. Even so, carpeting still provides potentially the cheapest form of floor covering available — especially the bonded cords which also happen to be reasonably hard wearing. Beware offers of free underlay and free laying; obviously these services are not free and the charge for them is included in the marked price. Usually priced by the yard, carpet laying can be subject to enormous wastage because of the limited roll sizes. The D-I-Y builder might be happier to lay carpet tiles, but if price is the only consideration, then it will still probably be cheaper to look out for the absolute basic ranges supplied and fitted by one of the carpet warehouses. Some of these carpets sell for a good deal less than a decent underlay (which can cost £3/m²) so you can imagine what the quality is like.

For the novice, buying carpets is a bit of a proverbial minefield with enormous price variations for apparently similar products. The British Carpet Manufacturers' Association runs a grading scheme as follows:
- Grade 1: suitable for areas getting low use (bedrooms)
- Grade 2: average use areas (dining rooms, studies)
- Grades 3/4: heavily used areas (halls, staircases).

This grading scheme would be more useful if every retailer abided by it but they don't — some use their own grading systems and others blithely ignore the whole procedure. It can all be a particularly taxing affair for the selfbuilder who is often under great pressure to move in quickly. There often isn't time to make an informed decision and rash choices here can be expensive and hard to live with. A *Which?* report (March 1994) into buying carpets provides good background reading. Key buying points to watch out for are:

- Don't be misled by incredibly low area prices quoted in newspapers and magazines. Get written quotations with details of underlay, fitting charges, and any extra that might get charged for gripper, door bars, delivery, etc. There are plenty of hidden costs for the unwary.
- Material. Wool is the traditional and natural material for carpets; it also tends to be the most expensive. Synthetics like nylon and acrylics are now commonplace and much carpet sold these days is a cocktail of wool and synthetics — and people walking on them would not know the difference. The very cheapest material is polypropylene which looks synthetic but may be fine for your needs, especially in bedrooms.
- Comparing prices over the phone is difficult because a lot of carpet is not branded and there are so many varieties on the market that very often no two outlets sell the same thing. Sticking to an established name like John Lewis will ensure that you are not ripped-off, but they are unlikely to be selling carpet below £10/m² which is higher than many people's budget will allow.
- Bear in mind this rule of thumb when estimating cost: you should double the advertised price of a fitted carpet to get an

9b: Floor Finishes Guide Prices

All costs are £/M²	PRICE	WASTE	EXTRAS	LAYING	TOTAL	BENCHMARK HOUSE COSTS
Cheap Carpet	£5.00	£1.00	£2.00	£3.00	**£11.00**	£1,800
Decent Carpet	18.00	3.60	2.00	3.00	**£27.00**	£4,500
Axminster Wool	35.00	7.00	2.00	3.00	**£47.00**	£7,800
Cheap Vinyl Tile	5.00	0.40	1.50	3.00	**£10.00**	£1,700
Expensive	50.00	4.00	1.50	8.00	**£64.00**	£10,600
Cork	14.00	1.40	2.50	5.00	**£23.00**	£3,800
Red Quarry Tile	12.00	1.80	4.00	10.00	**£28.00**	£4,700
Cheap Ceramic	7.00	1.05	4.00	10.00	**£22.00**	£3,700
Expensive Ceramic	40.00	6.00	4.00	10.00	**£60.00**	£10,000
Softwood T&G	7.50	0.75	7.00	5.00	**£20.00**	£3,300
Junckers-style Beech Floor	32.00	3.20	2.50	5.00	**£43.00**	£7,200
Reclaimed Boards	22.00	4.40	8.00	7.00	**£41.00**	£6,800
Wood Block	10.00	1.00	8.00	10.00	**£29.00**	£4,800

Timber floors have a hidden cost advantage in that they can be laid straight onto timber joists without the need for any decking; a potential saving of £5/m², but not without its problems. See text.

idea of what it will all cost when laid on your floors. This will allow for offcuts, underlay and laying costs.

Bathroom Carpeting

Avoid woollen carpet in bathrooms as they will tend to go mouldy, especially if they have a hessian backing. Polypropylene carpets with foam backings are cheap and durable and will survive many years of bath time frolicking.

Tiles

There are many different materials used to tile or sheet floors and there is not space to cover them all here. In particular, there are any number of synthetic rubbery plastic type floor coverings which are generally more at home in an industrial or commercial setting than a house. If you want to know more, check out your Yellow Pages > *Flooring Services*. Here I look at just the three most popular tiled finishes.

Vinyl

The very word vinyl sounds cheap but don't be misled, it's not. Either in sheet or tile form, this can vary between the very cheap marble effects (like *Polyflex*) costing less than £5/m² — these tiles usually have only a small percentage of vinyl in them — to Amtico floor tiles costing over £50/m². The best results are to be had when the immediate sub-floor is covered either with a 5mm latex screed or hardboard sheeting. Adhesive adds around £1.50/m², laying costs between £2.50 and £5.00/m².

Cork

Cheap cork tiles can be purchased in the D-I-Y sheds, but they do not last very long. In any area receiving reasonably heavy wear, use

vinyl covered and backed tiles. Wicanders is the main producer: their top of the range *Cork Master* costs around £30/m²; the same company produce a cheaper version called *Ipocork* at around £15/m², which is adequate for all but the most demanding situations. Best laid on board; if laid on a cement screed ensure that it's completely dry — this takes around eight summer weeks. Adhesive adds £2.50/m², laying costs around £5/m².

Ceramic/Quarry Tiles

Laying costs are higher when specifying ceramic tiles because it is a more involved process, requiring time-consuming cutting and a second pass to grout up the results. Adhesives and grouts add around £1.50 to £2/m² to prices. The very cheapest floor tiles are usually imported from Italy or Portugal and are displayed under little known brand names in the D-I-Y sheds and discount tile shops at less than £5/m². The cheapest British quarry tiles — which are made from reconstituted stone rather than baked clay — are available in red at around £10/m², whilst Cristal, Pilkington and Wooliscroft produce popular floor tiles from around £9/m² upwards. At the other end of the scale, Fired Earth and numerous imitators sell a dazzling array of terracotta floor tiles, many of them reclaimed, from around £35/m² upwards.

Timber Flooring

Many people are attracted to the idea of having exposed wood floors but are put off by the price. Some have experimented using painted or sealed boards, like chipboard and plywoods, as a floor finish but, though these are cheap and initially cheerful, by and large they do not wear very well. Alternatively you can lay a new tongued and grooved pine floor; materials can be bought from as little as

£7.50/m² but these need sanding and sealing — allow around £5/m² for this — when laid and will almost certainly shrink dramatically, opening up unsightly cracks between the boards. This shrinkage problem is a feature of all wood floors — though it is insignificant when using well-seasoned hardwoods — and the only way to ensure it doesn't happen is to let the timber dry out in your centrally heated environment before laying — rather impractical for most builders.

Another approach is to use a reclaimed board which has been stored undercover and is, hopefully, dimensionally stable. These vary in price from around £6/m² up to £30/m² and will almost certainly involve you in a lot of extra work (denailing, sanding, hole filling, more sanding, sealing). The huge variation in prices for reclaimed boards is of course an indication that there is a huge variation in quality as well. If you go to one of the better salvage yards, such as Machell's, near Leeds (0113 2505043), you'll find good quality board but prices to match new planks. Another option is to use wood blocks — reclaimed oak can still be picked up from salvage yards for less than £10/m² — but again be prepared to have to carry out a lot of extra preparation work. However, a wood block floor (sometimes known as parquet) has to be laid on a solid backing, which will generally involve laying some form of extra screed or decking beneath, especially as floor insulation is now virtually mandatory.

If price is no barrier to you then you'll most probably be looking to lay a new hardwood floor. The best known brand names are Junckers, Tarkett and Kars, all widely available, material prices starting at around the £30/m². You can save a little on this by specifying a veneered hardwood floor rather than a solid one — IKEA has such a range costing around £20-25/m². On the other hand, you can of course choose all manner of weird and wonderful patterns, inlays and borders. Laying hardwood flooring is a job well within the capabilities of most competent DIYers but it is worth noting that, when laid professionally, hardwood flooring work has a very high callback rate — hardwood floors behave temperamentally, frequently squeak and often open up. Look in your Yellow Pages under *Flooring Services* for local contacts.

A reclaimed timber floor usually looks stunning when laid — but also requires a great deal of work

Second-fix carpentry is a bit of a rag-bag of different activities that covers just about everything that carpenters get up to after the plasterers are finished. It usually includes door hanging and staircase fixing, as well as fixing skirtings and architraves and pipe boxings; often it also includes fitting kitchens and vanity units in bathrooms and putting up shelves. Prices in this section are mostly just material prices; for an inkling of the current fixing costs refer to the Chippies Rates Table 11c in Chapter 11.

Internal Doors

The world of the internal door is split between the hollow and the solid. The hollow doors are like sandwiches; the casings are layers of board and the filling consists of a material very similar to egg boxes. Where you would normally place the handle and latch, they put a solid hunk of wood called the *lock block* and foolish would-be chippies (like me) have been known to hang these doors in a hurry, only to find that the lock block is on the hinge side of the door. If you are observant, you will hang the door on the correct side — there is only ever one lock block in a hollow door.

This all sounds very cheap and tacky and, generally speaking, eggbox-style doors are, but they can also be purchased with expensive hardwood veneers, usually from some environmentally incorrect species like sapele (pronounced *sa-pee-lee*), and this pushes the price up to levels at which you can buy solid softwood doors, around the £25 mark.

The very cheapest doors you can get are eggbox-filled doors which are encased in, wait for it, hardboard. Expect to pay around £12 for one of these but don't ever kick it. A popular variation on this theme is the embossed or moulded door; they are no stronger but they imitate the fielded panels found on timber doors and some of them imitate wood grain texture. The simpler ones cost between £30 and £40 each and they look quite acceptable when painted, which is what they are designed for. Some superior ones use a type of fibreboard for the casing and they are strong enough to take glazing, although doors with glazing panels are much more expensive — around £70. All the major joinery manufacturers have a selection of these doors and, if you want to select a door, get hold of one of their catalogues. Crosby and Magnet both have good ranges. Most designs are also available in bi-fold format for use as sliding cupboard doors.

Solid Wood Doors

For people who like their doors to go clunk rather than thwack when they shut. Not that these doors are that much heavier than their eggbox counterparts; indeed there are a number of incredibly cheap (i.e. less than £30) imported timber doors available in the D-I-Y sheds which look as though they might actually disintegrate if you shut them too hard. They are usually stored about ten feet above ground level and when you get to see them close up you realise why.

Generally, internal timber doors fall into two categories; stainable and paint-only grade. The paint-only ones are made from inferior timbers that may well have dead knots — which are given to working loose — and are frequently made up of short sections of timber which are finger-jointed together. If you are planning to paint the doors you might just as well settle for a paint-only grade door costing around £40; the better quality, stainable doors are more than twice as much.

Hardwood is an option as well. Oak and meranti are widely available but expensive at around £150/door. The hardwood veneered hollow doors are about half this price and are solid enough for most people's demands.

Cottage Style Doors

An increasingly popular option is to fit ledged-and-braced doors to all internal openings. This style of door used to be exclusively associated with back doors and outbuildings, but with the fashion for all things cottagey, they are beginning to move indoors. External doors are manufactured with a moisture content of around 18% whereas the ideal moisture content for internal doors is around half this amount. Hanging an external door inside tends to result in them twisting out of shape.

The joinery majors such as John Carr now carry internal cottage doors (in their case known as an *FL&B* for Framed Ledged & Braced) but they cost twice as much as the ones designed for exterior use. Alternatively, seek out one of the small specialist suppliers such The Real Door Company; they will tend to charge between £140 and £200 for softwood doors.

MDF Doors

Another approach which is gaining in popularity, especially as regards fitted cupboard doors, is to make them on site using MDF (medium density fibreboard). MDF is a

Contrasting styles of door beget contrasting door handles. Above - hollow, moulded, cheap: below, authentic timber.

9c: Benchmark House: Door Furniture

	NUMBER	UNIT	UNIT COST	TOTAL
EXTERNAL ITEMS				
Hinges	4.5	prs	£5.00	£23
5-lever Mortice Locks	3	No	15.00	45
Night Latch	1	No	18.00	18
Rebate Sets		No	2.00	
Handles	3	prs	5.00	15
Letter Plate	1	No	4.00	4
Door Knocker	1	No	5.00	5
Slide Bolts	6	No	5.00	30
Security Chain		No	5.00	
2 point locking system		No	50.00	
Door Bell	1	No	3.00	3
EXTERNAL TOTAL				**£140**
excluding garage side door			*Allow £30*	
INTERNAL ITEMS				
Hinges	22	prs	2.00	£44
Latches	10	No	2.00	20
Rebate Sets		No	2.00	
Handles	10	prs	9.00	90
Privacy Locks	3	No	2.00	6
Slide Bolts	2	No	2.00	4
INTERNAL TOTAL				**£160**
GRAND TOTAL				**£280**
Cheapest alternatives (Aluminium)				*£175*

manufactured timber board which can be worked like natural timber; the finish can be sanded to accept paint or even, at a pinch, stain. Mouldings can be either routed into the board or stuck on to the surface. This is obviously rather labour intensive and the doors tend to be a bit on the heavy side but it is cheap. If you have nonstandard sized doorways, which often occurs with alcove cupboards and the like, then MDF is often a good solution. You need a board that's at least 25mm thick or else you won't be able to hinge it; alternatively, you can stick two thinner boards together and cut bits out of the top one to make decorative panelling effects. A good timber merchant will be able to dimension MDF for you, a facility not to be sniffed at.

Door Furniture

Door furniture is the phrase used to describe just about everything to do with doors excluding the door itself. That usually means all the bits made of metal and *door ironmongery* would be a much easier to understand expression, but the building trade likes the word *furniture* to be used. I really don't know why. Perhaps it adds to the mystique of the whole thing or maybe they are just being pig-ignorant. Anyway, I digress.

The point to cotton on to here is that some door furniture is purely functional in that you don't see it or, if you do, you don't notice it; however other bits are very visual and — wait for it — tactile. Yes folks, door handles are sexy. Developers know this and consequently are prepared to spend above the bare minimum to create an impression on the would-be house purchaser. Door handles may indeed be the only part of the house that the viewer actually touches during an inspection and women in particular are reckoned to be impressed by something strong and solid which responds readily to their grasp. No doubt about it, cheap and flaccid door furniture is a turn-off. Not for nothing is (was?) the UK's largest specialist retailer in this area called Knobs and Knockers.

Quality

And there is a wide range of quality available. The accompanying table shows the kind of money spent on the door furniture for the 3 external and 10 internal doors of the benchmark house. Without looking for more than ten minutes, I was able to re-specify at less than half price. And of course it would be just as easy to more than double the price to over £500. Quality here is a complex field; there are numerous manufacturers and several different materials to choose from. Each material is available in a wide range of grades —

there are no generalisations to be had in this game. The very cheapest handles may well be aluminium or plastic or brass-plated: equally well, these three materials may feature in some of the most expensive furniture available. If there is a discernible rule it is this: the British manufacturers are expensive. They will claim that this is because they are producing a quality product and that's bound to cost more, but isn't that exactly what the British motorbike manufacturers claimed in the 60s? Unlike most building materials, door furniture is small enough and expensive enough to be readily tradable along the world's shipping lanes and the signs are that overseas competition is putting the drops on us again. Most of the domestic grade stuff you can buy in the UK is imported.

Style

Most developers fit brass-plated furniture to their doors. There are two basic styles: Victorian (or plain) and Georgian (frilly bits added). Both styles are catered for by builder's merchants and D-I-Y sheds who sell shrink-wrapped pre-packs at fairly reasonable prices. These pre-packs have one big advantage going for them in that they've got all the bits you need in the pack; you may be able to buy at keener prices but you risk a) forgetting vital bits, b) having to overbuy on items like screws and c) buying the wrong bits — classic one here is to get the wrong-sized hinges. If your tastes veer away from these mainstream choices you'll have to brave it and go and order your very own door furniture.

Our benchmark house is fitted out with brass furniture on the external doors and white ceramic knobs by Gainsborough on the internal doors.

Door Security

Door security features are dealt with in the following Security section in this chapter. To summarise — if you can't be bothered to find this section — current NHBC guidelines recommend fitting 5-lever locks to all external doors but also recommend that the main exit door should be protected by a Yale type night latch which can be readily opened from inside without a key; this is to make escape easier in case of fire.

Espagnolettes

These are fancy multi-point locking systems that are fitted, as standard, on uPVC doors, but this is because the basic material is so flexible that it would not be secure without bolts top, middle and bottom. The use of espagnolettes is creeping into the world of timber joinery and you can fit your own to any timber door simply by routing a slot down the closing edge. The espagnolettes cost around £55; they have an integral handle but they don't replace the 5-lever lock necessary on any external door.

Buying Tips

As already mentioned, the door furniture pre-packs are a moderately good deal if you are happy to stay within a limited range. If you want more unusual fittings then the D-I-Y sheds have a surprisingly varied range; if you want wood or ceramic knobs this is a good place to look. More specialised still are the Architectural Ironmongers: check the Yellow Pages in your area. Clayton Munroe make one-off wrought iron door furniture which is both traditional and very different.

Another tip well worth pursuing is to order your door locks "to pass." This means that all your 5-lever locks can be opened with just one key. Its not exactly the automated house but it's a big improvement on lugging around identical looking keys each of which will only open one of your doors. A good merchant will be able to sell you locks "to pass" at no extra cost though they will take an extra day or two to sort it out.

Knobs

Sorry to bring up this sordid subject again but the observant amongst you may have noticed that there are two distinct styles of door opening levers, otherwise known as handles and knobs. Whatever the merits and demerits of the two, there is one painful little trap to watch out for if you go for a knob — you need to fit a longer latch otherwise you will scrape your knuckles every time you open the door. For the technically challenged, the latch, in this instance, is the metal tube that fits inside the door and the hole in the latch determines exactly how far the handle or the knob sits from the edge of the door. The standard tubular latch is 63mm long and it's designed for handles; when fitting a knob on an internal door, fit a 75mm latch and an external door knob will require an even longer latch — say 95mm. The pre-packed knobsets normally include 75mm latches, but if you are buying independently then watch out.

Stairs

By far the cheapest staircase you can specify is the straight-flight with 13 steps and a total rise of 2600mm, which is the industry standard distance between floors. Timber staircases like this can be picked up off the shelf for as little as £180; they are also much quicker to install and, generally, have far less in the way of newel posts and balusters. A straight flight staircase with all the trimmings is going to take a good chippie no more

How stairs stack up

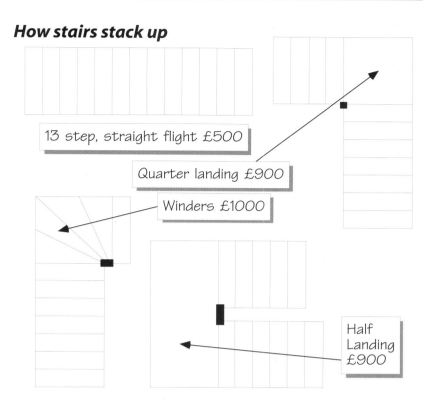

13 step, straight flight £500

Quarter landing £900

Winders £1000

Half Landing £900

than two days to put in, and so anticipate a cost (without decoration or carpeting) of just £450 (M £300, L £150). The cheapest source of straight stairs is the Magnets and Boulton & Paul's of the joinery world; for more complex arrangements, a local joiner may well be very competitive, though note that Boulton & Paul's bespoke staircase production is excellent.

Half Landings

The commonest alternative is to split the staircase into two halves connected by a half-landing. This arrangement is better when you want a more open stairwell design and often makes it much easier to design the internal layout of the house. Half-landings (and the related quarter-landings) tend to double the overall staircase costs; the staircase at our benchmark house has a half-landing built to a non-standard rise by Boulton & Paul at an installed cost of around £800 (M £500, L £300).

Winders

Winders (pronounced *wine-ders*, not *winders*) is the name given to steps that turn corners whilst still climbing; a spiral staircase consists of nothing but winders but a more conventional arrangement uses three winder steps (usually at the top or the bottom of the flight) to navigate a 90° turn. They are space efficient and so are normally used in situations where space is tight. These days they are most commonly used with loft conversions, precisely because of this reason. They

are not cheap — the staircase alone will cost £600 plus — and in many ways they are best avoided, especially when you want to move furniture up or downstairs.

Spirals

The ultimate in winding-staircases is the fully fledged spiral staircase. Usually done in steel, they are expensive and enormously impractical. The logic behind spiral staircases is that they save space but in reality the amount of spaced saved is minimal. They *do* certainly impose a style and in certain, modern looking interiors, they are just so. Realistically, the average UK housebuilder is going to find them far too ostentatious. Expect to pay over £1000 for a very simple steel spiral staircase.

Fittings

At least as significant visually as the shape of the staircase is the specification of all the little bits that go with the stairs; the banisters, the handrails, the newel posts. These days banisters tend to get called balusters which is, perhaps, something to do with European integration, but the details remain wedded to the turn of the century (last time around). As with so much else in UK housebuilding, the standard options all hark back to our dearly beloved bygones: Georgian, Victorian, Colonial, Fluting, Rope Twist, etc. Easily the least fussy — and the cheapest — are the peasant variety known as Plain Balusters. The plain arrangements cost around £30/lin.m whereas the fancy turned timber bal-

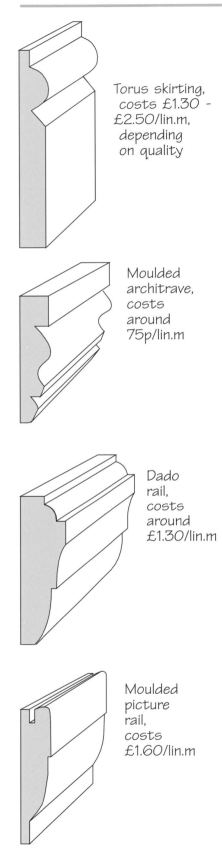

Torus skirting, costs £1.30 - £2.50/lin.m, depending on quality

Moulded architrave, costs around 75p/lin.m

Dado rail, costs around £1.30/lin.m

Moulded picture rail, costs £1.60/lin.m

usters start from around £45/lin.m. Even on a relatively straightforward staircase, the fittings will often cost as much as the stairs.

Galleries

A surprising number of otherwise very conventional new homes incorporate an open-plan gallery area which links the two floors with a grand staircase arrangement. Typically there will be an area of hallway around the front door which is open right up to the upstairs ceiling or even the underside of the roof, lit by a Velux rooflight. It makes for a very impressive entrance with dramatic overtones of minstrel's galleries and the like. In a way it's pure theatre; it is an extremely impractical arrangement and it doesn't owe much to traditional housing styles which we British seem so keen to ape in other respects. Done out using acres of glass, white walls and chrome staircase, we would say "It's far too open plan for us"; however, dress up the same idea with pile carpeting and traditional looking balustrading and we react quite differently — "Gosh! Isn't that just like Gone With The Wind."

However you finish it, the gallery/open-plan stairwell arrangement is *space hungry* and is, therefore, a luxury. In itself it's not a particularly expensive detail (unless you start curving the staircase and the balustrading) but before you embark on a maximum impact entrance, first consider whether you wouldn't rather have an extra room or two instead. Chances are that if you want that kind of entrance then, frankly, you don't give a damn.

Skirting/ Architrave

The amazing thing about skirtings and architraves is that we don't really need them at all. Indeed, many countries have already done away with them. Yet a glance at the building costs table generated by the benchmark house will reveal that Complete Fabrications, in common with every other major UK builder and just about every selfbuilder, spent good money (£800 or 1% of the total building costs) on fixing largely superfluous bits of timber to the base of all the walls and around all the internal door openings.

There is (or rather was) a logic behind fitting skirting boards. It used to be standard building practice to leave a 50mm gap between the floor and the bottom of the plaster on the wall so as not to breach the damp-proof course placed in the wall; however, damp-proofing techniques have changed and now floor membranes are lapped into wall membranes and the damp never (in theory) penetrates the room space at all. It still leaves the problem of filling the unsightly crack be-

tween wall and floor but the widespread incorporation of fitted carpets has made even this problem a thing of the past.

Not that I've anything against the skirting board; I love 'em — the wider the better. They look great and any room without them will look cold and, worse still, European. Both skirtings and architrave are available in a range of styles varying from the very plain to the thick moulded sections beloved by the Victorians. Fixing times don't vary much (prices usually hover around £1/m) but as regards material costs, the fancy sections are two to three times more than the utilitarian versions which are around 40p/m. To some extent this can be offset by specifying moulded sections from timber "fifths" (see section on buying timber in Chapter 11, Shopping), which are perfectly adequate for most people's needs. On the other hand, you can go for hardwood skirtings which — in my book — is pure unadulterated ostentation.

If you are in a hurry you can use prepainted MDF sections, which are now becoming widely available at builder's merchants. These are best nailed into the walls but, alternatively, can be stuck on with an adhesive like *Grip-fill*, a "mastic glue" which can be used to bond all kinds of materials. Not only could you use it for all your skirtings and architraves, but it's fantastically useful for sorting out little problems like squeaky stairs. A true friend to the bodge merchant.

Dados and Picture Rails

You may find it hard to believe that skirtings and architraves are purely cosmetic, but even the most sceptical amongst you will have to agree that dados and picture rails are not essential. However, they were regarded as essential in polite Victorian parlours. The dado rail was placed at waist height, the picture rail just a few inches below the ceiling. Their chief function was to provide a visual break in the eye feast that was the Victorian living room, whose walls consisted of two different kinds of wallpaper as well as (starting at the bottom) skirtings, dados, picture rails and plaster covings. Despite the fashions for all things Olde Worlde, this level of detail in new housing is now extremely uncommon. Nevertheless, good timber yards still keep these sections, mostly for restoration work, and you may choose to fit them in a new house if you are looking for a bit of style.

Loft Hatch

Every house has one (unless you have a room in the loft) and they are not the most demanding of features. But take a little care in fitting a loft hatch as it is frequently a weak point in your home's battle against draughts. Furthermore, being an outlet for draughts rather than an inlet, you are never likely to be aware of just how much warm air you may lose through the loft hatch. Many an otherwise fastidious greenie (myself included) have insulated the top of the loft trap door — Gripfill is brilliant for this job as well — but neglected to effectively draught proof the strips of wood on which the hatch door sits. In terms of heat loss through loft hatches, effective draught proofing is ten times more important than the insulation. You don't have to do anything dramatic; just make sure it sits tight. If you are particularly fussy, you can buy proprietary loft hatches made from uPVC which clamp shut. Marley make one — street price around £50.

Loft Ladders

Not essential but nevertheless incredibly useful, even if you only go up there once a year. A decent aluminium sliding loft ladder will cost around £50 and take a competent D-I-Y boffin around 2hrs to fit. However, if you are interested in making your loft hatch draught proof, it is really worth carrying out the installation of a loft ladder first because it usually leads to you having to make significant adjustments to the trap door housing.

Whilst we're on the subject, it's worth installing a permanent light in the loft just to make life easy when fixing a loft ladder. You won't regret it.

Airing Cupboard

Airing cupboards are not actually required in houses with central heating but they are still very commonly fitted. There is one major drawback to the contemporary airing cupboard and that is that with the new generation of super-lagged hot-water cylinders, you no longer have a creditable heat source in the airing cupboard; hence, perpetually soggy towels. Well that's not quite true; any new house will enjoy a much higher ambient temperature than an old wreck and this will tend to dry damp clothes, albeit rather slowly. You can, of course, just put fully dried clothes in the airing cupboard, but this rather defeats the purpose of having an airing cupboard in the first place. Alternatively, you can fit a mini-heater or a 150w light bulb inside. It all seems a bit futile when the cause of your problem is the fact that you've wrapped up the hot water cylinder so well that it no longer gives off any heat.

What's really needed is an effective way of lagging and unlagging your hot water tank, controlled automatically by the relative humidity of air inside the cupboard. But this sounds very expensive and surely the world is full of more pressing problems. Still it's one to ponder on during those long sleepless nights.

Boxing

Boxing in the pipes is a new facet of housebuilding that now forms a significant bit of a second-fixer's work. In the good-bad-indifferent-Olde days the pipes were left naked for all to see. The stench pipe in particular was usually run down the outside of the house. Current fashions are for internal stench pipes — *concealed* internal stench pipes — and this means boxing is de rigeur. Now, depending on your disposition, this type of job can seem like an incredible almighty drag or a marvellous opportunity to show the world just how creative you can be with a bit of dead space. Whichever camp you fall into, it helps to plan your pipe runs and attendant boxings well ahead so that the boxing can be incorporated into the overall scheme of things rather than sticking out into rooms like an ugly carbuncle ("monstrous," I hear you saying). Bathroom boxings are often best tiled over, but you must allow at least some of the panelling to be removable — a trick that's accomplished with mirror screws and flexible mastic joints. If you are painting the finish, then MDF is probably the best material to use, but if you plan to stick ceramic tiles on, then a waterproof 18mm plywood would be a better choice.

Boxing is also widely used in bathrooms to create a fitted vanity unit effect. There are a range of basins (known as semi-countertop) that are designed to sit over a boxed unit and there are also concealed cisterns which will be proud to flush behind your mini-wall. The usual choice of wall finish will be ceramic tiles but pine matchboarding is becoming fashionable once again, albeit painted not varnished.

Shelving

The only quotation that The Duchess of Windsor is remembered for is "You can't be too rich and you can't be too thin." Had she been a keen builder, she might have added "You can't have enough shelves" because it is an axiom that, however many shelves you put up, you will still need more. I can discern three approaches to shelving:
- **Buy some:** go out and buy some ready made up units. D-I-Y sheds have some pretty basic ones; IKEA has some basic ones which are a little better designed.

Department stores like Habitat and John Lewis have some very nice expensive shelving systems. Free standing shelving units are not especially cheap but they are removable.
- **Bash them up:** utility shelving can be extremely cheap to fit. If you use one of the proprietary steel bracket systems like Spur or Element 32 you pay a lot more but you get a system that's very quick to install and easy to alter. It is also readily removable. Materials for a steel bracket shelving system work out at around £30/lin.m which is cheaper than almost any ready made system.
- **Labour of love:** design your shelving to fit a particular alcove or sit at a certain height. Think a little of the finished look; perhaps add some sort of pelmet and possibly some lighting as well. This sort of detail does not have to be expensive but it does require a certain amount of forethought. If you know what MDF is and know how to wield a router, you should be able to erect bespoke shelving (with no metal brackets showing!) for less than £20/lin.m (materials only).

Airing cupboard in benchmark house: all that's missing is warmth

Bedrooms

For developers, bedroom space is cheap space. All that really has to be provided is enough room to fit a bed and an item of furniture plus enough space to manoeuvre about between them — the technical term for this is *swinging a cat*.

Design Considerations

You can of course give far more consideration to the whole issue. It's worth visualising the layout of the bedroom furniture so as to work out where to place radiators and power sockets. Also it's a nice touch to arrange light switching so that it can be reached easily from the bed. On the other hand, if you want to maintain maximum flexibility, then fit power sockets on every wall so you can accommodate various layouts. In reality there may only be one sensible place where a bed can go, but there may be other considerations. What is appropriate as a nursery for a toddler is unlikely to suit a teenager and you should consider how the uses a bedroom gets put to will change over the years. Don't always assume that a bedroom will remain a bedroom.

Size

It is conventional to rank bedrooms by size. Now, you might think that in a four-bedroom house you would provide a double bedroom for mum and dad (or whoever tickles your fancy) plus three smaller but similar sized rooms for the children. But no; the British way of doing it is to build bedrooms in ever decreasing sizes. It's also the British way of doing things to rank houses according to the number of bedrooms they have. Almost all developers switch to four bedrooms when the overall floor size creeps over 110m², and perhaps the most remarkable single fact about our benchmark house is that it breaks this rule, putting just three bedrooms into a floor area of 166m², a size at which conventional developers would be thinking of switching to five bedrooms. Now you might think "Where's the problem?"; you might be right. The majority of today's housebuyers are not families with three or more children, so why the fascination with bedrooms?

Nevertheless, this house took months to sell and the agent reckoned it was because people thought it looked overpriced for a three bedroom house. In fact while it was on the market, it had very few visitors, despite the house market being pretty hot at this time (Spring 97). It seems that housebuyers use bedroom numbers as a shorthand for size and that they therefore concluded, wrongly, that a house with three bedrooms must be small. If the agent had advertised the house as 166m² or 1800ft² most punters would not have known what that meant. Incidentally, as outlined in Chapter 2, the reason the house has just three bedrooms is because it was not originally envisaged for re-sale at all but was built with someone in mind who didn't want more than three.

The Eltisley benchmark house bedroom sizes are as follows:
- MASTER BEDROOM
  4.8x3.6m   17.3m²
- BEDROOM 2
  3.9x3.5m   13.6m²
- BEDROOM 3
  3.2x4.1m   13.1m²

A more common arrangement would be to split the 45m² of bedrooms something like 15/12/10/8. This may suit you fine, but I think you should at least think about it before accepting it on the nod. Many standard house plans are drawn with this exaggerated size spread between bedrooms and they can be fairly easily redrafted to get sizes which better suit you.

Wardrobes

Not usually included by developers and not usually included in any summary of building costs, the wardrobe is, nevertheless, a near essential item in any bedroom. As with shelving, outlined in the previous section, there are basically three approaches to creating bedroom storage space:
- Use free standing furniture: it costs but you can take it with you
- Use specialist bedroom fittings
- Make your own.

The last method has one major advantage, recently agreed by Customs & Excise, in that it is regarded as zero-rated for VAT purposes. Typically you would design your bedroom wall partitions with various strategically placed kinks into — see the plan of the benchmark house which uses this technique — which you slip a hanging rail and a few open shelves and then hang a door or two in front. It's probably the cheapest option for new housebuilders as the cupboards can be created as you go rather than being added on afterwards. Budget between £100 and £250 per fitted wardrobe, depending on the size, finish and complexity of the design; this would include shelving, hanging rails and a door or two. Magnet and the D-I-Y sheds sell melamine wardrobe fitting kits, complete with hanging rails, at around £35ea.

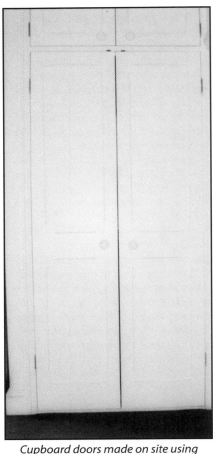

Cupboard doors made on site using two sheets of MDF glued and screwed together. This is a useful technique when you want to fill a gap that isn't an industry standard one.

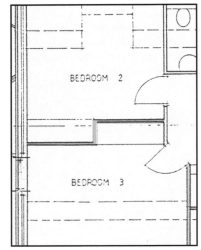

Benchmark house uses the kinked bedroom wall technique to create wardrobe space — and avoid VAT.

Bathrooms

Bathroom fixtures and fittings is an area where standards have risen dramatically in the last century; the provision of a bathroom only became obligatory in the 1985 Building Regs and there is still no minimum size for bathrooms nor any obligation to build in more than a bath (or shower) and a loo. (This standard rises to a bath and two loos in houses where five or more people might be expected to live).

The basic minimum standard adopted by new housebuilders is way in excess of this. All contemporary bathrooms include washbasins and virtually all houses with four bedrooms or more have a second bathroom, usually known as the *en-suite* and accessed directly from the master bedroom. A downstairs cloakroom is also now an extremely common feature in family homes. Professional housebuilders are not known for their largesse and they would claim that the effective standards are those imposed by the house buying public, which seems to be about thirty years ahead of the building regulations in this instance.

Costs

The bathroom is a multi-trade zone. Do not be fooled into thinking that bathrooms are all about plumbing-in sanitaryware: that's just the beginning. Ventilation, wall tiling, mirrors, accessories, obscured glazing, enclosed light fittings, pull switches, towel rails (heated or otherwise) and specialised floor coverings all combine to make bathroom fitting a complex and elaborate process — and one that is easy to neglect in the hurry to finish a house. Bathroom planning is even more important in timber frame buildings because timber bearers should be present in the walls to secure all the fittings.

Bathrooms are expensive. The accompanying table shows costings for the two bathrooms plus downstairs cloakroom in the benchmark house. This is a typical installation with a bath in the family bathroom and an enclosed shower in the en-suite bathroom. Bear in mind that it's not the size of the bathroom that is expensive but the fittings in them. Big bathrooms are becoming very popular: many people want to fit cupboards and furniture in their bathrooms: the en-suite bathroom in particular seems to be getting bigger and bigger, eating chunks out of its attached bedroom.

9d: Benchmark House: Bathroom Costs

ITEM	FAMILY	EN SUITE	CLOAK ROOM
Loo (inc. Pine Seats)	£140	£130	£140
Basin (inc. Taps)	45	45	40
Bath (inc. Taps)	160		
Shower Tray		70	
Shower Door		90	
Shower		140	
Copper Pipe/Plastic Waste	80	80	40
Labour To Fit	220	250	130
Soil + Vent Pipe	80	50	
Labour To Fit	100	50	
ACCESSORIES (inc. Fitting)			
Pipe Boxing	40	40	
Vanity Units		100	
Fans	100	100	
Wall Tiling (14m²)	220	340	50
Enclosed Light Fittings	60	60	
Shaver Sockets	40	40	
TOTALS	**£1285**	**£1585**	**£400**

Conclusions

11% (19m²) of the overall floor area of our benchmark house comprises bathrooms and it's an expensive 11%; the combined bathrooms cost £3200 in excess of ordinary bedroom space. If you want to save money, don't build more than one bathroom. A bedroom costs about £300/m² to build; a fairly basic bathroom will add £160-£200/m² to that price and specifying fancy period fittings or modern continental styling, together with matching towel rail and tiling, could easily double the cost of a basic bathroom.

Shower cubicles are three times the price of a bog standard bath. Don't think you are saving water (and therefore money) by showering; an enclosed shower space is a luxury, and the extra £250-£300 over and above the cost of a cheap bath will not be paid for out of water saved, especially if you fit a power or mains pressure shower which uses a bath load of water in three minutes.

Bathroom Suites

Budget bathrooms are most usually sold as three-piece suites. Normally a bathroom suite includes:

• Bath, bath taps, plug
• Bath panels (to conceal the fact that the bath is plastic)
• Basin and supporting pedestal
• Basin taps and plug
• WC, cistern, seat, handle.

If you don't buy a suite, you'll have to remember to get all these items separately — items like cistern levers are easily overlooked. If you want to opt for a separate shower instead of a bath you may be able to find a two-piece "cloakroom suite" (*be warned*: cloakroom basins are often minute). A very basic bathroom suite will cost £200-£250. You won't get high style at this price but you will get a choice of six or seven pastel colours which can be coordinated with tiles to, at least, suggest that you've tried. Most bathroom outlets have a range of four or five suites going up in price to around £400; after that you get into more upmarket designs where all items come priced individually. Prices tend to get softer as they get higher and trade discounts of "no more than 10%" on budget lines suddenly rise to 30% or more when your spend rises above £1000.

Accessories

Most suites offer a wide range of matching accessories (shelves, soap holders, loo roll holders, toothbrush holders, toilet brush holders, towel rails) at prices well over the odds for what you would pay in a D-I-Y shed. Even on a fairly basic suite, you could easily spend over £100 on buying matching fittings, adding another 20% to your suite price. If you want a bidet, expect this to add around 30% to the basic three-piece suite price.

Visit any bathroom showroom or trade fair and it immediately becomes apparent that there is a style war in progress. Top: the Continental look, all sleek lines and curves. Bottom: Ancient British look, profoundly Eurosceptic

Authenticity comes at a price; the Victorians never had mahogany bath panels nor glazed shower screens. To get the full period effect, attention must be paid to the detailing throughout the bathroom. A roll-top, cast-iron bath that can stand on its own will cost £500 plus; a *Dorchester* heated towel rail £400. There are small craft producers, like Sanitan and Vernon Tutbury, producing authentic designs but such a bathroom can cost £3000 just for the sanitaryware.

The Modern Look

This is the other dominant style in contemporary bathrooms. The porcelain styling is all curves and pastel colours, the taps look like mushrooms and lavatory cisterns are concealed. Basin vanity units can be purchased from the merchants (from £70) but a more pleasing alternative is to build tiled work surfaces on to which you place a semi-countertop basin (like Ideal Standard's *Tulip*, £70 plus taps).

Colour Coordination

The essence of this style of bathroom is, not surprisingly, to match colours. If you want to do this, check that the British Standard colour numbers are the same — don't assume that "Ivory" or "Misty Peach" is the same colour for tile producers as it is for bathroom suppliers. You can also have your heated towel rails spray-painted to match bathroom suites (costs about £40 extra).

Top of the Range

Whirlpool baths like the Jacuzzi will cost £2000+ though the plumbing in is relatively straightforward. Other ideas that you may come across are building in saunas or gyms; all of which will cost a great deal of money and good luck to you.

Styles

There are currently two discernible streams of bathroom styling, mirroring the fashion in contemporary kitchens. One is towards modern looking, built-in fixtures; the other is harking back to Victorian and Edwardian times. The more money you spend, the greater the divergence of styles become. The major UK producers (Armitage Shanks, Ideal Standard, Shires, Twyfords) all plough this well worn furrow. If you want something that transcends these styles, you'll have to look at continental brands names like Sottini or Roca or, if you want to get thoroughly minimalist, check out Vola UK (01525 841155) who import all manner of weird and wonderful sanitary sculptures like glass sinks. Sales literature is available at most plumber's merchants and many builder's merchants; also check out the growing number of bathroom boutiques — try looking in the Yellow Pages under *Bathroom Eqpt*. If you want something out of the ordinary, be aware that it may take many weeks for it to be delivered.

Period Styling

Up till fifteen years ago, people were still stripping out period porcelain and nothing new had been produced since the 50s. The return to fashion of these styles (always white or off-white) has been the one big success story for sanitaryware producers in the last few years and now every manufacturer produces sanitaryware to fit the period. The cheaper suites are priced at £350-£400 but they don't look very authentic (Plumb Center's *Bramham Suite* is as good as any). Ideal Standard have produced suites in four period styles (Victorian, Edwardian, Art Deco, Country Cottage).

Showers

A rapidly growing market, showers are popular both as attachments to bath taps (known as shower mixers) and in their own right in stand-alone shower cubicles. Apart from style — and there are showers to fit every style — there are two things to look out for; thermostatic control and adequate flow rate.

Thermostatic Control

Thermostatic control automatically adjusts the balance of hot and cold water flowing through the shower head as other taps in the house turn on and off. It is expensive, usually adding around £70 to the cost of a shower. A cheaper alternative is to have a shower with a high-temperature limiter which will avoid scalding but may still leave you drenched in cold water when a hot tap opens somewhere else.

Shower Power

There are many routes to getting a good pressure through your shower head. The most effective are to install a mains pressure hot water system or a thermal store (see section on Domestic Hot Water in Chapter 8, Services). The least effective are to install an electric shower or a combination boiler, both of which heat water instantaneously and therefore suffer from low flow rates. In between these extremes come a whole gamut of power showers which aim to add whoosh to feeble pressure from tanks in the loft. There are single impeller pumps which boost the water after the mixing valve and double impellers which boost both hot and cold before they enter the valve. Which you choose is partly dependent on the layout you have and prices are largely dependent on the power of the pump. They can be purchased for just over £100, but a pump delivering 30lts/minute (equivalent to a good mains pressure system) will cost £180plus. Leading manufacturers: Mira, Aqualisa.

There are a also number of integral pumped shower valves like the Triton *AS 1000* (£140). These tend to be a cheaper option (the styling is naff) and you end up with an unsightly box of tricks in the shower cubicle. There are also electric showers which work entirely off the cold main and don't need a hot water supply and electric showers like the Triton *T90* (£305) which heat, pump and make thermostatic adjustments. The most ingenious (and probably the cheapest option) is the Aquadart *Hyrdoflow* (£100) which uses the pressure from the cold main to force the hot water flow rate up. Alone of the power showers it doesn't need a power supply, but there's no thermostatic control.

If you want a power shower in a new house, you would be well advised to avoid all these products and go for a mains pressure or near mains pressure hot water system.

Shower Trays

Acrylic trays can be had for under £50 but they are not recommended because of problems with leaking caused by the trays flexing. The most popular option is the *ceramic stone* trays: Matki's is good (cost £75). For another £12 you can buy them with an under-tile upstand which will eliminate any possibility of leakage. The standard size is 760mm square (which suits the standard pivot doors). There is a significant (100%) cost penalty if you want a larger tray.

Advanced Showers produce this all in one moulded shower enclosure. Included is this gizmo for clearing hair out of the trap.

Shower Doors

You have a choice of building the shower into an alcove (with three side walls tiled), into a corner or free standing against one wall. Pricewise there is little to choose — the cost of a tiled wall being similar to the cost of a glazed side panel. The alcove option usually looks the most professional; you finish the opening with either a pivot or a bi-fold door which will cost anything from £80 (Elbee, Laconite, Ram Niagra) to £200 or more (Matki, Daryl, Showerlux, Nordic). Matching side panels tend to be 60-80% of the door price. If your shower is incorporated with your bath, then you have a choice of a simple shower curtain hung from a rail (from £30) to a glazed shower screen (£50 upwards).

Alternative Designs

Open showers running into a floor drain is a style more often seen in warmer countries than ours, but with effective space heating, there is no reason for not building it into a British bathroom. Well, actually, there is a good reason for not doing so and that is that the tiled surfaces have to perform a very good job if you're not to get leaks through your bathroom floor. In theory, this is no problem; in practice, tiled shower cubicles often ship water where they shouldn't and tiled floors will tend to fare even worse. It really is worth paying a lot of attention to the construction of shower enclosures generally because their failure is one of the commonest faults in new buildings. Don't skimp on the linings — use a water proof plywood rather than plasterboard — and use the best adhesive you can afford to fix ceramic tiles with. The key failure point, however, is the joint between the

walls and the floor (or more likely tray) and with most designs you are dependent on a bead of silicone mastic to stop water finding a route through the defence. Your silicone sealant will stand a much better chance of success if the joint is tight and even, something which is likely to be the result of your carpenters work.

One ingenious way around the problem of leaking showers is to install an all-in-one moulded cubicle. Advanced Showers (01483 295930) produce a range of elegant, standalone enclosures which, whilst not cheap (costing upwards of £1000), are very quick and easy to install and will be valued by all those who have experienced the frustrations of shower leaks. Another option is to avoid timber joists in your first floor: it's the shrinkage in these joists (often as much as 8mm) when the house is drying out that causes all these shower leaks: specify either a beam and block first floor or something like a Trus Joist floor (see Chapter 7, section on Floors).

Kitchen Design

The kitchen is easily the most expensive part of the house to build. Whereas unfurnished spaces (such as bedrooms and living rooms) clock in at around £300/m^2 and bathrooms at around £500/m^2, the spend on the kitchen area is likely to be in excess of £750/m^2.

This is perhaps a slightly misleading statistic because only the kitchen and bathrooms are finished at the building stage; everywhere else has to be furnished by the homeowner. But even so, if insurance company figures are anything to go by, the average home has just £20,000 of stealable fittings and, looked at on a £/m^2 basis, that only adds £250/m^2 to floor area costings. So, whichever way you look at it, kitchens remain far and away the most expensive item in the contemporary house.

The kitchen has come a long way in a short time; the Victorians regarded the kitchen as "below stairs" and, even in humble homes, it was relegated to the backroom status along with the dunny and the coal house. Today, it is not unusual for the kitchen to receive pride-of-place treatment in any showhouse; for housebuilders this is the place to put on the dazzle. Furthermore, this trend is entirely market driven; the NHBC's regulations for kitchen fitting are covered in just 100 words, none of which could be said to be onerous on the housebuilder. What we have here is what a sociologist would call "a profound social change" but what in anyone else's terms is business, business, business.

Benchmark Kitchen

Robin Gomm, proprietor and designer of Complete Fabrications, the benchmark house builders, has been designing and building kitchens for 20 years. In some ways it's what he does best and he's forever doodling over little design details to improve on his system. Typically a Gomm kitchen is made up on site and incorporates lots of hardwoods (maple and iroko are two favourites) and open shelving. However, the kitchen in the benchmark house did not get the Robin Gomm treatment. By the time the kitchen came to be fitted, it was realised that the house was going to put on the market and price took a front seat. Not that Gomm's kitchens are that expensive — they have been fitted into several other spec. houses so they can't be — but here the client wanted a simple off-the-peg solution and the solution chosen was a Shaker style kitchen from Arena. The appliances are German (Neff) and, perhaps unusually for a developer, include a dishwasher as well as the

obligatory cooker, hob and hood. The utility area was, however, was kitted out with two matching base units and a second stainless steel sink unit. Other essential appliances — cold storage, washing machine, tumble dryer — were left to the house buyers.

The overall kitchen layout is unusually large including, as it does, a meals area at one end almost as big as the dining room located off the hallway. What prominence you decide to give to the kitchen is the most difficult internal design decision that you will be faced with. The two extremes to opt for are:
- the kitchen as utility area (hidden from view and servicing a separate dining room)
- the kitchen to be the main living area of the home, typically called an open-plan arrangement.

The trend is towards the open-plan kitchen; this suits the kitchen suppliers as it means a) bigger kitchens and b) consumers are more conscious of the way their kitchens are going to look. If you accept the notion that you want your kitchen to be the most important room in the house, then you are probably prepared to spend a much larger sum on making it beautiful. On the other hand, if you want to keep costs down, design your kitchen more as a utility area and have a separate dining room where you eat.

Grasping the Kettle

When you've come to some conclusion about how you want your kitchen to work with the rest of the house, you can then get down to the nut and bolt design matters of what goes where. It is usual to start with a list of household appliances. If you have opted for a separate utility area, this will be the natural home of washing machines and tumble dryers and, possibly, freezers. The kitchen proper must have a sink, some sort of cooker and a fridge. Dishwashers are increasingly sought after and are conventionally placed close to the sink. The positioning of your appliances around the kitchen becomes the skeleton on which the kitchen furniture is hung. There are some conventional dos and don'ts to consider:
- DO locate sinks and plumbed-in appliances where waste pipes can get to the drains. Usually this means placing them against an outside wall.
- DO locate cooker hoods against an outside wall where exhaust fumes can be evacuated. You can run ducting to get around this problem but it is a fiddle best

avoided.
- DO leave worktop space either side of both the sink and the hob (or cooker top).
- DO keep the sink, the hob and the fridge reasonably close to each other. Simply for the sake of convenience. Some kitchen planners will go on at length about the importance of the *work triangle* in the kitchen. Politely ignore them.
- DON'T place a hob or a sink in a corner unless you consider an angled corner arrangement (expensive); corners tend to make poor working/storage space.
- DON'T place a fridge or freezer next to or under a heat source (hob, cooker, radiator).
- DON'T forget to consider the boiler if it needs to be in the kitchen. Not only will it be hot but there are rules concerning just where you can and can't place boiler flue terminals (see Chapter 8, Services, section on boilers).
- DON'T put wall cupboards over the sink; conventionally, sinks go under windows and for most small- or medium-sized kitchens this will always be the most practical location.

If you're a neat, logical kind of person, having got this far you should be able to draw a layout plan on some graph paper and begin to get an idea of the number of units you will need. Congratulate yourself because you're the kind of client any kitchen supplier would be pleased to have — you actually know what you want!

9e: Benchmark House: Kitchen Costs

	NO.	NOTES	VALUE
APPLIANCES		Cooking gear is NEFF	
Kitchen Sink	1	1.5 Bowl/Single Drainer in St. Steel	£60
Utility Sink	1	1 Bowl/Single Drainer in St. Steel	£40
Taps	2	Aquadisc Mixer Taps @ £40ea	£80
Hob	1	Electric, 4-ring Sealed (inc VAT)	£80
Hood	1	3-speed, Ducted to Outside (inc VAT)	£60
Oven	1	Electric Double, Integrated (inc VAT)	£450
Dishwasher	1	Integrated, Under Sink (inc VAT)	£350
KITCHEN UNITS		Arena Sherborne Shaker style	
FLOOR STANDING			
Full-height Housing	1	Oven Housing	£190
U/worktop Housing	2	Dishwasher/Cold Store @ £70	£140
Corner Units	1	1000mm wide	£110
Drawer Unit	1	600mm wide	£130
Drawer Units	2	300mm wide @ £110	£220
Base Units	3	600mm wide @ £100	£300
Base Units	2	300mm wide @ £60	£180
Base Unit	1	400mm wide	£90
Sink Unit	2	1000mm wide @ £160	£320
WALL UNITS			
Cooker Hood Unit	1	600mm	£40
Wall Units	2	600mm wide @ £95	£190
WORKTOPS		38mm thick laminate	
Kitchen and Utility	4	4100mm @ £90	£360
FLOOR PLINTHS	4	Sections: total 5620mm	£90
KITCHEN FITTING		including appliances	£900
TOTAL COST OF KITCHEN WORKS			**£4,380**
plus			
WALL TILING		10m² ceramic tiling	£ 420

Floor plinths run along the foot of floor units similar to skirting board. Often sold separately and fitted to unit legs with spring clips. They have to be returned back to the wall at open ends

Pelmets do much the same as plinths but run around the top of the wall units instead of along the floor. This kitchen didn't have any pelmets.

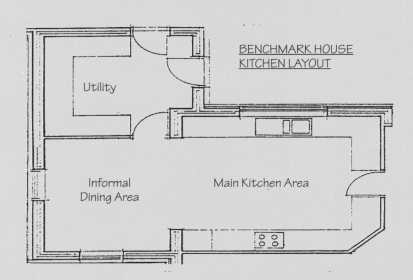

BENCHMARK HOUSE
KITCHEN LAYOUT

Utility

Informal
Dining Area

Main Kitchen Area

Kitchen Units

The fitted kitchen market is a postwar phenomenon and even as recently as the 60s most people still thought a kitchen cabinet was something to do with Harold Wilson. The 70s saw the start of the totally fitted kitchen, initially with an ultra-modern look using entirely man-made materials, but it has since grown to include semi-natural timber finishes.

Flat Pack v Rigid

A flat pack kitchen is one that arrives on site as a kit to be assembled. Anyone with the skills to assemble a house is not going to be overwhelmed by having to put together a flat pack cabinet and, not surprisingly, the flat packed kitchen (which is much cheaper to transport) has 75% of the market and is increasing. It is dominated by UK manufacturers, notably MFI. In contrast, the rigid carcass market, which is seen as more upmarket, is dominated by imports. In the past some commentators sought to denigrate the UK producers for always aiming cheap and leaving the cream to be exploited by the French and Germans. There is, however, no particular reason why a flat-packed kitchen should be inferior to a rigid one and, in many ways, it makes a good deal of sense to buy a flat pack which should always work out a little cheaper.

Just Shelves with Fancy Doors

When we think of fitted kitchens, we think of how the door fronts look. The kitchen dream sellers are well aware of this and, although the actual units may make up only 25% of the final bill for a fitted kitchen, these are how kitchens are sold to us. The explosion in the number of manufacturers and stylings has really only happened since 1970 and fashions have come but they've never really gone, so that each few years kitchen design expands to incorporate new ideas whilst it continues to recycle the old ones. The basic manufacturing process is relatively simple and cheap so that no new successful idea can be free of imitators for more than a few months at most.

The kitchen business is fully metricated and works in modular units which increase in 100mm intervals. Thus any given range of floor units or wall cupboards will be available in widths of typically 300mm, 400mm, 500mm and 600mm. In various combinations they can fill any space on any wall to the nearest 100mm — and they sell blanking-off pieces to cover any gaps left in the corners. The appliances, like cookers and fridges, are made to fit into 600mm gaps. So

give a kitchen designer a space that's 3600x2400mm and they will tend to think of it as 6 units long and 4 across. Anything that doesn't fit into this neat configuration tends to get thought of as infill space.

Materials

All but the most expensive kitchen unit carcasses are made from a wood pulp board like chipboard or MDF (medium density fibreboard), usually covered with a melamine veneer which serves both to make them stronger and moisture resistant. The cheaper doors, which are hung over these carcasses, are made of similar materials, though here the melamine covering is usually decorated with some trim. Solid timber is a more upmarket door option and there are more adventurous designs using such materials as steel and plastic.

Styles and Outlets

MFI and the D-I-Y Sheds

The mass market producers are inclined to be incredibly conservative in taste, tending to plain-coloured laminates with a wood trim for their cheaper ranges and fielded wood panelling for their more expensive lines. They would have us believe that pine is now rather dated, but in truth they never really succeed in making pine look good; despite its low price and ready availability it doesn't take well to mass production of this kind — though it can look stunning when done out in a rough and ready style. IKEA, the Swedish megastore which currently has six UK outlets, has been a leader amongst the mass market producers in designing some of their ten ranges in the "Continental" style and it is noticeable how the arrival of IKEA as a force to be reckoned with has caused other outlets like MFI to broaden their range of styles.

The Continentals

The more innovative and interesting designs tend to remain the preserve of the upmarket kitchen. The Germans were the first into this pond in the 70s when names like Wellman, Allmilmo and, most notably, Poggenpohl came to the UK. Like all things German, they have built up a reputation for superbly designed — "engineered" is possibly a better word — kitchens. In terms of style however they've been left in the slow lane. The high-tech, Continental look is now led by the French and, especially, the Italians — look out for Boffi's futuristic designs (Alternative Plans 0171 228 6460).

Smallbone, etc.

Despite exporting barely any kitchens at all (we import about 20%), the British have responded to the threat of mainly upmarket invasion by inventing a whole new romantic theme — now known as the English style or, more often, *doing a Smallbone*. Smallbone — which started as an antiques business in Wiltshire — have consistently led the way in creating a new vernacular kitchen, which manages to strike some chord in the English middle-class psyche and leads people to pay good money to recreate a past that never existed. Using many revived techniques and idioms (rag rolling, marbling, Welsh dressers), they manage to create a magnificent, seductive illusion. To purchase the actual Smallbone marque is now outrageously expensive — though not necessarily poor value — but the style has spawned hundreds of imitators. This school of kitchen design has grown away from providing modular boxes towards what has become known as the *unfitted kitchen* — an Aga here, a beech block table there, terracotta tiles on the floor, whicker baskets hanging on rails, you can almost smell the garlic and olive oil.

Some of these upmarket companies must be approached directly, many have just one UK outlet. The nearest thing to a directory exists in the back of *Kitchens, Bedrooms and Bathrooms* magazine which will give you an overview of the market's top end.

Kitchen Boutiques

Another approach is to ignore the plethora of manufacturers and concentrate on your local kitchen specialists. Most small towns have at least one left and a regional shopping centre will have several — check Yellow Pages. Most will stock only three or four manufacturers' products but as manufacturers offer sometimes hundreds of options (especially in door colours) this can still be quite bewildering. Typically, they will stock a mass-produced British flat-pack product (like Ram Kitchens or Symphony) which they will use to try and compete with MFI and co, but the bulk of their showrooms is given over to displaying a middle market Continental range. They make more money on the more expensive kitchens so it is understandable that it is these that they promote, even though they may sell only one or two a month.

Many people are rather reluctant to set foot inside a kitchen specialist as they think it would be a) too expensive and b) involve high-pressure selling. By and large, this is not the case; though they probably cannot compete with MFI on kitchen unit price alone, they are usually owner-managed and tend to give a very high level of personal service without resorting to any pressure tactics. If there is a drawback to using this route, it is that you have to get into bed (i.e. arrange a site visit) to be able to get prices, and some people will feel it is hard not to consummate the deal having got that close. Unlike the major retail outlets, prices are usually negotiable and this makes it hard to compare on a like for like basis.

Almost all kitchen specialists are tied to certain manufacturer's products: there are very few independent fee based advisers and easily the best known is Roma Jay Designs (0181 886 1850) who offer a very competitive postal design service for £60 — but note that a full design resulting from a site visit with working drawings would be very much more expensive.

The Builder

Another route often used when kitchen work is being carried out is to ask the main building contractor to supply and fit. There are several outlets (principally builder's merchants and joinery centres) which aim to sell mainly to builders and they will have kitchen catalogues available to browse through and sometimes showrooms to visit. The major joinery firms — Boulton & Paul, Magnet, John Carr — all produce fitted kitchens — though, stylistically, they tend to be the most conservative of all — and their catalogues are easy to get hold of and clearly priced. The builder can buy these units (and the accessories) at discounts of between 20 to 40% off list price and

many will be happy to negotiate to share at least some of the discount with you — see section on Contracts in Chapter 5, Project Management, in particular find out what a PCSum is. Even so, the prices from the volume joinery majors, even with full discount, will be slightly more than the cheapest available from the likes of MFI; but there is one big advantage if your builder fits the units and that is that he will remain responsible for sorting out any snags. If, on the other hand, you supply your own units to your builder and, say, the hinges work loose or there are unsightly gaps here and there, then you'll have your work cut out trying to convince him it's his fault: indeed you'll have fallen into one of the contractual traps placed along the route.

Direct Sell

There are a number of kitchen manufacturers who sell, largely to the replacement market, via a direct sales force. Kitchens Direct is the biggest name in this business. The product tends to be good; Kitchens Direct make every kitchen to order and are unusual in not using modular units. However, cost comparisons are woefully difficult to make as there really is no such thing as a fixed price. Suffice to say that a large amount of the kitchen price goes to the salesperson and that they are given discretion over what price the bargain should be struck. They concentrate on the aspirational purchaser who is unlikely to look elsewhere — and is unlikely to have read this.

Bespoke Kitchens

Before the advent of Smallbone, getting a joiner to make up a kitchen for you was always thought of as the most expensive option. If you choose to have doors made up out of gale-blown timbers, etc., this can still prove to be expensive enough but, with the advent of MDF (Medium Density Fibreboard), simple handmade and handpainted kitchens can be surprisingly cheap. Almost all kitchen carcassing (i.e. the bits you don't see) is made up of MDF (or sometimes chipboard, which is structurally inferior). You can buy 18mm thick MDF board in 2.4x1.2m sheets for as little as £14/sheet and get it machine cut for under 50p/cut. A sheet will make up an averaged-sized kitchen carcass and door; add a little for ironmongery and knobs, paint or varnish, design a simple trim and plinth detail and — lo and behold — you've got all the materials for our standard kitchen at less than half the price of MFI's cheapest.

Even though a competent joiner would take little longer to assemble this kitchen than he would a flat-pack, there are still remarkably few takers for such a design. This is probably a result of marketing failure as much as anything else. There are many economies in fabricating on site but most people are simply unaware what they might be. There are substantial design limitations — glass doors, friezes, fielded panelling and other complicated motifs are best carried out in factories — but there is, however, undoubtedly a niche for kitchen designers to create simple made-on-site kitchens which will accommodate the limited budget. This would be much closer to the ideal of the Shaker kitchen than those maddeningly expensive ones that carry that currently fashionable title.

Benchmark house: the Shaker-inspired kitchen, made by Arena, is nearing completion

Sinks and Worktops

Sinks

Stainless Steel

Stainless steel sinks now represent the cheap and cheerful option, which is perhaps surprising because in many other contexts stainless steel is regarded as an expensive material. Steel is actually a very good choice of material for a sink; it's strong, lightweight and easily cleaned. However, it is something of a victim of its own success because stainless steel sinks became so ubiquitous in the 60s and 70s that people started to choose other materials just to be different. It also suffered from the fact that it was a one colour product at a time when kitchens were becoming colour coordinated.

The very cheapest kitchen sinks now tend to be stainless steel; single bowl/single drainers can be picked up for less than £30, a set of taps for less than £20. However, the products from the big names in kitchen sinks (Fordham, Leisure, Carron, Franke, Blanco) can be every bit as expensive as the multicoloured ones touched on in the next section. Expect to pay £120plus for something as good as a Franke one-and-a-half bowl sink.

Asterite

Asterite (which is made by ICI) is just the best known of many resinous silicone-based materials, all of them revolutionary and all with names that sound like bit players from Star-Trek: Resan, Sylaca, Silquartz, Silacron, Novean, Astracast. Every sink manufacturer seems to have developed their own material (mostly made in conjunction with ICI). Whilst steel became stigmatised as being downmarket, these synthetics, typically coloured white, brown or something in between (usually christened Mocca or Cappuccino to add sophistication), took off in a big way. In terms of performance they offer no advantages over steel — in fact they are a damn sight harder to clean — but they do look good in kitchen showrooms, particularly with colour coordinated taps.

Asterite sinks are most commonly sold in packs. What this means is that you'll get a bundle of extras like sink racks, drainers and (maybe) a hardwood chopping board thrown in along with taps and waste fittings. If you don't mind obscure brands, then expect to pay around £135 for a one-and-a-half bowl sink pack. Generally it's worth paying an extra £15 to get taps with ceramic discs which, it is claimed, never drip.

Butler's Sinks

The old fashioned butler's sink also tends to look a wow in the kitchen showroom, particularly when it is inset in a hardwood surround with drainage grooves. It's not changed from the original Victorian design (i.e. a large white rectangular box) and this adds an air of authenticity to it which nothing else in a modern kitchen can touch, not even an Aga (which hails from the 30s). Consequently, it's become an item in all Smallbone-inspired kitchens and its very size and weight stand as statements of contempt for the standard mass produced fitted kitchen. Butler's sinks, such as the Armitage Shanks *Belfast*, cost between £110 and £150 depending on size. Taps and waste are extra: these sinks are most definitely not sold in packs.

Kitchen Worktops

The worktop is the name given to the main shelf in a kitchen where all the action happens — the food preparation, the cooking and the cleaning. Everything else is just storage. Getting the worktop right is a crucial part of kitchen design and, though it may not be the first thing you think about when selecting a kitchen, it will be the single most important element in your kitchen. The standard width for laminate worktops is 600mm which is sufficient for most kitchen configurations. Peninsulas, islands and breakfast bars may all require wider surfaces; there are a few extra-wide sizes available with two good edges, designed for these types of applications. The cheapest option is 28mm thick white or near-white laminate which costs around £20 for a 3m. length, available at D-I-Y sheds or trade outlets like Magnet. However, if you want irregular shapes or fancy trims then you will need to go via a kitchen specialist and probably have to buy a more expensive laminate.

Expensive Laminates

The patterned varieties are what the kitchen showrooms push. There are a few well known names like Formica, Polyrey, Resopal, Duropal and Beaumel; the showrooms often try to sell their own versions. They are usually sold in 40mm thicknesses which gives them a beefy feel — though provided the front is supported every 600mm the extra thickness is unnecessary. There is a far wider choice of colours and patterns but prices will be around three times the cheapest options — i.e. they start at around £60 for a 3m length or, if you prefer, £20/lin.m.

Hardwood

These usually appear as thick strips of woods such as beech or oak which are glued and laminated into a solid board. Both Junckers and Texwood produce a range of worktops, available in a 27mm and a 40mm thickness in beech, maple, ash and oak. They look fantastic but cost around £70-£80/lin. m. It's not particularly difficult to build your own hardwood worktops but you will probably need the skills of a good joiner's shop to enable you to work the wood into a useable 600mm wide strip.

Marble/Granite

Costs for marble or granite range from £150-£300/m^2 (£90-£180/metre run of worktop). Normally this supplies a 20mm thick slab which is usually fitted on to a timber sub-

A Corian sink-cum-worktop: notice there is no join between the two

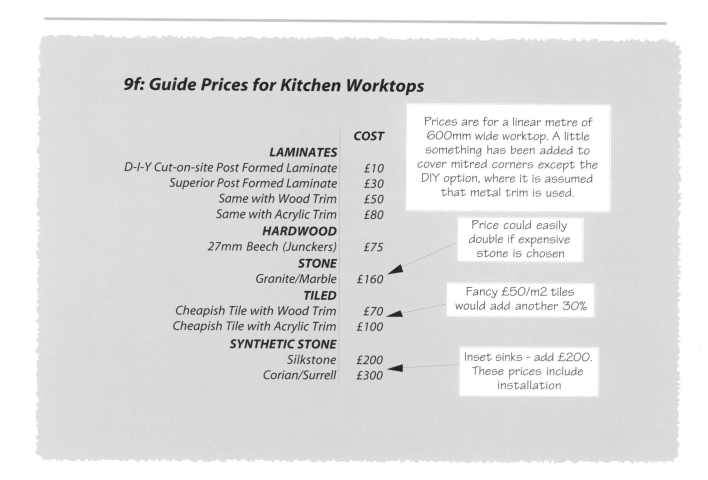

9f: Guide Prices for Kitchen Worktops

	COST
LAMINATES	
D-I-Y Cut-on-site Post Formed Laminate	£10
Superior Post Formed Laminate	£30
Same with Wood Trim	£50
Same with Acrylic Trim	£80
HARDWOOD	
27mm Beech (Junckers)	£75
STONE	
Granite/Marble	£160
TILED	
Cheapish Tile with Wood Trim	£70
Cheapish Tile with Acrylic Trim	£100
SYNTHETIC STONE	
Silkstone	£200
Corian/Surrell	£300

Prices are for a linear metre of 600mm wide worktop. A little something has been added to cover mitred corners except the DIY option, where it is assumed that metal trim is used.

Price could easily double if expensive stone is chosen

Fancy £50/m2 tiles would add another 30%

Inset sinks - add £200. These prices include installation

base for extra support. Holes can be cut for sinks and hobs (at around £50/hole) and intricate moulded edges can be applied at £10/lin.m; drainage grooves can be cut at around £20 each. Marble is not a particularly good choice for worktops as it stains and reacts to acids like lemon juice and vinegar (though some would regard this as "patina"). Granites are the preferred option for those wanting stone work tops. Whilst marbles tend towards whites and pinks, granites naturally tend to blacks and greys, which makes a granite worktop too dark for many people's tastes.

Tiled Worktops

A base is built of ply or blockboard (cost £4.20/lin.m) on to which tiles are stuck. The cost largely depends on the type of tiles chosen: budget perhaps £20/m² to lay, more if it's a complex pattern, and for tiles anything from £10/m² for mass produced plain tiles up to £40-£80/m² for something which would look good in a Fired Earth showroom. They can look spectacular and can be run in or set off against tiled splashbacks, but the irregularity of the surface (particularly on the more expensive tiles) can become an annoying feature and tiled worksurfaces are much harder to clean. Tiled worksurfaces look best when combined with a wood trim surround.

Corian

Corian is a new product which is used to make both worktops and sinks. It is best known for making it possible to "weld" sinks seamlessly into the worktop so they appear to be one and the same item. It remains a bit high-tech for many people's tastes and a bit high priced for many people's pockets. What is it? Well, it's an inert mineral filler fixed in a matrix of methyl methacrylate polymer. Nuff said? It's a synthetic panel product but unlike the regular melamine laminates (which are actually just thin coverings stuck on chipboard) these boys are solid, heavy and smooth. Every kitchen specialist showroom boasts a Corian (or Corian look-alike such as *Surrell*) sink-cum-worktop but they don't actually shift very many. There are an increasing number of alternative makes and some are beginning to get very much cheaper than original Corian. Look out for *Silkstone* which looks very similar but costs something akin to a mere £100/m run, about half the price of Corian.

Trim Options

The standard edge detail for laminate worktops is what is called Postform, which gives a curved finish to the front edge. You can get square-edged finishes but they are not recommended unless you are going to add some sort of trim to it. An otherwise cheap and cheerless laminate top can be made to look very much more attractive with the addition of an edge trim. These can be applied by hand but it is difficult to do a professional job on site; if factory applied, it will approximately double the cost of a laminate worktop (budget £50/lin.m). Even more expensive trims are available — like Corian — which would push the price up by over £70/lin.m.

Jointing Options

One of the problems in specifying laminate worktops, particularly ones with curved, postformed edges, is how to get around corners. The cheap option is to use metal jointing strips which stand up proud of the worktops and cover the gap where the two worktops meet. They are cheap, at around £3 each, but seamless they are not. Worktop fabricators offer various options for jointing worktops so that they appear to be one piece; straight runs are butt jointed from about £10; angles get a mason's mitre for around £15. If you are not going through a kitchen specialist then a useful contact is Allied Manufacturing who supply a wide range of kitchen fittings besides worktops.

Kitchen Appliances

All prices quoted in this section will include VAT. Trade prices invariably exclude it whilst retail outlets invariably include it. Whichever way, you cannot reclaim VAT on kitchen cookers or appliances.

Cookers

The bog standard route is to buy an oven/hob/cooker hood package. There will be a choice of gas or electricity for your hob without any effect on price, but a gas oven is much more expensive than an electric one. The budget developers' packages (Ariston, Ignis) are priced at around £290ea: you can buy similar packages from MFI or Comet for under £250. If a prestige marque is important, Neff do a developer's package at around £350. In the table below, the prices are drawn from cheap and cheerful sources like MFI and built-in makes like Ariston and Ignis.

Other Options

Stand Alone/Slot-in Cookers

These are not noticeably cheaper than built-in ones, though they do have the advantage of being removable; also they do not require £200's worth of kitchen units to house them in. One drawback is that cleaning will almost certainly be harder. You can still get very cheap gas cookers with eye-level grills (from £200) but these cannot really be incorporated with a cooker hood.

Double Ovens

The conventional British arrangement is to have the smaller oven doubling up as a grill and placed on top. The conventional "Continental" arrangement is to have the smaller oven underneath; eye-level grilling is much easier with the British arrangement. Most double ovens have one chamber with a fan and the other statically heated. Note that many single ovens have grill capabilities and many people would find a microwave stacked over a single oven more convenient and no more expensive.

Microwaves

Despite being limited in their uses — all they actually do is heat water — microwaves are excellent in a number of areas (cf. cooking casseroles and fish, boiling vegetables, reheating, defrosting) where conventional cooking is cumbersome. They are quick, clean and energy efficient. As an alternative to fitting a separate microwave unit, there are a number of multi-function ovens that include a microwave function. Panasonic's *Combination* (£550) is a single oven which can work static *or* fan assisted *or* grill *or* microwave, and can be built in at eye-level.

Gas Ovens

Built-in gas ovens are uncommon (though note that MFI stocks them); they are more expensive and don't have many of the features of an electric oven like fan assist. They also tend to produce much more moist waste than an electric oven — especially on grill settings — which ideally should be extracted from the kitchen. Their big selling point is low running costs — around 25% of conventional electric cooking. The extra cost of a gas oven will pay for itself within 5 years if burning mains gas and 10 years if burning LPG. Only Stoves make a true gas double oven: more usually you get a grill compartment set over a separate oven but the grill chamber cannot be used to cook conventionally.

Ceramic/Halogen Hobs

They look smart and are easy to clean but they perform only slightly better than conventional electric plates and they may cause you to replace all your cookware. Halogen heating areas, despite being advertised as "superfast response," are actually no quicker than the cheaper ceramic zones; they do, however, make a pleasing orange glow. Gas remains the fastest, cheapest and most responsive direct heat source: its drawbacks are harder cleaning and a dislike of pans boiling over. If mains gas is unobtainable, then consider having bottled gas just for the hob; propane is better than butane for this purpose.

Cooker Hoods

There is no actual requirement to have a cooker hood at all, but building regs do insist on some sort of extract fan in the kitchen so a ducted cooker hood is much the easiest way of satisfying the requirements. In a new, draught-free house, condensation and cooking smells will not easily disperse without opening windows, so a cooker hood is nigh-on essential. The standard cooker extractors are open to view, have three fan speeds and a light (very useful); there are "integrated" versions which get concealed behind a matching kitchen door and slimline or telescopic versions which are no more than 25mm deep and come on when you tug them towards you. The most upmarket option is to go for a canopy cooker hood which acts more like a conventional chimney: finished in stainless steel, look to pay around £350. There are a few heat recovery cooker hoods available, but they are expensive and are prone to greasing up unless very well maintained. Actually all cooker hoods require regular maintenance but few are lucky enough to get it.

9g: Guide Prices for Cookers
Prices include VAT @ 17.5%

OVEN	
Basic Single Built-in Static Electric	£140
Same with Fan (aka Circotherm)	£200
Same, either Static or Fan (aka Multi Function)	£230
Double Electric Oven - (One Static, One Fan)	£320
Double Electric Oven with Built-in Microwave	£370
Basic Single Gas Oven	£300
Double Gas Oven	£400
HOB	
Basic Four-ring Hob (Gas or Electric)	£80
Ceramic Hob (Electric only)	£260
Ceramic/Halogen Hob (Electric only)	£300
COOKER HOOD	
Basic Three-speed Hood w/light	£50
Integrated (or Concealed)	£70
Slimline, Telescopic	£110

Which Make?

There is an awful lot of snobbery about kitchen appliances. Top of the pecking order are the German (or at least German sounding) names like Neff, De Dietrich (French), AEG, Bosch, Miele and, especially, Gaggenau. British manufacturers like Hotpoint, Tricity Bendix, Creda have reputations based on price rather than quality, as have Philips Whirlpool and most of the Italian manufacturers. The very cheapest appliances often come with little-known brand names and obscure East European origins.

Getting confused? It gets worse. White goods branding is an extremely complicated area. There is much cross-manufacturing of parts and "country of origin" labelling should more correctly read "country of final assembly." As an example, most European cooker hoods are made in Italy and perform to much the same (rather noisy) standard whether they are branded Candy, Neff or Creda. Much of the upmarket German kit is actually assembled in Turkey or Portugal.

No wonder purchasers subcontract the decision making as well as the installation. Broadly speaking, if you want to create an impression then the brand names have to be German. The very best cookers tend to be German, but don't assume that a German brand name is necessarily a sign of quality. Also, if you want anything unusual like a built-in griddle you will need to seek out the high quality brand names. However, if low price is your main concern, then you should check out Curry and Comet own brands or alternatively, if you want integrated appliances, look at MFI or specialists selling to developers — phone Arrow, Allied, BDC or Crangrove.

Agas

The Aga remains *the* item for the complete country kitchen. Despite their exorbitant cost (nothing less than £3000 to purchase plus the need for adequate foundations, suitable chimney arrangements and £300 fitting costs) and their exorbitant running costs (nothing less than £7/week in fuel), otherwise rational people still salivate at the thought of having an Aga in the kitchen. To quote the sales blurb: "It transforms even the most functional kitchen into a warm and welcoming gathering place for all the family. It becomes the heart and hub of your home." The fact that this description is often spot on usually says more about the state of the rest of the house than any unique attributes of the Aga. Any large radiant heat source will be immensely attractive on a bitingly cold day and it's this aspect of the Aga — over one

tonne of hot cast-iron — which fuels its seemingly unending popularity. A large storage heater would fulfil the same function at a fraction of the cost but, I'm afraid, it would completely lack the necessary style.

It is uncommon to fit Agas into new housing because there is very little grand housing currently being built — and Agas look at their best in large kitchens. If you are contemplating an Aga for your home, you must plan for it from the ground upwards. Though not designed as water boilers, for an extra £200 you can go for an Aga with a boiler capable of heating not less than 400lts of water/day (i.e. enough for about eight people) *and* — provided yours is a new house qualifying for VAT zero-rating — you can reclaim VAT on the purchase which instantly saves around £500. Customs & Excise are usually happy to accept this distinction and they cannot insist that the boiler is ever connected to your hot water cylinder. Agas come in gas-fired, oil-fired, solid fuel and electric (Economy 7) versions. Contact Glynwed for sales literature.

There are alternatives between the splendour of the Aga and the industry standard "tin boxes" which are sold as part of a fitted kitchen. Rayburn and Stanley make cast iron cookers and water heaters which start at around £2700. Also look at the gas-fired hobby cookers which are a must if your culinary aspirations are to eclipse the Roux brothers; the most famous is La Cornue which will make an Aga look cheap but there are others selling at under £2000 like the *Double Bocuse* oven by Rosieres. In the last two years, every manufacturer seems to have jumped on this bandwagon and there are now dozens of ranges on display in kitchen showrooms, starting at around £1200.

Dishwashers

A fairly basic, reliable machine like the Candy *Ecosystem* will cost around £280. If you are prepared to pay over £350, you can buy a better thought of name like Ariston or Whirlpool. The Bosch *SMS 4472* (£350) is the only widely available model with a delay timer, which gives potential savings on running costs of £30-£40/annum.

Integrated (or built-in) versions are retailed from £420, though builders can get hold of makes such as Ariston for £310.

Washing Machines

Hotpoint sell over 50% of all washing machines in the UK. Their basic standalone models start at around £280; their *Aquarius* range starts at £400 and incorporates a number of green features (less water, less power, less powder). Hoover are one of the very few to offer a machine with a delay timer. A recent *Which?* report (Jan97) liked the Bosch WFF 2000, but it's pricey at £520..

Tumble Dryers

Full-size, air-vented dryers (like Creda's *Reversair* or Zanussi's *TD523*) cost around £180. There are condensing dryers available which do not need ducting to outside, but they are expensive — over £300. Cannon and White Knight make reasonably priced (£300) gas-fired dryers which are said to be quicker and will be much cheaper to run; whilst they may cost an extra £50 to plumb in, they will save that in running costs within two years. Note that washing machines, dishwashers and fridges sold by gas showrooms are not gas-fired even though they are branded New World or Cannon, names usually associated with gas appliances.

Washer-dryers

The trend towards separate utility areas in larger houses has meant that there are very few built-in washing machines and no built-in tumble dryers. Instead there are a large number of extremely expensive washer dryers costing from £500 upwards. They do save space but they are not as convenient as you might hope — they are only capable of tumble drying half a wash load at a time so they need unpacking between programs. They are also the most unreliable of all kitchen appliances.

Cold Storage

There are numerous options of above- and below-freezing point storage and there are also numerous arrangements for their hous-

9h: Integrated v free standing units

	FREE STANDING	INTEGRATED
Fridge only	£180	£300
Freezer only	£180	£300
Fridge/freezer	£260	£550

ing. Really, only the larder fridge — that is the term normally applied to above-zero storage — needs to be in the kitchen and if you want an integrated look then you can save money by placing your free-standing freezer elsewhere (utility?). Prices in Table 9j below are for basic appliances by Whirlpool, who have a good reputation for cold storage.

Integrated v Free-Standing

A built-in cooker/hob/hood package is basically no more or less expensive than its free-standing equivalent. However, with almost all the other kitchen appliances, the built-in versions are very much more expensive. Table 9h highlights the imbalance with regard to cold storage, but the same sort of discrepancies occur with dishwashers and washer-dryers. This is a blatant example of an industry squeezing profit out of a new market by charging a premium rating for what is in effect an inferior product; after all, the built-in versions have much less casing and must be cheaper to produce. My analysis shows that while a kitchen load of fairly basic free-standing appliances will cost around £1300, the built-in versions of the same kit will cost perhaps £1700. As the product choices move upmarket, the gap in the price becomes still greater.

Developers can overcome these price imbalances, to an extent, by buying from trade sources such as Arrow or Allied which are geared up to supply built-in appliances. Ariston, in particular, price their built-in ranges more competitively than most. This route is not open to selfbuilders unless they can convince the suppliers they are genuine trade. Even if they can, they will still be paying more than they would for free-standing equivalents from Comet or Currys.

Another effective counter to this overcharging ploy is to specify a large utility room. Move washing, drying and freezing appliances out of the kitchen where they are not essential.

Finally, consider an unfitted kitchen with free-standing appliances standing naked as God intended. Ignore the first law of MFI which is "Try to hide away as many appliances as possible." You save on housing costs, concealer door costs as well as overpriced appliance costs. Furthermore you can take the appliances with you if you move.

Salvage?

The used gas and electric cooker market is well organised, there being shops specialising in such gear. However, it is mostly free-standing stuff. Integrated cookers (and washing machines and tumble dryers) are harder to track down though they have been around long enough for people to throw them out; look out in your local paper for private sales.

9j: Reliability Tests for Kitchen Appliances

	Washing Machines	Tumble Dryers	Washer Dryers	Dishwashers
MOST RELIABLE	Miele (1 in 12) AEG Ariston Candy Indesit Tricity Bendix Zanussi	Whirlpool (1 in 100) Electra White Knight (Electric)	Whirlpool (1 in 9) Tricity Bendix Zanussi	Neff (1 in 50) Bosch Indesit Siemens
AVERAGE	**1 in 5** Bosch Creda Electra Electrolux Philco Servis Whirlpool	**1 in 10** AEG Creda Servis Tricity Bendix	**1 in 4** AEG Ariston Bosch Candy Creda Indesit Miele Servis	**1 in 9** AEG Ariston Bauknecht Candy Hotpoint Miele T Bendix Whirlpool Zanussi
LEAST RELIABLE	Hoover Hotpoint (1 in 3)	Hotpoint White Knight (gas) Zanussi Hoover (1 in 6)	Hoover Philco Hotpoint (1 in 3))	Creda Hoover (1 in 4)

Chances of a breakdown in any 12 month period

Source: Which? Magazine Feb 97

Kitchen Waste

The average kitchen design pays far too little attention to the dirty business of waste disposal. The standard solution is to fit a 20lt plastic bin behind the door of the sink unit and to leave it at that but this is hardly ideal even for one-person flats. Large kitchens produce large amounts of waste and processing this waste efficiently should be part of a good kitchen plan. Growing interest in waste recycling means that more people are paying attention to separating waste and this means separate storage areas being made accessible. There is often no need for anything more complicated than a cardboard box, but boxes tend to take up space and become untidy.

Organic Waste

There are two reasons for wanting to separate organic waste from the rest:
- you can't stand the smell or the mess
- your garden or your chickens love it being thrown over them.

The two approaches call for radically different solutions. The *Clean Jeans* will be fitting a waste disposal unit under their kitchen sink. This is a gizmo which macerates all animal and vegetable remains fed to it and then pumps it out into the foul drains. Cost from £100 to £300 depending on power and capabilities. Leading makes Tweeny, Maxmatic, Waste King.

The *Smellie Nellies* will be going for a compost bin, which will also probably be located under the sink, conventionally in a 20lt plastic bin. Leading make: Addis, cost £3.50. More elaborate bins are available which clip on to the back of the door and have a cunning lid which lifts up only when you open the door. It pays to keep it pretty simple and have a bin which you can wash frequently.

There are some very fancy "green" sinks which have extra holes down which you can put organic waste which falls seamlessly into plastic-lined bin below — look for a Blanco *Box Sink*, prices start at £300, (0181 450 9100). This is a composting option for the *clean and green Jeans* but they will have to pay dearly for this ability to keep the surfaces spotless.

Other Recycling Options

Visit your local recycling centre and decide what it is that you can or want to recycle. Glass, aluminium, newspapers (but not cardboard), cork, batteries, clothes are the most frequently observed bins in my part of the woods, but your local council may have different priorities. It is worth giving some thought as to how you will store these items until you next visit a bottle bank. It seems absurd to use up expensive kitchen space which has no doubt been ergonomically planned so that not even the spice rack is out of place. The utility room may be the place but note that if you've got dogs or children they may appreciate boxes filled with all kinds of interesting things stored at ground level. Garages or external covered bin spaces may be better solutions but bear in mind that the further away from the kitchen you get, the more likely it is that everything will get chucked in the bin marked "General." A little thought at the design stage can make all the difference. Note that the most frequently recycled materials — glass and paper — are also two of the least cost-effective to recycle. There is a good market for clear glass but green and brown glass is almost valueless and many bottle banks don't differentiate; and newspaper recycling is itself a difficult and polluting process of doubtful economic value. In contrast, plastics and metals — especially aluminium — are well worth somebody recycling. If you are serious about recycling, find a centre that takes many different kinds of waste — and don't drive twenty miles out of your way to get there!

General Advice

Don't be fobbed off with a mini-swing bin of 20lt or less. Even the greenest households need a waste bin that will hold a dustbin liner. If storing this quantity of waste is a problem, you can get over things with a rubbish compactor which reduces the volume four or five times. They are an expensive option, costing around £700 and taking up as much space as a large bin! Contact In-Sink-Erator (01371 873073).

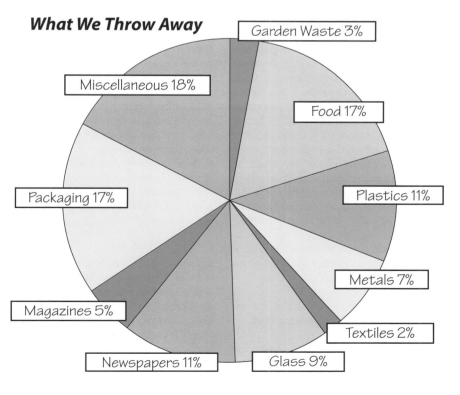

What We Throw Away

- Garden Waste 3%
- Food 17%
- Plastics 11%
- Metals 7%
- Textiles 2%
- Glass 9%
- Newspapers 11%
- Magazines 5%
- Packaging 17%
- Miscellaneous 18%

Security and Safety

The average private dwelling currently suffers an attempted break-in every 12 years and over half of these attempts are successful. Furthermore, the amount of burglary has nearly doubled since 1983 and if the crime rate continues to grow at this extraordinary pace, then by 2025 the rate will have risen to one attempted break-in at every home every year.

Whether this Doomsday scenario ever comes about is open to doubt because it would involve an army of a quarter of a million burglars each breaking into a house every week. Whatever the future holds, burglary is not a problem that is likely to go away and anyone considering building a new house would be foolish not to consider the matter very carefully. Some inner city areas already suffer appallingly high burglary rates, making house contents insurance extremely expensive and sometimes even impossible to obtain.

The Burglar

As you might suspect, the typical burglar is a young male but you might be surprised to learn that he is not part of a well-organised gang but usually a lone wolf whose break-in is often done almost on the spur-of-the-moment, when he sees the opportunity arise. There is really no reason to adopt a fatalistic attitude because, although it's entirely true that if someone really wants to get into a house they can, 90% of the time they won't bother if you go to the trouble of making life difficult for them. Our young burglar's main concern is not to get caught in the act and to this end he values being able to get in, and out, quickly and preferably unseen. Another surprising statistic thrown up is that as many as 20% of burglaries take place while the home is occupied. You'd think this would be amazingly risky for our burglar but it only takes a few seconds to come in through an open door and walk out again with something like a radio or a camera and you may not even realise that you've been burgled. If you are worried about this sort of thing happening, get a dog.

With regards to new housebuilding, current thinking focuses on the following areas:
• Site layout
• Preventing access to the rear of the house
• Decent locks fitted to ground floor windows and doors
• Burglar alarms where risk is high
• Security lighting.

Site Layout

Though this area has more relevance to estates than to single dwellings, it's worth mentioning what they are on about. Dark corners and unlit alleyways should be avoided and houses should be sited where their neighbours can see who is coming and going. There is often little the individual housebuilder can do about this, though it is possible that consideration can be given to the issue when there are two or more houses to be sited near each other.

One obvious point that the professionals have tended to overlook is to locate the most widely used room in the house — usually the kitchen — at the front of the house, so that the occupants can see who is coming and going out on the street. However, this arrangement remains an extremely unpopular layout in this country; we still prefer our kitchens to be by the back door.

Restricting Access

The rear of the house is the preferred area of entry for burglars. This is largely because the back of the house is almost always more private and is often very well screened from neighbours. A burglary often starts with a casual casing of the front of the house; if it looks as though there is no one at home, the second stage will be to go round the back and take a closer look. Only when they're convinced the coast is clear will the break-in proceed. If access to the back of the house is impeded, then the would-be burglar may abort the job at this early stage in the hope of there being easier pickings further up the road. A 2m fence and a stout gate — even without a bolt — will provide a considerable measure of defence against unwanted prowling. Back gardens can be protected, to a lesser extent, by walling or hedging them in. Plan in any obstructions that will at least slow down the progress of a potential burglar. On to the next line of defence.

Robust Locks

It is now an NHBC standard to have 5-lever locks on all external doors and to have window locks as well. At least one exit — usually the front door — must be protected by a night latch (Yale-type locks) which can be opened from the inside without a key; this is to aid escape in case of fire. The idea is to lock the door on the night latch when the house is occupied and to use the 5-lever mortise lock when the house is empty. Window locks are now fitted as standard on most volume joinery, so all new houses will — or should — be built to these security standards now and there is no further action that need be taken at the design stage.

French and Patio Doors

It is marginally easier to force a door inwards than to prise it out but it is likely to be rather noisy. Most front doors open inwards. However, note that double-doors (french doors) are particularly easy to force in or prise outwards; most French doors open outwards and if you fit them be sure to fit decent sliding bolts to the top and bottom of both doors. For extra security, make these lockable bolts. Sliding patio doors are generally a much more secure (and draughtproof) alternative (though not half as elegant); however, many break-ins have occurred where the patio door frame has been levered out of its seating, having only ever been held in by six short screws or, sometimes, nothing more than mastic sealant.

Glass

The recently upgraded building regulations will ensure that you have to fit double-glazed sealed units and the safety standards on glazing insist that safety glass is fitted to all doors, windows next to doors and all glazing less than 800mm above the internal floor level. Safety glass is expensive, costing nearly twice as much as ordinary float glass and now it has to be double-glazed it becomes doubly expensive. It comes in two varieties, toughened or laminated and they perform slightly differently. Toughened is harder to break but when it breaks it collapses into small nodules, whereas laminated glass has a sheet of plastic sandwiched between two layers of ordinary glass; this makes it harder to break through (from the burglar's point of view) and is therefore slightly more secure. The police are big fans of laminated glass, suggesting that it should be fitted wherever there is glass next to an accessible lock but as this includes virtually every ground floor opening window it would be an expensive option

Burglar Alarms

There are a number of different systems on the market, including some which can be plugged into the mains and work on FM or AM radio signalling. It is usually cheaper to install a wired system which is particularly well suited to new housing as the wiring can be concealed during first-fix stage. Installation quotes for a four bedroom house are likely to vary from £500 for a system based on a mixture of internal infra-red detectors and contact points — which are triggered by internal movements and doors opening respectively — to £700 for an external vibration detection system which is triggered by interference with doors and windows. Should you not want to go to the expense of installing an alarm, as an alternative, the wiring can be first fixed-in a day for between £100 and £200, so that the intruder detectors can be fitted at a later date without disruption to the decorations. A recent concession by the government has made burglar alarms eligible for zero-rating of VAT when building a new home.

If you've never lived with a burglar alarm, you might be forgiven for thinking that they are the last word in home security. However, the consequences of fitting an alarm can be fairly tortuous for the householder.

All systems are set to make a loud noise for around 20 minutes; false alarms will make you very unpopular and false alarms do happen so a burglar alarm is not without its problems. A recent police estimate reckoned that no less than nine out of ten ringing alarms are actually false alarms and the police in some areas are now refusing to respond to ringing alarms, particularly if the alarm in question is known to be a repeating offender.

Monitored Alarms

If you have a very remote site or are not entirely happy about a 105 decibel alarm ringing when a mouse crosses the floor, the next step up the security ladder is to get a monitored alarm. These link your house via the phone lines either to the local police or a security firm. Monitored alarm systems tend to be way more expensive than bell only systems (a *Which?* report in Nov 94 reckoned on them costing about double) and they carry an annual charge which is likely to be in excess of £150; they are only available if two key holders besides the occupants live close by and are prepared to be called out in the middle of the night. If you are worried about cowboys, look for NACOSS approval of your installer.

If you can't make up your mind about whether you need an alarm or not, you can always delay the decision until after you get burgled and then fit a wireless alarm. Both Wickes and Response Alarms (01372 744330) have simple systems that cost less than £200, can be installed by DIYers and the only hard wiring they require is one mains outlet to plug the base unit into.

Car Parking

Both integral and detached garages can be included in whole house intruder alarm systems, but this tends to be very inconvenient; the car has to be left outside whilst the alarm is deactivated (usually inside the house). It rather defeats the purpose of these remote control devices for garage doors.

Other Measures

Door chains (from £3) and viewers (from £4) are becoming more common, and are recommended by the police. Surely the most cheeky is the fake "Protected by Burglar Alarm" bell casing which you screw on to your outside wall. Available at around £8 from D-I-Y sheds.

Security Lighting

Passive Infra-Red (PIR) detectors, similar to the ones used on internal movement sensors in burglar alarms, are also used on external lighting. These can be very useful around dark entrances although the halogen bulbs (sometimes 500w) can be so bright that you dazzle passers-by and tend to make them think you live in a high-security prison. Installation of a good PIR security light will cost around £80 (Mats £40, Lab £40). There are some very cheap versions on the market (at around £10-£15) which are best avoided; at around £30 you start to get ones where it is possible to change the bulb. Better forms of external lighting exist which can be wired to PIR switches, as well as manual override switches, which give pleasant external illumination as well as some form of security (see section on lighting).

There are also a number of products (widely available at the D-I-Y sheds) which can be used to give the effect of occupation when the house is empty. For around £20, you can buy a gizmo which fits in between a lightbulb and its lampholder which acts as a light-sensitive switch, useful for simulating occupation when you are away.

Shutter Protection

Fitting metal roller shutters around the external openings is an expensive option. It doesn't work well with outward opening windows (think about it) and is best designed around either sliding sash style or tilt and turn windows. To fit security roll-down shutters to every opening on the benchmark house would cost over £6000.

Safes

Home safes are available from £150 for a wall fitting one and from £200 for one bolted to the floor. Placing a safe in an existing house can be awkward but in a new house it's a

doddle — if you've planned ahead for it.

"Secured by Design"

This is a new homes marketing campaign sponsored by the Police. It highlights seven points for attention; houses which meet all seven points are eligible for the "Secured by Design" logo. Whilst this campaign is aimed at professional developers, the details are of interest to all. These points are:

- Smoke alarm fitted, one per floor (now standard building regs)
- Substantial door locks fitted on external doors (now standard)
- Window locks fitted (now standard)
- Door chain and viewer fitted to front door
- Boundary fencing and bolted gates — limiting rear access
- Option for an alarm to be fitted (i.e. first-fix wiring present)
- Security lighting front and back.

For the new housebuilder, the additional costs of upgrading to meet "Secured by Design" standards are between £300 and £400 plus the fencing costs which will obviously vary from site to site — a 1.8m-high close-boarded fencing has a budget cost of £25/lin.m (M £15, L £10).

Look out for this natty police logo which designates that a house or, more likely, an estate meets the Secured by Design criteria

Fire Safety

The purpose of the fire safety regulations is not to stop buildings burning down but rather to allow the occupants time enough to escape from them when they do start burning down. One of the long held prejudices against timber-frame building is that people think it will be more likely to catch on fire but this really is not so as the timber elements are almost always enclosed in a layer of inert plasterboard which is enough to delay the onset of fire by half an hour. The real danger in house fires is caused when soft furnishings catch fire and the smoke quickly engulfs the occupants. Whilst there has been a steady introduction of inflammable materials into the home furnishing market, the biggest change to affect housebuilders has been the mandatory introduction of smoke detectors. Since 1992, all new homes have been required to have smoke detectors fitted; what's more these are required to be mains operated with a battery backup. These start at around £18 and can be wired into the house lighting circuit. Electricians are by now pretty au fait with what's required. The regs are that there should be smoke alarms on each storey and that they shouldn't be further than 3m from any bedroom door, so that some larger designs will require two or more on the upstairs landing.

Other safety features you might choose to look at are the provision of fire blankets in the kitchen (around £30) and extinguishers in garages and near open fires (£70-£100). Your best bet is to stick with local firms which offer maintenance; look in Yellow Pages under *Fire Extinguishing Eqpt*.

Three storey Houses

Provided every room opens onto a hallway or corridor, a two storey house is not going to have any problems meeting fire safety regulations. But there is a critical safety level, defined as having a floor 4.5m above ground level, when it becomes necessary to beef up your escape procedures. Either you have to fit an fire escape or you have to ensure that your main stairwell is fireproofed: this in turn means enclosing it and ensuring that doors into it are fire resistant and have automatic closers fitted. It also limits the layout somewhat because the staircase must exit into a hallway next to the main entrance. A third storey in a house is usually more than 4.5m off the ground, so only in these situations do you have to consider designing a fireproof stairwell.

Incidentally, meeting the provisions of this regulation is one of the big hidden costs of doing a loft conversion in an existing two storey house. Another problem to be overcome is that fire doors are usually pretty awful looking things: one way around this is to apply intumescent paints to ordinary doors, a solution which most building control departments are now happy to accept.

Painting & Decorating

Exterior Work

You can, of course, avoid exterior decorating altogether by specifying pre-finished materials like uPVC. Indeed many are doing just that: Wimpey Homes, our largest volume housebuilder, has recently switched to no timber exteriors. The windows, fascias and bargeboards are uPVC; the doors are steel; the garage doors are GRP.

However, most housebuilders are still choosing timber doors and windows as well as timber roof edgings and all these need some form of protective covering. The main choice is now between traditional paint (usually white) and woodstains. Even though woodstains are more expensive to buy, the cost difference between the two systems is negligible because there is such a high labour content in decorating and, if anything, stains are slightly quicker to apply. What really causes decorating costs to tumble is to reduce the number of coats needed to get a decent finish. Many builders do this with stains by dispensing with the third coat, which would be difficult with conventional paint, but there are now a number of one coat paints (e.g. Crown *Solo*) which enable you to dispense with the third coat — at a price.

Wood Paints

The traditional way of finishing external timber is with oil-based gloss paint. This is applied in a three coat system, primer, then undercoat, then gloss. If you want to use a traditional paint finish you can save money and time by specifying that your joinery arrives on site primed with paint instead of the current industry standard of a basecoat of honey-coloured stain.

Which paint to use? There is now a bewildering array of paints available: traditional oil-based gloss, non-drip gloss, one-coat gloss, microporous paints, acrylic paints to name but a few. Coupled with the fact that every manufacturer seems to use a different naming system to describe their product and it's no wonder the poor consumer gets confused. *Which?* magazine carries out an annual review of exterior paints (and stains) but it only scratches the surface of the paint market; their survey is just not comprehensive enough to provide a complete picture and, in any event, the canny manufacturers are forever reformulating their products and giving them new brand names so that the chances are even if you went around B&Q armed with the latest *Which?* survey in your hand, you'd still not find their recommendations. Or if you did, how would you know it was the same as it was five years ago when *Which?'s* test started. One fact does stand out from their surveys — which is also borne out by personal experience — and that is that Akzo don't make bad paint. Akzo is the Dutch company behind many popular brand names — *Permoglaze, Sandtex, Sikkens* — and they also make contraceptives so it stands to reason that they should know a little bit about protection. There are, of course, many other good paints on the market but no other company achieves such consistently good ratings on all their products.

Water-based Acrylics

Two factors have combined to increase the sales of these paints and they are both to do with user friendliness. Firstly, they are very easy to apply — afterwards the brushes can be washed out under a cold tap; secondly, there are increasing concerns over the health

9k: Painting and Staining Guide Prices

	UNIT	COATS	MATERIALS	LABOUR @ £6.00/hr	TOTAL/m²
1 COAT EMULSION	m²	1	£0.15	£0.38	£0.50
3 COAT EMULSION	m²	3	0.45	1.14	£1.60
3 COAT GLOSS (inc. preparation)	m⁴	3	0.63	4.00	£4.60
Strips (in linear metres)	lin.m	3	0.16	2.00	£2.20 /lin.m
Windows (both sides)	m²	3	0.31	30.00	£30.00
Doors (both sides)	m²	3	1.25	20.00	£21.00
Balusters	m²	3	0.63	17.00	£18.00
3 COAT VARNISH/STAIN (+ prep)	m²	3	1.50	4.00	£5.50
Strips (in linear meters)	lin.m	3	0.38	2.00	£2.40 /lin.m
Windows (both sides)	m²	3	0.75	30.00	£31.00
Doors (both sides)	m²	3	3.00	20.00	£23.00
Balusters	m²	3	1.50	17.00	£19.00
2 COAT MASONRY PAINT	m²	2	1.73	4.00	£5.70
EXTERNAL STAINING (3 Coat)	m²	3	3.84	4.00	£7.80
Strips	lin.m	3	0.96	2.00	£3.00 /lin.m
WALLPAPERING (1 layer)	m²	1	1.10	1.20	£2.30

STRIPS refers to narrow sections such as skirtings and fascia boards. Here prices are worked out in linear metres rather than square metres. For windows, doors and balusters prices are given for painting/staining both faces-i.e inside and outside.

risks of using the traditional oil-based gloss paints. The people most likely to benefit from both these factors are the professional painters and decorators yet, paradoxically, they are the ones who are most resistant to using water-based paints, reckoning them to be useless. Expensive more like. Though they are still a comparatively new system (first introduced in the 70s) the indications are that water-based paints perform rather better than many oil-based alternatives. What they won't give you is a high-gloss sheen finish, but then the matt look is preferred by most people these days.

Masonry Paints

As if to emphasise the last point about the durability of water-based paints, standard masonry paints, which are used to cover external render and masonry, are all water-based and many will claim to last for 15 years before needing recoating. They are easy to apply but their application should not be rushed; the underlying cement render must be allowed to dry out thoroughly. This is a drag because many builders are itching to strike the scaffolding by the time the external rendering is done and waiting for render to dry can take forever. Take the scaffolding down and it'll take you three times as long to paint the house. The moral? Only build houses with external painted panels when the sun shines.

Stains

Woodstaining is one of the very few continental ideas to have really caught on in British housebuilding. The habit of applying woodstains has been a hit with the wood stripping Habitat generation despite the fact that it's anything but a traditional British practice. This popularity is largely because the stains enable you to see the natural grain of the timber which they are covering. Generically, stains are divided into two subgroups, *low build* and *medium build* but you are unlikely to hear these terms bandied about on a building site where they are known by their brand names. The build rating refers to the thickness of the stain and the higher the build the better the protection but the less you see of the underlying wood. The biggest names in this business are Sadolin (Swedish) and Sikkens (Dutch), though the British manufacturers are at last getting their act together (Ronseal, Dulux, Hicksons, Cuprinol). Sadolin's low build stain is called *Classic* and is most widely used on sawn timber which drinks it like a Dublin bar on St. Patrick's night; their medium build stain is called *Extra* and this is much more oily — treacly almost — and you use this for covering timber joinery. All these stains are available in a range of woody colours but the really jazzy colours are usually restricted to the low build ranges.

Conventionally, stains have been spirit based but, as with paints, you can now buy water-based acrylic stains. Sikkens' *Cetol BL* range is reckoned to be one of the best.

Creosote?

There are a number of wood preservatives which are way cheaper than the commercial woodstains. And of these, creosote stands out as being much the cheapest — you can pick up 25lts of the stuff for £15, which makes it six times cheaper than a Sadolin wood stain. The trouble is that creosote stinks and it goes on stinking for years. Use it out in the garden and even on the garden shed but don't ever put in on your house.

Interior Work
Walls and Ceilings

Most interior walls are finished with emulsion paints which are very cheap and very easy to apply, being water-based. The standard choice you need to make is between a matt finish and a silk finish. Matt finishes are characterised as being thicker (more opaque)

9l: Paints and Stains: Guide Prices and Coverage

All prices exc VAT: coverage and m2 rates for one coat only.
All prices are for whites and magnolias

Some outlets supply clours for the same price. Usually standard colours are 15% more expensive. A colourising machine is 40% more than white.

	REGULAR SIZE	PRICE	COVERAGE	COST/m²
Contract Emulsion (non-vinyl)	10 lt	£ 10.00	12 m²/lt	£0.08
Vinyl Matt Emulsion	5 lt	£ 9.00	12 m²/lt	£0.15
Vinyl Silk Emulsion	5 lt	£ 10.00	12 m²/lt	£0.17
Masonry Paint	5 lt	£ 13.00	3 m²/lt	£0.87
Regular Gloss/Undercoat	5 lt	£ 12.50	16 m²/lt	£0.16
Eggshell	5 lt	£ 14.00	16 m²/lt	£0.18
Acrylic Gloss or Eggshells	5 lt	£ 18.00	12 m²/lt	£0.30
Wood Primers	5 lt	£ 13.00	10 m²/lt	£0.26
SADOLIN CLASSIC on sawn timber	5 lt	£ 32.00	5 m²/lt	£1.28
SADOLIN CLASSIC on planed timber	5 lt	£ 32.00	10 m²/lt	£0.64
SADOLIN EXTRA on joinery	2.5 lt	£ 18.00	15 m²/lt	£0.48
Polyurethane	2.5 lt	£ 15.00	12 m²/lt	£0.50
Floor lacquers	1 lt	£ 10.00	10 m²/lt	£1.00

All prices in this column are for single coats only

SADOLIN (together with SIKKENS) are the market leaders for wood stains. Much cheaper alternatives exist (i.e. Kalon own brand)

9m: Benchmark House: Painting Costs

Trade rates are all-in labour and materials rates

WHAT	QUANTITY		TRADE RATES	TOTAL
WOOD STAINS				
Fascia 25x200	54	lin.m	£ 2.40	£130
Ventilated Soffit	42	lin.m	2.40	£100
Barge Boards 25x150	57	lin.m	2.40	£140
Dormer Cheeks	4	m²	5.50	£20
Porch	10	lin.m	5.50	£60
External Doors and Frames	5	m²	21.50	£110
Windows	20	m²	31.00	£620
Featheredge cladding	95	m²	7.80	£740
PAINTS				
Masonry Paint	46	m²	5.70	£260
Emulsion Walls/Ceilings	490	m²	1.60	£780
Internal Doors and Linings	22	m²	21.00	£460
Balusters	7	m²	18.00	£130
Skirting	185	lin.m	2.20	£410
Architrave (25 sets)	133	lin.m	2.20	£290
Window Cills	14	lin.m	2.20	£30
Vanity Units/Boxings	10	m²	1.60	£20
Mastic	10-15 tubes, various applications			400
TOTAL				**£4,700**

Various items in this table need decorating on two faces - doors, windows, balusters. The areas in the quantity column are measurements for one face only but the trade rates for these items are for both faces.

Still not clear? Well if you laid all the windows together on the ground they would cover an area of 30m²; but the rate of £31.00/m² is a trade rate for staining both the inside and outside of a window. Estimating can be a real hassle sometimes.

and softer; silk finishes produce a harder, glossier look that has the added advantage of being more readily washable. There is no difference in price. Satin finishes are a half-way house between matt and silk. One tip for new housebuilders is to apply your emulsions immediately after plastering or dry-lining is finished. You can get in and have a relatively free run at bare walls without having to fiddle around with skirtings, architraves, socket boxes, switch plates and radiators.

Another tip, this one for the stylistically challenged housebuilder, is to slap magnolia on everything. White is a bit too clinical for most people's taste; in contrast magnolia has enough cream in it to soften the overall effect without making any loud statements that will clash with furnishing choices made later on. If you are in a hurry and don't want to be bothered planning colour schemes, then magnolia is the answer. Dull but true.

Woodwork

Interior woodwork gets very similar treatment to exterior woodwork. Traditionally, that meant a three-coat gloss paint system. Increasingly it means that woodstains are used instead. Interestingly, the benchmark house which is positively bathed in woodstain on the outside gets treated to a traditional paint finish on the internal woodwork.

Varnish

I'm tempted to say that varnishing is vanishing but I wouldn't be so daft; its use is, however, much more limited than it used to be. Externally — where it is prone to blistering and flaking — it has been replaced almost entirely by the woodstains. However there is still a place for varnishes indoors on any exposed timbers. The fashion these days is to use matt lacquer varnishes (like Sadolin's excellent *Holdex*) which give a subtler, understated sheen. And there are also now acrylic varnishes (like Cuprinol's *Enhance*) which are so subtle you'd hardly know they were there. Wood floor finishes are another area where clear seals get used, usually with rather poor results. It looks fantastic when first applied but after a depressingly small number of weeks it comes to look worn and tired. If you are looking for an alternative to wax, check out Dulux's *Diamond Glaze*, a water based lacquer said to be ten times harder than conventional floor varnish.

Specialist Finishes

Artex Textured Ceilings

Don't think that Artex is a replacement for painting as well as plastering. It has to be painted to stop the smell, and emulsioning Artex is a good deal more time consuming than going over a flat surface. Many of the big housebuilders still specify Artex on their ceilings throughout, presumably because of problems they have experienced with cracking in plastered ceilings. Dry-lining, which is now prevalent on internal walls, can of course be applied to ceilings as well but the taping and jointing work needed to finish it is more complicated because there is always a much higher number of cuts and joints on ceilings than on walls.

Wallpaper

Summary Table 9k just about says it all. Or at least it covers the basics. The price of £2.30/m² is for a very basic covering and obviously the sky is the limit when it comes to buying wallpaper. It is worth noting that a basic wallpaper is not so very expensive; you could wallpaper the benchmark house throughout for around £500 over and above the cost of slapping on a basic emulsion.

Paint Effects

There has been a considerable revival of interest in near-forgotten painting techniques like stippling and rag rolling. If you are at all interested you will probably already have a book by Jocasta Innes and there's really nothing more to add. However, if you want to dip your toes in it but are afraid that you might get stoned on scumble glazes then you can cheat and use one of the new proprietary two tone paints like Dulux's *Duet* or Sikken's *Alphadecor* (guide price around £30/5lt). How they get a two tone stipple effect inside one can is beyond me but the results aren't bad. However, I don't think Jocasta would approve somehow; if you want to get a more authentic look you could do worse than shop at the great lady's emporium, Paint Magic, 0181 940 5503 — mail order sales available.

Mastics

Mastics are something of a new feature in building, or at least the ways we use them today are new. They now tend to get applied to just about every conceivable join between materials; so wherever timber joinery meets brickwork or a tiled surface meets a worktop or a bathtub, there's a bead of mastic. There are mastics for sealing between plasterboard sheets and decorator's mastics for filling cracks (*Painter's Mate*); just about the only thing that is common to them is that they are packaged in tubes. Where water penetration is a problem — and that includes most external applications — it is worth paying more for the silicone based ones which, whilst remaining flexible, are less likely to break down.

It is said by some that mastics are the bodger's friend and that if you build to very high standards your joints will all be tight and you shouldn't need mastics at all. While there is some truth that good building standards are usually reflected in tight joints, mastics, particularly the silicone based ones, are now so widely used that it is inconceivable you will not have any need of them at some point. It is, however, very difficult to estimate just how much mastic you will need — that, at least, often depends on how wide your gaps are. And it is also true that mastic is a whole lot easier to apply against tightly fitting backgrounds. My figures for mastic work on the benchmark house, showing costs of £400, is much higher than average: it is inflated by the need to mastic the joint between the external render and the plinth brickwork beneath it. Note that if you are subcontracting decorating, you should make it absolutely clear where you want mastic to be applied and which type of mastic you want to be used.

Benchmark house again: note the mastic bead between brick and render gets wider as it travels right

Curtains & Blinds

It hardly seems like building but it's still a cost to be considered: a development cost for sure. Normally you buy curtain material by the yard (or metre) and this is the price that tends to stick in the mind. Yet on all but the most expensive materials, this is only about a third of the final cost if you include making-up costs and curtain rails.

Now for many D-I-Y enthusiasts, these costs are absorbed in their own time. You put up all the curtain rails while your husband runs-up all the material on the machine. But to pretend these costs are not there would not be in the spirit of the rest of the book, which assumes that your time is worth something (albeit not very much).

Curtain Rails

Unlike the materials which hang from them, curtain rails are zero-rated for VAT purposes and so, if you are a selfbuilder, it is worth buying these before any reclaim is made. The rails look best when they are at least 400mm longer than the opening they cross and they don't look out of place if they are much longer. The usual materials are plastic (£3/m), wood (£9/m) and brass (£10/m) — though watch out for whether things like rings are included: the raw price of a wooden pole can double by the time fittings and rings have been added.

Curtains

As a rule of thumb to establish the overall widths of curtain material needed, double the length of the track from which you are going to hang it. Most curtain material comes in 54" or 136cm (1360mm) widths and to work out how many widths of material you need, you divide your doubled track length by the width of your chosen material. The table shows a worked example of costings for a standard bedroom window.

Making-up costs are also usually worked out on a width basis; Star Curtains of Newmarket (01638 666642) charge around £8/width — the length of the curtains is immaterial. Some sort of lining material is recommended (though not essential) and also a taped heading is standard for a pencil-pleated finish. Thus the costs for a reasonably good but not extravagant material, like Jonelle's *Bergereac* which retails at £10.00/metre run, on a 1200x1200mm window work out at just over £100 and, if you transpose these prices on to our benchmark house, you would expect to pay around £1500 to curtain the whole house.

You can, of course, buy ready-made curtains and these can be much cheaper. But will they actually fit your windows? Good luck when you go looking. Alternatively, many selfbuild-ers will have curtain material available from their old house and, using their own labours, will be able to drape all their windows for much less than this figure. On the other hand, I'm not being in the least bit extravagant in my choice of materials (less than £10/m) or fittings. Fancy designer-label fabrics, Austrian blinds, cast iron hanging rails — this sort of detail could easily double or even treble the cost.

Blinds

The cheapest type of blind available is the roller blind. It's also the cheapest way of providing a window cover as it comes with its own integral hanging brackets. A blind in a 1200mm-wide bathroom window will set you back no more than £40 and possibly a lot less — some manufacturers produce roller blinds in standard widths which you can then cut to size. Venetian blinds are a shade more sophisticated; in aluminium they are two to three times the price of a roller, in wood they are around five times the roller blind price.

9n: Estimating for Curtains

TRACK LENGTHS and MATERIAL QUANTITIES for a BEDROOM WINDOW

Window Width		1200mm
Curtain Track Length	add 400mm	1600mm
Standard Curtain Width		1360mm
Total Width of Curtains	Twice the curtain track length	3200mm
No. of Standard Widths Needed	Total width divided by standard width	2.35
	Rounded up to nearest half width	2.5
Window Height		1200mm
Curtain Drop	add 300mm	1500mm
Extra Material for Repeat Pattern	add 200mm	1700mm
Curtain Material Needed	2.5 widths x 1700mm drop	4250mm or 4.25m
COSTS		
Wooden Curtain Pole	1.6m @ £9/lin.m	£14
Wooden Fittings, Rings		£10
Curtain Material	4.25m @ £10.00/m	£43
Lining Material	4m @ £2.00/m	£8
Taped Headings	3.2m @ 70p/m	£2
MATERIALS		**£78**
Costs for Making-up Curtains	3 widths @ £8/width	£24
Fitting Curtain Rails	0.5hr @ £8/hr	£4
Fitting Curtains	0.5hr @ £8/hr	£4
LABOUR		**£32**
ALL-IN TOTAL		**£110**

Driveways & Pavings

Driveways are included on the list of external works which are exempt from VAT on new buildings, so there is every reason to finish the drive before occupation. Almost invariably these days, planning permission for new homes requires provision for off-road car parking and this means that some attention has to be paid to both where and how this is to be accommodated. So whilst a garage is arguably a luxury you could dispense with (or postpone), driveways and hardstandings must be accommodated within the initial design and costings.

Foundations

Whatever drive finish you decide on, the base you lay should essentially be the same: ideally 100-150mm of *hardcore* (which can consist of a number of different materials, none of which should cost much more than £7/tonne). A 1m^3 void needs 2 tonnes of hardcore to fill it, so:

- To lay hardcore 100mm thick, 1 tonne will cover 5m^2 — budget £1.20/m^2
- To lay hardcore 150mm thick, 1 tonne will cover 3.3m^2 — budget £1.80/m^2.

A superior method, particularly recommended on clay sites, is to use a *Terram* or *Geotextile* sheet underlay beneath the hardcore layer. These cost around 90p/m^2 but they allow water to pass through whilst stopping mud mixing in with the hardcore overlay. Laying hardcore can be done by hand but this is backbreaking and time-consuming. The most efficient method is to use machines to spread and tamp hardcore — digger buckets are particularly effective tampers. It is very useful to have hardcore laid as early as possible on a building job as it aids access

and stops the site becoming a quagmire, but drain-laying timetables do not always allow this use of machinery and whether it is worth getting machinery in later just to lay hardcore depends on the size of the driveway.

- Budget £1/m^2 for spreading hardcore with excavating machinery
- Budget £100 for getting a JCB to come in especially
- Budget £2/m^2 for barrowing, spreading and hand tamping.

Overall, laying hardcore on already dugout ground should not cost more than £5/m^2. If you dispense with or skimp on this hardcore sub-base, you will end up with a drive which will initially look good but will rapidly disintegrate. The other problem to be aware of here is rainwater drainage; on flat sites, water will tend to pool if it is not adequately planned for. To this end, it is normal to lay the drive so that rainwater collects in certain points then drain the water away off to a soakaway. Whilst the falls can usually be constructed when the actual driveway is being laid, the drainage obviously has to be installed before the sub-base. A minor detail? You won't think so if you overlook it.

Concrete Block Paving

This is becoming an increasingly popular way of finishing the front access (and also for doing paths and patios). There are large price breaks available for bulk orders and full loads (144m^2) should be available at less than £5/m^2 in greys or buffs (which makes them as cheap as plain concrete paving slabs and almost as cheap as wet concrete laid 100mm deep). They are usually laid *dry* (i.e. without any cement) on a 50mm bed of sharp sand,

and finished with jointing sand brushed over them and *whacked* with a compactor plate: dry laying is cheaper than wet and this makes them a cheap and attractive option for patios and paths as well as drives.

Supply and fix prices tend to come in around £15/m^2 (excluding hardcore foundation preparations). Kerb work obviously has a big impact on the overall costs and the value of this varies from site to site but averages about 20% of the overall costs. More elaborate pavers than the bog standard found on garage forecourts will bump the overall price up by 50-100%. As with bricks and roof tiles, there is a choice between clay and concrete; clay invariably costs more but is said to look better or, more accurately, to *wear* better.

Builders can usually make significant savings by negotiating paver prices off the back of brick and block orders placed at the beginning of the job and thereby taking advantage of full load deliveries. Money can also be saved by using machines (JCBs, etc.) to place pallet loads at convenient places; later on this work can often only be done by hand.

Tarmac

The preparation is much the same as for pavers; kerbs need to be set in concrete round the perimeter, though these are usually cheaper than the special kerbings used with block paving. A pukka job should consist of a 80mm base course laid below a 35mm top course, known as the *wearing course*. A 50m^2 driveway with 20m kerbings should cost around £14/m^2 (M £6, L £8, hardcore works excluded). This would fall to around £10/m^2 for areas over 100m^2. Some tarmac prices

9p: Guide Prices for Driveway Finishes

	MATS	LAB	COMBINED	BENCHMARK HOUSE COSTS	
				PER ITEM	OVERALL
Hardcore foundations/m^2	£3	£3	£5	£430	£430
Concrete Block Paving/m2	6.00	4.00	10.00	860	
Kerb Work/lin.m	4.00	3.50	7.50	240	£1530
Tarmac/m^2	4.80	4.00	8.80	760	
Kerb Work/lin.m	2.00	2.50	4.50	140	£1330
Concrete/m^2	4.50	3.00	7.50	650	
Kerb Work/lin.m	1.00	1.50	2.50	80	£1160
Shingle/m^2	1.00	4.00	5.00	430	
Kerb Work/lin.m	0.50	1.50	2.00	60	£920

Hardcore foundation costs are common to all applied toppings and additional to other costs

Assumes 86m^2 driveway with 32m kerbs

Key Drive Prices

Concrete Block Paving

Pavers: £5.00-£8.00/m² (down to £4.50/m² in full loads)

Matching kerbs: £5.00/lin.m (down to £3.00/lin.m. in full loads)

Labour rates for laying pavers: £4.00/m²

Labour rates for setting kerbs: £3.50/lin.m

Allow a contingency for levelling hardcore, setting falls and moving blocks around the site.

Incidentals include 50mm sharp sand bed (12m²/tonne @ £10/tonne) and jointing sand (15m²/50kg bag @ £3.60/bag). Recessed manhole covers which can be filled with blocks are available at £75 .

Tarmac

Tarmac (base or wearing): £24/tonne 1 tonne of base coat will cover 7m² at standard 50mm depth: 1 tonne of wearing coat will cover 14m² at standard 25mm depth.

Materials cost of base and wearing course: £5/m²

Labour rates for laying: £4/m² (more on small areas).

Wet Concrete

PAV 1 Readymix : £40-£50/m³ or £4-£5/m² at standard 100mm depth

Labour rates for laying: c. £3/m² (rising to £5/m² on small areas)

Edging formers: c.£2.00/lin.m.

For quotations and for other finishes, check your Yellow Pages under Paving Services.

appear to be far lower than this — this is the Wild West of the building trade remember — but the specification is unlikely to be the business and the finished drive may not last very long.

Concrete

Base preparations are similar to pavers and tarmac; kerbs can be ignored in favour of shuttering (or road forms) for which steel formers are available to hire. The designated readymix for driveways is PAV 1 — strong and relatively expensive — and it is normally laid at 100mm depth. Reinforcement should not be necessary. A 50m² driveway with 20m edgings should cost around £10/m² (M £5, L £5, hardcore works excluded). This would fall to around £8/m² for areas over 100m².

Patterned Concrete

A number of specialist operators now offer patterned concrete paving where imprints of pavers are set into wet concrete to give a pave effect drive. This technique is widely used elsewhere around the world but is having difficulty catching on in the UK because of the low (depressed) prices for standard concrete block paving. Patterned concrete drives start at around £20/m² (excluding foundation work) which, if anything, is rather more expensive than concrete block paving.

Shingle and Gravel

This is the cheapest option and, in many rural situations, the most attractive. It's particularly suitable for long drives. However, note that the better gravel driveways are actually labour intensive as they involve laying three or four layers of stones, each rolled and then left for a day or two between coats. Edgings need to be placed — treated timber strips are adequate — and the success of the drive overall depends on good hardcore beneath. Top coat materials shouldn't cost much more than £1.00/m² but laying costs are likely to be high, especially if there's no mechanised plant available.

Quotes to supply and lay a gravel drive often specify a simpler two layer application as this keeps the price down to around the £7/m² mark (excluding foundation works).

Resin Bonded Driveways

Available from specialist firms, these work by sticking small stones into a rigid sheet to give a shingle-look driveway which is as hard and durable as concrete or tarmac. Prices tend to start around the £20/m² mark (excluding hardcore foundation work).

Fancy Paving Options

There are many other materials available to lay paths and, in particular, patios. Labour costs for laying vary widely (£5-£15/m²) de-

pending on whether they can be laid wet or dry and whether they need pointing-up afterwards. Wet laying involves using cement (albeit usually a dryish mix) and tends to be very much more labour intensive. Some hardcore backfill is usually advisable though when it is designed for foot traffic only it does not need to be laid as deep as it is under driveways. Materials choices include:

- Plain paving slabs — £4.00-£5.00/m²
- *Riven* paving slabs (textured surface) — £6.00-£7.00/m²
- *Heritage* paving (simulated natural stone) — £13/m²
- Natural York stone flags (the real McCoy) — £40/m²
- Granite sets — £35/m²
- 75mm Beach Cobbles — £15/m²
- Reconstituted stone — £25/m².

Marshalls of Halifax are the largest supplier of manufactured pavings (and garden walling effects). Their brochures, which are widely available at builder's merchants (Travis Perkins, Harcros), are a good starting point in assimilating some possibilities. They also have a wide choice of block pavers (both concrete and clay) and paving slabs.

Natural stone slabs, setts and cobbles are widely available though you have to search them out from smaller suppliers and quarries: try Harris & Bailey (0181 654 3181). Blanc de Bierge (01733 202566) produce an attractive honey coloured range of reconstituted stone slabs and sets which cost around £20/m². Be aware that prices are usually quoted ex-works and that transport costs are likely to add between £100 and £250 to the total depending on amount and distance.

Specialists

Laying a drive should not be beyond the competence of a good builder yet many people prefer to subcontract the whole process to a specialist, typically found in the Yellow Pages > *Asphalt and Macadam* or *Paving Services*. Before you do this, you would do well to refer to a recent *Which?* report (Drive Carefully, Nov 95). This revealed a staggering range of prices as well as some uncompromising high pressure selling tactics which, to be fair, are usually associated with national companies advertising through magazines and usually (but not always) selling patterned concrete or resin-bonded driveways. In this *Which?* report, prices for one 60m² driveway varied from £329 to £6210! The accompanying table gives a flavour of the middle range of driveway prices. I would tend to steer clear of both the very cheap quotes and the very expensive ones.

Fencing & Turfing

Fencing

If you just want to mark a boundary and are not too bothered about privacy or security then the cheapest permanent option is the timber post-and-rail fence. This arrangement shouldn't cost more than £8/lin.m (Mats £4, Lab £4); it looks fine and is easily maintained. If you have longish (30m plus) lengths to erect, then the cheapest suppliers are to be found in the pages of *Horse & Hound* (down below £6/lin.m). Alternatively, a chain link fence will cost a similar amount and, though less attractive, is more secure and should stop dogs and children straying to boot.

1.2m-high chestnut palings are another cheapish option (costing around £5/lin.m) which, being vertical, are much harder to get over. They are easily fixed — just whack posts in every 2m or so — but have a temporary air about them which may not appeal to all. The picket fence is similar in design but altogether more permanent in appearance but it costs around £14/lin.m (M £9, L £5).

If you require privacy and security then you will have to go for a solid or near solid fence with a height of 1.8m (above head height). The traditional way of doing this is to erect something similar to a post-and-rail fence and then to cover it with vertically fixed, featheredge boarding. This is known as a *close-boarded* fence. Expect it to cost around £25/lin.m (M £15, L £10). It is a little cheaper to use ready-made panels of the type you see in garden centres but the result is very flimsy in comparison. There are many variations on the theme of boarded fences; you can set the boards horizontally or diagonally, or alternate the boards between the inside and the outside of the fence posts (called *hit and miss* fencing). You can achieve quite stunning effects very simply and they don't have to be stained dark afterwards. If you want to investigate further, I recommend you get Jackson's Good Fencing Guide (01233 750393). They also deal with wire fencing which, I am assuming, is of lesser interest to would be housebuilders.

Brick Walls

Whilst timber fencing is getting expensive at around £25/lin.m, you are not going to get even a whiff of a brick boundary wall under £90/lin.m. This is a different animal altogether and ideally should be erected along with the main house so as to combine economies of scale — not to mention getting JCBs into the back garden. A 1.8m-high brick wall is actually a rather vulnerable construction, prone to blowing over in howling gales, and best practice advice now recommends that all unsupported walls over a mere 650mm high should be built two brick skins thick (225mm). In exposed locations, a 1.8m-high brick wall should be built 330mm thick. Whether your wall is freestanding or is being built as a retaining wall against some high ground, your building inspector will advise you as to the exact requirements needed.

Turfing

A detailed look at landscaping lays beyond the scope of this book, but I feel I must cover turfing at least because most developers consider it part of their remit to make a garden look acceptable, if not exactly inspired. Indeed, as with fencing, the VAT office allows you to reclaim VAT on purchases of turf when erecting a new house: unfortunately for keen gardeners, the VAT line is drawn at turf.

Of course there's more to it than just laying the turf. After the builders have done their bit, the average plot resembles a World War One battle ground and the site has first to be cleaned of debris. Usually, it is then rotavated, levelled and rolled, and normally a selective weed killer is applied to prevent thistles taking over. Turf itself usually costs around £1.15/m^2 to purchase; the preparation work and the laying will cost around £1.50/m^2, more if the work is particularly arduous or if there are slopes involved. If extra topsoil is needed, this costs around £10-£20/m^3. You can halve the cost of turfing if you seed the area instead but this can be a bit hit and miss: it's best carried out in March or April and you need to be lucky with the rain or else you will have to water for about eight weeks.

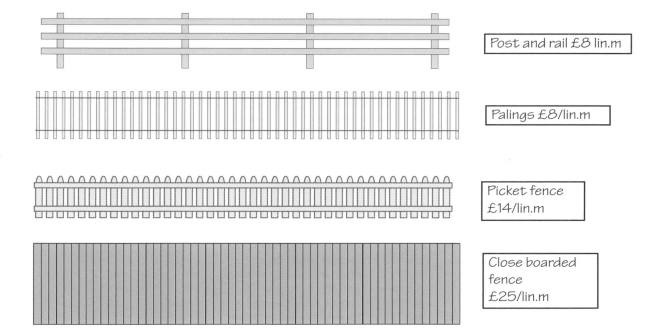

Post and rail £8 lin.m

Palings £8/lin.m

Picket fence £14/lin.m

Close boarded fence £25/lin.m

Working from Home

Pick up any paper or magazine and you're likely to find articles about working from home, as if it had just been discovered as the panacea of all modern ills. This is completely daft. Working from home is what most of us always did, long before they invented factories and offices and there are still loads of trades and businesses which have always worked from home. What is new is that there is a whole raft of office workers who would previously have commuted some distance to work now padding a few feet down the passageway. Journalists in particular are able to work from home which is, just possibly, why you read so much about it in the newspapers and magazines. But my farming friends just scratch their heads and wonder what everyone is talking about.

What's the upshot of all this? Well, what most people think when they think of working from home is that they need an office, or at least some office space. The physical requirements for all this are remarkably small, usually satisfied by a few shelves and a working space serviced by a couple of power outlets and a telephone socket (two if you are greedy). There really isn't much designing to be done, you just take over the box bedroom and have done with. Even if you are inclined towards the hi-tech office with PCs, faxes, printers, scanners, copiers, modems and the like, you still don't really need anything more in the way of infrastructure.

However, for many others, working from home will need considerably more thought. You may require meeting space or consultation rooms which are best kept quite separate from the rest of the household in order to maintain a professional atmosphere. On the other hand, you may need workshop space which will create dust or noise or smell and which is ideally situated in a separate building. These are specialised concerns and really no one is going to understand them better than yourself, so it is pointless me whittling on. What I should point out though is that the more specialised and separate your workspace becomes, the more problems you are likely to encounter at the planning stage.

These problems are likely to hinge on whether you can extend the terms of the planning permission to include non-residential uses. Solo home office working is frankly not going to be an issue but anything that a) makes a lot of noise or smell or b) attracts a lot of visitors is not going to be passed through on the nod; in fact, it's probably unlikely to get passed at all if the area is zoned purely residential. However the buzz word of contemporary planning, sustainability, is on your side here. For decades the planning system has worked to separate the residential zones from the industrial zones on the premise that the two don't mix well, but as much of our working activities have become cleaner and quieter, the wisdom of this zoning has been called into question. Now the boot seems to be on the other foot because the car — more particularly the car journey — has become the *bete noir* of planning departments. Anything which can be done to reduce the number of car journeys is said to be sustainable, which is planning speak for a good thing.

There is an awful lot of hot air being blown off by politicians and environmentalists about how bad the car is and how we need to invest much more in public transport. It won't work. For public transport to take the place (or even a significant slice) of private car ownership, you would have to have so many damn buses running along the roads that you would end up with a far greater number of vehicles on the road overall. Public transport only works well when you have large numbers of people wanting to travel to the same place, but our planning system has actually done it's utmost to ensure that our work places are now scattered all over. And our working lives are no longer spent working for one organisation in one location: long gone are the days when you could sensibly choose to live near a bus route or railway station that connected to your place of work because the chances are in two years time you will have changed jobs, or your business will have changed location.

We have become a society hooked on mobility. Car journeys are but a symptom of this, they are not the problem. If we want to address these issues, then we have to re-invent the way we live and the way we work and one very obvious way to do this is to increase the amount of home working. There are many many jobs which could be done from home or at least partly from home. And as the information highway improves, the range of jobs which can be done from home will increase. As our admin moves, albeit rather hesitatingly, from paper to digital, so our flexibility grows as to where and when we need to process it. Similarly, our shopping habits will probably become more orientated towards phone ordering/home delivery which will obviate the need for so many shopping trips and for so many sales staff. But to set against these brave predictions of how life might be conducted 20 or 30 years hence, bear in mind that as of now the amount of home/mail order shopping going on is actually in decline at the moment and attempts to get us to shop via the internet have been spectacularly unsuccessful.

Whether you need to plan ahead for any of this if you are designing a new house is a moot point. As I have already indicated, no one knows your circumstances like you do and only you can take a guess as to how much, if any, work you are likely to be doing from home and, if so, what sort of space and resource requirements you will need. Spec. housing is still being built with separate living rooms and dining rooms plus every room upstairs being classed as a bedroom: it can't be long before this rather old-fashioned arrangement is replaced with one with dedicated office space, either replacing the dining room or one of the bedrooms. If you are designing for yourself, it would be as well to bear in mind that though you may not want any home office or workshop space, future purchasers are likely to have such space high on their wish list. If there is a lesson to be learned here, it is to plan a little flexibility into the scheme you are designing. If you definitely want a home workspace then all well and good, but many people are not altogether sure that they do: instead of fitting one out from the word go, instead identify which room you think would be best for this purpose and specify a couple of extra power sockets and maybe first fix an extra phone line in. More elaborate specifications are touched on at the end of Chapter 8 in the section TV and Telecoms.

Chapter 10
Green Issues

Most of the interest in this field — and indeed, most of this chapter — is to do with saving energy. Interest in this subject really began during the 1974 oil crisis when people assumed — incorrectly — that we were facing a permanent fuel shortage and consequentially rocketing fuel prices. However, in more recent times, concern has grown among scientists that the ambient temperature of the entire planet Earth is gradually increasing, a phenomenon, known to us all now, as global warming. Why this should be is not yet understood but a very large finger of suspicion is pointing at us and, in particular, our habit of burning masses and masses of fossil fuels and thereby releasing carbon dioxide (CO_2) into the atmosphere. This may (or may not) be causing a greenhouse effect which, in turn, may (or may not) be causing temperatures to rise which, in turn, may (or may not) have catastrophic effects on Mother Earth. It's only a theory; all that's known for certain is that a) there is much more CO_2 in the atmosphere than there was even

50 years ago and b) global temperatures have been rising. The crux of the problem is that we won't know how much of this theory is accurate for another 50 years from now by which time it could be too late to do much about it.

Reckoning that it is probably better to be safe than sorry, governments the world over have been signing accords — most notably at the Rio Earth Summit — to reduce levels of energy consumption though, as environmentalists point out, not by very much and sometimes by nothing at all. As private households contribute about a third of our national CO_2 emissions, the effect of these undertakings is beginning to trickle down to the Building Regulations in the hope that stricter codes for new building will bring about some reduction. Hence all of the recent changes to the building regs are to do directly with reducing CO_2 emissions, though you won't see any mention of CO_2 in the regs. What is interesting to the new housebuilder is

that many of the energy (and therefore CO_2) saving features that can be built into a new home are also money saving features, and if you are concerned with ongoing running costs, then you can build energy saving into your home knowing that you will be saving money as well as possibly saving the planet. Whilst speculative developers are still primarily interested in keeping construction costs low, selfbuilders and housing associations are two groups that are just as concerned with ongoing running costs and they have not been slow to see the importance of energy saving. In the rest of this chapter I'll try and avoid mention of CO_2 and concentrate on filthy lucre, but the more high-minded of you can rest assured that saving one almost always means saving the other. Energy saving is, however, not the be-all and end-all of environmental concerns and I'll start the chapter by taking a look at some of the other issues, including an assessment of how much energy is used in actually constructing a new house.

Construction Audit

Trade Balance

Materials going into our benchmark house weighed around 260 tonnes, the vast majority of which will have been produced within 200 miles of the house. Timber (6 tonnes) is the only significant import by weight, though copper (used extensively in plumbing and wiring) and kitchen appliances were also imported. Traditional house building remains an overwhelmingly British business. It is low-tech and uses a lot of very bulky materials which are costly to transport. Even where foreign companies achieve market penetration in Britain, production is usually UK based — cf. Celcon (Danish), Osma (Dutch), Lafarge (French), Knauf (German), Sadolin (Swedish), Akzo (Dutch), Velux (Danish).

As a rule, Britain runs a trade deficit in building materials. We are net exporters of steel, wallpapers, paints, sanitaryware and even bricks (mostly to Japan) whilst timber accounts for around 90% of our net imports with heating and plumbing gear being the only other significant contributor on this side of the account. Take out timber from the equation and everything else pretty much balances out.

Energy Audit

Energy use involved in building any house can be divided into three areas, material production, transport and construction. Broadly speaking, the less a material is processed, the less energy it takes to produce and the less distance a material travels the less energy is used in getting it there. On-site energy use is remarkably low, unless heating and lighting are employed which is unusual when doing spec. housing. Table 10a summarises the energy used in constructing the benchmark house and it is based on the following figures:

- NATURAL MATERIALS take the least energy to produce. Sand, stone, slate and timber come into this group: production costs might be typically 100kWh/tonne.
- CEMENT-BASED PRODUCTS like concrete and render are low on energy use because they have a high proportion of natural sand or stone mixed in with the cement. They consume around 300kWh/tonne to produce.
- CLAY-BAKED products like bricks and clay roof tiles use around 800kWh/tonne. Also included in this group are plasters and plasterboard. Note that the manufacture of concrete products

consumes just half the energy of their clay equivalents.
- GLASS: uses 9000kWh/tonne
- STEEL: uses 13,000kWh/tonne
- COPPER: uses 15,000kWh/tonne
- ALUMINIUM: uses 27,000kWh/tonne
- PLASTIC (inc. uPVC): uses 45,000kWh/tonne — but a tonne goes a long way.

Transport

In addition to the manufacturing costs, there are energy costs involved in getting the materials to site. As previously mentioned, most of these materials are locally produced. The one big exception is timber which almost always is imported. Our joinery grade softwoods come mostly from Scandinavia, our carcassing from N. America, Scandinavia and Russia, timber boards can come from anywhere though note that Sterling Board is produced in Scotland and most of our MDF comes from Ireland.

Comparisons

The table breaks down the embodied energy that went into the benchmark house, which I calculate at around 160,000kWh, very similar to that used on my previous benchmark house. The current one used more concrete in the foundations but gained from having a reclaimed slate roof cover.

160,000kWh is equivalent to the amount of energy the house will take to heat, light and cook during its first five and a bit years of occupation (30,000kWh/annum) or, looked at another way, about ten years motoring in the family car doing 12,000miles/annum. The table indicates the difference between a house which just passes building regs and one that is incredibly energy efficient; in fact the benchmark house scored somewhere between these two extremes, having an NHER rating of 8.7. The current building codes mean that even a house which scrapes through the regulations is saving as much as 20,000kWh/annum over the average of what older housing stock would consume; that means that the energy consumed in production is recouped within ten years. Arguably, many of the improvements built into new housing can be easily transferred into the existing housing stock, but on balance new housebuilding is still an energy saving activity.

Environmental Audit

Extraction of Aggregates

Around 200 tonnes (over 80% by weight) of the benchmark house is composed of sands and gravels mostly bound together with cement. With 150,000 new houses being built in the UK each year, around three cubic miles of materials are being extracted annually to meet this demand. That's an awful lot of holes in the ground and it's one area where new house building is particularly greedy. Quarries pose no long-term health risks and, arguably, the scars of quarrying are actually healed remarkably quickly. However, that doesn't make quarries attractive to nearby residents

Timber

The weight of timber used to construct houses is minute in comparison with masonry/concrete products. The benchmark house uses about 10m^3 (6 tonnes) of wood and wood-based products. Were it timber framed, this figure would rise to around 17m^3 (10 tonnes) and if the entire house was built from wood — cedar shingles on the roof, weatherboarded exterior and pine panelled interiors — the volume of timber would still only be around 40m^3 (24 tonnes), less than a quarter of the equivalent weight if masonry products were used. On the face of it, building from a renewable resource like timber would seem to be very desirable but there are a few snags:

- Logging often has more in common with mineral extraction than agriculture; even so-called sustainable sources are often permanently damaged after the virgin crop is removed to be replaced by monotonous, species-thin plantations.
- Almost all structural timber has to be imported into Britain, making it the one major building component not to be sourced in the UK.
- Exterior timber and structural elements of timber frame housing has to be treated with preservatives, thus causing the manufacture of chemical nasties with all their associated health risks.

Tropical Hardwoods

The problem with using tropical hardwoods is to do with the way in which they are harvested (or plundered) with acres of virgin rainforest being destroyed often to fell just one particularly nice mahogany tree. By and large this land is then cleared and used for rather poor cattle grazing. This sort of wan-

10a: Benchmark House Construction Audit
Material Quantities and Energy Used to Construct House

MATERIAL	ENERGY USED in MANUFACT-URING (in kWh/tonne)	MATERIAL QUANTITY		WEIGHT (in tonnes)	ENERGY USED (in kWhs)
Concrete	300	50	m^3	90	27,000
Bricks	800	7000	No	18	14,400
Lightweight Blocks	300	600	m^2	50	15,000
Concrete Floor Beams	1,000	5	t	5	5,000
Sand	30	40	t	40	1,200
Cement	800	7	t	7	5,600
Concrete Tiles	300		No.		0
2nd hand Roofing slates	40	4200	No.	6	200
Concrete Pavers	300	106	m^2	15	4,500
Hardcore	30	20	t	20	600
Timber	100	10	m^3	6	600
Chipboard/Plywood	300	2	m^3	1.1	300
Plasterboard	800	300	m^2	2.9	2,300
Steel	13,000	2	t	2	26,000
Glass	9,000	13	m^2	0.3	2,700
Plastic/uPVC	45,000	0.25	t	0.25	11,300
Sanitaryware	5,000	0.2	t	0.2	1,000
Others	10,000			0.2	2,000
Timber Transport		10,000km			12,000
Heavy Goods Transport		5,000km			30,000
TOTAL				264	160,000

COMPARISONS Energy used/annum	NHER Score	kWh/annum
Benchmark House built to Bld Reg standards	8	35,000
Benchmark House Built to Energy Efficient Standards	9.4	24,000
Average for UK Housing Stock of Similar Size	4.5	55,000
Family Car doing 12,000mls/year		15,000

ton destruction is going on all over the tropics and, in truth, is as much to do with burgeoning population growth as it is with extracting hardwoods, but there is no doubt that the hardwood trade plays a significant part. The building trade is, as ever, very slow to pick up on the potential problems here and long after retailers have been selling furniture "Made from Renewable Resources", there is little sign of any green awareness from timber merchants, possibly because tropical hardwoods are a nice little earner.

However, the environmental problems resulting from using these hardwoods in new housebuilding should not be exaggerated because their use is rare precisely because of their expense. Brazilian mahogany is specified as standard as a cill detail on door frames — currently there are no alternatives offered by the major joinery manufacturers — but otherwise you have to go looking for materials — chiefly joinery — made out of tropical hardwoods. Another area where you may stumble across them is as constituents of better-grade plywoods (Far Eastern) and blockboards, but these are more commonly used for shelving than construction; MDF can be used as a cheaper substitute.

Health Risks

Formaldehyde

This glue is used to bind timber panel products, chiefly chipboards, MDF and plywoods. Some people are known to react badly to the fumes which are released very slowly over a period of months after manufacture, a process known as off-gassing. However, adverse reactions are rare and exact causes are difficult to pinpoint. Almost all volatile synthetic compounds (VOCs) have come under suspicion — including carpets and clothes — and it remains a complex and poorly understood area. You can, of course, build and furnish a house from entirely natural materials but it is an expensive option.

Solvents

Solvents are used in oil-based paints, stains and varnishes, as well as adhesives and mastics. Many people actually like the smell of solvents but long-term exposure to them has been linked with brain damage. Occasional users probably need not be alarmed, but be aware that solvents are likely to be far more damaging to young children than to adults;

if youngsters (and pregnant women) are present then you would do well to consider using water-based paints and stains indoors.

Wood Preservatives

One normally associates timber treatment with remedial work carried out on old houses but a great deal of new timber gets pretreated with either water-based tanalith or solvent-based protim. The tanalising treatments are based on the copper-chrome-arsenic compounds (CCAs) whilst the spirit-based systems use a cocktail of chemical nasties such as lindane, pentachlorophenol (PCPs) and tri-butyl-tin-oxide (TBTOs). They serve a dual purpose; one is to reduce risk of fungal infestations such as dry rot, the other is to reduce risk of insect attack such as woodworm and death watch beetle. The idea is that treated timber will taste so foul that insects and fungus will steer well clear: the danger is that these chemicals won't do us much good either.

External joinery is pre-treated as a matter of course and NHBC regulations require that timber in exposed walls is treated. There is a potential long term hazard, although this is rather along the lines of the formaldehyde and VOC threat — i.e. no one can say what it is — but there is also a more immediate danger to site carpenters who inevitably come into physical contact with treated timbers. Wearing gloves is not really an option for a chippie: the best precaution is to ensure that the timber is dried properly before it is worked — sometimes it arrives on site still dripping with the chemical preservatives, having just come out of the vacuum tank. Some commentators maintain that if the design detailing is good, then the timber does not need preserving but preservation is now an industry standard; note that timber frame kit houses tend to come with pre-treated timber specified everywhere, whether it's actually needed or not.

Asbestos

In many ways, asbestos is a great product — lightweight, stable and has incredible fire resistance. But, and it's a big but, asbestos dust particles are a proven killer and great care should be taken when handling the product. Although asbestos is tending to be phased out, it is still present in a number of building products on sale today (cf. certain damp proof courses, artificial slates and other roofing products). However, you are at greater risk when removing asbestos products from old houses because this is where you are most likely to come into contact with the dust. Asbestos was extremely common in houses built from 1920-1980 and care should be taken if demolishing something from this era — watch out particu-

larly for things like textured Artex ceilings. The risks of removing asbestos should not be underestimated and if you encounter it, or anything suspicious-looking dust forming material, you should look to call in specialist help — start with a call to your local Environmental Health Office.

MDF

The problems related to formaldehyde have already been touched on and are not unique to MDF. However MDF is the board that gets worked most and it tends to produce the finest dust which sails through the average dust mask as if it's not there. This combination is reckoned (by some) to make MDF a hazard on a par with asbestos and moves are afoot to produce a similar board made with safer resins. Passive consumers of MDF products are unlikely to be at risk but you should look out if you work with a lot of MDF dust.

Cement

Human skin does not react well with wet cement and concrete mixes; there is no instant sign that burning is taking place and many people assume that it is therefore harmless. It's not; prolonged exposure will cause very nasty burns.

Fibreglass

Fibreglass insulation, together with the closely related mineral wool, are unpleasantly itchy on skin, and eyes like it even less. Thought by some to be similar to asbestos in effect, others claim that the fibres are generally too large to cause lethal irritation. Whoever proves to be correct, it makes sense not to be macho about it. Wear gloves and a mask when insulating.

uPVC

The use of uPVC has been growing steadily in housebuilding. You will find it in plastic guttering and drainage pipes, in electric cable and, of course, uPVC windows and doors. However there is a growing campaign (led in this country by Greenpeace) against the use of uPVC, principally on the grounds that its production is a dirty, polluting business leading to the release of dioxins and thalades, not to mention the dumping of chlorine. What is not clear is whether uPVC manufacture is any worse than the rest of the chemicals/plastics industry.

Site Safety

See section on Running a Site, in Chapter 5, Project Management.

BREEAM

This is short for the Building Research Establishment Environmental Assessment Method. This is produced by the people at the BRE in Watford who are better known for

their work on energy efficiency (under another hat called BRECSU). BREEAM attempts to quantify the good and bad points surrounding the whole issue of housebuilding in relation to the environment. The issues addressed and the maximum points you can score for specifying a particularly green solution (according to BREEAM) are as follows:

- CO_2 emissions resulting from energy use in the home (6)
- CFC and HCFC (hydro-chloro-fluoro-carbon) emissions (1)
- use of natural resources and recycled materials (5)
- storage of recyclable materials (1)
- water economy (1)
- ecological value of the site (2)
- ventilation (2)
- control of volatile organic pollutants of indoor origin (1)
- wood preservatives (1)
- man-made mineral fibres (1)
- asbestos and lead (1)
- lighting (3)
- smoke alarms (1)
- storage of hazardous materials (1).

These factors are all summarised in an interesting booklet called *Homes for a Greener World*, available from CRC (0171 505 6622) for £16.50 (inc P+P), though for just 33 pages this is unlikely to appeal to the casual housebuilder. Many of its conclusions are common sense but there is much background that is extremely informative, although I'm not sure I like the idea of giving greenie points for being good; it seems a bit Nannyish. Many environmental issues are not at all clear cut and involve a series of trade-offs and compromises. For instance, they state that the environmentally correct use of wood preservatives should be "to reduce the unnecessary use of wood preservatives while maintaining essential protection of vulnerable timber." Now, if we want to avoid specifying wood preservatives, we have to use better timber which, by and large, tends to mean the timber which remains in the virgin forests...oh but we don't want to cut those down, do we? You can have one or the other but not both and each route is severely environmentally compromised so why pretend, as BREEAM does, that there is a greenie point to be had here at all, especially as the conclusion is identical to that sought by conventional housebuilding. Notwithstanding my carping, the purpose of BREEAM is to draw attention to the fact that there are many more environmental issues surrounding new housebuilding than just energy saving and in this it succeeds; doubtless in the future it will become more refined.

1995 Building Regs

In 1995 there was a considerable uprating of the regulations concerning the energy efficiency of houses. These changes involve some subtle and possibly over-complex changes to Parts F (ventilation) and L (thermal efficiency) of the Building Regulations. For new housebuilders the key points were as follows:
- New dwellings must be energy-rated
- U value calculations are to be tightened up to take account of cold bridging (mortar joints, lintels, timber joists, etc.)
- Methods of heating and ventilating are to be taken into account
- A thermal break is now required around window and door openings to limit the effect of *cold bridging*.

Surprisingly, the maximum U values allowable were not changed (though, as indicated, their method of calculation was) and it is still possible to build in traditional brick and blockwork without any dedicated insulation materials present in cavity walls or under the ground floor. However, in order to do this, attention will have to be paid to heating efficiency and it is likely that this will mean having to go to the expense of fitting a high-efficiency condensing boiler.

Housing associations, selfbuilders and others concerned with running costs, not just the capital costs of building, have long been specifying high insulation levels as well as high-efficiency heating systems and were largely unaffected by the changes, but many speculative builders have had to rethink their basic construction methods.

Current Requirements

What, you will be wondering, exactly are the current requirements for thermal insulation. The building regulators have boxed clever on this one — possibly under pressure from the block manufacturers — and there are a series of trade-offs available so that, for instance, you can keep lower standards of thermal insulation if you have high-efficiency space heating. There are in fact three different routes to satisfying the thermal building regs and only one of them, the so-called elemental method, actually goes as far as specifying maximum U values. Having said that, the elemental method is by far the easiest to understand and many people will adopt its higher insulation standards as a matter of course — see accompanying diagram. But now that energy assessments have been made

mandatory, and a SAP rating of 85 out of 100 (for a large house) will on its own be deemed to be good enough to satisfy building regs, many builders may be tempted to look at other methods of getting such a high score.

Notes for Converters

 You don't need to do an energy rating if you are extending an existing house (though you do have to build to the higher U-value standards). But if you are converting an existing building into a dwelling you are regarded in the same manner as a new housebuilder, which means that a SAP rating is needed. And note that, whereas it is relatively straightforward to build a new house to the improved standards, it can be much trickier (and more expensive) to incorporate them into an existing structure. Indeed the more of the original structure you retain, the bigger the problems you will face as you have to change floor levels and wall thicknesses. To some extent these sorts of problems can be overcome by using thinner sections of better quality insulants but these tend to cost three or four

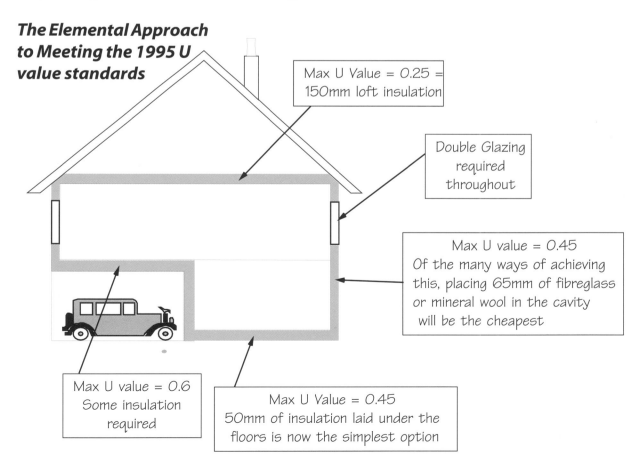

The Elemental Approach to Meeting the 1995 U value standards

Max U Value = 0.25 = 150mm loft insulation

Double Glazing required throughout

Max U value = 0.45
Of the many ways of achieving this, placing 65mm of fibreglass or mineral wool in the cavity will be the cheapest

Max U value = 0.6
Some insulation required

Max U Value = 0.45
50mm of insulation laid under the floors is now the simplest option

times as much as the industry standard solutions. If you experience problems trying to squeeze insulation into spaces that really aren't wide enough or deep enough, then you will appreciate the flexibility of the current regs in that they don't prescribe minimum insulation levels but allow you to trade-off a weakness in one area (say no underfloor insulation) with strength in another (say Low E glass or a condensing boiler).

SAPS

There are several different energy rating systems kicking around at the moment, although all of them are based on the original BREDEM model created by the BRE. The system selected to be embodied within the building regulations is known as SAP (Standard Assessment Procedure) and SAPs are scored from 0 (awful) to 100 (excellent). It's one of the more basic rating systems, taking account only of energy required for heating and hot water. The more sophisticated ones, like the NHER rating, include calculations for lighting, cooking and appliance use as well. As already mentioned, designing a house with a high SAP rating will be enough on its own to pass muster with the current building regs and designing in a high SAP rating is easy. The benchmark house achieved a SAP rating of 97 and that was not designed as a particularly green structure; its insulation levels are the ones specified in the Elemental Approach diagram (i.e. pretty basic), it has

no Low-E glazing, no condensing boiler, the blockwork is not aerated but simple, cheap lightweight concrete. If just the thermal spec. of the blockwork has been upgraded, the SAP rating would have hit 100 which begs the question why the SAP ratings stop at 100 when a really green house would score 120 or more.

Limited Effects

If you are intending to build to a reasonable level of energy efficiency, the upgraded regs will probably make no difference to your plans at all — excepting that you now need to carry out an energy rating. The builders who will most likely be affected are those who build in brick and block and who like to keep empty cavities. When this latest change in the regs was mooted in 1992, the block manufacturers must have been quaking in their boots thinking that the whole world and their aunt would switch to timber frame in 1995, but, in reality, it couldn't have turned out better for them with an ever expanding market for their added-value aircrete blocks. To ice the cake, you are now able to satisfy the elemental floor insulation requirements by using just super-lightweight blocks in the footings and as floor blocks in a beam and block floor.

The responsibility to calculate SAPs has fallen on the shoulders of the building inspectors. For instance my local authority is now issues a three page SAP questionnaire which they ask designers to complete as a matter of course when applying for building regulations approval; the questions are not particularly difficult and many of them will be satisfactorily answered with the phrase "Refer to Drawings." What is new is the requirement to be specific about space and water heating systems at this early design stage — in the past, house designers have generally left these details to the plumber.

People are wont to compare the process of home energy assessment to the mileage performance fig-

ures on new cars, but, unlike new cars, new houses — even estate-typed new houses — are unique and each will perform differently so each will require its own assessment. The government's expressed hope is that the SAP rating on new and existing homes will become a widely accepted measure of performance and that consumers will thereby exert pressure for higher and higher SAP ratings, thus enticing the market to build to higher standards of energy efficiency rather than forcing them to do so by forever tightening the thermal building regs. The danger is that the implementation of compulsory SAP ratings for new dwellings will just introduce a new ream of pointless and expensive paperwork.

Energy Ratings

Now that the building regs are insisting on energy assessments being carried out on all new dwellings, it is worth examining just what an energy rating consists of and what we can learn from them. There are at least four organisations offering home energy ratings but they are largely targeting the existing housing stock. However one of the groups, National Energy Services, works closely with the NHBC and provides a bolt-on energy audit for NHBC registered new homes. Currently the NHBC charges just £10 for upgrading the obligatory SAP rating to a full NHER audit — about £90 less than having an NHER audit done from scratch.

An energy rating basically consists of carrying out a whole house heat calculation based on the U values of all the various different elements of the house and an assessment of how efficient the heating system will be. In theory it's a precise calculation but there are loads of assumptions made about how houses actually get occupied and how draughty they will be once built and, coupled with likely human error in taking the measurements, energy ratings have a reputation for being a bit hit and miss. *Which?* magazine (Feb 96) laid the boot into them, claiming that energy ratings were not only inaccurate but that, for the individual consumer at any rate, a complete waste of money. They used two guinea pig homes to compare the results of the four licensed assessment companies and they showed there was a huge variance between the results - as much as 20% above or below the correct figures. None of the companies stood out as being better than the others. I am not altogether surprised. It is notoriously easy to make large errors when measuring up a house, particularly when it is being done in a hurry, and the

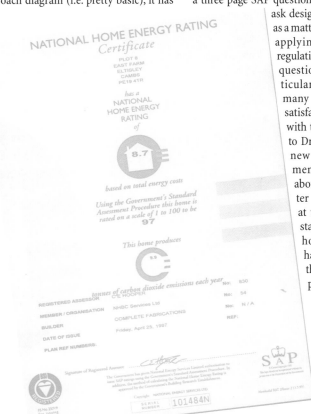

prices being charged for energy assessments are not enough to ensure that the job is done methodically.

NHER Ratings

So much for practise, what about the theory. Well it is just worth a closer look because there are some useful lessons to be gleaned for new home specifiers. The NHER rating (as the NES system is known) is an index of fuel cost/m² of floor space and it takes account of literally hundreds of variables in house construction and specification. Its fabric loss calculations are extremely precise — for instance, each window is individually assessed according to its orientation; however, its assumptions over boiler efficiency and ventilation rates are only based on observed averages achieved in British buildings and its assumptions over things like occupancy patterns and actual user-demand can only be extrapolated from average use data. Obviously, a house which is constantly occupied is likely to use more energy than one which is occupied intermittently.

In contrast to the basic SAP rating (0 - 100), The NHER rating system scores housing from 0 (awful) to 10 (very green). And an NHER 10 is considerably greener than a SAP 100. By way of example, the benchmark house's 97 SAP rating converts to a measly 8.7 NHER rating. Housing built to meet but not necessarily pass current building regulations tends to score between 7.8 and 8.7. The addition of various energy saving features will of course add to the score; for instance, a condensing boiler on it's own will add 0.5 or 0.6 points in a new house. But NHER assessors reckon that a conventionally designed house hits it's top limit at around 9.4 and that to get a full 10 rating, you would have to redesign from the ground up.

Bills Remain High

What is interesting about analysing the results of an NHER energy rating is that, whilst space heating and DHW costs can be reduced by 40% through carrying out super-insulating and heating measures, the electricity bills for lighting, cooking and appliances remain stubbornly high: 55% of total fuel bills in a house scoring around 8.0 and 65% in the energy-efficient version scoring over 9.0. There has been much less attention on these areas of energy saving — indeed they are much harder to tackle and I attempt to redress this lack of balance in two sections later in this chapter, *Energy Efficient Lighting* and *Kitchen and Laundry*. There is as much money and energy to be saved by designing good lighting and detailing good use of cookers and household appliances as there is in

10b: Benchmark House: Likely Fuel Bills

Figures for 166m² house	To BLD REGS	ENERGY EFFICIENT
NHER RATING	8.0	9.4
Central Heating	£270	£150
Open Coal Fire	50	0
Water Heating	100	70
Electric Cooking	70	70
Appliances	200	160
Lights	135	100
Standard Electricity Standing Charge	25	25
Additional charge for Economy 7	0	15
ANNUAL FUEL BILLS	£ 850	£ 590
COSTS INCLUDE VAT @ 5%		

10c: Where the Heat Goes?

Figures are for the 166m² house	To BLD REGS	ENERGY EFFICIENT
NHER RATING	8	9.4
Lost through Walls	£40	£25
Lost through Roof	10	9
Lost through Ground Floor	20	15
Lost through Windows	40	30
Ventilation and Draughts	30	25
Lost up Chimney	20	0
Boiler Inefficiency	80	40
Heating Control Inefficiency	10	8
ANNUAL TOTALS	£250	£152
COSTS INCLUDE VAT @ 5%		

the much better known methods of increasing insulation levels and having energy-efficient heating.

Summary

One of the most interesting points to come out of the NHER's energy rating scheme is the analysis of just where all the heat goes. The accompanying table attempts to clarify the issue; out of it several interesting points emerge:

- The single most effective action to take is to improve boiler efficiency; by and large this means fitting a condensing boiler.

- The so-called fabric heat losses (i.e. walls, roof, floor, windows) are really fairly insignificant — £120/annum on the standard house, falling to £75/annum on

the super-insulated house. Before you fork out good money for an energy-efficient super house, realise that if you reduced fabric heat loss to near zero your anticipated annual savings would be lucky to get you half way round Sainsburys — once a year.

- Losses through ventilation are also fairly insignificant. But here there is often a huge variation between the expected heat loss and the actual heat loss which is not infrequently three of four times the figures outlined in the table. For more detail see the Ventilation section in Chapter 8, Services.

Wot's a U Value?

Get on to the subject of energy efficiency and insulation and it's not long before you hear the term *U value*. The time has come to take a closer look. Like most of the other values in our society, U values are declining; however, in this case, declining values are broadly welcomed. You see a U value is a measure of heat loss and a material with a low U value loses less heat than one with a high U value. Low U value materials are said to be thermally efficient and, therefore, green. In many ways, that's all you need to know and if you are not interested in fathoming the depths of this subject then move on. However, a U value is not like a moral value which you either have or haven't got; it's actually a scientifically derived measurement and knowing your U values will help you make a whole lot more sense of your decisions about how to build and how to heat your house.

Definitions

A **U value** is a measurement of the **heat flow** (measured in watts) through **a square metre** (m^2) of a building element **in one hour** for **every 1°C temperature difference** between the inside and the outside. That reads like the horrible sort of definition you had to learn for Science A-levels, which is why you never did one. It's actually got four different bits to it and in an algebra lesson they'd call them **a, b, c** and **d** and make it even more unintelligible. However the point that it's trying to make is dead simple: some things are better at retaining heat than others. It's something you know instinctively without ever having to ascribe a value to it — afterall you know just how many clothes you need to wear to feel comfortable. The U value is just some poor sod's attempt at quantifying this fact.

In fact the U value of just about everything you could ever think of using to construct a house has been worked out under laboratory conditions. It's a three stage process. Step one is to establish how well each material holds on to heat — the boffins call this **thermal conductivity.** Thermal conductivity is an innate property of each material but how it actually performs in situ depends on how much of it there is. So the next step is to define the **thermal resistance** or **R value** of each layer of material. The R value is calculated by dividing the thickness of the material (expressed in metres) by the thermal conductivity of the material (expressed as watts/m^2x1hrx1°C — see previous definition). This is a strictly proportional relationship so that

the R value of 100mm of glass fibre insulation is twice as much as the R value of 50mm of the same.

Now, buildings are made up of layers of different materials and each of these individual layers will have its own R values. Not only do solid materials have R values but also air gaps in cavities and even internal and external surfaces are all deemed to have some (albeit not very much). The higher the R values, the better the elements perform as heat insulators. Total the R values for each layer and you get an R value for the whole wall/roof/floor or whatever. The diagram shows how it works in a common external wall arrangement. You might think this is enough, but there is one final step to the calculations and that effectively turns the whole thing on its head.

R Values become U Values

To work out the U value for a given element, the R values are added together and the result is divided into 1. The higher the R values total, the lower the U value. Why bother to fiddle around with the values like this? Isn't the R value measurement perfectly adequate? Well not quite. Let's look at three examples of the relationship between R values and U values:

- Take a wall with a cumulative R value of 1.5; its U value is 1/1.5 = 0.67 (fails building regs).
- Double the R value (by adding lots of insulation) to 3.0; its U value is now 1/3.0 = 0.33 (about standard Swedish levels, easily passes our current regs).
- To hell with the cost, increase the cumulative R value to 4.5; the U value is 1/4.5 = 0.22 (lower still, but not that much lower).

What I'm trying to illustrate here is that U values are subject to the law of diminishing returns. Doubling the R values halves the U values. However large your R values get, your U values can never fall to zero so you have to make some sort of decision about just where to stop.

Commentary

Table 10d, overleaf, covers most of the regular building elements that you might meet in constructing a new house. You can use it to work out your own construction's U values by adding all the R values together and dividing 1 by the result. I have used the most regular thicknesses, but if you are not using one of these, remember that R values can be

scaled up or down directly in proportion to the thickness of the material so that you can readily calculate your own.

What's noticeable about these R values is that the specialist insulating materials perform brilliantly and that just about everything else sucks. Although it is a principle that every little bit of a wall/floor/roof construction helps to stop heat loss, it is also true that 80% or more of the insulation is actually achieved by the dedicated insulation materials. The only thing that comes close to achieving good U value rating that isn't specifically an insulation material is the low density, super-lightweight block which many developers prefer to use instead of filling cavity walls with insulation.

Eagle-eyed readers will be asking "Where's the glass?" and the answer is back in the glazing section of the Superstructure chapter. Glazing is a bit of a special case, sometimes it is able to gain heat. Also note that ground floors are seen to behave rather differently from the way that just the sum of their R values might suggest; they tend to leak more heat around their edges than they do in the middle. This has given rise to the supplementary Table 10e, for calculating heat loss through ground floors.

Section through a Brick and Block Cavity Wall, showing the R values of each element

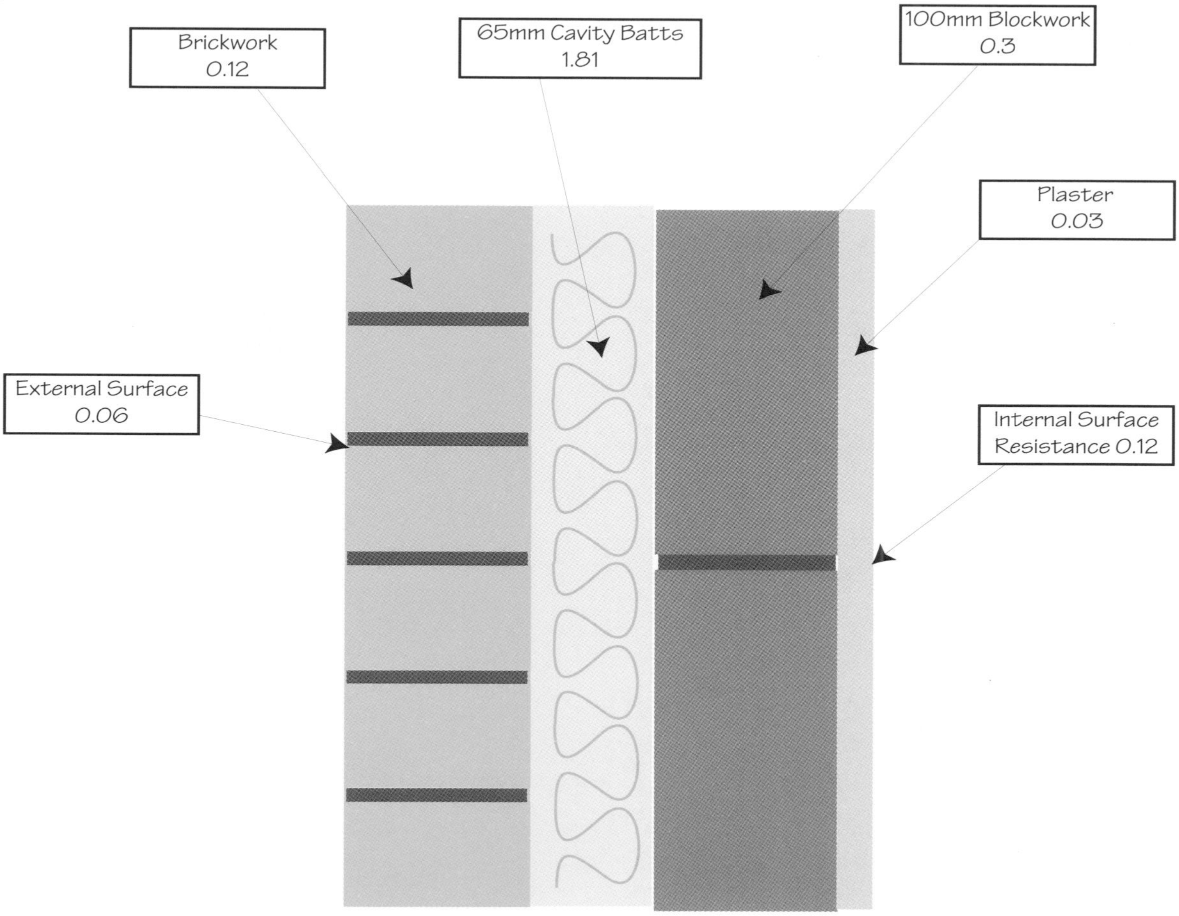

Brickwork
0.12

65mm Cavity Batts
1.81

100mm Blockwork
0.3

Plaster
0.03

External Surface
0.06

Internal Surface Resistance 0.12

External Surface	0.06
Brickwork	0.12
65mm Cavity Batts	1.81
100mm Blockwork	0.30
Plaster	0.03
Internal Surface Resistance	0.12
Total of all R Values	**2.44**
U Value of Wall	**0.41**

To calculate the U value, you first total all the R values of your wall/roof/floor

Step two is to divide the number 1 by the total of all the R values

10d: R values

INSULATION	THERMAL CONDUCTIVITY	THICKNESS in MM	R VALUE
Fibreglass/Mineral wool			
Loose quilt	0.04	100	2.50
	0.04	150	3.75
	0.04	200	5.00
Cavity Batts	0.036	50	1.39
	0.036	65	1.81
Timber Frame Batts	0.04	90	2.25
	0.04	140	3.50
Expanded Polystyrene	0.037	25	0.68
	0.037	50	1.35
Extruded Polystyrene	0.03	25	0.83
	0.03	50	1.67
Polyurethane	0.023	25	1.09
		38	1.80
	0.023	50	2.17
Vermiculite	0.075	100	1.33
OTHER MATERIALS			
Softwood	0.13	25	0.19
	0.13	50	0.38
Hardwood	0.15	25	0.17
	0.15	50	0.33
Plywood/chipboard	0.13	9	0.07
	0.13	18	0.14
	0.13	22	0.17
Plasterboard	0.16	9.5	0.06
	0.16	12.5	0.08
add for Foil Backing			0.20
uPVC	0.4	2	0.01
Clay Brick	0.7	102	0.15

BLOCKS	THERMAL CONDUCTIVITY	THICKNESS in MM	R VALUE
Dense Blocks	0.6	100	0.17
Clinker Blocks	0.25	100	0.40
Aerated	0.19	100	0.53
Super-Lightweight	0.15	100	0.67
Super-Lightweight	0.15	115	0.77
Artificial Stone	1.3	100	0.08
Granite	2.9	100	0.03
Limestone	1.6	100	0.06
Sandstone	1.3	100	0.08
Clay Tile	0.8	10	0.01
Concrete Tile	0.8	12	0.02
Roofing Felt	0.2	2	0.01
50mm Screed	1.3	50	0.04
65mm Screed	1.3	65	0.05
100mm Concrete Slab	1.3	100	0.08
150mm Concrete Slab	1.3	150	0.12
Render	1.2	12	0.01
Finish Plasters	0.9	3	0.00
AIR GAPS			
Cavity 25mm plus			0.20
10mm or less			0.10
Ventilated loft space			0.20
SURFACE RESISTANCE			
External			0.05
Internal			0.10

10e: Additional R values for Ground Floors

EDGE:AREA RATIO	R VALUE
0.3	2.0
0.4	1.6
0.5	1.4
0.6	1.2
0.7	1.1
0.8	1.0

Worked out by dividing the ground floor perimeter (in lin. m) by the floor area (in m²)

These R value figures are additional to R values for actual flooring materials used

D-I-Y Energy Assessment

If you go back to the definition at the start of the last section, you will notice that in order to define a U value, you had to set a number of constants. To recap, a U value is a measure of heat loss **through a square metre, in one hour, through 1°C.** Having got a figure for your U values, you can then use it to work out both your home's heating requirements and its energy rating.

Heat Loss Calculations

Buildings loose heat in two different ways:

- **Fabric loss** occurs as heat is dissipated slowly through a wall, roof or floor because the outside air temperature is lower than the inside and left to itself the house will naturally cool down, just like a hot bath does.

- **Ventilation loss** occurs as air moves in and out of the house through air gaps and ventilation holes. The warm internal air gets replaced by the cold external air.

In working out whole house heat loss, the two types of heat loss are assessed quite differently. If you have taken measurements of your house (see the first section of the next Chapter, Shopping) then you will have most of the information you need to hand. The missing ingredients are your building's U values and you can either work these out from the R values table or cheat and look at the typical U values achieved in the following Table 10f.

Fabric Heat Loss

The "watts lost" is calculated by multiplying the area (in m^2) of each element (i.e. walls/roof/floor) of the house by its relevant U value. The answer is the number of watts lost through each particular element of the construction for each 1°C difference between inside and outside temperatures. Therefore if, as in the benchmark house:

- House ceiling area is $93m^2$
- Roof has a U value of 0.30
- Roof loses 93 x 0.3 = 28 watts/1°C temp. difference.

If you repeat these steps all the way around the external fabric of the house, including external walls, windows, external doors and the ground floor, you will arrive at a figure for the total fabric heat loss for your house, albeit for a measly 1°C temperature difference between inside and out.

Ventilation Heat Loss

The calculations here are involved with establishing how much air is leaking out of the building and how much heat is needed to heat up the infiltrating cold air. The only relevant measurements you need are the volume of air inside the house and the rate of air flow through the house. Combine these with the useful nugget of information that it takes 0.33w to heat 1 cubic metre (m^3) of air through 1°C — this is known as the specific heat of air — and you're away. Again, figures from the benchmark house:

- Volume of air in the house is $410m^3$
- Hoped for number of air changes/hr. is 0.5
- Ventilation heat loss = 410 x 0.5 x 0.33 = 68 watts/1°C temp. difference.

Heating Standards

Combining the totals for each type of heat loss gives us the amount of heat needed to keep the inside of the house 1°C hotter than the outside — not really very useful when you've got a snowman on your back lawn and you haven't seen the sun for three weeks. In designing a heating system you have to make some assumptions about just how warm you want to be. Though you are under no obligation to stick to them, the industry standards for desired temperature in each room are as follows:

Living rooms/kitchen	21°C
Bedrooms	18°C
Hall/stairs	16°C
Bathrooms	22°C

Standard external temperature to design heat loss to is -1°C (though in Scotland it's -4°C). Therefore potential heat loss from (an English) bathroom would be 23°C whilst heat loss from a bedroom would be 3°C less, or 19°C.

From the point of view of calculating your whole house heat loss, you can average out the designed room temperature standards and reckon on a whole house standard of 19°C; this suggests a designed for temperature difference of 20°C (-1°C+19°C). Therefore you multiply your figure for heat loss from both fabric and ventilation (watts/1°C temp. difference, remember) by 20 and you get the maximum heating load required; the answer is in watts, and it is usually surprisingly low. For the benchmark house the result is just over 5400w (or 5.4kW).

This total figure can also be expressed in watts/cubic metre. In our case that's 5400 divided by 410m^3 = 13w/m^3. This watts/m^3 figure is useful: it gives you a relative idea of just how much heat you need for each room; for instance, a bedroom measuring 3x3m which is a standard 2.4m high is 21.6m^3 and would therefore need just 285w to keep it 20°C warmer than outside. You can also use it to assess your plumber's radiator and boiler sizing proposals. The industry doesn't really accept these comparatively low heat requirements; for instance, the standard British Gas installation is capable of belting out over 60w/m^3, four times the amount needed in a new house. As discussed in the sections on Boilers and Ventilation (both in Services chapter), there are good reasons for specifying space heating at higher levels than the heat calculations suggest, but a figure of around 25w/m^3 should be adequate for most new houses for space heating purposes.

Full Energy Assessment

What has been covered so far is the basic heat loss calculations. They are concerned primarily with assessing how large the heating system needs to be. The energy assessors take the process several stages further and convert the figure for rate of heat loss into a quantity of heat lost through time (usually a year). They also add in energy used for things other than space heating and then get very green and convert this into the amount of CO_2 that you are filling the atmosphere up with. For the record, the full NHER survey reckoned that our benchmark house will release 9.9tonnes of CO_2/annum.

Now such calculations are really beyond the scope of this book. If you are interested you can commission an energy survey from MVM Starpoint or an NHER energy assessor; if you think a survey is too pricey you can get hold of a calculation sheet (either paper or computer disc) from CRC (0171 505 6622) called the "Energy assessment for dwellings using BREDEM worksheets."

There are any number of factors which effect the energy performance of each individual house. Unfortunately U values are only the beginning and you need to take into account:
- location (a house in the Scilly Islands requires just 60% of the heat of an identical house in the Shetlands).
- orientation (south facing windows are good news)
- space heating efficiency (can vary from 50%-100%)

• heat gain from occupants (bonking indoors during the heating season is good for the environment).

Table 10f summarises some of the "what-ifs" for the benchmark house. As I have already stated, every house is an individual case and the relationship between area of building element and annual heat loss varies with the factors already mentioned. Having said that, the variations are unlikely to make the results radically different from this table and, if you use a bit of the commonsense you were blessed with (otherwise you wouldn't have got to this page), you can refer to this table to help you make those tricky command decisions about just what specification you should build the house to. Remember that the benchmark house is a 166m² affair and you should scale your own calculations up or down depending on whether your house is bigger or smaller.

10f: Energy Saving What-ifs for Benchmark House

CONSTRUCTION METHOD	AREA in m²	APPROX. U VALUE	WATTS LOST/m²/hr/1°C	kWhrs LOST/ANNUM	STANDARD HEATING COSTS	ENERGY EFFICIENT HEATING COSTS
ROOF	**93**					
150mm Quilt		0.30	28	1004	£21	£18
200mm Quilt		0.25	23	837	£18	£15
300mm Quilt		0.15	14	502	£11	£9
EXTERNAL WALLS	**159**					
Empty Cavity/Insulating Block		0.60	95	3434	£73	£60
Fully Insulated Cavity		0.45	72	2576	£55	£45
90mm Timber Frame		0.35	56	2003	£43	£35
140mm Timber Frame		0.25	40	1431	£30	£25
WINDOWS, FRENCH DOORS	**18**					
Single Glazing		5.60	101	3629	£77	£64
Double Glazing		3.00	54	1944	£41	£34
Double Glazing/Low E Glass		2.00	36	1296	£28	£23
EXTERNAL DOORS	**7**					
44mm Timber		3.00	21	756	£16	£13
Insulated Core		0.60	4	151	£3	£3
GROUND FLOOR	**93**					
No Insulation		0.73	68	2444	£52	£43
25mm Expanded Polystyrene		0.50	47	1674	£36	£29
50mm Expanded Polystyrene		0.35	33	1172	£25	£21
75mm Expanded Polystyrene		0.27	25	904	£19	£16
	HOUSE VOLUME (in m3)	NO. of AIR CHANGES/ HOUR				
VENTILATION	**410**					
Very Leaky		2.0	271	9742	£207	£171
Leaky		1.5	203	7306	£156	£128
Average		1.0	135	4871	£104	£85
Good		0.5	68	2435	£52	£43
Heat Recovery System		0.3	34	1218	£26	£21

10g

	Cost	Saving
EXCELLENT		
Do without Open Fire and Chimney	Save £1400	£50
Passive Solar design	No cost	£30
Run Appliances on Off-Peak Electricity	£30/annum	£70
Use a Gas Tumble Dryer	£50	£25
Cook by Gas instead of Electricity	£150	£50
Choose the Right Fuel	zero-£400	£90
Fastidious Draught Proofing	£200	£50
Fit a Gas-fired Condensing Boiler	£300-£500	£60
Buy Efficient Electrical Appliances	£200	£40
MODERATE		
Switch to Timber Frame Construction	£0-£3000	£50
Add an extra 25mm of Ground Floor Insulation	£60	£10
Add Extra Cavity Wall Insulation	£150	£20
Put 200mm of Insulation in the Roofspace	£40	£5
Fit Better Space Heating Controls	£200	£20
Design an Energy Saving Lighting Scheme	£500	£45
Fit a Super-lagged, Quick Recovery Cylinder	£50	£5
POOR		
Fit better cold bridge insulation	£150	£5
Fit Argon-filled, Low E Double Glazing	£150	£15
Fit High Performance Windows	£200	£10
Fit Solar Panels	£2000	£40
Fit a Heat Recovery System	£1500	£0

The NHER assessment of the benchmark house, as built, scored it 8.7 out of 10, rather better than the average for houses constructed to the 1995 building regulations. This equates to an annual fuel bill of £850 including VAT at 5% — see Table 10b a few pages back.

Now the benchmark house was never designed as a "green" house which would have fantastically low running costs, and yet it is interesting to note that the combined bills for space heating, water heating and coal come to just 50% of the total fuel bills. Much of the literature and advertising you see aimed at selfbuilders and professionals alike goes on and on about *thermal-efficiency this* and *energy-saving that* and how you must have this gizmo to have low heating bills and save the planet; but a balanced view of all this will show you that you already have low heating bills in a new house and that if you want to lower overall fuel bills then it is best to concentrate on other areas.

Table 10g summarises twenty-one commonly considered energy saving measures that can be taken by the householder wanting a low energy consuming house with low fuel bills. Details on most of these measures are looked at in greater depth in their relevant sections in other parts of the book, but here they are grouped together for easier comparison. The results I find rather extraordinary; the most cost effective measures are generally the least talked about and the least advertised and, conversely, the products which tend to get "sold" to us as being ultra-green are often of very doubtful value.

Open Fires

The single most effective energy saving measure a new housebuilder can take is to do away with an open fire at the design stage. Fires are a costly feature to build (£1200 in the benchmark house), they are inefficient in terms of heat output and, when not in use, the chimney sucks up warm air like a vacuum cleaner. Despite this, people (otherwise known as the market) love real fires and they are unlikely to go out of fashion for a while to come. Using an enclosed stove doubles the heating efficiency of an open fire but halves the enjoyment value. See the sections Fires and Chimneys (Chapter 7, Superstructure) and Alternative Heating (Chapter 8, Services).

Passive Solar Design

Sounds very grand but all it means is orienting your dayrooms so that they face south. Usually the possibility of doing this is dictated by the site and, given the choice, most people would opt for it instinctively. A good passive solar design will save around £30/annum in fuel bills.

Off-peak Electricity

Switch to an Economy 7 meter and, for an additional standing charge of around £20/annum, you get 7 hours night-time electricity at under 40% of peak-rate cost. Buy appliances with timers (or buy separate timers for £20) and run appliances at off-peak rates. Potential saving: £50/annum.

This is saving you money but isn't, strictly speaking, saving energy. Night-time electricity use is no different to daytime use in this respect. However the reason night-time electricity is cheap is that there is comparatively little demand for electricity at night and yet they can't shut down all the power stations — especially the nuclear ones — at the flick of a switch. So using electricity at night is

Running power hungry appliances like tumble dryers at night requires a delay timer and a little discipline. An accessible wall socket helps too.

saving energy indirectly because it would otherwise probably be wasted. See following section, Kitchen and Laundry.

Gas Tumble dryers

Buying a gas-fired tumble drier will pay for itself within two years. One for gas customers only. See following section, Kitchen and Laundry.

Gas Cooking

Gas cooking is much cheaper than electric. Gas hobs are priced the same as electric ones but gas ovens are considerably more expensive. Even so, it is well worth buying one. See following section, Kitchen and Laundry.

Fuel Choices

Oil and gas are currently the two most efficient fuels. Specifying one of these fuels will save around £90/annum, though installation charges will offset this to an extent — see section on Fuel Choices in Chapter 8, Services.

Draught Proofing

Table 10f shows the costs of having a leaky house. Paying proper attention to draught proofing is well worthwhile and not expensive. See also section on Ventilation in Chapter 8, Services. Unplanned ventilation, as it is sometimes known, is likely to be a much bigger problem in complex shaped homes with lots of junctions.

Condensing Boilers

A gas-fired heating system run off a condensing boiler will cost an extra £300-£500 to install and should save £60/annum on heating and hot water costs. Really alone of the high-tech green gizmos, the condensing boiler is genuinely cost effective. Oil-fired condensers are very much more expensive and are, therefore, only rate moderate. See section on Boilers in Chapter 8, Services.

Efficient Appliances

Washing machines, electric tumble dryers, dishwashers, each cost around £40/annum in electricity to run. Fridges and freezers cost around £25 each. Specify "low energy" models when buying new and you could save 25% on these annual costs. See following section, Kitchen and Laundry.

Floor Insulation

The benchmark house was built with 50mm of floor insulation; anticipated annual heat loss through such a groundfloor would be £25. Until 1995, you could build a ground floor with no insulation, but the amended regs make floor insulation virtually mandatory. Expanded polystyrene floor insulation is cost effective up to 75mm. See section on Sub-floors in Chapter 7, Superstructure.

Extra Cavity Wall Insulation

It is now very unusual to build a house without external wall insulation, but many people are building with the bare minimum needed to get a U value of 0.45 — this tends to equate to 65mm of glass fibre. Increasing the insulation width to 100mm or more is going to reduce the U value to 0.3 which will save around £20/annum. The cost of the extra insulation will be about £1/m², equivalent to £150 on the benchmark house. Furthermore you should be able to build with a cavity of this width without adding to other costs, though expect to pay a bit more for longer wall ties. NB. This section does not apply to timber frame walls.

Extra Loft Insulation

Standard practice in lofts now is to install 150mm of insulation: anticipated annual heat loss at this level is just £20. Increasing the insulation to 200mm thick will cost an extra £42 and reduce annual heat loss by £3 to £4. Above 250mm thick, the payback period extends well beyond 10 years.

Heating Controls

Almost all central heating controls are cost effective, though the savings are hard to quantify. Generally speaking, it is worth spending money on good controls though some of the more advanced controls, like boiler managers and zone control, are not appropriate to every situation. Thermostatic radiator valves (TRVs) will cost an extra £90; system managers are available for an extra £100. See section on Heating Controls in Chapter 8, Services.

Low-energy Lighting

Annual electricity bill for lighting a four-bedroom house is likely to be around £120: compact fluorescent "energy saving" bulbs are cost effective, but are not suitable in every situation. A well designed lighting scheme might save £45/annum in running costs but is likely to cost £500+ to install. See following section, Energy Efficient Lighting.

Better Hot Water Cylinders

All new cylinders are pre-lagged to reduce heat loss to a minimum, though some are better than others: look for one with 50mm of polyurethane insulation. A "quick recovery" cylinder will cost an extra £50 to buy but will save £5/annum in making better use of boiler output. See section on Domestic Hot Water in Chapter 8, Services.

Low E Glass

Using Low E glass sealed units on the benchmark house would save around £15/annum over ordinary double glazing. However, the extra cost is likely to be £250. (£500 v £700). If you do go for Low E glass, the argon filled units are only slightly more expensive and do improve performance significantly, but they need to be seated in joinery that can take a 20mm thick unit and such joinery is 20% more expensive than the industry standard. See section on Glazing in Chapter 7, Superstructure.

Avoiding Cold Bridges

Cold bridges occur where the outer skin of the house is returned to meet the inner skin: they occur around windows and doors and reduce the overall thermal efficiency of the walls by about 5% (although much less in timber frame construction). This form of heat leakage has been addressed in the current building regulations which now insist on there being at least a thin strip of insulation to provide a thermal break between the masonry skins. There are a number of different products on the market which you can use to do this job. Costing around £2/lin.m (£150 overall on the benchmark house), *Damcor* is reckoned to be the cheapest — it's basically just an inch of polystyrene stuck onto a plastic DPC. There are better made alternatives such as *Thermabate* (a plastic filler) but they cost twice as much and as the total heat leakage through cold bridging on the benchmark house would have been in the order of £5 without any form of thermal break, it is hard to justify spending more than the bare minimum. Of course, you don't have to use a proprietary product and ingenious builders should be able to improvise this detail without too much trouble.

Timber Frame Walls

90mm timber stud walls perform very well thermally, reducing annual heat loss from around £55 (masonry construction with 0.45 U value) to around £40. Also timber frame housing tends to be less draughty than masonry construction: if this sounds confusing you'd do well to refer to the section on Ventilation. There is, however, often a cost penalty for building in timber frame. Expect to pay at least £2500-£3000 extra for building in timber frame if you are adapting a masonry design, much more if building with a pre-designed kit home. Note, however, that there are some house designs which will be cheaper to build in timber frame so it's hard

(meaningless?) to try and put a figure on the capital costs. See Inner Skin section in Chapter 7, Superstructure.

Solar Panels

Don't be tempted by solar panels unless they cost less than £300, not on cost grounds at any rate. Annual savings are likely to be less than £40. See Alternative Heating section in Chapter 8, Services.

High Performance Windows

These are timber windows which will accept double-glazed sealed units with air gaps of 12mm, which are around 25% more thermally efficient than the standard air gap of 6mm: there is no added cost in making the sealed units thicker, and the annual heat saving would be in the order of £10-£20. However, whilst the glazing units may not cost anymore, the high performance windows

themselves cost 20% more increasing the window budget by around £200. See Windows section in Chapter 7, Superstructure.

Heat Recovery Systems

These are justifiable in terms of energy savings but not in terms of financial savings. They cost a great deal (£1500+) and they cost more to run than they could possibly save. Even a system which saves three times the amount of energy it consumes is still going to cost you, because the energy saved costs around 2p/kWh whilst the energy used to run the thing costs over 7p/kWh (i.e. peak-rate electricity). See Ventilation section in Chapter 8, Services for a more information about MVHR (as it gets referred to) and also passive stack ventilation, a non-mechanical alternative which is more cost effective.

Energy Efficient Lighting

The annual cost of lighting the benchmark house will be around £135, which is 16% of the total fuel bill and is larger than the bill for domestic hot water (£100) and exactly half the cost of the space heating (£230). Lighting is expensive because a) it is inefficient (95% of the energy coming out of a standard GLS light bulb is heat) and b) it is using peak-rate electricity at around five times the price of oil or gas. If you are considering spending a lot of money on energy-saving features, then you would do well to examine your proposed lighting scheme.

Saving that Juice

The benchmark house has 25 light outlets fitted and in normal usage patterns about a third of these will be heavily used, a third will be lightly used and a third rarely used. On occupation it is likely to gain a few more lamps with the furniture and could be expected to have around 35 lamps to burn when occupied. A typical usage pattern would look something like this:

12 lamps @ 60w, ea. 2000hrs/annum
 1500kWh used, cost £110
12 lamps @ 60w, ea. 500hrs/annum
 350kWh used, cost £25
10 lamps @ 60w, ea. 50hrs/annum
 30kWh used, cost £2.

Anyone wanting to attack these costs would of course do well to concentrate on the areas of heavy usage, which are generally kitchens, living rooms, hallways, stairwells and stud-

A compact fluorescent lightbulb: they produce real enough savings but you need to give careful consideration to their installation

ies; even the areas of light use (typically bedroom and bathroom lighting) unlikely to produce any significant savings. You could simply substitute your 12 most heavily used GLS bulbs with compact fluorescent, energy saving bulbs — for an explanation of what these are see Chapter 8. Extra cost around £120: annual saving as much as £60. Problem is that energy saving light bulbs are not always particularly suitable as direct replacements for GLS bulbs; they cannot be easily dimmed, the light quality tends to be a bit

too cold for most people's taste, and they are generally not compatible with standard lampshades. Some years back, a Blue Peter survey found that 70% of UK households had one low-energy light bulb and that, of those, 70% would never buy another one. Substituting fluorescent light for tungsten light makes for subtle changes in atmosphere, and ill-planned installation can end up putting people off energy-saving light bulbs for good. Energy efficient lighting doesn't have to be bad lighting but for too many people this is exactly what it becomes when they swap over to a compact fluorescent bulb.

The second most efficient light source (after the sun) is a pendant light hanging centrally in a room. A medium-sized room can get adequate ambient (background) light from this source and no more. Spotlights, uplighters and especially downlighters are more specialised fittings with more specialised functions but using them exclusively for general lighting becomes expensive to install and expensive to run. However, central pendant lighting is also rather bad lighting and is definitely unexciting; almost all lighting consultants will bat off about how it is to be avoided at all costs and perhaps they are right but only you can decide.

Kitchens

Fluorescent lighting can work well in the kitchen — specialised lights can be used for both task and background lighting.

Living Areas

In contrast, fluorescent lighting will not work well in living rooms and dining rooms. Low-voltage downlighting is an option (they use roughly half the power of a GLS bulb but twice the power of a fluorescent) but because of the tightly focused nature of the beams, you will end up using twice as many fittings which neatly cancels out their 50% efficiency rating over GLS bulbs. Low-voltage does not have to be confined to downlighters and a well-de-signed scheme could achieve adequate lighting from half the number of lamps by using mini-spots and/or uplighters.

Hallways and Stairs

The other areas of heavy use tend to be in hallways and stairwells. Arguably light quality is not so important here and there are numerous compact fluorescent (CF) fittings which will fit the task. Whilst you may struggle to get a CF bulb to look good in a lampshade, the small 9w bulbs do fit into most uplighters and there are an increasing number of specialised low-energy light fittings becoming available; downlighters, glazed ceiling fittings and wall lights. They tend to cost around £30 where the conventional fittings might be had for under a tenner and so they need to be heavily used to justify the extra expense.

External

If you plan on external lights either control them with timed passive infra-red (PIR) switches or, if you want them on permanently, use low-energy fittings. As for utility rooms and garages, fluorescent lights are commonly used here in any event and they can't readily be improved on.

Intelligent Switches

Don't overlook the fact that one of the best ways to save lighting bills is to turn lights off when they are not being used. However, if you've got a house full of stroppy teenagers this may not be quite as easy as it sounds. You can of course fit time switches in hallways and stairwells but they tend to be a bit institutional. We are now quite used to seeing PIR switching used for external security but its use indoors to control lighting is still rare, but no more expensive than external PIRs (prices from around £25). Home Automation (01249 443422) produce an informative price list which includes such things as well as dimmer switches for low-voltage and compact fluorescent lighting.

Summary

A low-energy lighting scheme needs to be carefully designed to be successful. With potential savings of £50/annum, it is worth spending money on too — which you will have to. There is precious little professional advice available on the subject — many lighting consultants will specify lots of low-voltage halogen fittings that will cost you much money but which won't save on running costs. Many architects know next to nothing about lighting design and electricians are taught only the rudiments of good lighting practice. How much you spend on energy saving features is entirely up to you but if your budget extends much past £500 on a four-bedroom house like the benchmark house, then you are unlikely to get cost effective savings.

Kitchen and Laundry

Together with lighting, household appliances are the great unseen energy consumers. An examination of the fuel costs for a new home reveal that, even without specifying super-insulation levels and condensing boilers, fuel bills are actually higher for cooking, kitchen appliances and lighting than they are for space and hot water heating. Yet with a little application it should be possible to reduce running costs by nearly half.

Table 10h includes a breakdown of estimated fuel costs for cooking and household appliances in the benchmark house using the standard arrangements and comparing them with the cheapest alternative. The "normal" arrangement assumes all electric appliances using peak rate power: the "cheapest" assumes a mains gas supply is available. These are very much notional average bills; a "dinky" house-hold, without children, might well run up bills less than half this amount whilst a large family could easily double the sums.

Cooking

Gas cooking is way cheaper than using electricity; cooking by gas costs almost a quarter of what costs to cook using peak-rate electricity. Many people prefer cooking on a gas hob (and most developer's packages offer them as an alternative at no extra cost) but gas ovens have an undeservedly poor reputation and they are now few and far between, particularly in the built-in market. Electric controls and electronic ignition have greatly improved the traditional gas oven and if you use a main oven or grill more than one hour a week, it will be worth paying the extra £150 to install a gas oven. Stoves, Canon, Parkinson Cowan, New World still produce them; British Gas showrooms (now called Energy Centres) display them but are an expensive place to buy. MFI has a number of cheaply priced gas ovens (made for them by Philips and Stoves). If mains gas is not available, then LPG models will still produce 50% savings on electric cooking.

If electric cooking is the only sensible option, there is currently very little one can do to reduce costs. Energy efficiency has yet to make any significant impact on this area, but note that microwaves are very efficient at cooking small quantities. Microwaves are quick and work at much lower power than conventional electric cookers: on the other hand, food bought ready for microwaving is expensive. It all depends on how you use them.

10h: Running Costs of Household Appliances

	USE	NORMAL	CHEAPEST
Cooking	400hrs/annum	£90	£25
Fridge/Freezer	Constant	£38	£25
Washing Machine	300 times/annum	£45	£20
Dishwasher	350 times/annum	£55	£20
Tumble Dryer	200hrs/annum	£35	£8
TV/Video	1500hrs/annum	£15	£14
Other Appliances		£20	£18
Electricity Standing Charge		£44	£65
TOTAL		**£ 342**	**£ 195**

Note that cast iron stoves — and Agas in particular — are very heavy users of fuel. A gas- or oil-fired Aga kept on all year would cost over £400/annum to run.

Tumble Dryers

If mains gas is available, then go for a gas-fired tumble dryer. Canon and Crosslee White Knight both produce reasonably priced gas tumble dryers. Expect to pay £220plus which is 50% more than the cheapest electric versions, and allow for gas plumbing, but they are very much cheaper to run — payback period is around five years.

Off-peak Electricity

If you are unable to get mains gas, then fit an Economy 7 meter and you can take advantage of electricity at around 40% of the peak rate by arranging to use your appliances during the off-peak hours. If you don't lead a nocturnal lifestyle, then buy equipment with delay timers (Bosch dishwashers, some expensive Hotpoint and Creda tumble dryers, some Hoover and Hotpoint washing machines) or make sure that you can easily access the sockets and fit separate delay timers (cost £15-20). Despite the large savings to be had, delay timers still hardly feature as a sales aid: you have to go looking for them.

Off-peak electricity charges are complex to understand; each supply company (REC) sets its own charges.

- All of them increase the standing charge (tariff) for letting you buy cheap rate supplies. These increased tariffs vary from £15 to £25/annum extra).
- All of them have an off-peak rate of around 2.5p/kWh (compared with peak rates of 7p/kWh or higher) at which you will be charged for all electricity supplies for seven hours each night.

The economies to be gained from using an off-peak tariff will vary from area to area, but if properly managed it should result in a reduction in electricity bills of 15%, perhaps more.

Hot and Cold Fill

Look for dishwashers and washing machines which can be filled from your hot water pipes rather than heating their own water. This is now standard on new washing machines but is still rare on dishwashers (though Ariston make one). If using machines on delayed night-time switching, then separate H&C fill is of little benefit as the disparity between the costs of off-peak electrically heated water and boiler heated water is much reduced.

Energy-efficient?

Many manufacturers are jumping on the bandwagon in claiming to produce machines which save on electricity, water and detergents. This is a complicated area and many of the claims are at best marginal and depend on the user understanding just what is expected of them. To help spread a little light into this murky area, fridges, freezers and washing machines are now routinely energy labelled to help the customer make an informed decision about how much power they use. A visit to my local Curry's revealed a wide range scores: a Bosch *Economic* fridge freezer scored A and reckoned to use just 120kWh/annum (cost £8) whilst a giant Hotpoint power guzzler scored G, estimated to use 544kWh/annum (cost £38). Whilst the accuracy of energy labelling (which is carried out by the manufacturers) has been called into question (Which? Jun. 96), the fact that there is now a comparative yardstick available on a range of white goods is a big boon.

Although these savings may not look individually very large, careful purchasing should be able to save £50 or more per annum of peak rate power and metered water. Water saving washing machines actually save remarkably little in cash terms and yet it is this feature which tends to be the strongest selling point on "Green" appliances.

For most buyers, there will be a number of other factors which will determine which machines they purchase — notably servic-

ing costs and standards, reliability record, easy-to-use controls or perhaps it just all came with the kitchen — and you may well be right to base your decision on these criteria, but don't be afraid to ask about water and electricity use. It is worth paying a little more for machines which perform well but, with the exception of cold storage, running the appliances during off-peak hours is by far the best option if you want to save on running costs. Don't be conned into paying out hundreds of pounds extra for "eco" products which bring minimal savings to you or the environment; instead, ask why it hasn't got a delay switch fitted.

Use of Appliances

Considerable savings can be achieved by using your appliances efficiently. Really these are no more than commonsense measures

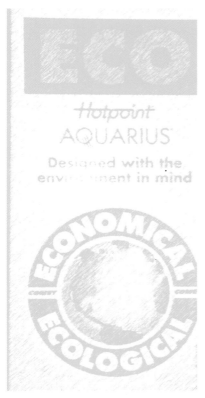

10j: Energy Efficient Appliances

	AVERAGE	BEST	ANNUAL COST SAVING
Washing Machine: Electricity Use	2kW	1.5kW	£12
Washing Machine: Water Use	90lts	70lts	£4
Dishwasher: Electricity Use	2kW	1.5kW	£12
Dishwasher: Water Use	35lts	25lts	£2
Electric Tumble Dryers	2.5kW	2kW	£10
Fridge/Freezers	500kWh	300kWh	£15

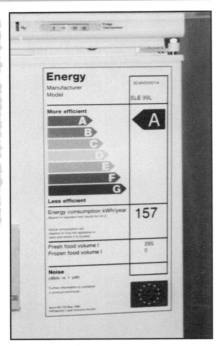

Energy labelling of electrical appliances is slowly catching on. To date it's mostly fridges, freezers and the odd washing machine

such as drying clothes on washing lines whenever possible, setting washing machine temperatures as low as possible and turning off lights when rooms are empty. If you've a genuine interest in energy conservation — or just don't like paying bills — then at least part of the solution is in your hands.

Summary

Energy-efficient appliances — or more particularly energy-efficient use of appliances — can be planned into a new house. The presence of gas on site makes for large cost savings but, even on remoter sites where gas is not available, there are numerous actions you can take to increase fuel efficiency. There is a cost penalty (though it is hard to quantify because there are so many variables) but there are also appreciable savings to be made. However, unlike installing insulation or efficient heating systems, saving energy in the kitchen requires you to interact intelligently with your machines and for many people this is just too much hassle.

Noise

Nobody wants a noisy house. Nobody wants noisy neighbours either. But very few people give much thought to either problem when they are designing new detached homes. There are regulations governing the control of noise levels — these are covered by Part E of the Building Regs — but these are largely concerned with the control of sound within buildings in multiple occupation, such as terraced housing and, in particular, flats where close attention is paid to these details.

If you are building a detached house in a reasonably quiet neighbourhood, then you probably don't need to be concerned with sound insulation. Yet there are many situations where correct detailing at the design stage would make for a considerably nicer house to live in. Detached houses can sometimes be in noisy locations such as under a flight path or close by a busy road and it is well worth specifying solutions that will cut down on noise.

Mass Law

The most fundamental principle in sound insulation is the so-called Mass Law. It's actually fiendishly complicated but in layman's terms it translates that heavy dense objects absorb sound much better than light ones. Deduce from this that masonry construction performs rather better than timber or steel frame constructions (which are both essentially hollow skeletons). Cavity walls are pretty good sound deadeners whatever the materials but two leaves of masonry (as in a brick and block wall) will always outperform a timber-frame and brick cavity wall construction. More importantly, if you are worried about sound transmission between floors, then you would be well advised to build your first floor out of concrete beams infilled with concrete blocks rather than the more usual timber joists covered with a layer of chipboard. However this is an expensive option, likely to add £500 or more to construction costs on a detached house and, of course, you can only build a masonry block

floor on top of masonry walls — i.e. it's not an option in a timber frame house where, arguably, the problem is going to be worse in any event. Not that timber frame houses perform particularly badly in this respect. I have found that the problems of sound transmission through timber stud walls are minimal, particularly now that nearly everyone is using building with 12.5mm plasterboard rather than 9.5mm — the extra thickness makes for big improvements.

Impact Sound

The sound that really does carry through a house is impact sound, caused by such things as stiletto heels walking across a hardwood floor or children banging toys. Sound moves in many mysterious ways; it's not just a question of volume or pitch and one of the ways that it makes its presence felt is via vibrations travelling along floors and up walls. Hard surfaces such as hardwood or tiled floors can transmit noises like footsteps right throughout a house, not enough to wake you up in the night but enough to make you wonder sometimes what it would have been like if you'd put carpet down instead.

There are numerous techniques for improving sound insulation in existing dwellings where it is not possible to replace major elements like floors but if you are starting from scratch and you are worried about noise levels, then go for dense masonry construction every time. If aircraft noise is a particular concern, then go for a heavy roof cover such as a clay or concrete plain tile (or thatch).

Windows

Double glazing is now mandatory in new build and one of the supposed benefits of double glazing is that it reduces sound trans-

mission. But whereas the optimum gap between panes for thermal insulation is between 12 and 20mm, the best gap for good sound insulation is around 150mm, the type of gap you get when you fit secondary glazing rather than the integral sealed units which are now required in a new house. The narrow gap sealed units do help sound insulation but not by very much (and at some frequencies they actually make matters worse). The little research that has been done in this area suggests that there is little difference between timber and uPVC frames and that seemingly incidental details like the quality of the gaskets or mastics surrounding the frames has a disproportionate effect on the sound reduction.

Bathrooms and WCs

There is a requirement for these rooms to be soundproofed rather better than other rooms. With masonry construction there is no problem but with timber walls you are required to either fix two 12.5mm sheets of plasterboard to each face of the wall or fill the void in the wall with mineral wool quilt such as Rockwool (which is a much cheaper solution and the one everyone now uses). Alternatively, use a superior wallboard such as Fermacell which allows you to a) use just one thickness and b) hang things like basins and loo roll holders off it without having to work out beforehand where to put the timber supports.

Saving Water

Although 95% of UK property is still charged for water and sewage by a rating system, newly constructed housing is invariably metered. Living with a metered water supply is a novel experience for most of us and it takes some getting used to. If you are connecting your drains into the main drains as well as tapping into the local water supplies, your bills will be broken down into four sections:
* Standing charge for water supply
  * Volume charge for water supply
* Standing charge for sewage disposal
  * Volume charge for sewage disposal.

Properties that dispose of waste by other means (usually septic tanks) will have other costs to pay instead of sewage charges — see section on Drains (Chapter 6, Groundworks).

Water Charges

Unlike fuel prices, water supply charges are on the way up. The average charge levied in England and Wales has doubled since 1989 and is only now beginning to level off. Average charge for water by volume is 65p/m^3, although this can vary between a high of £1.09/m^3 (Mid Sussex) to a low of 41p/m^3 (in nearby Portsmouth). In addition standing charges average £23/annum.

Sewage Disposal Charges

Average charge is 64p/m^3, but this varies from 40p in Northumbria to £1.49/m^3 in the South West. Welsh and Anglian also charge well above average. Annual standing charges payable for sewage disposal vary from £9 to £64 with an average of just over £30. As a rule, companies with high standing charges have low volume charges and vice versa, so it does tend to even out.

1000lts of water = 1m^3 = 220 gallons = 12 baths = 120 flushing loos. When metered, this much water costs between £1.50 and £2.50 to use and pour away.

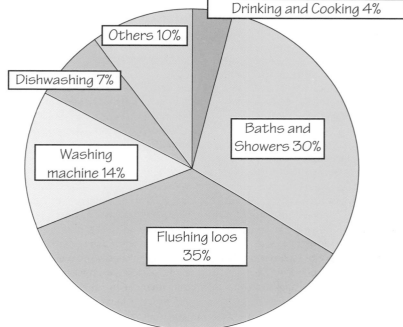

Drinking and Cooking 4%
Others 10%
Dishwashing 7%
Baths and Showers 30%
Washing machine 14%
Flushing loos 35%

Metering: how it works

Only the water supply is metered. The volume of discharge you pour back down the drains is worked out from the amounts of water you consume: some companies reckon it to be 100%, some 95% and some 90%. If yours works on a 95% figure then, if you were to consume 100m^3 of water, you would be charged for 95m^3 of sewage.

A four-person household will typically use and discharge 185m^3 of water/annum (equivalent to 2300 baths, that's just over six baths a day). This is likely to cost them between £300 and £450/annum depending on how much their water company charges. This

185m^3 figure is very much an average and a new house with lots of thirsty appliances like dishwashers and power showers, not to mention children, could easily use 50% more. (Incidentally our household of five has all these thirsty appliances and we consistently consume 230m^3 of water per annum). Heavy demand from swimming pools, garden sprinklers and the like would be in addition to these figures.

Comparisons

The charges for average water usage are larger than the anticipated heating bills for a new home. Assuming the average 185m^3/annum is consumed by our notional four-person

10k: Water Appliance Consumption

Av. Consumption/head	*150lts/day*
Flushing a Loo	*7-10lts*
Taking a Bath	*80lts*
Ordinary Shower	*10lts/min*
Power Shower	*30lts/min*
Washing Machines	*70-100lts/wash*
Dishwashers	*25-50lts/wash*
Garden Hose/Sprinkler	*10lts/min*
Tap Dripping Once a Second	*5lts/hr*

household, the average bill, including standing charges, will be just over £300/annum. However, in some high charging areas such as the South West this could rise to over £450 for the same volume of water. In comparison, the estimated space *and* water heating costs for the benchmark house are £330 — including 8% VAT which is not levied on water and sewage services. With so much attention focused on saving energy, let us try to redress the balance and look at reducing water consumption. The pie chart illustrates how we consume our water.

What immediately stands out about these figures is how little water actually passes into our bodies (4%) compared to how much is consumed largely to keep us and our homes clean and hygienic. Part of the justification for higher water prices is that our drinking water standards are too low but, on reflection, it seems extraordinary that we should go to such trouble to purify our water supplies in order to pour 95% back down the drains. In theory, at least, there is ample scope to use non-potable water and ample savings to be made by avoiding relatively expensive metered supplies.

Use Less

Before delving into esoteric water-saving schemes, there are a number of common-sense ways that water consumption can be reduced without making you smell:

- Wash yourself under showers, not in baths (impractical with small children)
- Don't fit a power shower
- Fit the smallest WC cisterns possible — the industry standard is now 7lt. cistern but the Shires Aqua uses only 6lt per flush and this would save around £10/annum
- Don't run washing machines and dishwashers unless they are full

- Don't water lawns; water plants in the evening to avoid evaporation
- Use water butts (though attractive ones are hard to find)
- Don't build a swimming pool
- Pee anywhere except in the loo — easier for some sexes than others.

Water Saving

Water-saving schemes are sommat else. They can be divided into two areas: rainwater collection which replaces water you'd normally buy through your water meter and grey water collection which recycles some of the water you have already used.

Rainwater Collection

Even in dry lowland England (average rainfall = 750mm/annum) a four-bedroom house plus detached garage will get around 100m³ of rain falling on to it during the course of a year. Add in a paved yard and a drive and potentially you could collect your entire 185m³ annual consumption from the skies overhead. In wetter areas to the north and west this figure could easily double as rainfall levels are so much higher. The potential is there; the problem is that rainfall is not only unpredictable but sporadic whereas household usage is basically quite constant. You need to build a reservoir capable of holding enough rainwater to supply basic household needs, which is exactly what your own water company does on a much larger scale. Starting your very own water supply business may be an appealing prospect for some but it is likely to prove expensive to build and time-consuming to run. The bigger your reservoir, the more effective your own supplies will be in replacing your metered supply, but the more problems you are likely to have with construction and maintenance. If you do decide to build a rainwater collection system,

you won't be alone. Hardy souls have ventured before you and they occasionally get written up in magazines like *Build It*.

Perhaps a more logical approach would be to use a swimming pool as a rainwater reservoir. If you are prepared to go to the expense of building a swimming pool (which has most of the infrastructure required to store rainwater), then combining it with a water-saving scheme would probably add just a few hundred pounds to the scheme as well as significantly reducing the cost of filling the pool each year. However, if you can afford a swimming pool the chances are you won't be too bothered by the size of your water bills, but there's no accounting for taste.

The obvious objection to collecting rainwater is that it might not be fit to drink; even if it was when it fell out of the sky, it probably wouldn't be by the time it came out of your tap. Installing a purification system is one possibility but realistically this is too much hassle for a single household; another approach is to ensure that these supplies are not used for drinking or cooking. Another problem to be addressed is that though your rain-saving scheme might significantly cut down on your purchases of water, you haven't decreased the amount you are dumping down the drains. As over half your water charges are levied in order to collect and treat your mains sewage, if your water company ever cottoned on to what was happening, they would have a case to penalise you by increasing the sewage charges.

Grey Water

Only a water recycling scheme will cut down both supply and discharge. Grey water is the term given to waste which is reusable, notably the waste from baths, showers and wash basins. There is potential to recycle this water in the garden and especially for flushing loos. Because the waste from baths and washing is much more regular than rainfall, the storage facilities do not have to be nearly as large to be effective. A large bath sized tank will be enough to flush ten loos and should get refilled most days.

Various designs are possible and whilst converting an existing dwelling so as to recycle bath water would probably be prohibitively expensive, it is a far different story when building a new house. The kit already exists in the form of bathroom pumps which are designed for getting waste up from basement bathrooms into drains; Pump Technology (01734 821555) produce a suitable unit called *The Drainmaster* (£380) which is capable of clearing waste water from baths and washing machines and pumping it up 3m to a con-

10I: Water Charges for New Dwellings

ANNUAL CHARGES			
	WATER	**SEWAGE**	**COMBINED**
Average Standing Charges	£23	£32	**£55**
Average Volume Charges	£0.65 m³	£0.64 m³	**£1.29 m³**

WATER USED BY 4 PERSON HOUSEHOLD			ANNUAL VOLUME CHARGES		
ACTIVITY	Litres/day	As %	WATER	SEWAGE	COMBINED
Drinking/Cooking	20	4%	£5	£5	**£9**
Baths/Showers	150	30%	£36	£35	**71**
Flushing Loos	175	35%	£42	£41	**82**
Washing Machine	70	14%	£17	£16	**33**
Dishwasher	35	7%	£8	£8	**16**
Others	50	10%	£12	£12	**24**
TOTAL	500	100%	£119	£117	**235**
STANDING CHARGES + VOLUME CHARGES			**£142**	**£149**	**£290**

VARIATIONS	
4 person household, Highest charging area (South West)	£450
4 person household, Lowest charging area (Northumbria)	£260
Average for 3 person household	£230
Average for 2 person household	£170
Average for 1 person household	£110

ventional 227lt loft tank (£100) which would provide adequate grey water storage. Gravity and ball valves would do the rest.

There are now proprietary grey water systems available using pumps and a small holding tank which can be placed in the loft. The grey water is treated with cleaning agents and passed through a carbon filter. I have come across two firms producing them, Aquasaver and WD Water Dynamics, and both are producing grey water units at just under the £1000 mark. If they are as effective as claimed, this will pay for itself in around ten years in a four-person metered household.

Potential

By combining rain-saving and grey water systems, the potential is there to reduce water demand in new housing by over 50%. Whilst the legislation dealing with carbon dioxide emissions (our thermal building regs) has grown steadily more onerous on the housebuilder, water saving has yet to be seriously considered. Yet the harmful effect of CO_2 — the so-called greenhouse effect — remains an unproven hypothesis (albeit with potentially catastrophic consequences), whilst the effects on the environment caused by reservoir building are all too tangible. The best that can be hoped for is that the whole area could be given a much needed boost by exempting developments incorporating water saving schemes from the perilous infrastructure charge — see Chapter 3, Pitfalls.

Still, despite the water shortages experienced during the summers of 95 and 96, interest in recycling water is virtually nonexistent other than people installing the odd water butt. There have been a range of pioneer schemes carried out by groups like the Centre for Alternative Technology but these have tended to focus on the potential to naturally digest foul waste by using a series of ponds, something which is not applicable to 98% of new housing because of the lack of garden space. But if we experience any more droughts the field is open for a rapid uptake of more simple grey water scheme, especially in new houses where the supplies are metered.

Paying for Leaks

Whilst the problem of a dripping tap is well known (and costly for metered households), it palls into insignificance compared to the potential nightmare of an underground leak. You, the householder, are responsible for all water consumption downstream from the water meter — which is conventionally located outside, close to the plot boundary. Spring a leak underground between the meter and your internal stop tap and you may know nothing about it until a massive water bill arrives on your doormat (as much as six months later); if you are lucky, the water company will let you off paying the sewage charge but even so a bad leak might lose as much as 20m³ of water a day which would cost £1500 by the time you get your water bill. Be warned that sloppy installation (and loose connections) of water mains can be very expensive once you are on metered supplies.

Boreholes

There is another way of avoiding water company charges — and infrastructure charges — and that is to sink your own borehole and draw your own water supply up from under the ground. It's where most of the water comes from in SE England and in many other areas besides and, whereas your local water company has a monopoly on piped supplies, there is nothing to stop you tapping into the enormous natural groundwater reservoir directly. That's an oversimplification; there is the small matter of installation costs which vary from £1000 and £10,000, depending on such matters as the depth of the borehole and the water pressure. For most people, that makes it an extremely expensive way of going about getting water and sends them straight back into the arms of their local water company.

If you are one of the small number who plan to draw their own water supply from under the ground, then you will be responsible for your own water quality. That's not to say that you won't have to submit your water for analysis to the local Environmental Health Inspector: indeed most councils will be around testing you every couple of years or so. Simple bacteria tests tend to be done in local hospitals and cost around £30, however tests for pollution are more expensive — I was quoted £100 for a nitrate test. The Environmental Health Inspector has the power to condemn your supply but this rarely happens because almost everything can be filtered out — at a cost. My local inspector reckoned that ground water pollution was something of an overstated problem and that when he did come across it it was very often the house itself that was the cause of the pollution; he advised not to use ground water supplies in conjunction with a septic tank. Obvious when you think about it.

Water Treatment

There are two very distinct processes here. You soften (or condition) water in an attempt to prolong the life of your domestic appliances, whereas you filter water in an attempt to prolong your own life. Both techniques are surrounded by a veil of mystery and intrigue which is hard to penetrate, and the whole subject is so rife with claim and counterclaim that it makes the job of the humble commentator akin to negotiating a minefield. Wish me luck as I go in.

Softening and Conditioning

If you live in a soft water area (which includes most of Britain above a line drawn between the Humber and the Severn) then this section is one to miss. If in doubt, phone your water company to get figures on local conditions. Even if you live in a hard water area there is no need to panic. Households have been known to function quite adequately for years without so much as a hint of any water softeners about. However, many sane people swear by water softeners and insist that they produce tangible benefits — even if it's only to reduce the amount of soap powder they use in their washing machines

Traditional Softeners

Permutit are the best known name here though there are a number of other manufacturers. For between £400 and £1000 you get a big box into which you add salt – you need around three 25kg bags of salt per person per annum, so this alone will cost you £20 each every year. Softeners work by sepa-

A phosphate conditioner plumbed into the feeder main to a mains pressure cylinder

rating out the hard bits in the water, exchanging them for softer sodium bits. The box needs an electrical supply and a drain-off point. The long-term benefits include reduced water heating bills and savings on soap powders (combined unlikely to be worth more than about £25/annum). Evidence that water softeners increase the lifespan of hot water appliances is — careful now — inconclusive but almost everyone who has one reckons they do make the water feel softer and the laundry appears cleaner.

As these boxes actually chemically change the water supply, their output should not be drunk or cooked with. Design your plumbing system so that the kitchen tap, at least, comes directly from the mains.

Phosphate Conditioners

These are a sort of junior version of the big water softeners. They are designed to stop hot water appliances from scaling up and they are usually sold in conjunction with combination boilers and/or mains pressure hot water cylinders. You will see them in plumber's merchants — look for names like *Combimate* and *Combicare*. They work by adding phosphate solution to the incoming water, which inhibits scale formation — they don't "soften" the water as such but they are reckoned to prolong the life of water-heating equipment in hard water areas.

They cost around £80 and they don't need power or drainage facilities but the phosphate cartridges need replacing every year (cost £15 a time). Again the treated water is not ideal for drinking but these conditioners are normally only fitted with water heating devices.

Inhibitors

Unlike the two preceding methods — which are chemical treatments — inhibitors act by passing a magnetic or an electrical charge through the water which — it is claimed — prevents the hard bits in the water from sticking to the pipes. They are relatively cheap (£30-£60), easy to install and need no maintenance. Also they do not affect drinking water qualities. Some need electrical power, most operate without. But do they work?

You may figure they are so cheap that there is nothing to lose in trying and you may well be right. But how will you know that your investment does the biz? Another thing to ponder on during those long dark nights. During 1995, *Which?* carried out a survey on

this very issue and reported back with a wide range of reactions from "very pleased" to "a complete waste of time and money." If there was any conclusion at all it was that they work in some areas but not in others. Not really very helpful. Leading names are Salamander and Liff, who both produce magnetic versions and electrolytic versions. If you want to know what the difference is (or what reverse osmosis is) then you sound like you're interested enough to make your own enquiries; start your investigations at the plumber's merchant.

Filtering

In the last few years, there has been an enormous growth of interest in the subject of tap water quality. Whereas the Victorians basked in the glory of the technical achievement of providing clean drinking water to all homes, we have now become blasé about this and tend to worry that much of this water runs through lead pipes and, in any event, doesn't taste very good. Added to which there are fears (in lowland England at least) that we are now getting nitrate and pesticide residues in our tap water.

There is now a huge choice of water filters available, ranging from the free standing plastic jug affairs which can be picked up in Boots for a few quid to expensive, in-line purifiers. There are no British Standards for water purifiers ("tap water's just fine, old boy") and there is little concrete evidence on the effectiveness of the various methods. There is also concern that many filters may themselves be health hazards, providing spawning grounds for micro-bacteria. Nevertheless, interest in water filters continues to grow and one of the more innovative companies working in this field is Liff (01484 512537) who supply the whole range of water treatment gizmos from softeners and scale reducers to filters and ultra-violet disinfection units. If you want to find out more, get hold of their *Practical Guide to Water Conditioning*.

Chapter 11
Shopping

Building a house is a complicated process and it involves a number of overlapping activities. Now it follows that writing a book about building a house is also going to involve describing any number of overlapping activities and I've reached the stage in the book where I have to tie together a number of loose strings. The book to date has been littered with contacts and tips, but in this chapter I am looking a little more systematically about how to arrange your purchasing and also covering a number of specific fields that simply didn't get a look in earlier on. First we'll dive in to the tricky matter of how much to buy.

Taking off Quantities

A bill of quantities is a fancy, construction professional's term for a shopping list. Making a comprehensive one is fundamental to controlling costs and is one of the major benefits to derive from having a properly designed, properly specified job. Many times in the past I have measured off plan to estimate a cost and then gone and measured again on site to order materials. I must also admit to having measured three or even four times when the bit of wood I write the measurements on gets nailed into some studwork or gets painted over. If I had taken the advice that I'm offering now I'd be a little bit richer and a little bit fatter. It may just be that you have built so inaccurately that your house does not resemble the plans that were drawn up, but if this is the case then you're playing in a different orchestra to me and there's no help to be proffered; go ahead and skip the rest of this section.

Now serious construction professionals will engage the services of a quantity surveyor (known on site as "the QS") to work out what is needed. However, QSs don't come cheap and many small builders work on their own rules of thumb for estimating the right quantities. These are not usually as accurate as a QS would get them but they are much better than nothing.

Free Take-offs

If you've no experience of this sort of quantification work, then I would tend to steer well clear unless you have loads of time and patience, particularly as many builder's merchants now offer a free take-off service ideally suited to the needs of rookie builders. Much of the repetitive grind of measuring and recording is carried out by computer and, provided the job is relatively straightforward, they are pretty accurate. The closer you stick to industry standard solutions, the better the outcome and they are quite capable of generating accurate results from a basic set of plans and elevations. The materials buying sheets generated for the benchmark house included amount for foundations, masonry work, joinery, lintels, roof covers, carpentry, rainwater gear and sanitaryware; not exhaustive but a good start.

Traditional Route

Let's compare it with the traditional way of doing a takeoff. Traditional here means that your source document is a written schedule of work (often known as the spec), not the plans. You use the plans to calculate the areas and volumes but you work methodically down the written list so as not to miss anything out. To give you a flavour of what I'm on about, here is a clause taken from the benchmark house spec.

• 7.1 External (house) walls of 275 - 280mm 3.5N clinker blockwork cavity work incorporating 75mm Rockwool or similar full fill cavity insulation and 200mm s/s butterfly brick ties at max 900mm horizontal and 450mm vertically and at every block course adjacent to openings. Additional 105mm skin of face brickwork (bricks to clients choice) forming plinth wall and tied to blockwork with s/s butterfly ties as described above. Plinth wall extends 10 courses above DPC.

Hardly a riveting read, but it's clear enough. The job of the QS is, if you like, to rewrite this specification with the quantities added in so that it might read:

• 7.1 158m^2 double skin external (house) walls of 275 - 280mm 3.5N clinker blockwork cavity work incorporating 145m^2 x 75mm Rockwool or similar full fill cavity insulation and 580No. 200mm s/s butterfly brick ties at max 900mm horizontal and 450mm vertically and at every block course adjacent to openings. Additional 55m^2 x105mm skin of face brickwork (bricks to clients choice) forming plinth wall and tied to blockwork with 130No. x s/s butterfly ties as described above. Plinth wall extends 10 courses above DPC.

You don't need any specialised equipment. All you need are your finished plans, a decent ruler, a calculator and a pen and pencil (rubber would be handy). And bags of common sense. If you've got a computer and you know your way around a spreadsheet you'll save yourself a bit of work, but not that much.

Measurements to Take

Take your measurements from your detailed plans (which are now conventionally drawn in metric scale which makes scaling up a damn sight easier). If the distance you want is referred to on the drawings then use it, otherwise you must measure off plan in millimetres and scale up to get actual sizes; thus, if drawings are 1:50, then you multiply your measurement by 50 to get the actual measurement.

Many of the dimensions you need will be written in on the plan so you won't need to measure. Where an area is needed you multiply the two sides together, but when this area is not a simple rectangle you must split the overall area into a number of smaller rectangular boxes and add these together. Remember that the area of a triangle = Half Base x Height.

For all but the very largest houses all this measuring should take about four to six hours. Complicated building details like split levels, curved work, dormer windows or raked ceilings make the measuring much more complex too and it is well worth double checking as a mistake here will have costly ramifications on down the line. Oh, and don't forget to write the answers down where you won't lose them.

I also find it incredibly handy to make little notes next to the calculations which remind me what assumptions I have made when doing the calculations. Typically these read as "have assumed no skirtings in conservatory" or "have allowed for three courses of face brickwork below DPC." It's a good idea to decide whether your derived quantities are "as measured" or whether you have added an allowance for waste. It really doesn't matter which method you employ but you must be consistent otherwise you will end up adding 15% to the quantities several times over and you will over order by miles.

The further your house gets away from the good old box shape, the more complicated it gets to measure out and, if a feature like a bay window or a fancy chimney is difficult to quantify, then you can bet that it will also be difficult to build.

Working Through the Spec

You work methodically through the spec quantifying everything that is quantifiable. You then have to sweep through the whole thing a second time to generate a shopping list; some of the things you have quantified will have to be amalgamated with other sections, others will have to be broken down still further.

Blockwork is a good example. The bulk of the benchmark house's blockwork appears in this section 7.1 that I've already highlighted, but there is more blockwork in the garage, in the internal walls downstairs and around the chimney. All these have to be totalled to get an overall total for blockwork. And then consider that blockwork includes not just the blocks themselves, but the sand and cement making up the mortar not to mention the labour to lay them with. These totals have to be extracted from the blockwork total and added to the brickwork total which, to add to the confusion, will have different square metre labour rates and uses different volumes of mortar.

Written Specifications

Well that's the traditional route. It's time consuming but it works. If you plan to do your own project management it may even be worth going through this exercise to familiarise yourself with the job in hand. However many housebuilders never bother with anything so elaborate as a written specification of works but just make do with plans on a couple of A1 sheets. This is fine if you know what you are doing but using a set of plans without a written spec can be a bit like trying to cook a new dish for which you have a list of the ingredients but no instructions on how they go together. Arguably it doesn't matter which order you measure quantities in but the danger is that if you don't work methodically through a list, you will miss whole chunks out. If you have skimped on this stage of the design process, then this is where your chickens come home to roost.

Applying Measurements

From all these measurements plus various details drawn in on the plans you should be able to construct a reasonably accurate bill of quantities. You may not actually want to make up a shopping list for paint at the planning stage, but the point is that by having taken all these measurements you shouldn't have to keep taking them throughout the job. You have the figures. From these figures plus a little close scrutiny of your house planned you can work out quantities for:
- Excavation
- Concrete (approximate)
- Flooring materials

- Walling materials
- Roofing materials
- Insulation
- Plasterboarding and plastering
- Decorating materials
- Skirting and architrave
- Covings
- Scaffolding
- Guttering and downpipes
- Whole house heat-loss calculations.

Joinery is treated rather differently. If you've got a pukka written spec, there will be a joinery schedule attached which will list all the opening sizes and the window and door styles which will fit in the openings — see Table 7g to see what I'm on about. I find it helpful to start with the joinery: I work out the overall areas and use this sum to subtract from wall areas. The joinery schedule can also be used to calculate approximate quantities for glazing, lengths for lintels and cavity breaks and a subsidiary schedule for door furniture.

If you are planning to project manage your own development, then getting a grasp of these quantities and the prices you should expect to pay for them is essential. Indicative rates for all these materials are to be found dotted about throughout the text. Space and printing costs preclude me from reiterating them here. The rates I quote later in this chapter are all rates that have been quoted or paid during 1997 for building work in either Cambridgeshire, Northants and London. Your area may (almost certainly will) have different prices in operation by the time you start building, but bear in mind that Cambridgeshire is close to the national average on building costs and I think you'd have to start building in Ireland to find many costs that would vary by more than 10% from these figures. As a rule of thumb, the further away

from London you go, the cheaper building becomes; however note that in many remote districts, and especially in Scotland, whilst labour rates may be approaching half those of what you might see in the Metropolis, the materials prices are often much higher because of the extra transportation costs. This results in overall building costs being remarkably uniform throughout the UK. In any event, my prices are intended as a guideline by which you can compare your own quotations; if you come in much cheaper you are doing well.

Wastage

If you manage to work out the theoretical quantities of just about everything you need, you are still faced with the problem of knowing how much extra to order to cover wastage. Wastage is a wonderfully vague term that covers just about any and every mishap that can occur on a building site from defective materials being delivered to perfectly adequate materials apparently walking off site. There's really no way of knowing in advance what your wastage rate will be, but experience suggests that you'd be wise to over order by between 8 and 10% on heavyside materials like bricks, blocks, sand and cement and also plastering materials. You should be able to work out timber quantities exactly, but here you will probably be blighted by timber quality not being what you require and again you would do well to add extra lengths to your totals. Buying more than you actually need is, of course, expensive but so are the frequent shopping trips which happen when you buy too little.

Entering the Bazaar

The British consumer is used to being able to see what something costs. Visit any high street or supermarket and the price you pay will be clearly labelled on the goods or, at least, on the shelf underneath. Haggling over the price is something that you might do on holiday in Morocco or Turkey but it's thought not to be part of the British way of life.

This is far from the truth. Step off the high street and into the world of commerce (or house buying or even car purchase) and we Brits are out there haggling with the best of

them. Generally speaking, when there are three or more zeros on the end of the price tag, the gloves come off and any pretence at civilised shopping goes out of the window. Anyone responsible for purchasing building materials would do well to bear this in mind because a well organised buyer can achieve savings of 20% or more over the unprepared novice.

It helps to be an established builder. To have a proven trading record stretching back over some years and, better still, to have had a record as a prompt payer will stand anyone

in good stead with their suppliers. But after the recent slump, merchants are keen to attract any custom (except the doubtful payers) and if you can establish your credit worthiness and the fact that you might be a substantial customer, if only temporarily, then you will have a strong bargaining chip.

Inside a Builder's Merchant

Like any business, builder's merchants and all the related building trade suppliers are buying in goods and selling them on at a mark-up. The services that a merchant pro-

vides for this mark-up are:
• accessibility
• delivery (usually free)
• advice.

There are a handful of national chains — Jewsons (which took over Harcros in 1997 and is now the largest), Travis Perkins, Grahams, Builder Center, Keyline — and around thirty regional operations (typically with 5-10 outlets). However, the largest number of general merchants come into the category of independents, one- or two-branch outfits which may well turn over less than £1million/annum. In addition, there are specialist trade outlets dealing with plumbing (cf.. Plumb Center), electrics, roofing, joinery, ironmongery and glass. Whether they are any good or not depends an awful lot on the quality of the staff working in any particular branch and, in particular, the branch manager. Needless to say the smaller operations tend to give a more personalised service but can't always match the prices offered by the large chains.

A general merchant will hope — indeed need — to make an average mark-up in excess of 50% to stay in business. Thus, if they purchase some paint for, say, £100 then they will need to sell it for £150. An awful lot of their business is conducted with preferred clients at mark-ups much lower than this 50% and so to balance this out they must sell a great deal at mark-ups of 70, 80 or even 100%. So, one of the keys to getting good prices from a builder's merchant is to become known as a preferred client. And the best way to do this is to get your works quoted for at the outset.

This practice of there being retail and trade prices is common to almost all areas of building supplies except the D-I-Y sheds (Texas, B&Q, etc.). It's partly volume driven (that is if you buy 150 sheets of plasterboard you'll get a better rate than if you buy just one), but it also has much to do with the cosy understanding that exists between builders and their suppliers which goes to make builder's rates look cheaper than they actually are — or to put it another way, to discourage the D-I-Y enthusiast from getting out of bed. The levels of discount vary from product to product and just to make it complicated some merchants operate two, three or even four levels of discount off the retail price. Some products are sold with a list price from which you have to negotiate the biggest discount you can get; other products have no list prices and the prices paid for them just come down to good old haggling.

A question you occasionally get asked over the phone is "Is this a job you are actually doing?" Probably sounds rather silly but they are sounding you out: if you're just estimating you get one price, if you are buying you get a better price. They quite expect you to go the rounds of local suppliers and they want to have a bit of fat they can lose on the next call. If in doubt, get your status across with your first breath and you could stop some meaningless toing and froing.

Now, as recently as the 80s what I have just written would have practically barred me from ever setting foot in a builder's merchant again. But slowly the worm is turning and the trade merchants are far more aware of a) the competition from the D-I-Y sheds and b) the

growth of the selfbuild market. Most merchants I talk to are only too willing to supply one-off builders at somewhere near their best prices. They have had too many cosy relationships with "trusted trade customers" turn horribly sour and now the order of the day is to do any business which pays. So even if you are a coven of Bangladeshi single-parent lesbians, don't feel you'd not be welcome — although you'll probably still get funny looks in the cement shed.

Buying Direct

This whole question of who supplies whom is still a pretty murky area. Most manufacturers take the view that they should support the established distribution channels (i.e. the general merchants) and consequently you will have to shop there for the product. For instance you can't buy plastic drainware direct even if you are Barratt Homes. On the other hand, there are manufacturers like Rytons (who produce roof ventilation) who readily sell via mail order to all comers but who, consequently, tend to get blackballed by builder's merchants so that their product is little known. As a general rule, manufacturers do not deal direct with end users except where they set up their own distribution channels, as have Hepworth and Magnet. To make the whole picture thoroughly confusing, you will find that some distributors (notably Jewsons) will have own brand items on sale which suggests that they are manufacturers. Just like Sainsburys are farmers. But this doesn't mean you are buying direct. What really matters is not which brand or where you bought it from but was it cheap and was it any good?

What about B&Q and Homebase?

One of the reasons for the success of the edge of town D-I-Y sheds is the perceived unfriendliness of the builder's merchant to non-trade customers. The Saturday afternoon patio-building brigade have long felt that they have been treated as second-class customers at trade outlets and, what is worse, have been forced to pay over the odds for this dubious privilege. How much more convivial to shop at a place where the prices are actually displayed, even if they aren't particularly cheap, and where the staff probably know even less than you do — "'ere, Sharon, do we sell rawlplugs?" " I dunno, tell him to look in lighting."

Until the recession, the sheds had it easy. Indiscriminate customers poured through an ever increasing number of doors. However, now price is back in the driving seat, these same sheds are struggling as they are no longer perceived to offer value for money.

Despite the tales of financial irregularities, Wickes remains a reliable source of cheap building materials, used widely by both the trade and DIY enthusiasts

Their response has been to slash prices and there are now many areas where they are actually very keenly priced: there has also been quite a shakeout in the industry and there has been a tendency for two or three suppliers to consolidate their hold on the available sites. As a rule the D-I-Y sheds are not very competitive on heavyside, bulky materials but tend to be pretty good on the finishes, provided you are not looking for anything fancy.

The one exception I've found is Wickes, whose prices are keen right across the board. Wickes is a hybrid between a builder's merchant and a D-I-Y shed; the prices are close to (and sometimes better than) a regular builder's merchant's trade prices but they are also on full display — a big advantage to rookie builders. Wickes are now a near-nationwide chain and, though they don't operate credit accounts like the trade outlets, they are well worth looking out for. In 1996, Wickes was embroiled in a financial scandal of its own making and for a while looked like disappearing altogether but at time of writing it continues to trade and continues to be good value.

Specialists

The general builder's merchant is to the building trade what a convenience store is to the high street shopper. You can get just about anything you want there and the prices are reasonable. However, for the serious shopper, intent on sniffing out bargains, there are any number of specialist suppliers who can usually undercut the general merchants in their own areas. The trouble is they take some hunting out, and often they don't want to be bothered by small fry, one-off housebuilders, let alone amateurs. You could spend an awful lot of time tracking down specialist suppliers and not save more than a few hundred quid overall, and it may well be that you decide the convenience (and often helpfulness) of a local builder's merchant is worth hanging on to.

However, I would not be doing my duty if I wasn't to make you aware of how the professionals do it. Where do they go shopping? Well you could do worse than let your fingers do the walking and look in the Yellow Pages; this is where you will find many of the best local contacts, and subcontractors too for that matter. The general builder's merchants do still get a look in. They are conspicuously strong when it comes to supplying cement, drains, timber, plastering materials and joinery, but they tend to be out-priced by specialists in most other areas. However, do bear in mind that whilst the general merchants are to some extent geared to wallies asking stupid questions, the specialists usually expect you to know what you are talking about. Ask a steel stockholder what you should use to reinforce your garage floor and you'll probably get told some awful mother-in-law joke.

Sand and Aggregates
Straight from quarries or via specialist hauliers. Check Yellow Pages under *Quarries*.

Cement, Lime
General merchants are usually the best place to buy.

Bricks, Blocks, Pavings
Besides the general merchants there are a number of specialist brick wholesalers (or factors) who specialise in supplying full loads direct to site. Look out for Brickability, particularly good for sourcing block paving. Also check Yellow Pages under *Brick Merchants*.

Building Stone
Either direct from quarries or via brick or stone merchants. Check Yellow Pages under *Stone Merchants*.

Readymix Concrete
Direct from readymix outfits. Check Yellow Pages under *Concrete — Ready Mixed*.

Drainage
General merchants do well, though there are some specialists who are worth checking out. John Davidson Pipes are good for Osma and Burdens are good all round groundworks suppliers.

Joinery
Mass produced joinery is usually best sought out via the general merchants. Magnet joinery, which is characterised by being "good value", is alone amongst the major producers in being only available from its own depots — and for not making any deliveries. For workshop joinery, look in the Yellow Pages under *Joinery Mfrs*.

Timber and Timber Boards
General merchants tend to do well here though some are conspicuously better than others. There are some specialist timber merchants and these are the places to look for unusual species. Check Yellow Pages under *Timber Merchants*.

Roof Trusses
Many timber merchants run up roof trusses as a side line and this is a good line of approach. There are specialists though they are few and far between. One with a good reputation and near nationwide coverage is Scotts of Thrapston.

Encon are a nationwide insulation specialist particularly well geared to the needs of small builders

Insulation
There are many specialist suppliers in this field and they usually undercut the general merchants. Check Yellow Pages under *Insulation materials*. Don't overlook the *Insulation Installers* section; many of these offer very good value either for supply only or supply and fix.

Roofing
Another area where specialists reign supreme both as suppliers and subcontractors. Most Yellow Pages have several pages of both *Roofing Materials* and *Roofing Services*.

Guttering
Buy from general merchants unless you want something better than the industry standard uPVC fittings.

Lintels
Again buy from general merchants.

Steel Beams, Reinforcing
Usually the steel stockholders offer the best value. They have their own Yellow Pages section.

Glass
Again the specialists usually offer the best value, certainly cheaper than buying your glass with your joinery. Check Yellow Pages under *Glass Merchants* and *Glaziers*. Unit 2 Glass have a good reputation for sealed units and supply to most of S.England.

Plumbing

Plumbers buy from specialist plumber's merchants who get their own Yellow Pages section.

Electrics

Look in Yellow Pages under *Electrical Supplies Wholesalers* or *Retailers*.

Kitchens

As the section on kitchens, hopefully, makes clear, your kitchen could come from any number of sources. Joinery shops, general merchants, kitchen specialists, you name it. There are also worktop specialists, appliance wholesalers and over 1000 kitchen unit manufacturers, many supplying direct. Details of many of these suppliers are in the kitchens section.

Plastering

General merchants pick up the great bulk of sales to plasterers. However the Yellow Pages, *Plastering & screeding*, is a good source of contacts for hiring plasterers and dry-liners.

Paints, Stains

Decorators' Merchants get a listing in Yellow Pages but for many people a general merchant or even a D-I-Y shed will be just as cheap and more convenient.

Ironmongery

There are specialist stockists offering wholesale prices but a one-off housebuilder is still going to do better by buying the right amounts rather than chasing extra keen prices. General merchants discount heavily on bulk orders and do well here. Also check local *Bolt and Nut* stockists in Yellow Pages. One firm which sells all manner of lightside building materials, delivered direct to small sites throughout England and Wales is R&J Builder's Hardware. Another is Screwfix who specialise in mail order nails and screws. Note that at most general merchants, price breaks for screws very often don't start till you've purchased more than 1000, so if you need just nine screws of a particular size there really is little point buying a whole box of 200.

Door Furniture

If you want anything unusual, check out *Architectural Ironmongers* in the Yellow Pages.

Ceramic Tiles

Check under *Tile Mfrs & Suppliers*. United Tile are a nationwide supplier and a very good source for basic ceramics — many builder's merchants buy from them

Garage Doors

Check under *Garage Doors*.

This list is by no means exhaustive but I hope you have gleaned that in many cases the Yellow Pages is an essential reference tool both for digging out materials and for finding subcontractors. For items like central vacuum cleaners, underfloor heating and heat recovery units, where there may well be no local agents, the obvious place to look is in the self-build magazines, where the nationwide businesses actively seeking work are likely to be advertising. The directory at the end of this chapter includes head office phone numbers for all contacts that I've mentioned.

Salvage

One other important area I've not touched on are the salvage yards. Time was when salvage yards were a source of cheap building materials, but there has been a flight to quality in this market and these days you are much more likely to be sniffing around expensive architectural gems which you probably won't be able to afford. If you are seriously into using salvaged building materials, you would do well to identify as early as possible what exactly it is you are going to get because incorporating changes to materials specification during construction can be very costly. There are hundreds of reclaimed building materials yards all over the country, varying in size from a couple of sheds in a back garden to multi-acre sites better equipped than the average builder's merchant. If you want to look further afield than your local Yellow Pages area, contact Salvo who keep a good database of material recyclers all over the UK. They are also one of the very few organisations in this book to run a cool web page — http://www.salvo.co.uk

Trading Accounts

For anyone planning to purchase materials for a project as large as building a new house, it is well worth opening a trading account with a couple of local builder's merchants. Most merchants are well aware of the growing number of D-I-Y builders and are only too keen to capture a share of this market. As a potential new housebuilder, you will be a valued customer and should get offered trading terms similar to a small builder.

To open a trading account, you would normally be asked for a bank reference and two trading references. The bank reference shouldn't be a problem (depending on your relationship with your bank of course) but trading references could prove difficult if you've never had a trading account. Instead, write a letter of introduction saying who you are and what your project is. This will carry far more clout if you include a copy of the plans, which they may well offer to quote on.

Say that a monthly trading account would be administratively convenient (it will be) and they should offer you trading terms. If they don't then you can console yourself that you wouldn't have wanted to trade with them in any event.

If you've never had a trading account (and if you are not in business on your own account there is no particular reason to have had one), they operate under a very simple code. When you pick goods up or have them delivered you get a *dispatch* or *delivery* note. The tax *invoice* arrives a few days later by post (this is the one you must keep for VAT records) and every month you are sent a *statement of account* which summarises all the invoices you have run up on your account in the previous month. Normal terms are that you must pay off the outstanding balance on your account at the end of each subsequent month; i.e. if you spent £500 on account with Jewsons during April, you would be required to give them a cheque for £500 at the end of May. In effect you get between 30 and 60 days credit depending on whether your purchase happened at the beginning of the month or the end of the month. Sometimes postponing a purchase by a day or two — so as to avoid the month end — can get you an extra 30 days credit. Builders merchants know all about these tricks and they consistently get more sales in the first week of a month than they do in the last week.

Don't assume that you'll get better rates just because you've got a trading account opened. However, you can much more easily take advantage of deliveries, which are a big time-saver, and you can easily order by phone which makes haggling easier. Understandably, merchants do not like to haggle at the counter in front of other customers: it is an essentially private matter.

Hiring in Plant

In the rush to get a selfbuild project up and away, tool and equipment hire is often overlooked in the planning stage. Yet, as with most things in the field of project management, a little planning beforehand will reap dividends along the way. What equipment you need to hire (or buy) depends very much on how you plan to manage your build. For instance, if you are entrusting the whole shooting match to a main contractor, then you really shouldn't need anything at all. But if you are acting as the main contractor and hiring subcontractors to complete the various trades, you will need to discuss each subcontractors requirements beforehand.

It can be a confusing area. For instance, some subcontractors — notably plumbers, electricians and most carpenters — tend to come fully fitted out with toolkits and access equipment: others, typically bricklayers, expect you to provide everything other than their trowels and their levels. With groundworks, you tend to hire the kit and the labour together as a single unit—thus when a JCB is quoted at £120 a day you are getting both a JCB and a competent driver for that price.

Scaffolding contracts usually stipulate extra charges if the scaffolding is up for more than 10 weeks

Scaffolding

A specialised area of plant hire that is normally undertaken by either dedicated scaffolders or sometimes roofing gangs. A standard scaffolding contract would specify an agreed price for a hire period of eight or, perhaps, ten weeks; if the hire continues beyond the agreed period, a surcharge is levied — typically 8% of the original price per week. The original price would include for three or sometimes four visits from the scaffolders to erect the different levels (known as *lifts*) needed for the other trades to put up the house.

Single-storey houses (and detached garages) will typically need only one lift but its level will have to be adjusted between brickwork and roofing; a two-storey house needs two lifts, each being adjusted in level at some point. Guide prices for scaffolding are £6 per metre run per lift and to calculate the relevant metre runs add 15% to the perimeter measurements of the buildings you wish to scaffold to get the scaffolder's lengths. A guide price for a four bedroomed house with detached garage would be around £800 for ten weeks hire, followed by a £64/week surcharge for longer hire periods.

If you want to take control of the scaffolding process itself, there is a system called *Kwikstage* by Kwikform UK (0121 275 0200) which just slots together, rather similar to erecting an aluminium tower scaffold, which makes it particularly suitable for those who are taking a more hands-on approach and who want to have scaffolding erected for much longer than the normal time span. Kwikform provide some training for people who have never used scaffolding before or, alternatively, can provide an erection service. Rental prices for a four bedroom house- sized project work out at around £50/week.

Skips

Part of your build plan should involve a close look at how you plan to dispose of waste and for many small builders a skip is a practical and economical solution. Even after the imposition of the landfill tax in 1996, which added something like 30% on top of waste disposal prices, a skip is still good value if you wish to run a clean and efficient building site.

Skips come in three sizes:

- LARGE hold 6.2m³ ("8 yards"), = around 7-8 tons and will cost £70-80 for one week and £4 extra for each subsequent week
- MEDIUM hold 3m³ ("4 yards"), = around 5 tons and will cost £50 for one week
- MINI-SKIPS hold 1.5m³ ("2 yards"), = up to 2.5 tons and are usually only hired for two or three days max. at a cost of £30.

It is worth saying that the main costs involved with skips are to do with delivery and disposal of the waste. The rental element is usually surprisingly small (typically £4/week) and so you don't save money by delaying the arrival of a skip—you simply end up having to handle your rubbish twice over. Given that all building sites produce copious quantities of rubbish, I think that having a skip on site (certainly during the latter stages of the build) is essential: if you disagree, then at least have some coherent alternative strategy worked out for waste disposal.

Site Fencing

There are an increasing number of sites where some sort of perimeter fencing is advisable, if only to stop unwanted visitors clambering all over your building sites and walking off with your tools. The introduction of new health and safety regulations has also meant that builders are being forced to examine their policies in these areas because of accidents occurring with children playing on sites. Though a self builder will be largely exempt from these regulations, that is no reason for ignoring their importance and if you are unable to provide round the clock supervision to a site, you should consider some form of site fencing if your site is vulnerable.

You can hire steel fencing for about 50p/metre/week (less for long periods) but it is the province of the specialist. One system we have used with success is SGB's *Heras Readifence* which is about six foot high and is very easy to assemble yet surprisingly secure. If you need security fencing for more than five months, it will probably pay you to buy it and resell when you have finished.

Tool Hire Shops

If you want to stay ahead of the game, then make sure you open trading accounts with a couple of tool hire shops as well because you will save yourself an awful lot of phaffing about. For many novice project managers, tool and plant hire is one of those things that you just stumble into once the project is up and running. But after you've been and hired three things and left £50 deposits which did or didn't get credited to your final bill and anyway you've gone and lost the paperwork which was in the front of the car but now you cant find it...you'll wish you had opened a trading account at the hire shop too. If you do, you will be able to take tools for as long as you want without having to pay any deposit. Deliveries and collections are also much easier to organise—most hire shops will deliver and pick-up for a small charge (around £5-£10). Generally, the hire charges are structured so that you pay the highest rate over the first 24 hours, then the daily rate falls significantly if you hire for longer periods. After about ten weeks you will have paid as much in hire charges as it would cost you to buy, so hiring really only makes sense over

shorter periods. The list of what you can hire never ceases to amaze me and rather than bore you with a long list, if you are interested get hold of a catalogue yourself—Hewden Stuart's is particularly good.

Hiring v Buying

Which begs the questions: what should you hire and what should you buy? There are a few basic bits of kit that it would seem near essential to have with you permanently and therefore you should buy if you haven't already got them. I would include in this basic hand tools like a 5m tape measure, hammer, saw, screwdriver, 1.2m spirit level, the sort of thing you need to put up shelves or assemble flat-pack kitchen units. I would also place a good, beefy (£70plus) power drill, a good extension lead (£10) and a 6m ladder (£120) on my list of essentials; this equipment will be useful for ongoing maintenance not just for housebuilding.

How much else it is worth buying is really only a question you can answer. It depends on how quickly you plan to build, how much direct involvement you will have in the building process and whether or not your selected subbies will have their own equipment. A brickie gang will, for instance, very often expect you not only to supply tea but also a cement mixer, and it may well make good sense to buy one that you can sell on at the job's end (though don't expect very much for a

used mixer). If you work in the trade or have serious D-I-Y pretensions, then you will probably have all of the above plus a lot more and you may view your project as a wonderful opportunity to expand you range of tools. But if you don't intend to carry on building after you've finished your house, then it is pointless to lay out thousands to buy tools which will only ever fill up your precious storage space and provide rich pickings for would-be thieves.

Whether you hire or buy, the cost of specialist tool provision is significant. Note that on the benchmark house the tool hire bill came to £2800, or 3.5% of the build cost total. Admittedly, 80% of this total was taken up by three items not normally associated with tool hire shops(being site fencing at £970, scaffolding £760 and skips at £460) but on the other hand, the job was undertaken by a regular building firm which has cement mixers, ladders, tower scaffolds and the like, not to mention chippies with literally thousands of pounds worth of power tools which a self builder would be unlikely to own. Whichever way you look at it, the proportion of your total bill going on either hiring or buying equipment is large and can be one major hidden cost to creep up on the unwary. Also note that selfbuilders are not able to reclaim VAT on tool purchases or tool or plant hire, including such items as scaffolding and fencing.

Trucking

Moving materials around the country is expensive. A lorry with an off-loading crane (usually a HIAB, pronounced *high-ab*) and driver will cost around £150-£250 to make a trip of more than half a day — although this will be less with an ordinary flat-back truck without a crane. This sum will be the same whatever the load and so from the buyer's point of view it makes good sense to get as near to a full load as possible. The best economies come when ordering 20 tonnes, which is usually a full payload.

What's in a Full Load?
A 20-tonne lorry can shift:
· about 8000 standard bricks
· or 7200 block pavers (=144m^2)
· or 1440 dense blocks (=144m^2)
· or 2400 clinker blocks (= 240m^2).

Aerated blocks (like *Thermalite*) are so light that the capacity constraint on haulage tends to be volume rather than weight. 20 tonnes of super-lightweight blocks would be about 6000 blocks, which would be 36 double packs.

There are no industry standards as to how masonry materials should be packed, although there is a tendency to use shrink-wrapped plastic (which keeps watertight) and to pack in weights and quantities that fit on to a pallet. A forklift can handle over two tonnes and a common pack size is around 1 tonne (which allows two packs to be lifted at once). When ordering direct loads, you'll have to accept the nearest pack size quantity so if, for instance, you wanted 8000 bricks and your selected brick is packed in 410s (many are),

you would have to settle for either 19 packs (19x410 = 7790) or 20 packs (20x410 = 8200).

Packs will either come palletted or with fork holes for forklift off-loading. The chances are a fully laden 20-tonner will not be able to get off the road and hire of a rough terrain forklift may be the best solution for unloading. A rough-terrain forklift and driver should be available at around £100 for a half day and is usually money well spent if the site is big enough to warrant one. Bricks and blocks can (sometimes) be set around site, making labouring much quicker and easier. A JCB with forks can be used as an alternative to a rough-terrain forklift.

Plasterboard

The plasterboard manufacturers all pack in the same sizes. Better prices are usually negotiable on full packs. A 22-tonne direct load would be enough for three or four large timber frame houses — probably a bit too much for your average individual builder — however, by buying in full pack sizes you should be able to make savings.

- 1200x2400x9.5mm plasterboard comes in packs of 80 (1.76tonnes)
- 1200x2400x12.5mm plasterboard comes in packs of 60 (1.66 tonnes).

Timber

Timber has to be purchased in 20m³ lots to take advantage of bulk discounts and 20m³ is an awful lot of timber. Furthermore, CLS studwork, which is perhaps the commonest size of timber used in timber frame buildings, has to be ordered in 40m³ lots. The average timber frame house uses around 1000m of CLS — a paltry 5m³! Full loads of timber can undercut merchants' best prices by as much as 30%, but you have to have some site going to justify such orders. By and large, you'd do better to try and concentrate on buying good timber rather than cheap timber.

Pallets

Many builder's merchants now charge a £15 deposit on pallets supplied to site with tonne loads of cement or whatever. This can soon mount up to a substantial sum. Reclaiming

Above: a HIAB crane at work. Right: may look like a pile of old pallets but if they were all dropped on your site, you'd have to pay a deposit of £2500 for the privilege

the deposit is straightforward if your paperwork is in order — i.e. you can't just take the pallets back, you need to prove that you actually paid a deposit before they will refund. This practise of charging a deposit on pallets does not yet appear to have extended to supplies direct from manufacturers so you may well end up with some pallets with a deposit on their heads whilst others are free spirits.

Concrete

Site mix v Readymix

One person working with an electric or diesel mixer will mix 1m³ of wet concrete in about an hour. Making concrete on site in a mixer will cost between £38/m³ (Mats £28, Lab £10) and £56/m³ (M £46, L £10), largely dependant on how cheaply the aggregates are bought, which itself depends on the quantity of aggregates bought. In largish (10 ton +) loads, they should be obtainable at around £6/tonne; in loads under 2 tonnes, this may rise to around £15/tonne. Another factor to consider is availability of mixers (usually hired at £10/day).

As a rule, readymix will be cheaper when more than 2.5m³ is needed. Readymix loads are always going to be preferable where consistent concrete strength is important.

Strengths

Traditionally the design strengths of concrete have been expressed in ratios of volumes *sand:gravel:cement* (as in 6:3:1). However, things are stirring in the sleepy world of concrete and there are now at least three other labelling systems in operation. If you are mixing concrete on site, the old ratio system, as described, is fine and is actually very useful as you can use it to gauge how many shovels need to go into the mixer, although

note that it is usually most convenient to have a sand and gravel mixture delivered to site — ask for "all-in ballast." If, however, you phone up for a readymix delivery you may do well just to explain what it is you want the concrete for and let them work out which mix it is you need:

- Foundation Mixes: 6:3:1 is traditional but the NHBC now insists on a stronger designated mix referred to as GEN 3
- Floor Slab Mix: 4:2:1: is traditional, the NHBC stronger version is known as GEN 4.

Each of these is capable of holding 6m³ of readymixed concrete at an average cost of £250/truckload. The benchmark house used nine loads.

The NHBC has been very hot on these new *designated* mixes — they suffer a lot of foundation failures and they insist on mixes substantial stronger than the ordinary building regulations. GEN 3 and GEN 4 are about 5-10% more expensive than the traditional mixes and if you are not building under the instructions of the NHBC then you can save a little money by pouring the long established mixes 6:3:1 for foundations and 4:2:1 for floor slabs. However, on a house the size of the benchmark house, you would save less than £100 overall and most people would reckon this to be a false economy — the NHBC did not increase their mix strengths for nothing.

Don't add water

When you add water to readymix, you weaken its strength. It often leaves the readymix yard in a perfect condition and is watered on site, making a joke of its original spec. Watered concrete is perhaps the biggest single cause of concrete failure.

Charging for Air

Readymix lorries charge not just for the concrete they deliver but also for the unused air space in their drums. The effect of this empty space surcharge means that readymix can be very expensive in small loads. The overall effect on price is shown in Table 11a, *Paying for Air* where empty space is charged at £12/m³. On quantities above 12m³, all deliveries on the same day will be charged at the basic rate.

PBF mixes

One way you possibly can save a little money without compromising quality is to specify a PBF mix. PBF (stands for Portland Blast Furnace) is a cement-like slag material which is a bi-product of steel manufacturing. It started being used in concrete mixes in the 80s as a way of making concrete cheaper — initially it was called *Cemsave*. Soon it was found that in many ways PBF performed rather better than ordinary cement in binding aggregates — it poured better, it tamped better and it only caused problems when power floating took place. Normally it is mixed in a 30:70 ratio slag:cement, but there is a configuration called LHPBF which is 70% slag; the Dartford bridge is built out of this so it does work. Because of the popularity of PBF slag, it's price has increased so that now the price difference between PBF mixes and ordinary (OPC) mixes is now quite slight but nevertheless worth investigating.

Readymix concrete is delivered to site in lorries that hold 6m³. A full load of GEN 3 concrete will cost around £250 (or £42/m³). The price variations in 1997 in the Cambs region were as follows:

- Add £1/m³ for GEN 4 mix
- Add 50p/m³ for every ten miles travelled from the yard
- Add £1.50/m³ for a concrete pump mix
- Less 70p/m³ for using a PBF mix
- Less £1.50/m³ for using an LHPBF mix
- Less £2.00/m³ for using the old 6:3:1 mix
- Add £14/m³ for space not used on first two loads.

Concrete Pumps

To hire a concrete pump, allow around £120—£150 per session. They pump a full load (6m³) in 20 minutes, about three times quicker than three men barrowing might do. Concrete pumps make financial sense on jobs with more than 30m³ of concrete to be poured but there are other reasons for using them, notably when speed is important or access is difficult. If using a pump be sure to let the readymix supplier know, because the mix design is wetter and the throughput of lorries is much faster than on a normal job.

11a: Readymix: Paying for Air

There is a large cost penalty when readymix concrete is ordered in small amounts

QUANTITY ORDERED	CONCRETE COST	CHARGE FOR AIR	TOTAL COST	COST/m³
FIRST LOAD				
1m³	£42	5x£14	£112	£112
2m³	84	4x£14	£140	70
3m³	126	3x£14	£168	56
4m³	168	2x£14	£196	49
5m³	210	1x£14	£224	45
6m³	252	£0	£252	42
SECOND LOAD				
7m³	294	5x£14	£364	52
8m³	336	4x£14	£392	49
9m³	378	3x£14	£420	47
10m³	420	2x£14	£448	45
11m³	462	1x£14	£476	43
12m³	504	£0	£504	42
THIRD and SUBSEQUENT LOADS–no air charge				

Steel

Steel can be used in a wide variety of applications in new housebuilding and there are moves afoot to introduce steel framing as an alternative to timber framing. However, most housebuilders use it sparingly, preferring to use the traditional materials brick, concrete and timber wherever possible. Steel is the No.1 choice for standard fixings like nails and screws but elsewhere its use is restricted to a few specialised areas.

Reinforcing

The commonest form of steel reinforcing used in housebuilding is *A142* anti-crack mesh, which is often set in concrete floor slabs to add strength. The mesh costs between 75p and £1.20/m^2, depending on quantity needed but note that you'll need bolt croppers on site in order to cut it. It is usual (though by no means universal) to lay this in garage floor slabs. There are many other forms of steel reinforcing used in concrete but you are unlikely to come across them in housebuilding unless you are having to lay specialised foundations.

Lintels

Though reinforced concrete is much cheaper, for many years now steel has been the preferred material for bridging the openings made by doorways and windows. The problem with concrete is that, in insulated new houses, it remains a large cold bridge through the wall which is bad news thermally and attracts condensation. Also, when viewed from outside, concrete lintels look crude and cheap. In contrast, steel can be insulated and the outer leaf support is hidden seamlessly over the top of the window or door. The market is dominated by two Welsh steel businesses, Catnic and IG, and designers usually specify their products. Alternative suppliers do exist and Dorman Long and Samsom can often be 10-15% cheaper. The most commonly used IG lintel is the L1/S, very suitable for bridging openings in cavity work with cavities up to 65mm. There is a heavy duty version, known as the L1/HD. They are made in lengths from 600mm to 4800mm and they increase in 150mm increments. The minimum end bearings must be 150mm so that an opening of 900 would need to be bridged by a lintel of 900 + 150 + 150 = 1200mm. Standard lintels tend to cost around £20-£25/ lin.m. The benchmark house spend on lintels was just under £500 and just under £300 for steel beams used over the garage doors and in the opening between the meals area and the kitchen.

In contrast, concrete lintels still tend to be the preferred choice to bridge internal doorways. Here the lintel is completely covered and the heat loss/condensation issue is irrelevant. The steel lintel manufacturers do produce an internal door lintel but it is not widely used. Timber framers tend use timber lintels, but note that where a brick skin is specified for the external wall, there are special steel lintels designed to do the job of just supporting the outer skin.

Cavity Wall Ties

Where the facing material is brick, block or stone you need approx. 3.5 wall ties/m^2. If the inner skin of the cavity is timber frame rather than blockwork, the wall ties are a different shape and you need slightly more (about 4/m^2). Look to pay between £8 and £20/100 for wall ties depending on type and quality. The benchmark house would have used around 600.

Cement

The standard building cement, packed in 50kg bags, is known as *OPC* which stands for Ordinary Portland Cement and sometimes this is referred to as Portland Cement. The cement (and concrete) market is dominated by a small number of firms (RMC, Rugby, Blue Circle, Castle) and, being a mature industry, you'll find that there is remarkably little variation in cement prices — though cynics may have an alternative explanation for this. By all means shop around — current prices are hovering around £75/tonne (£3.75/bag, little changed in ten years) — but note that it is worth sticking with the same manufacturer once you've made your decision; cement colours vary and you can ruin face brickwork with a nasty change in mortar colours. Our benchmark house will have absorbed something like 4 tonnes of cement (excluding concrete) so, with a total value of under £300, cement purchase is never going to be a bank-breaker.

Mix Designs

How strong do you want it? Strong mixes (1 part cement to 3 parts sand, henceforth 1:3) are used where the mortar must stand on its own (i.e. a floor screed) or is likely to get very wet (i.e. some underground work); for brick and blockwork and for wall renders, it is important *not* to get an over strong mix and also to get some plasticity into the mix. This is usually accomplished by using additives (such as *FebMix* or *Cementone*) or by substituting lime for some cement. Given the choice most bricklayers would prefer to lay with lime in the mortar but its not universally admired; it's bulky and easily wasted and transporting split bags is a pain. Also mixing has to be carried out more accurately as the addition of a third ingredient adds to the likelihood of changes in mortar colour.

Masonry Cements

There are several other options available, all designed to make on-site gauging a little easier and a little more accurate. *Wallcrete* masonry cement is probably the best known; it consists of 85% OPC and 15% filler, usually crushed limestone. It's not as strong as OPC and doesn't behave as well as a sand:lime:cement mortar. This is because the modern, pure limes, when gauged, behave in a way that makes the mix "fatty" and they help to cure the finished mortar, leaving it ever so slightly plastic enabling movement joints to close up. Wallcrete's fillers do not do this. A better alternative is a product from Buxton Lime Industries called *Limebond* which, as its name suggests, uses lime and not fillers and is, in effect a pre-gauged package to which you just add sand. Note that *Limebond* is relatively new and many merchants have never even heard of it; call 01298 768444 to find a local stockist. Yet another option is to use a premixed mortar (i.e. even the sand is mixed in for you)— RMC can supply these at around the £15-£20/tonne mark either in skips or tipped-off lorries.

Idiot Proof Cements

All these masonry mortars are designed for low strength applications like brickwork, blockwork and renders and their mistaken use in concrete mixes can present major structural problems. In contrast, Blue Circle's *Mastercrete* and Castle's *MultiCem* are designed to be completely idiot proof. They can be used in all the major cement applications (concrete, brick mortars, renders and screeds) and will go fatty enough in a mixer to be used without any additional additives. One brickie I know is very uncomplimentary about them, to the extent that if I was to print his comments, all you would see would be a whole bunch of asterisks.

Lime

There is no compulsion to use cement for the construction of new buildings and there are many restoration projects where it would be advisable to avoid it altogether. Although cement has existed for 150 years, its use in housebuilding did not become widespread until the 1920s. Before that people used lime-only mortars which never set as hard as cement and one of the big advantages of lime mortars is that the mortar can be cleaned from the brick, making it possible for some bricks to be reused in other buildings. In contrast, cement mortars cannot be removed from bricks and cement-bedded bricks are

good for nothing more than hardcore. Another advantage is that lime mortars remain plastic and this provides a certain amount of flexibility to walls which helps to withstand subsidence and cracking. Whilst new builders would be best advised to stick with lime and cement mixtures for their above ground work, if you are restoring a pre-cement building then you should at least consider using all lime mortar. Real lime mortar (known as *lime putty*) is not cheap because very little is produced nowadays but it is arguably a better way to build all round. If you wish to know more, phone the Lime Centre in Hampshire (01962 713636) and go on one of their lime days.

Quantities

I find it helpful to calculate how many cubic metres (m³) of mortar are needed in each application and this is how Table 11b works.

I have made some assumptions about just how far a m³ of mortar will go; if, for instance, you are laying a double-thick 215mm block-wall rather than the normal 100mm thick one, you would do well to adjust your quantities so that your coverage is halved. The table is also complicated by the fact that there are several different mortar mixes commonly used on building sites; if you want to convert volumes (by which they are gauged) into weights (by which they are bought), look at the section called Crucial Measurements at the end of this chapter. Another big imponderable is waste; just how do you go about allowing for it, how much will you waste. Usually a surprisingly high amount though this figure varies substantially. My coverage rates are fairly conservative, allowing for between 15-30% of the m³ of mortar to end up somewhere other than you intend.

11b: Sand and Cement Estimating Guide

	Soft Sand	Sharp Sand	O.P. Cement	Lime	Plast-iciser	Mortar Costs
	kg	kg	kg	kg	lt	
LIME MIXES (1 Cement: 1 Lime: 6 Sand)						
1000 bricks (= 16.6m2)	1000		150	63		£ 29.00
1m2 x single skin bricks	60		8.7	3.8		£ 1.70
1m2 x 100mm Blocks	36		5.2	2.3		£ 1.00
1m2 x 12mm Render		24	3.5	1.5		£ 0.70
CEMENT/PLASTICISER MIXES (1 Cement: 6 Sand)						
1000 bricks (= 16.6m2)	1140		166		0.8	£ 26.40
1m2 x single skin bricks	69		10.1		0.05	£ 1.60
1m2 x 100mm Blocks	41		6		0.03	£ 0.95
1m2 x 12mm Render		27	3.9		0.02	£ 0.63
SCREED MIXES (1 Cement: 3 Sand)						
1m2 x 50mm Screed		80	24			£ 2.60
1m2 x 65mm Screed		104	31			£ 3.40

Worked Example on Benchmark House

	Amount	Soft Sand	Sharp Sand	O.P. Cement	Lime	Plast-iciser	Mortar Costs
	in m²	kg	kg	kg	kg	lt	
Brick Footings	86	5934		869			£ 140
Face Brickwork	97	5820		844	369		£ 160
100mm Blockwork	438	15768		2278	1007		£ 440
External Render	46		1242	179		0.90	£ 30
65mm Screed	93		9672	2883			£ 320
TOTALS		**27,522**	**10,914**	**7,053**	**1,376**	**1**	**£ 1,090**

Bricks

Bricks remain the preferred material for external walls throughout England and Wales. They are reasonably cheap, they are well understood by the building trade, they can look attractive and, above all, they are durable. Not only should a brick wall not need any further care after construction, it should actually improve with age.

Selecting the Right Brick

There are dozens of brick manufacturers and thousands of bricks to choose from. There is also a substantial business in reclaiming bricks from old buildings — though it only amounts to 1% of total brick sales that's still 40million bricks reclaimed each year. If you are limited by budget you will probably find your choice is rather narrow, but if you are prepared to pay more than £250/1000 (that's 25p/brick) then a whole world of choice opens up. Choosing a brick is quite an involved process and it is notoriously difficult to visualise what a brick wall will look like from a manufacturer's display board. Most British bricks are baked clay and these are the ones to go for if you are seeking out a *character* brick. There are other materials, notably concrete and sandlime, that get used to make bricks but the overall effect tends to be industrial looking and, crucially, there are no great price savings to be had — unlike in the world of roof tiles and block paving where concrete is invariably cheaper than clay.

Classified

There are two technical ratings for clay bricks to do with frost resistance and salt content. The frost rating is broken down into three categories being F (high), M (medium) and O (appalling), and the salt rating is split into just two categories, L (low) and N (normal). What does it matter? With frost, the problem is spalling, where the face of the brick starts crumbling away. Very soft bricks, rated O, would not be acceptable in any situation in the UK where they would be exposed to the elements — i.e. outside — but only severe frost areas (Scotland, the Welsh mountains and the English Lakes and Pennines) would require a brick rated F. M-rated bricks are fine for almost all applications outside these areas, but note that in certain exposed applications (notably chimneys) you will be asked to add copings and overhanging courses if not using an F-rated brick.

The matter of low or normal salt content is not as important to housebuilders. In very wet areas (usually within sight of the Irish Sea) it is advisable to avoid bricks with an N rating as you may be asked to use sulphate-resisting cement. A merchant will be able to advise as to a brick's rating — but what if you're using second-hand bricks? You'll have to check your source and convince the building inspector that they are suitable for outdoor use. The building inspector will very probably have seen the brick before and will be able to assess its suitability. But do check before forking out. Take samples into the building control office if necessary.

Engineering Bricks

These are particularly hard wearing and strong. Not only do they offer much greater structural support (and so they are a natural choice for supporting steel beams) but they are also extremely moisture-resistant. This second quality, combined with some very low prices (under £120/1000), has seen engineering bricks being widely used as a damp-proof course (DPC). The semi-gloss finish on the bricks (which are either blood red or slate blue) can be used to good effect in creating two-tone effect brickwork both at DPC level and elsewhere on brick elevations.

Specials

This is the term given to bricks that aren't a standard rectangular box shape. These get used, typically, on details like cills and brick wall cappings where you want to stop rainwater pooling. Some of the more common specials are readily available but many have to be made to order which is a) expensive and b) time-consuming. If your chosen design incorporates specials then don't assume that they will just turn up with the rest of the bricks; you may have to wait another two months.

In response to these problems with procuring specials, there are now brick-bonding services which will cut and glue ordinary bricks into out-of-the-ordinary shapes. At between £3 and £4 per brick they are a little cheaper than unusual specials and with a turnaround of two weeks they are somewhat quicker. It's a particularly useful service if you are using a second-hand brick from which you could never otherwise hope to obtain specials. Try Brind Products (01773 836960).

Brickies Rates

As of 1997, our local rate is around £200/1000 face bricks laid, back up to late 80s prices having been down as low as £150/1000 in the depths of the recession in 1990. On typical British residential sites, a two-and-one gang (that's two brickies serviced by one labourer) will lay 1200 bricks a day — though normally they alternate between brick and blockwork. A rate such as this would normally include extra work like corners and reveals and fixing joinery and insulation, but not overly-fiddly details like dogstoothing gables which would be negotiated separately. If paying brickies by the square metre, be clear whether or not your square metres are "solid" (i.e. include openings).

Two courses of engineering bricks used as a damp course is in most ways preferable to fiddling around with rolls of plastic DPC...and it is likely to cost less.

Soft bricks are prone to frost attack, called spalling

Brick factors

55% of British bricks go into new houses and the suppliers have developed specialised antennae for detecting new house building activity: note that if you phone up a factor or a merchant inquiring after bricks, the first thing you get asked is "Where is the site?" Why do they all want to know? Well, brick merchants get money for simply identifying (or "covering") a new site, even if they don't get the subsequent order. So the moment they inform the manufacturer that there is a new house going to be built in Pig Lane, they clock a commission (rumoured to be 2.5% of the value of the brick order).

As mentioned in the section on shopping a few pages back, there are a number of specialist brick suppliers known as factors. Now the good factors survive by having ever such long antennae and by having deals going with all the major suppliers. A factor will wave brick panels in front of you with gusto and the bricks will not be identifiable as Ibstocks or Blockleys but have names like Mellow Red or Autumn Gold, renaming the bricks to make it harder for you to get alternative quotes. Don't get me wrong: dealing with brick factors can be fun and some of them do terrific deals, but there is more than a hint of the Middle Eastern souk about the whole process.

Blocks

With blocks, there are two qualities that concern us: the first is strength and the second is how well it insulates. In many countries blocks are manufactured with feature finishes and are used extensively, instead of bricks or stone, as external wall finishes in their own right but in Britain this hasn't proved to be a popular technique, except where cheaper substitutes for stone are sought. So when we look at building blocks we are analysing how well they perform structurally, not how good do they look.

Block Strength

Block strength is calculated in Newton/mm^2, known in the trade as "Newtons" or just plain "N." Roughly speaking the more cement in the block, the higher the strength (or the more Newtons it is said to have). Most blocks qualify for the basic 3.5N strength, though some applications require 7N blocks (i.e. below ground and, some say, floor blocks). You will find a number of *utility blocks* on the market, often at a price less than £4.00/m^2, but their strength is not guaranteed.

Block Types

There are many shapes and sizes of block made but there is an "industry standard" which is 440x215mm. This is the equivalent of six standard bricks and you need 10 of these blocks to build a m^2 of wall. They are usually 100mm thick, though some of the super-lightweight varieties are thicker in order to get their insulation values up to par.

The Dense Block

Uncomfortably heavy to lift, they are usually used below ground, often at 7N strength. Cheap — full loads cost just around £5.00/m^2.

Lightweight Clinker Blocks

Almost half the weight of a dense block, these are often used on the inner leaf of insulated cavities and in partition walls. They provide an excellent keying surface for plasters. They are also widely used in beam-and-block flooring; they are very similarly priced to dense blocks.

Aerated Blocks

These are used as an alternative to clinker blocks. They were widely used in the 80s to provide the requisite U values needed to gain building regulations approval, but the increasing standards of insulation required have rather limited their use. Aerated blocks tend to cost about 50% more than their more basic clinker cousins and they have a tendency to not key plaster as well and also to show more settlement cracks.

Super-lightweight Blocks

Celcon call them *Solar*, Thermalite call them *Turbo*, Tarmac call them *Toplite*, Durox call them *Supablox*, yet they are all variations on the same theme, a sort of son of the ordinary aerated blocks designed to meet the insulation standards of the 90s. At 125mm thick, they will (just) meet the 1990 building regs and so the block manufacturers have been pushing these at the expense of the standard

aerated blocks. However, current thermal building regulations, which came into effect in 1995, mean there is very little point in using super-lightweights at this sort of thickness because you still need to add insulation to get your U values up to par. One interesting development has been the introduction of 250 and 265mm super-lightweights which enable you to build solid walls without any additional insulation and still get the wall U value down below 0.45.

Fair-faced Blockwork

As already mentioned, fair-faced blockwork is not a popular option in the UK. There are, however, a number of manufacturers, such as Forticrete, specialising in this type of finish, though the overall effect is usually hard and modern. One area where concrete blocks are commonly used in exterior applications is when people are looking for a cheap substitute for stone. Reconstituted stone blocks can look like a convincing imitation of real stone at a fraction of the cost. Check RMC Peakstone and Marshalls of Halifax.

Trade Rates

An all-in rate of between £5 and £6/m^2 for laying internal blocks is OK. *All-in rate* means that your brickies would fix wall ties, cavity wall insulation, joinery, lintels, airbricks, DPCs, etc. as they go. Also using an all-in rate saves the hassle of measuring non-standard runs like chimneys. A two-and-one gang should be able to lay between 30 and 40m^2/day.

Timber

You rarely see the price of timber advertised and you rarely see it on display in timber yards. This is because there is a wide range of prices charged for timber. The regular trade prices are usually around 33% less than those charged to casual in-off-the-street customers and large orders will get another 5-10% off the regular trade prices. The way to get good prices is invariably to send your (hopefully) large order in for quotation at least two weeks before you require it. By all means include second-fix items like skirting boards which you may not need for several months; it makes you look more like a serious customer.

Carcassing

Most construction grade carcassing timber is spruce, usually referred to as carcassing, whitewood or deal — presumably because it's a good deal. It is relatively cheap and easy to work but it suffers from being one of the least durable timbers available. Of more interest to the builder is the strength of any particular piece of timber and there are several grading systems run by the timber trade for assessing this. The commonest form of grading at present is to see timber labelled as *SC3 or SC4*. SC4 timber is the stronger and the advantage of paying the 3-5% more for SC4 timber is that you are allowed to use them over longer spans. For instance the longest distance you can bridge with a 50x175mm section of timber is 3170mm in SC3, but this length rises to 3380mm in SC4.

Kiln-dried Timber

In 1995 it became compulsory to use low moisture timber in all internal structural applications — which means joists, studwork walls and roofs. Low moisture is defined as having a moisture content below 20% and in effect this means using kiln-dried timber. The advantage of kiln dried timber is that it is dimensionally stable — it will not twist or warp as cheaper timber will, especially if it's been treated — and that it is regularised, which means that it has all been milled to an accuracy of 1mm. It is thus very much quicker and easier to put up accurate studwork and to fix flooring joists; non-regularised timber can sometimes vary in depth by 5mm or more and this is very noticeable when flooring is being laid over it. The main disadvantage with kiln dried timber is cost; its introduction, coupled with a global increase in demand for building timbers, means that the price of structural timbers hasn't benefited from the currently strong pound. Some timber merchants now differentiate their carcassing timbers as either *Wet* or *Dry*.

IIc: Chippies Rates

	EACH	LIN.M	m²
Joists		£1.25	
Joist Hangers	£1.20		
Joist Notching	0.35		
Straps	0.50		
Chipboard Floor			£2.00
Plywood Floor			£3.00
T+G Flooring			4.20
Wallplates		1.25	
Roof Trusses	14.00		
Cut Roof		1.35	9.00
Fascia		1.60	
Soffit		3.75	
Bargeboards		1.60	
Studwork		1.00	
Noggins		1.00	
Windowboard		2.25	
Door Linings/Stop	5.50		
External Doors	30.00		
French Doors	50.00		
Internal Doors	15.00		
Architrave		0.90	
Skirting - Nailed		1.35	
Skirting - Screwed		2.85	
Clapboard			7.00
Sheathing			1.50
Timber Panel Erection			1.50

This table is, hopefully, self-explanatory. It covers most of the regular activities of the carpenter engaged in new housebuilding. However, it is a fairly basic summary and there are many complicated details which cannot be so easily summarised.

Prices include both hanging and furnishing doors

Timber Treatment

Spruce is not classified as a durable timber and this means that it is liable to rot if exposed to continuous damp. This has led to the increasingly widespread use of timber preservatives to add durability. These preservatives can be applied by brush on site but more normally the timbers are immersed in a vacuum-pressure tank, which leads to them being referred to as having been "vacuum treated." There are two rival systems in regular use, *Tanalising* and *Protimising*. There is little to choose between them in price — they add around 10% to the cost of the raw timber — but they do perform rather differently. Tanalising is a water-based treatment which

tends to dye the wood a light green colour although there is now a brown-dye version as well (useful if you plan to use brown or black stains); Protimising is spirit-based and usually leaves the wood uncoloured, although sometimes a red dye is added. You can usually tell if timber has been Protimised from the pungent, petrol-like smell. Generally tanalising is preferred in applications where there is contact with the ground like fencing and protimising is preferred for structural timber (and joinery) because it is less likely to cause the timber to twist.

11d: Guide Prices for Sawn and Treated Timber

Prices are per lin. metre

	25mm Raw	25mm Treated	38mm Raw	38mm Treated	47mm Raw	47mm Treated	75mm Raw	75mm Treated
19mm				£0.18		£0.21		
25mm								
38mm		0.22	0.35	0.40				
50mm		0.30	0.40	0.45	0.50	0.55		
75mm		0.50	0.55	0.65	0.65	0.75	1.20	
100mm	0.55	0.60	0.80		0.95	1.05	1.60	
125mm					1.20	1.35		
150mm	0.80	0.90	1.20		1.45	1.65	2.20	
175mm	1.10	1.25			1.60	1.90		
200mm	1.30		1.65		1.85	2.15	3.50	
225mm	1.50		1.90		2.20	2.50	4.00	

11e: Guide Prices for Planed Timber

Prices are per lin. metre

	12.5mm	16mm	19mm	25mm	32mm	38mm	50mm	75mm	100mm
25mm	£0.24		£0.32	£0.40					
38mm	0.32	0.42	0.45	0.55		0.60			
50mm	0.40		0.55	0.65	0.75	0.70	1.05		
75mm			0.80	0.95	1.10	1.10	1.25	2.15	
100mm			1.05	1.25	1.50	1.60	1.50	3.00	4.85
125mm			1.30	1.50	1.80	1.75	2.15		
150mm			1.50	1.85	2.05	2.20	2.55		
175mm				2.15	2.70		3.00		
200mm				2.65			3.50		
225mm				3.70			4.50		

11f: Guide Prices for Timber Board

Prices are for individual sheets or boards

	BOARD SIZE in mm	THICKNESS 9mm	12mm	18mm	22/25mm
Standard Chipboard	2440x1220		£5.00	£8.20	£13.50
T+G Green Chipboard	2440x600			4.80	6.00
Sterling Floor	2400x600			5.75	
Isoply/Sterling Board	2440x1220	4.80	6.50	8.40	13.50
Sheathing Ply	2440x1220	8.00	10.00	14.00	
Sturdifloor Ply	2440x1220			16.40	
Premium Ply	2440x1220	13.00	17.00	26.00	35.00
Birch Plywood	2440x1220	16.00	20.00	30.00	40.00
Blockboard	2440x1220		17.00	22.00	34.00
MDF	2440x1200	8.00	10.00	13.50	19.00

Joinery Grade Redwood

The other commonly used wood in UK housebuilding is pine, or *redwood* as it is known. This is a denser and slightly more durable timber than spruce, and it is commonly used to manufacture windows and also for internal applications like skirting boards, floorboards and matchboard walling. It is more easily worked than spruce and it is most frequently seen in timber yards with a planed finish, usually referred to as Planed All Round (PAR) or Planed Square Edge (PSE). Scandinavia is the major supplier of redwoods.

You can use cheaper whitewoods for internal applications but they suffer from having what are called *dead knots,* which tend to work loose and fall out with time. Your mice may appreciate the odd dead knot in your skirting board but you will probably prefer to have timber with live knots which move with the timber as it expands and contracts.

Buying Redwood 5ths

Scandinavian timber is quality graded into 6 groups, 1 being the highest and 6 being the lowest; 1 will be clear knot free timber, 6 will have large knots and possibly waney edges as well. Most planed timber sold in the UK is sold as "Best" and includes anything from grades 1-4, weeding out only grades 5 and 6. Increasingly we are seeing grade 5 coming on to the market — known as "5ths" — and it sells for 25% less than the normal, unsorted timber. Grade 5 timber is very much more knotty but most people find it perfectly adequate for their purposes. It is increasingly available for fascias, barge boards and skirtings. And whilst I'm on about skirtings, consider that there is another new development in this field and that is the use of MDF boarding to replace internal joinery items such as skirtings, architraves and windowboards (and soon door linings as well). MDF mouldings are about 15% more expensive than best redwood (therefore about 50% more than fifths); but it comes in lengths of 5.4m which can be a boon AND it comes undercoated ready for topcoat. If you are planning on a painted finish to your interior woodwork, then MDF is going to save you time and money.

Specialist Softwoods

There are a number of more specialised softwoods available:

- **Douglas Fir** is particularly resinous and durable and it performs as well as many hardwoods. It is a favourite in high specification windows though one problem is that it doesn't hold paint well — wood stains are the solution.
- **Hemlock** is another North American speciality softwood which is mostly used in door construction.
- **Cedar** is particularly durable and really doesn't require any sort of on-site treatment at all. However, it is very limited in what it can be used for and its use tends to be restricted to external claddings such as garage doors and roofing where it is known as shingles.
- **Parana Pine**. This is a lovely looking South American timber, popular in several internal applications such as window boards and staircases. It is anything but durable and is very prone to buckling.

Hardwoods

Generally, hardwoods are not an alternative to softwoods. Rather, they tend to get used in particular applications like flooring and kitchen worksurfaces where softwoods are not commonly used. Joinery is the obvious exception to this rule and it's in the joinery sections that you'll find informed comment on the state of play with hardwoods. Also check the Green Issues chapter for the lowdown on tropical hardwoods.

11g: Guide Prices for Timber Mouldings
Prices are per lin. metre

DOOR LININGS		
32x115mm	£1.70	Usually sold in sets of 5.1m @ £10.00
32x138mm	2.00	Sets inc. doorstop
SKIRTINGS		
16x75mm Plain	0.45	
16x100mm Plain	0.60	
25x125mm Moulded	1.40	Cheaper moulded sections are available
25x150mm Moulded	1.80	Ask for FIFTHS Save 25%!
25x175mm Moulded	2.10	Also available in pre-painted MDF
ARCHITRAVE		
16x50mm Plain	0.35	
25x63mm Moulded	0.88	
WINDOWBOARD		
32x225mm	3.00	MDF boards available.
TONGUED + GROOVED MATCHBOARDING		
12.5x100mm	0.54	
16x100mm	0.61	
TONGUED + GROOVED FLOORBOARDING		
25x125mm	1.15	Prone to shrink and open up
25x150mm	1.30	Re-used boards cost £1.50-£2.50/m
PLANED EXTERNAL BOARDING (SHIPLAP)		
19x125mm	0.90	Sawn Featheredge = alternative
19x150mm	1.10	Costs around 55p/m
FASCIA 5th Grade, treated, slotted		
25x175mm	1.55	
25x200mm	1.80	
25x225mm	2.00	
BARGEBOARD 5th Grade, treated		
25x150mm	1.30	
HARDWOODS		Around 4 - 5 times as much as softwood

Buying Joinery

The volume joinery business works very much on the principle of publishing list prices so that all and sundry can see, but then, in private, haggling over discounts obtainable off these list prices. Discounts are partially volume driven (i.e. the more you buy, the bigger the discounts) but they are also very sensitive to what the opposition are doing. To the novice builder this might appear to be a stumbling block because their design will more than probably specify a certain manufacturer's product and there may be only one supplier in the area. However, each manufacturer will almost certainly be producing a similar product which can be substituted. It's a complicated business because although the sizes and styles are often nearly identical, the reference codes are not. What, for instance, Boulton & Paul refer to as a *Regency* style window, John Carr call *Edwardian* and most other manufacturers call *Victorian*. (They can't all be right and in this case they're all wrong: they are mock sliding sash windows, very much of the late 80s.)

Discounts

Most small builders will expect to get 30% off the list prices shown in the catalogues as a matter of course and a selfbuilder should expect to get as much. The big boys will be looking to get 50% off, and if your order is big enough (say 15 windows or more) you ought to be able to negotiate a discount larger than 30%. Often the merchants will be more flexible than the direct outlets and they also often stock two or more manufacturers. For instance, Travis Perkins, as a group, deal with Boulton & Paul, John Carr and Crosby and, even though most branches only stock one, every branch can supply every manufacturer.

Service

A further consideration is the speed and quality of delivery. In my experience this can vary enormously; sometimes the wrong items turn up, sometimes stock is damaged or parts are missing, often they are supplied later than promised. Furthermore, there seems to be little consistency; a factory or depot can supply everything correctly on time for one order and make horrendous cock-ups two months later. A lot obviously depends on the staff at the dispatching end, and what state they are in one cannot know. Ordering and correct delivery of joinery is one of the most crucial elements in the managing of a construction project because its absence can throw the job programme out of the window (or should that be window opening); on the other hand its presence on site too early creates storage problems — joinery is prone to site damage, to warping if poorly stored and to theft. If you do negotiate some whammo deal, check to see if you have to take all the items in one delivery because that may well not be the smartest move.

Delivery Times

Another frequent problem comes when ordering some of the more obscure items from the catalogues. Delivery times of six weeks are sometimes quoted — which in reality means they haven't got a clue how long it will take. Even slump conditions in the building trade don't help much because joinery factories are then prone to taking longish holidays — watch out for the extended August break. You can spend a long time and burn up your phone bill being shunted around from depot to depot trying to find out what has happened to your hardwood imperial French door frames. You'll get to talk to a lot of Geoffs, Steves, Daves, Sharons and Mandys but getting a fix on your missing order can prove virtually impossible. If speed is of the essence it will pay you to stick to readily available products: the catalogues make it clear which they are.

One way around the problem of coordinating joinery deliveries is to have the items delivered to your nearest depot (or builder's merchant) and then either pick the stuff up yourself or arrange a second delivery. Note that some suppliers will not do this (as it obviously adds considerably to their transport costs) but note also that Magnet have no site delivery service at all and that if you purchase from them they will be obliged to hold the stock for you until you want it (unless of course they sell it on to another customer!).

Comparing Costs

Another problem is trying to evaluate the cost of finishing the joinery once it's installed in the building. Time was when it all arrived on site in the same condition; softwood frames with a single coat of primer on. Now things are a lot more complicated. The penchant for staining doors and windows instead of painting them has meant that the primer coat has been dropped in favour of a base coat of honey coloured wood stain which can be either painted over or stained. However, timber joinery is now facing stiff competition from other products, most notably uPVC, which tend to get delivered to site ready glazed and pre-finished. As a result you can now buy timber joinery pre-finished (if you don't mind waiting for it); it's also usually available in an in-between state with some extra coats of paint or stain applied in the factory, all designed to reduce your on site decorating costs. Whether these pre-finished or semi-finished options are worth paying extra for rather depends on how much time and money you are prepared to bestow on the naked versions of your joinery; the pricing of these pre-finished units is usually set to make it as cheap as paying someone to decorate them. The accompanying table may help you make your mind up.

11h: Joinery Painting Costs

Allows for a 3 coat finish

	SIZE M²	MATS	LABOUR ALL RATES=M²	TOTAL
Small Window 630x1050	0.66	£ 0.50	£ 20.00	£ 21.00
Bedroom Window 1200x1200	1.44	£ 1.10	£ 43.00	£ 44.00
Triple Window 1770x1350	2.38	£ 1.80	£ 71.00	£ 73.00
Single Door 806x1994	1.6	£ 4.80	£ 32.00	£ 37.00
Double Doors 1106x1994	2.2	£ 6.60	£ 44.00	£ 51.00

Around 80% of the cost of decorating joinery is labour. The more fiddly the work gets the higher the labour content grows. Lots of small glazed units (as in Georgian windows) can add 50% to basic decorating costs.

Plumbing and Heating

Plumbing and heating, together with roofing and electrical work, is conventionally undertaken by specialist subcontractors who usually supply materials as well as labour. In analysing the labour costs, I've subtracted from quotations the amount a general contractor would hope to spend on materials: this leaves a labour rate of nearly £20/hr which is rather more than a plumber would charge. The difference is explained by the mark-up a plumber would normally put on materials, so that though he would expect to be buying somewhat cheaper than a rookie builder, he would price the job as if the materials were list price. The difference is perhaps academic but it explains why the rate/hr looks so high. You should be able to hire a one-man-band type plumber for nearer half this rate but he might not be happy for you to buy materials. However, if you are working on a zero-rated job (new build and barn conversions) and you hire a non-VAT registered plumber (or for that matter any other tradesman), you should insist on buying the materials yourself otherwise you will not be able to reclaim the VAT.

Plumbers Tasks

Conventionally, plumbers are hired to fit heating and sanitaryware; this includes all above-ground waste fittings, but rarely underground drainage or rainwater goods. Traditionally, plumbers also undertook sheet-metal work on roofing, but now this is tending to be carried out by roofers. There are a couple of grey areas that it is good to be aware of. The first concerns the wiring of heating controls (which is sometimes carried out by the electrician) and the second concerns the installation of kitchen sinks and dishwashers, which is sometimes undertaken by specialist kitchen installers. Be clear, when you are hiring, who is to do what. The table runs through these tasks on an hour and cost basis; one of the plumbers who've checked over this, commented simply "I wish it was always that quick!"

Check the Spec

Many contractors have only the vaguest understanding of the ins and out of heating and plumbing systems and are more than happy to let their plumber design, price and install whatever system they like and plumbers have become quite used to acting almost autonomously, as long as the kit works and the price is about right. Comparing quotations between plumbers is consequently a very difficult business because the specifications of the competing heating systems are almost bound to be different unless a professional has been employed to design the system beforehand, something which hardly anyone bothers with on smaller residential construction jobs.

Points to watch out for when comparing quotations are:

- Are the design considerations identical? What temperature is each room to be heated to? How many air changes an hour have been assumed in the calculations?
- What fuel is being specified to run the system? Have the costs of connecting to or storing the fuel been fully taken into account?
- What controls are being provided? How efficient will the system be? How easy will it be to service the system? Will pumps and cables be concealed? What insulation is being provided to the hot water pipes?
- What sort of emitters are being specified? If standard panel radiators, where will they be sited and who is responsible for painting them? Will they have TRVs fitted as standard? If so will these be in addition to or instead of a whole house thermostat?
- What provision has been made for towel radiators? Heating airing cupboards?
- What arrangements will be made for hot water storage? What will hot water flow rates be like?
- What sort of pipework will be used? Where will the overflows run to?
- What sort of guarantee is offered? Does the business offer any form of regular servicing contract?

11j: Typical Plumber's Labour Charges

FITTING A WET CENTRAL HEATING SYSTEM TO A 4-BEDROOM HOUSE	HOURS	EFFECTIVE CHARGE
Fit Boiler + Balanced Flue	8	£160
Fit Cylinder	4	£80
Fit Tanks in Loft	6	£120
Run Cold to Loft	2	£40
Connect Primary Pipework	8	£160
Fix 14 Radiators	8	£160
Flow and Return to 14 Radiators	14	£280
Fit Heating Controls	6	£120
Commission System	8	£160
TOTAL FOR WET CENTRAL HEATING	**64**	**£1280**
FITTING A BATHROOM		
Fix Bathroom Suite (Bath/Basin/WC)	6	£120
H+C Plumbing to Same	4	£80
Waste from Suite to Stack	2	£40
Fit Waste Stack (Ground to Roof)	4	£80
TOTAL FOR ONE BATHROOM	**16**	**£320**
ODDS N SODS		
Shower Fitting (inc H+C, Waste)	8	£160
Bidet Fitting (inc H+C, Waste)	4	£80
Fix Cloakroom Suite	4	£80
H+C Plumbing to Same	2	£40
Waste from Cloakroom to Stack	2	£40
Fit Kitchen Sink (inc H+C, Waste)	5	£100
Fit W/M or D/W (inc H+C, Waste)	2	£40
Fit Outside Tap	2	£40
Place and Plum Oil Tank	6	£120

Prices are labour only and do not include any material costs

Crucial Measurements

Weight

1lb = 0.454kg
1kg = 2.2lbs
1cwt = 112lb = 50.9kg
1 ton = 20cwt = 1.016tonne = 1016kg

Length

1millimetre (mm) = 0.039inches
1 centimetre = 10mm = 0.394inches
1 metre (m.) = 100cm = 1000mm = 39.4inches
1 inch = 25.4mm
1ft = 305mm
1yard = 914mm = 0.914m

Area

1 hectare = 10,000m^2 = 2.47 acres
1 acre = 4047m^2 = an area 64m x 64m
1m^2 = 10.76ft^2 = 1.20yd^2
Area of a triangle = Half (Base x Height)

Volume

1m^3 = 1.3yd^3

Circles

Pi ( ) = 3.14, r = radius
Circumference = 2 r
Area of circle = r ^{2}
Volume of a pipe = Length x area

Liquids

1 gallon = 4.5lts
1m^3 = 1000lts = 220gallons

Heat

1kiloWatt = 3410 BTU (British Thermal Units)
1kiloWatt Hour (kWh) = 1kW burned for one hour
1 Joule = 1 watt x 1 second
1 GJ = 278kWh
Specific heat of air = 0.36

Material densities

Sand : 1m^3 = 1.6 tonnes (20% less when wet)
All-in ballast: 1m^3 = 2tonnes
OP Cement: 1m^3 = 1.4tonnes
Hydrated lime: 1m^3 = 0.6tonnes
Dense concrete blocks (+ paving): 1m^3 = 2tonnes
Clinker blocks (lightweight): 1m^3 = 1.2 tonnes
Aerated blocks: 1m^3 = 0.65tonnes
Super-lightweight blocks: 1m^3 = 0.48tonnes
Face bricks: 1m^3 = 1.2 – 1.6tonnes
Softwood: 1m^3 = 0.6tonnes

Getting It Square

Only in a right-angled triangle is the square of the hypotenuse (the long side) equal to the square of the two shorter sides. This basic rule of geometry (*Pythagoras' Theorem*) allows us to get our corners dead square using nothing more than a tape measure. Most carpenters are taught this bit of geometry via the 3-4-5 rule which they use for squaring up frames but it is just as useful when setting out foundations. The classic 3-4-5 triangle calculation is demonstrated in the diagram but, of course, the calculation will work with any lengths, just as long as you can work out the squares — tip: get a calculator with a square root function.

What's in a Ton?

Conventionally when the word is written TON it refers to an imperial ton. When it's written TONNE, it's a metric ton(ne). The old imperial ton was 20cwt (hundredweight): the metric tonne is made up of 1000 kilogrammes. The imperial ton is just 1.6% heavier than the metric tonne and therefore, to all intents and purposes you can ignore the difference.

Not so the differences between cubic metres and tonnes. Now quarries or merchants can sell by using either method. In fact many suppliers use both — volume up to 10 m^3 and tonnes above that level. The conversion on sand is 1m^3 = 1.6tonnes but be warned that sand is much heavier when wet and so you'll be getting up to 20% less if you are buying by weight in wet weather. However, at £6-£10/ tonne for 10 tonne loads, it's cheap enough to not worry unduly over.

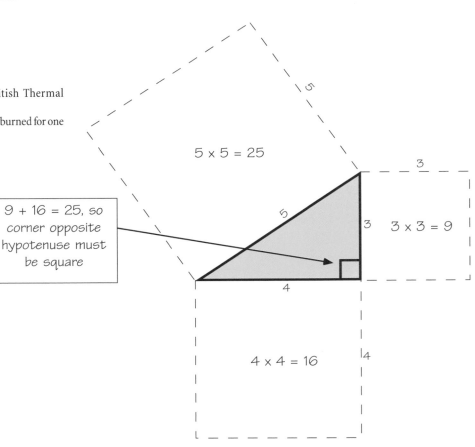

5 x 5 = 25

3 x 3 = 9

4 x 4 = 16

9 + 16 = 25, so corner opposite hypotenuse must be square

Contacts

6: GROUNDWORKS

AWD Contractors	Groundworks specialists	01794 388610
Caradon Terrain	Plastic drainware	01622 717811
Conder Products	Septic tanks/treatment plants	01962 863577
Earthspan	Beam and block floors	01223 837838
Klargester	Septic tanks	01296 630190
Marley	Plastic drainware	01622 858888
Mini Piling	Foundation piling	01527 529555
Naylor	Clay drainage	01226 794059
Osma	Drainware	01249 654121
Polycon	Sewage pumps	01278 425804
Pump Technology	Water Pumps	01734 821555
Pumping Systems	Sewage pumps	01480 435725
Rackhams	Beam & Block Floors	01924 455876
Sparkbrook Contractors	Groundworks specialists (Midlands)	0121 707 8379
T-T Pumps	Sewage pumps	01782 812231

7: SUPERSTRUCTURE

Abbott Joinery	Timber/uPVC joinery	01825 872567
Alcan Metal Centres	Conservatories	01992 904100
Andersen Windows		01283 511122
Beco Wallform	Hollow insulation moulds	01652 651641
Boulton & Paul	Joinery and kitchens	01603 706000
Celcon	Aerated blocks	0800 614652
Conservatory Fittings	Conservatories	0117 9639523
D W Pound	Garages	01299 266337
Dale Joinery	Joinery	01706 350350
Durox	Aerated blocks	01375 673344
Earthspan	Beam and block flooring	01203 393200
Eternit	Roof tiles	01782 750243
Excel Industries (Warmcel)	Insulation	01495 350655
Farmington Stone	Cotswold stone/fireplaces	01451 860280
Forticrete	Blockwork, concrete roof tiles	0151 521 3545
Glynwed	Cast Iron Rainwater Gear	01952 641414
Hill Leigh	Joinery, Roof Trusses	01179 822375
Horman	Garage Doors	0116 286 1404
Howarth	Windows and doors	01469 530577
Hunter Plastics	Rainwater gear	0181 855 9851
IG	Weatherbeater Doors	01633 486486
Isokern	Chimnies	01202 861650
Jablite	Insulation	01322 626600
John Carr (Rugby Joinery)	Timber/uPVC joinery	01302 39400
Keymer Roof Tiles	Clay roof tiles	01444 232931
Kingspan	Insulation	0800 610061
Kolind	Pumice stone chimnies	01926 842545
Leofric	Garages	01203 301301
Lindman	Fiber-Classic Doors	0117 961 0900
Marley	Roof tiles	01675 468400
Marshalls Jet Floor	Insulated Beam and Block Flooring	01636 832020
Owens Corning	Polyfoam Insulation	0800 627465
Pilkington Glass		0800 556000
Redbank	Roofing/flues/chimney pots	01530 270333
Redland Roofing systems		0990 601000
RMC Peakstone	Stone	01298 22244
Rockwool	Insulation	01656 862621
Rytons	Ventilation	01536 511874
Scotts of Thrapston	Roof trusses, windows	01832 732366
Seconds & Co	Insulation "seconds"	01544 260501
Selkirk	Chimney flues	01271 22551
StormKing	GRP Mouldings	01827 896441
Thermalite	Blocks	01675 462081
Trus Joist MacMillan	Floor Truss System	01527 854853
Tudor Roof Tiles	Clay roof tiles	01797 320202
Velux	Windows	01592 772211

Aga	Cast iron ranges	0345 125207
Baxi	Fires, boilers	01772 695555
Beam	Built-in Vacuum System	01905 611041
C&S Installations	Intelligent Switching	01442 232255
Charringtons	Solid fuel	0800 585372
Clyde Combustion	Traditional cast iron radiators	0181 391 2020
David Robbens	Underfloor Heating	0800 454569
ESWA	Electric heating	0171 735 0043
Evolution Systems	Home phone networks	01480 493655
Faral Radiators		01342 410188
Flexel	Electric underfloor heating	01592 757313
Gledhill	Hot water storage	01253 401494
Green Island	Low voltage lighting	01872 262228
Harrison McCarthy	Plumbing supplies	0161 794 9021
Heatrae Sadia	Megaflow water cylinders	01603 424144
Hellfire Combustion	Condensing Boilers	01400 250572
Home Automation	Lighting controls	01249 443422
Honeywell	Heating Controls	01344 656000
IPPEC	Underfloor Heating/air cooling	0121 622 4333
Johnson and Starley	Warm air heating	01604 762881
JSB Electrical	Safety lighting	01477 537773
Malvern	Boilers	01684 893777
Maplin	Home Electronics	01702 554000
Marlin	Lighting	0181 894 5522
Maxol	Boilers	01282 427241
Nu Heat	Underfloor Heating	01395 578482
Pendock Profiles	Underfloor ducting	01952 580590
Plumb Center	Plumbing supplies	01765 690690
Potterton Boilers		0345 697509
QVS	Electrical wholesale	0800 7310011
Stovax	Multi-fuel cast iron stoves	01392 474056
Sutherland Associates	Energy consultants	01737 370077
Thermalpanel	Radiators	01705 671821
TLC	Electrical wholesale	0181 646 6866
Trane	Air Conditioning	01256 306000
Valor	Gas Effect Fires	0121 386 6260
Willan	Whole house ventilation	0161 962 7113
Wimtec Environmental	Air Pressure Testing	01753 737744
Wirsbo	Underfloor Heating	01293 548512
Worcester Bosch	Boilers	01905 754624
Yorkpark	Condensing Boilers/unvented tanks	01494 764031
Zehnder	Towel radiators	01252 515151

9: FINISHES

Allgood (Modric)	Door furniture	0171 387 9951
Advanced Showers	Leakproof showers	01483 295930
Allied Manufacturing	Kitchen Suppliers	0181 205 4188
Alternative Plans	Italian Kitchens	0171 228 6460
Aqualisa	Showers	01959 560040
Arrow Distribution	Kitchen Appliances	01905 754200
Artex	Plastered finishes	01273 513100
Bathroom Store		0181 874 4000
Blanc de Bierge	Stone pavings	01733 202566
Blanco Sinks	Sinks	0181 450 9100
British Gates and Timber	Doors	01580 291555
British Gypsum	Plasters and plasterboard	0115 945 1000
Carlisle Brass	Door Furniture	01228 511770
Civil Engineering Developments	Stone factors	01708 867237
Clayton Munroe	Door furniture	01803 762626
Farrow & Ball	National Trust paints	01202 876141
Fermacell	Wallboard	0121 321 1155
Fired Earth	Handmade tiles	01295 812088
GJD	Security Lighting	01204 363998
Harris & Bailey	Stone factors	0181 654 3181

IKEA		0181 208 5600
ISE	In-Sink-Erator Waste Disposal Units	01371 873073
Jacksons Fencing		01233 750393
Kitchen Specialists Assoc..	Regulatory Body	01905 726066
Knauf	Plasterboard	01795 424499
Lafarge	Plasterboard	01737 243324
Marshalls of Halifax	Blocks, paving	01422 306000
Miscellanea	Bathroom supplies	01428 714014
Paint Magic	Decorating	0171 354 9696
Petersons	Chestnut Flooring	01263 735384
Real Door Company	Internal Doors	01462 768324
Response Electronics	Burglar Alarms	01372 450960
Roma Jay Designs	Kitchen designer	0181 886 1850
Sadolin	Woodstains	01480 497637
Sikkens	Woodstains	01480 496868
Star Curtains of Newmarket	Curtains	01638 666642
Vent Axia	Extractor Fans	01293 526062
Vola UK	Exotic bathroom gear	01525 841155
Wholesale Kitchen Appliances		0800 074 2074

10: GREEN ISSUES

Aquasaver	Grey Water	01288 354425
Energy Savings Trust	Grants	0345 023005
Liff	Water Softeners and Filters	01484 512537
MVM Starpoint	Energy ratings	0117 974 4477
National Energy Services	Energy ratings	01908 672787
Powertech Solar Systems	Solar power specialists	0700 0710150
Rainwater Harvesting		01452 770629
WD Water Dynamics	Grey Water	01622 873322

11: SHOPPING

Brickability	Brick factors	01656 645222
Brind Products	Brick bonding	01773 836960
Burdens	Groundwork suppliers	0117 9861766
Buxton Lime Industries	Cements and limes	01298 768444
Encon Insulation	Insulation supplier	01937 580228
Hewden Stuart	Tool Hire	01827 715255
John Davidson Pipes	Plastic drainware	01228 791503
Kwikform UK	Independent Scaffolding	0121 275 0200
Lime Centre		01962 713636
Machells	Salvage, reclaimed floors	0113 2505043
R&J Builder's Hardware	Ironmongery	01254 52525
Salvo	Directory of Salvage Yards	01668 216494
Screwfix	Wholesale ironmongery	0800 317004
SGB Scaffolding	Scaffolding/ Security Fencing	01403 790456
Solopark	Reclaimed builders yard	01223 834663
Tiptree Trading	Salvage Yard in Essex	01376 573555
Travis Perkins	Merchant/Tool Hire	01604 752424
Unit 2	Glass Merchant	01536 402244
United Tile	Ceramic Tiles	01384 480221

Index

loft
  hatches 127, 148
  plumbing 120
loft space 47
  planning concerns 28
low emissivity glazing 89, 188
low-voltage lighting 133

M

main contractor 52, 61
mains pressure hot water systems 120
manholes 70
Marshalls jet floor 93
masonry cement 207
masonry paints 167
mastics 169
matchboarding 141
MDF
  doors 145
  health risks 178
  kitchens 157
  shelving 149
  skirtings 148
mechanical ventilation 126
meter boxes 130
microwaves 160
mineral wool 81
mining subsidence 67
money
  borrowing 9
mortar 207
motorised zone valves 122

N

NHBC 38, 52
night-storage heaters 124
noise reduction 192

O

obscured glass 91
off-peak electricity 124
OFWAT 69
oil 112
optimisers 123

P

package build 39
painting 166, 202
pallets 205
Parana pine 213
pargetting 77
partial fill insulation 74
passive infra red
  detection 165
  switching 134, 190
passive solar design 90, 187
passive stack ventilation 126
patio doors 87, 164
patios 172
PC sums 56, 157

pea shingle 72
phones 135
picture rails 148
piling 67
Pilkington K glass 89
pipe boxing 149
planning
  drawings 34
  fees 36
planning permission 35, 44
  concerns 27
  outline 36
plant hire 64
plasterboard
  buying 205
  finishing 140
  formats 140
  insulated 74
plastering **140**, 202
  external 77
plumbing 215
polychip floors 93
polystyrene 81
polyurethane 81
power showers 153
powerlines
  overhead 31
Prime Cost sums 56
programmable thermostats 123
programmers 122
project management 49
property
  developing 13
protimising 178, 211
provisional sums 56
public liability 60
pumps
  central heating 122
  concrete 206
  drainage 30, 70
  shower 120

Q

quantity surveyors 40, 49
quarry tiles 144
quotations 52

R

radiators 118
  efficiency 116
radon 29, 67, 127
rafts 67
rain penetration 76
rainwater
  collection 194
  disposal 104
  drains 70
RCDs 130
readymix 205
reconstituted stone 79, 172
recycling 45, 163
  water 194

reinforcing 201, 207
remote controlled door operators 108
rendering 77
renovation 45
renovations 26
reserved matters 36
retaining walls 66
retention 55
retro-fill insulation 74
rights of way 27
road openings 70
roof
  carcassing 95
  covers 98
  trusses 95
  ventilation 97
roof pitches 28
rooflights 96
roofs
  buying tips 201
  trusses 201
rough casting 77
rubble walling 78

S

safes 165
safety 58
  glass 89
  health risks 177
  heating controls 122
  house wiring 131
  power tools 59
salvage 202
sand 201
satellite TV 135
scaffolding 59
screeds 92
security 164
  doors 146
  fencing 173
  site 58
Segal, Walter 10
selfbuild 10
septic tanks 30, 71
service connections 69
services
  problem connections 30
sewage 193
  infrastructure charges 69
shelving 149
shingles 100
shiplap 78
shopping 201
shower pumps 120
showers 152
silicone sealers 169
single storey houses 48
sinks 158
site diaries 60
skirting 148
skirting radiators 119
slate 99
slopes 29, 66